New Strategies
for
Public Affairs Reporting

second edition

New Strategies for Public Affairs Reporting

INVESTIGATION, INTERPRETATION, AND RESEARCH

GEORGE S. HAGE   *University of Minnesota*

EVERETTE E. DENNIS   *University of Oregon*

ARNOLD H. ISMACH   *University of Minnesota*

STEPHEN HARTGEN   *Twin Falls Times-News*

PRENTICE-HALL, INC.,   *Englewood Cliffs, New Jersey 07632*

Library of Congress Cataloging in Publication Data
Main entry under title:

New strategies for public affairs reporting.

Includes bibliographies and index.
1. Reporters and reporting.   I. Hage, George Sigurd.
PN4781.N33   1983   070.4'3   82-18567
ISBN   0-13-615740-8

Editorial/production supervision and interior design by Natalie Krivanek
Cover design by Jeannette Jacob
Manufacturing buyer: Harry P. Baisley

Printed in the United States of America

10   9   8   7   6   5   4   3   2   1

ISBN: 0-13-615740-8

Prentice-Hall International, Inc., *London*
Prentice-Hall of Australia Pty. Limited, *Sydney*
Editora Prentice-Hall do Brasil, Ltda., *Rio de Janeiro*
Prentice-Hall Canada Inc., *Toronto*
Prentice-Hall of India Private Limited, *New Delhi*
Prentice-Hall of Japan, Inc., *Tokyo*
Prentice-Hall of Southeast Asia Pte. Ltd., *Singapore*
Whitehall Books Limited, *Wellington, New Zealand*

Contents

8 COVERING GOVERNMENT AGENCIES AND SERVICES

9 COVERING POLITICS AND ELECTIONS

10 COVERING THE LEGISLATIVE PROCESS

11 URBAN JOURNALISM

12 COVERING BUSINESS, LABOR, AND CONSUMER NEWS

Preface

Journalism in the 1980s doesn't lend itself to easy classification. The journalistic manifestos of yesterday have lost much of their relevance and authority at a time when explosive change has come to the news media. No longer are there universal truths and simple models of accepted practice to guide the news worker.

Instead, journalists—particularly those in newspaper work—have been forced to explore new approaches to defining, processing, and presenting news to their audiences. In an age of expanding information resources and competing delivery channels, newspapers are reexamining past practice and dicta in the light of increasingly selective readers.

The move from certainty and uniformity to uncertainty and diversity has come rapidly in the past decade. For some in journalism, it has been growth through pain. Cherished beliefs about the selection and production of news have been abandoned, replaced by experimentation with new forms. Many newspapers have diminished their coverage of "hard" news and expanded their coverage of "soft" news.

Public affairs coverage still remains the core of the newspaper, however. Yet it, too, has undergone substantial change. Since publication of the first edition of *New Strategies for Public Affairs Reporting*, there has been a marked expansion of interpretive and investigative reporting. Traditional coverage of spot news is still fundamental to most newspapers, but the emphasis is now on relevance to the reader. That means less mechanistic coverage of isolated events and more effort to examine trends and conditions that bear directly on the lives of readers. Precision journalism, the use of social science research methods to provide information for news stories, has gained more adherents in the past few years. And more reporters are becoming trained in specialized areas such as economics, environmental sciences, computer technology, municipal finance, and urban social problems.

The second edition of *New Strategies* recognizes these developments as well as the practicalities of the contemporary newspaper. It attempts to bridge traditional practice with the cutting edge of innovation in the 1980s. We offer several chapters on new strategies for public affairs reporting as they apply to all journalistic settings. They include an examination of the important role of audience factors in news decision-making; techniques of investigative reporting and their relationships to conventional methods, and the practice of precision journalism.

Part two examines the specific settings of the public affairs arena. The legal process, executive agencies, politics, lawmaking, and several other areas of specialization are presented in terms of their unique problems and opportunities.

Throughout the text, strategies for innovation are suggested, and examples from both large and small newspapers are presented. The examples demonstrate the wide applicability and acceptance of the new strategies they illustrate.

New in this edition are chapters on investigative reporting; business, economic, and consumer reporting; science and medical reporting, and the reporting of urban problems. We have written this book for advanced students of reporting. In many schools, the course that we address ourselves to is called "Public Affairs Reporting." But whatever the name, it is usually the second writing course for the journalism student. Thus, we have written the text with a minimum of review material and have concentrated on the substantive issues and problems that the public affairs reporting student will face in the classroom, in community assignments, and eventually on the job. By emphasizing *strategies* and *settings* and de-emphasizing a review of remedial reporting practices, we have tried to avoid becoming a superficial civics book. Though we do touch on the unique problems of news settings (and in some instances that requires special training), we have attempted to show how a reporter can become a sophisticated investigator-researcher in evaluating public affairs. To do this, it is understood that a full grounding in state and local government, economics and law, as well as in other subjects, is needed. We suggest ways in which the student, and eventually the reporter, can become proficient in covering such specialized areas as courts, but we stop short of synthesizing a civics course. This, we feel, is the function of a liberal education that can only be reinforced in public affairs reporting.

It is our hope that the book will enhance the values of social responsibility taught elsewhere in the journalism and mass communication curriculum, and lead students toward a thoughtful and analytical approach to public affairs reporting, one that will help them adapt to and cope with change.

We are grateful to many editors, reporters, and broadcast journalists from whom we have drawn examples. We are also grateful to several generations of students in public affairs reporting classes whose questions and critical comments have helped shape our perceptions. For critical reading and contributions to Chapter 6, our special thanks go to John R. Finnegan Jr. of the University of Minnesota. We are also grateful to the following journalism educators for their helpful reviews of the manuscripts of the first and second editions: Benjamin H. Baldwin, Northwestern University; Jim Davis, California State University at Long Beach; Robert E. Drechsel, Colorado State University; David Grey, San José State University; John Griffith, University of Florda; Albert L. Hester, University of Georgia; John Kaufman, California State University; Don R. Pember, University of Washington; Ed Weston, University of Florda.

Acknowledgments

The authors are grateful for permission to quote or paraphrase excerpts from the following sources:

JONATHAN D. CASPER, *American Criminal Justice: The Defendant's Perspective* (Englewood Cliffs, N.J.: Prentice-Hall, Inc., 1972). By permission of Prentice-Hall, Inc.

EDWIN DIAMOND, "Fairness and Balance in the Evening News," *Columbia Journalism Review* 11 (Jan.–Feb., 1973). By permission of the *Columbia Journalism Review* and the author.

DORIS A. GRABER, "Press Coverage Patterns of Campaign News: the 1968 Presidential Race," *Journalism Quarterly* 48 (Autumn, 1971). By permission of *Journalism Quarterly.*

STEPHEN HARTGEN, *A Guide to Public Records in Minnesota* (Minneapolis: Minneapolis Star and Tribune Company, 1975). By permission of the Minneapolis Star and Tribune Company.

PHILIP MEYER, *Precision Journalism: A Reporter's Introduction to Social Science Methods,* Copyright © 1973 by Indiana University Press. Reprinted by permission of the publisher.

JAMES O. MONROE, JR., "Press Coverage of the Courts," *Quill* 61 (March, 1973). By permission of the *Quill,* published by The Society of Professional Journalists, Sigma Delta Chi.

"The Newsman's Guide to Legalese." By permission of the Pennsylvania Bar Association.

WILLIAM J. VANDEN HEUVEL, "The Press and the Prisons," *Columbia Journalism Review* 11 (May–June, 1972). By permission of the *Columbia Journalism Review* and the author.

VICTOR F. ZONANA, "Jogging's Fade Fails to Push Nike Off Track" *The Wall Street Journal* (March 5, 1981). Reprinted by permission of *The Wall Street Journal.* Copyright © Dow Jones & Company, Inc., 1981. All rights reserved.

About the Authors

George S. Hage is professor of Journalism and Mass Communication at the University of Minnesota. He has taught Public Affairs Reporting for twenty-five years and has been an active participant in public affairs as a member of the Minneapolis Planning Commission for eight years. Before joining the Minnesota faculty, he was a reporter on the *Columbus* (Ohio) *Citizen.* His most recent newspaper experience was an acting readers' representative on the *Minneapolis Tribune.* He is the author of *Newspapers on the Minnesota Frontier* and holds a Ph.D. from the University of Minnesota in American Studies.

Everette E. Dennis is dean of the School of Journalism at the University of Oregon. Prior to that he was professor and director of graduate studies in the School of Journalism and Mass Communication at the University of Minnesota. Dennis was the first journalism educator to hold a Liberal Arts Fellowship at Harvard Law School (1978–79) and a Visiting Nieman Fellowship, also at Harvard (1980). A well-known commentator on journalistic issues and problems, he is author and co-author of eight books and many articles and book chapters. His books include *Understanding Mass Communication, Reporting Processes and Practices, The Media Society,* and *Justice Hugo Black and the First Amendment.* Dennis has worked as a reporter and government information officer. He earned a Ph.D. in mass communication from the University of Minnesota, an M.A. from Syracuse University and did undergraduate work at the University of Oregon.

Arnold H. Ismach is an associate professor and chairman of the news-editorial sequence in the School of Journalism and Mass Communication at the University of Minnesota. He was a reporter and editor on daily news-papers in Washington and California for 15 years. He holds a B.A. degree from the University of Oklahoma, an M.A. from UCLA, and a Ph.D. in mass communication from the University of Washington. His other book credits include *Enduring Issues in Mass Communication* and *Reporting Processes and Practice.*

Stephen Hartgen is managing editor of the *Twin Falls* (Idaho) *Times-News* and has worked on several other newspapers, including the *Bangor* (Me) *Daily News,* the *Minneapolis Star,* the *San Diego Union* and the *Casper* (Wyo.) *Star-Tribune.* He has covered a number of public affairs beats, including courts, municipal politics, corrections and legislative issues. He holds an M.A. from Brandeis University in American history and a Ph.D. in American Studies from the University of Minnesota, where he taught interpretive and investigative reporting. He has also taught at Ohio State University and the University of Wyoming. He is the author of *A Guide to Public Records in Minnesota* and a contributor to *On the Record: An Investigative Reporting Manual.*

New Strategies
for
Public Affairs Reporting

1

The World
of the Public Affairs
Reporter

> Our society needs an accurate, truthful account of the day's news. . . .
>
> *Commission on Freedom of the Press (1947)*

> I grew up in a little town in East Texas, population about a thousand. One gas station, one grocery store and one newspaper. The gas station fueled my car and the grocery store fueled my body. But the newspaper fueled my mind.
>
> *Sissy Spacek, actress, in the* Houston Chronicle *(1980)**

A democratic society depends on an educated and informed electorate. This fundamental premise of democratic theory is the rationale for the American system of freedom of expression, which is guaranteed by the First Amendment. It is the main reason why journalists argue, and courts usually agree, that there should be no interference with the news media in their pursuit of a full and robust discussion of public events and issues.

The public, of course, needs accurate and timely information to make decisions of daily life, whether in voting, an economic trend, or navigating through heavy traffic on the way to work. Without doubt, the news media are the principal providers of that information, although they are not simple conduits for its free flow. Whether newspapers, broadcast stations, magazines, or cable news operations, the news media are dynamic organisms made up of people who think and plan and execute strategies that lead to news gathering, news writing, and eventually, the processing and dissemination of that information.

The public affairs reporters who work for these organizations act as representatives or trustees for the public.[1] In order to get the information that society needs—and sometimes wants—they go into places where the

*Reprinted by permission of the *Houston Chronicle*.

average citizen can't or won't go, and they do hard work that the public can't or won't do.

Just what is public affairs reporting? Who does it? And how do the reporters make their reports palatable for a less than fully attentive public? At first glance it would seem that public affairs reporting is simply coverage of the public sector, of government and government-related activities. Indeed, this reporting has usually meant coverage of courts and legal institutions, legislative bodies, government agencies, the executive branch, and the political process. However, the public and the private (usually meaning business and industry) often intersect. Government agencies contract with businesses to carry out their functions. The actions of corporations often have an important public impact and sometimes stir legislative action. Thus, public affairs reporting has come to mean anything that affects the public or is related to the public interest. The alert public affairs reporter must be especially observant in an era when activities in the public and private sector are not clearly delineated. For example, in the early 1980s, American cities were being wired for cable television. Private, profit-making companies were competing for franchises to operate local systems. In doing so they were guided by the rules of the Federal Communications Commission, sometimes governed by state cable authorities, and always subject to decisions of city councils which awarded the franchises. What unfolded was a complex series of public and private transactions, the result of which would determine the kind of cable system and the kinds of services the public would get. Naturally, public affairs reporters watched attentively, providing the public with reports of specific events relating to local cable franchises as well as stories dealing with long-term implications of city council decisions about cable operations.

The people who wrote these and other public affairs stories vary somewhat from one news organization to another, but most of them have a college education with a liberal arts background and some journalistic training. They know how to gather information, they know how to write in the conventional journalistic form, and they know how to work with their fellow reporters and with editors and other news managers. The best of them have a keen knowledge of public affairs: They know how government works, they understand the political process, they are aware of intersections when the public and private sectors meet, and they know about lobbies and interest groups.

Public affairs reporters also should have diplomatic relations with their audiences. They must know and understand differing needs, interests, and demands. They must prepare their reports so that they will be read, listened to, or viewed attentively—which may mean creating a vivid way to report a budget or improvising a technique for drawing out a dull but important politician. It assuredly means knowing who the audience actually is, what they will understand, and what information they need.

Although there may be ideal standards that all of us would like to apply to public affairs reporters, in reality they are human beings with human limitations who work for people and organizations that also have limitations.

Four types of such reporters are examined here.

In a medium-sized Southern city, a tough-minded young man walks briskly into the city hall hearing room. At twenty-six, Tom Greene has spent five years as a reporter for the city's 10,000-plus circulation daily newspaper, most of them as city hall correspondent. Greene observes the zoning commission as it considers public opposition or support for a proposed change in one of the city's residential zones. It is the first time a public hearing has been held on the issue—just two procedural steps away from final approval or denial by the city council.

As the doors of the criminal courts building in a large Northeastern city open, forty-six-year-old Susan Kahn, whose salt-and-pepper hair is the only hint of her age, walks toward a cavernous room labeled "Court Chamber No. 6," where a bank vice-president and civic leader, charged with a $450,000 embezzlement, will go on trial. The jury has been chosen, and today's session will hear opening statements by the attorneys. Kahn is an expert reporter who earned this assignment after years of metro daily desk and reporting experience.

Shaking dust from yellowing file folders, Harold Copeland searches laboriously through land records as he traces the ownership of several parcels of land that have recently risen in value because of major county road improvements. The thirty-five-year-old Copeland scans page after page of deeds and other land and property descriptions. As editor and part owner of a 4,500 circulation Midwestern weekly, Copeland is in pursuit of a story that will determine the "real" owners of fertile farmland scheduled for development by an out-of-state firm.

In the regional office of the state health department, twenty-one-year-old Chester Bond enters a door marked "Chief, Preventive Programs." He has arrived for an interview with a public-health planner who is developing a new program for exceptional children. Only three months out of journalism school, Bond is preparing a series for a Western triweekly that circulates mostly among suburban families.

Each of these four reporters has gone to a public office or proceeding because he or she believes that a worthwhile news story is likely to result. Even though there are potentially hundreds of other places in the community where these reporters might be pursuing the news, their decisions to cover these stories are not accidental.

On the morning that Tom Greene decided to spend two hours with the zoning commission there were three other meetings of interest at city hall. Susan Kahn's assignment was only one legal proceeding out of eight in her city that day. Harold Copeland might have spent his time with several hundred different kinds of public records. Chester Bond selected one social problem out of hundreds, one agency out of dozens.

Varying degrees of personal initiative helped to account for these selections. City editors assigned Tom Greene and Susan Kahn to their particular stories—although both were regulars covering city hall and courts. Harold Copeland picked his story on the basis of a healthy suspicion of corruption. Chester Bond presented an idea to a news editor who nodded approval.

Every public affairs story, from idea through development to finished copy, is the result of several levels of decision making. Editor Ronald Buel, who learned his craft at the *Wall Street Journal* and later founded *Willamette Week*, a high-quality alternative paper in Portland, Oregon, speaks of five layers of journalistic decision making:

1. Data assignment: who decides what is worth covering and why?
2. Data collection: who decides when enough information has been gathered?
3. Data evaluation: who decides what is important enough to be put into a story?
4. Data writing: who decides what words to use?
5. Data editing: who decides which story gets a big headline and goes on the front page, which stories to cut, which stories to change?[2]

Similarly, reporting has been likened to a manufacturing process. It is "a series of steps that begins with an idea and ends with a completed product—in this case, a story ready to be consumed by the reader, listener or viewer. Reporters, of course, live and work within this production system."[3] For the public affairs reporter, it is important to remember where they are in this system at any given time and what they need to do to cope with the particular demands of the moment. Sometimes that means arguing with an editor to justify a story; sometimes it means cajoling a news source or listening to a reader's complaint. Whatever else it may be, public affairs reporting is rarely boring.

PORTRAITS OF FOUR NEWS STORIES

Suppose you as a student had the opportunity to ask the managing editors of the previously mentioned newspapers why each of the four situations is deemed *newsworthy*. Tom Greene's editor would tell you that zoning meetings are always covered by his paper because they are public business. If a zoning variance is approved at today's hearing—and subsequently approved by the city council—it will have an impact on the city. It will change a neighborhood by mixing commercial purposes with residential. This alteration, the editor asserts, may have a positive or negative effect depending on how you look at it and what you think public policy should be. He tells you that the zoning hearing is likely to draw a large group of citizens, mainly residents of the neighborhood where the zoning change would be implemented. "People are interested in this zoning issue," he might say, "and because it has an impact on the lives of people, we should and will cover it." And furthermore, he might add, the zoning hearing is the most important thing happening in city hall today—surely it ranks above a citizens' committee planning a May Day parade, a meeting of the city council safety committee, and a group of businessmen discussing a preliminary plan for a campaign to renovate storefronts on Main Street.

No doubt Susan Kahn's editor would think you naïve if you were to ask why the paper had decided to cover the trial of an accused embezzler, who happened to be a prominent citizen. Few details of the embezzlement have been disclosed, the editor explains, but now, presumably, all of them will be made known, and thousands of depositors have an indirect interest.

Harold Copeland is his own editor. His search of records is important to his paper because it may disclose a conflict of interest. Did the county commissioners line their own pockets by ordering extensive road work in an area in which some of them had commercial interests? As a first step, Copeland says, it was necessary to search county land records. The land in the area was owned by several local and out-of-state corporations—but who owned the corporations? That question, thought Copeland, might lead him to an important revelation. In this instance, a thorough investigation, based on an educated suspicion, was the impetus for the story, and its public policy and public interest implications are evident.

As a college student, Chester Bond took courses in abnormal psychology. His personal interest in exceptional or retarded children led him to suggest the story he was seeking in the interview with the health department official. As his editor put it, "This is a good story for our readers. It affects thousands of them directly or indirectly. And since retardation is so often a family problem and our paper is directed to the suburban family, the newsworthiness of this story is clear."

ON THE NATURE OF NEWS

On the surface, the editors' explanations are logical enough. They say they chose the four assignments because they (1) were important, (2) affected people in the community, (3) would arouse public curiosity, and (4) would serve what they believe to be "the public interest." But clearly, neither reporter nor editor in any of the four cases was thinking of theoretical definitions of news. They were instead thinking of how their papers could present an "image of reality" of their community. For news is "in the largest sense that material which is most likely to be looked to and accepted as the image of reality."[4] There are, of course, many images of reality; thus the editor and reporter determined which image would constitute the news of the day. In a perceptive essay, sociologists Raymond and Alice Bauer observed that "the concept of 'news' which dominates our reporting media dictates that an event is newsworthy only if it is discontinuous with preceding events and if it is relatively recent in occurrence."[5] Although some stories, of course, linger on for second and third day treatment, in general, issues, events, and happenings in the community that do not meet these criteria are usually not deemed to be newsworthy.

It is possible to find many lofty, theory-laden explanations of what *is* and *is not* news, but there is really only one operational definition of news: It is the editorial content of what appears in the newspaper or on the radio or television newscast. Items selected for inclusion in the media are news; those rejected or otherwise excluded are not. As Buel's five layers of decision making indicate, news is also human interaction and conflict. The result of the compromise between and among the various individuals involved in the news story from conceptualization to the final rewritten words on paper is *news*. Political scientist Leon V. Sigal says that "the ability to get information into the news and to prevent rivals from doing so is at once a tactic and a stake in that fight [for news]."[6] Sigal continues,

> Four bargaining games run concurrently: those among newsmen inside their organizations, among reporters on the beat, between the reporter and his news sources, and among those sources, mostly officials in various government positions. Outcomes in one game can affect outcomes of the others. From the standpoint of bureaucratic politics, then, news is an outcome of the bargaining interplay of newsmen and sources.[7]

Thus, news is a highly complex concept, not easily categorized or abstracted. And yet, the content of most newspapers and newscasts has remarkable similarity, which is due to the conventions of news-gathering and the use of the standard journalistic form by news gatherers. With these thoughts about the nature of news clearly in mind, we return to the four public affairs stories.

WHAT THE REPORTERS DID— AND WHY

The zoning hearing that Tom Greene attended was like a thousand others in as many cities across the country. The meeting was called to order by a lean, angular man who served both as chairman of the zoning commission (a committee of the city council in this case) and as a member of the city council. He explained that a request for a change in the R-1 zoning regulations for residential areas in the northeastern section of the city was being considered by the commission. In measured language, he explained that the commission would hear both from proponents and opponents of the measure.

A well-dressed man, a consumer-relations director for a major oil company, strode to the front of the room. He explained that his firm wanted to build a large central pumping facility (a service station designed to serve a large community area) on the edge of the northeast neighborhood. As the energy crisis of the 1970s and 1980s brought the closure of small stations, larger central facilities allowed the oil companies greater economies, the man explained. Anticipating objections to the plan, the man said the building would be "architecturally consistent" with the neighborhood. It would have no gaudy signs but a pleasant neo-Colonial façade. He offered copies of engineering studies that dismissed the idea of extra noise in the neighborhood and promised that the pumping station would close every night by ten. His presentation took twenty minutes. It was highly professional and accompanied by visual aids and a handsome model of the proposed station.

The chairman said the commission would then hear citizen response to the proposal—to both the firm's specific proposal and the general idea of varying the zone. Six citizens testified. One represented the neighborhood improvement association, another the parent-teacher association. Others spoke for themselves, and one man testified for the chamber of commerce.

The testimony was mixed. The neighborhood improvement spokesperson said the station would deface and degrade the neighborhood. It might, he said, lower property values and cause danger in the event of an explosion. Others objected to the potential noise and the additional traffic flow into the quiet neighborhood. Only the chamber of commerce representative saw any virtue in the plan, but even she was careful to qualify her statements, "allowing as how the citizens did have a point." For two hours there was heated debate as the oil company spokesman was called back for cross-examination. First, the four commissioners quizzed him, then members of the audience of about 150 persons. Eventually, a commissioner moved to recommend approval. The motion failed three to one.

Tom Greene left the meeting thinking about the result, the discussion, and how he would write his story. By the time he reached his desk in the newspaper office he had a lead in mind. Eyeing the sheaf of notes he had taken, along with reports distributed by the various spokespersons, he began to write his story. It began as follows:

> The City Zoning Commission today rejected a plan that would have allowed construction of a gasoline pumping facility in the city's northeast corner.
>   By a vote of 3-1, the commission rejected a request by the Moon Oil Company. The firm had asked for a change in the present zoning from residential to a mixed commercial-residential designation. In a spirited meeting that

attracted 150 persons, Moon representative Robert Stevens argued that the proposed facility "will enhance the neighborhood, both in terms of convenience of gasoline and architecturally." Stevens presented a model of the proposed station and various reports.

Michael Malloy, president of the Northeast Improvement Association, disagreed sharply, saying that the station would "deface the neighborhood and cause great inconvenience, especially noise."

Malloy and several others who testified also maintained that there was potential danger to the community should the gasoline tanks explode.

Citing engineering studies, Stevens discounted this claim. "An explosion is virtually impossible," he said.

In this vein, the story continued for nearly twenty column inches, adding more quotations, more details, and eventually explaining the background of the zoning issue, how it occurred, and other concerns.

After leaving the meeting, Greene had nearly two hours to complete his story, and he had the assurance of the city editor that a twenty-inch story was desired. A facile writer, Greene was able to go over his notes and consider which quotes to use, which to discard. Because his story would fill a news hole on page one, he chose a conventional news style. He made only one phone call to check a factual detail but otherwise relied completely on his notes and memory.

Susan Kahn knew that court would convene at 9:30, allowing time to file a breaking story for the first edition at 11:15. She hadn't expected, however, the kind of information she got as the prosecution outlined its case. It would show, the prosecutor said in his opening statement, that the accused, as manager of branches, had taken an average of $50,000 a year for nine years by making out loans to fictitious persons and covering them with "repayments" from new fake loans. Revealed for the first time in the prosecutor's statement was the information that senior bank officials had tried to cover up the loss in the hope that the accused would be able to repay the sums he had taken. Only when it became apparent that he couldn't did they notify authorities. The accused, said the prosecutor, had used the money to live up to the image of the prosperous banker—large home, summer place, cars, and boats—on a salary of $18,000. While the prosecutor was still talking, Kahn had gone to a phone in the clerk's office and dictated the following lead:

> Top officers of the Blank National Bank tried to cover up an alleged $450,000 embezzlement by one of their vice-presidents in an effort to avoid adverse publicity, District Attorney John Jones said today as the vice-president went on trial in County Court.

In his search of land records, Harold Copeland learned that three of the six tracts of land affected by the road improvements were owned by the Resthaven Land Corporation, a local firm. The others were owned by two local men and an out-of-state firm, Cable Development Company, of Houston, Texas. A labored check of public records indicated that both Resthaven and Cable were owned by a holding company in the capital city. A telephone call to an attorney in the secretary of state's office brought him the information he wanted. Among incorporators in Post Road Holding Company were two members of the county board of commissioners and a private citizen who owned one of the six tracts. Copeland checked and rechecked the records, interviewed a knowledgeable and friendly local banker, then confronted the three men involved. One of them called him a "damned snoop" and all refused to confirm the report. But neither did they deny it. So Copeland wrote,

> Two members of the county board of commissioners and a local real estate broker may have benefited financially from road improvements the board approved recently.
> The three, supervisors Richard Bemis and Sidney Cohen and realtor James Hoffmeister, are incorporators of the Post Road Holding Company, which controls 500 acres of land in the Post Road area, according to state corporation records and county land records. The county commission, with both commissioners voting "yes," approved extensive road construction in the Post Road area last spring, and as a result the assessed valuation of the land increased about 30 percent, according to the county assessor's office.

The story continued with heavy documentation. Copeland cited authority for his explanations but carefully refrained from specific charges. He reported the unwillingness of the three men to discuss the land ownership with him. Although Copeland saw a number of other potential conflicts of interest in the case as he searched public records, he could not get corroboration and thus left them out of the story.

Chester Bond spoke to the public-health planner who briefed him on the problems of mentally retarded children in the suburban area where his paper circulated. He got facts and figures about the state's program and how the planners proposed to extend and accelerate services. From the planner's office he visited two psychiatrists who treated retarded children, the president of a parents' association, two day-care centers for the retarded, a state hospital, and a convention of the state psychological association. The interviews were coupled with considerable reading about the problem and a call to the state department of mental health, which provided state and national statistics and a statement about the nature and scope of the problem. After three weeks of interviews and research for background information, done while covering other, routine stories, Bond was ready to write. He sent his editor this memo:

> I'm planning a five-part series, each story running 20-25 inches. They would be (1) "The Plight of the Retarded—A Family Dilemma," which would outline the nature of the problem and have several good anecdotal examples; (2)

"What's Being Done," which would focus on present treatment practices and programs; (3) "Who Are the Retarded?"—their lives and potential; (4) "From Back Wards to the Community," a story looking at the changes in care and treatment of the retarded with an emphasis on community centers and home-visiting programs; (5) "What of the Future?"—a look at the state plans and reaction of citizen groups.

The memo continued, detailing the series, indicating what sources had been consulted and why. Bond began his first story:

Jack Brown is a 37-year-old family man with three healthy children, a working wife, and a promising future. Unusual? No, except for one thing—thirty years ago, Jack Brown was diagnosed as "mentally retarded."

The story continued (Jack Brown was a pseudonym), humanizing the problem, explaining the potential of retarded persons. Bond wrote expansively. He was not worrying much about space limitations because his belief that he was writing about a major public-health problem was buttressed by the knowledge that the publisher's wife was a board member of the state association for retarded children—and the chances of full use of the story were excellent.

A LOOK AT THE STORIES

Returning to Buel's five layers of decision making, it is evident why each of the stories was assigned—at least in terms of the editors' surface rationale. Obviously, a small daily should give considerable attention to a zoning meeting that will have an impact on a number of local citizens. When 150 of those citizens appear at city hall on a weekday morning—in a small city—that itself is news. It shows the intensity of concern. But such rationale was not really in play when the city editor agreed with Greene that the story should be covered. Zoning meetings are standard fare for public affairs reporters, and barring another, more important assignment, Greene always covers the zoning commission, especially when it is about to make a decision.

To some extent Susan Kahn's presence at the courtroom was also routine. Following up a continuing story on her criminal justice beat is standard practice. That she would be present in the courtroom was guaranteed by the coverage already given to the case. However, even the most vital cases sometimes get diminished treatment if a major, national catastrophe, such as a presidential assassination, occurs. The degree to which news values inhere in any story depends on what else is happening—in the community, state, and nation.

In deciding how much information to gather for their stories, the four reporters were all guided by constraints of time and space. In two hours, Greene could hardly write a short history of zoning. He decided to concentrate only on the meeting and what happened there. Of course, as the regular city hall reporter, he went to the meeting with a considerable fund of knowledge about the subject. What was a routine assignment for him might not have been routine for a new reporter.

Similarly, Susan Kahn had already covered the pretrial aspects of the embezzlement story, so she had no trouble composing a conventional lead under pressure of an early deadline. Harold Copeland concentrated only on those records relevant to his suspicion that there might be potential conflict of interest on the county board of commissioners, and he used only those items that could be confirmed elsewhere.

Chester Bond had the luxury of writing a multisource story in which he was able to spend several weeks tracking down information, conducting interviews, and thinking about what he was going to write.

In all these instances space was pretty much guaranteed, barring last-minute developments. Not one of the reporters had to fight with the city editor to get the story into the paper.

All the reporters had to sort out the trivial from the significant. This process was especially true of the zoning meeting, the transcript of which would have covered several newspaper pages. At the other extreme, the retardation story was the product of considerable planning. Bond spent little time with irrelevant sources, although he collected a large stack of written material that required sorting and sifting.

In writing the story, Greene hurriedly prepared his copy with little thought and time for rewriting. The story was routine and it was handled with dispatch. Similarly, the trial story was quick and to the point. Copeland was much more careful in his use of language. The potential for a libel suit, even though his subjects were public officials, was great and he didn't want to take any chances. The economic constraints of a possible suit were very real to him as an owner of the paper. Thus he took special care in checking and rechecking the information. Bond, in the retardation study, had more research time, which permitted the use of anecdotes, case histories, description, and dialogue. Finally, each of the stories was published with only a few editing changes.

The four stories presented here are typical assignments for public affairs reporters. Like these stories, every news story has many complex variations, and depending on newsroom interactions, space, time, and other constraints, the results may vary considerably. The lot of the public affairs reporter is dynamic, one that requires an inquiring mind, specialized knowledge, and an ability to adapt and adjust as news changes and situations alter.

The four hypothetical case studies are an introduction to the goal of this book: to provide a thoughtful framework for consideration of public affairs reporters—their problems and priorities. The book follows the reporters and their search for news, and it moves toward a new definition of news, one adaptable to change and geared to the future. It analyzes approaches to the coverage of public problems, including traditional strategies (for example, beats), direct and indirect observation, the search of public records, interviewing, and the writing process. Variations in the approach to coverage and writing style are also considered. Differences in reportorial practices demanded by different kinds of media and different time restrictions are also examined.

Attention is next directed to ways in which public affairs reporters can enrich their work by using social science methods such as surveys and field experiments. Similarly, the utility of understanding social indicators and statistical methods is stressed.

After considering the strategic problems in public affairs reporting, we turn to public affairs news settings, placing special emphasis on coverage of the legal process, government agencies and services, politics and elections, and the legislative process, and specialized coverage of such areas as business, urban crises, science, health, and the environment. Finally, we discuss the future of public affairs reporting as it appears from the contemporary vantage point.

Our emphasis is more on strategy than setting because it is clear that many of the techniques and thinking processes useful to the public affairs reporter in one setting apply to other news settings as well. Where there are differences and a need for specialized skills particular to a field, we will discuss them.

Thus, this book is developed not as a rigid road map for the public affairs reporter but as a stimulus to thinking and analysis. That is the point. Reporting is not an automatic reaction wherein a trained reporter always follows the same course. Reporting is a dynamic process best done when the reporter has an overall plan that assumes little and is open to new ideas and other changes. In short, reporters need strategies for their work as well as mastery of their tools and techniques. What follows in this book is directed to the student who wants to be a thinking reporter keeping pace with the future demands of the communications industry regardless of the form it takes.

NOTES

[1] For a discussion of the role of the press as a representative of the public, see Everette E. Dennis, "The Rhetoric and Reality of Representation: A Legal Basis for Press Freedom and Minority Rights," in ed. Bernard Rubin, *Small Voices and Great Trumpets, Minorities and the Media* (New York: Praeger, 1980), pp. 67–88.

[2] Ronald A. Buel, *Dead End: The Automobile in Mass Transportation* (Baltimore, Md.: Penguin Books, 1973), p. 220.

[3]Everette E. Dennis and Arnold H. Ismach, *Reporting Processes and Practices* (Belmont, Calif.: Wadsworth, 1981), p. xi.

[4]Raymond A. Bauer and Alice H. Bauer, "America, 'Mass Society' and Mass Media," *Journal of Social Issues 16,* No. 3, (1960), 50–51.

[5]Ibid., 52.

[6]Leon V. Sigal, *Reporters and Officials: The Organization and Politics of Newsmaking* (Lexington, Mass.: D. C. Heath, 1973), p. 5.

[7]Ibid.

2

Toward a New Definition of News

What is history but a fable agreed upon?

Napoleon Bonaparte

The parson, the geologist, and the cowboy were all standing together and gazing for the first time at the Grand Canyon.
"One of the wonders of God," said the parson.
"One of the wonders of science," said the geologist.
"What a helluva place to raise a cow," said the cowboy.

So much for objectivity.

With that bit of pointed whimsy, Detroit newspaper executive Derick Daniels dismissed a bit of hard-core journalistic dogma: that objective reporting is the one path to truth and reality.[1] The long-running debate about objective versus interpretive reporting is largely over. Interpretation has earned a secure place as an accepted member of the journalistic family. There are, of course, those who retain an uncomplicated faith in the sublime dynamics of objective reporting to fulfill adequately society's needs for information. The columns of newspapers are still largely populated with the classic, one-dimensional objective story in which the reporter serves as uncritical transmission belt, giving equal weight to all positions presented at an event.

Still, few editors today deny the need for reporting that goes beyond the immediate event, adding meaning to complex news situations. Journalistic excellence in the 1980s combines devotion to the factuality of objective reporting *and* recognition of the need for interpretation. It rejects the ritual model of journalistic objectivity that grew with the rise of the scientific method in the nineteenth century. That model, in its purest form, called for faithful recording of the observed event and suppression of the observer's prior knowledge of the subject.

14

Rejection of the pure objective model, however, doesn't mean approval of *subjective* reporting. Personal bias, unsupported assertions, and one-sided presentations have no place in news stories. The happy marriage of objectivity and interpretation demands factual observation along with a balanced presentation of pertinent background and contextual information. Because of the difficulty of arriving at that balance, many in journalism still cling to the ideal of the traditional objective report.

One reason for the survival and dominance of the objective form is the history of its hard-won acceptance. Herbert Brucker, former editor of the *Hartford* (Conn.) *Courant,* summed up the virtues of objectivity with this observation:

> No one can argue away the fact that American journalism has now struggled for a century and a third to replace partisan propaganda with reporting that gets within hailing distance of the truth. And that kind of reporting is too valuable, not only to journalism, but to self-government itself, to be discarded now in an emotional reaction fueled by the current political distemper.[2]

But objectivity, long the Eleventh Commandment for journalism's faithful, is now often regarded with the same irreverence as other mortal rules. Outside press critics and inside professionals alike are subscribing in increasing numbers to a new orthodoxy which argues that interpretation is needed in the reporting of *all* public affairs. The complexity of contemporary life, the diversity of modern society, the rapid changes brought by new technology and shifting cultural values—all demand explanation if the public is to be adequately informed. Yesterday's one-dimensional journalism yielded not neutrality but superficiality. The news media, both print and broadcast, deluged their audiences with what Eric Sevareid once termed "the daily needle shower of unrelated facts." They reported the events—especially the sensational and the graphic—but ignored the antecedents of those events. They covered the visible artifacts of society's turmoil but not the conditions responsible for that turmoil.

Communications researcher James W. Carey goes a step beyond criticizing objective reporting for what it hasn't accomplished. He believes it has also compromised the independence of the journalist and allowed news sources to use the press for their own purposes.

> First, as an adjunct of objective reporting there developed norms and procedures governing the manner in which reporters could utilize sources. The net effect of the press conference, the background interview, the rules governing anonymous disclosure and attribution of sources, and particularly the growing use of the public information officer within government, is to routinize the reporter's function and to grant to the source exceptional control over news dissemination. As a result, not only can government and other sources deliberately place messages, without alteration, before the public, but through the "leak" and other forms of anonymous disclosure, they can utilize

the press as an alternative channel for diplomatic and other private communication. The "canned" press conference in which questions are planted and to which "safe" reporters are admitted by pass further strips away the independent, critical function of the journalist.

Second, the psychology of the reporting process also chips away at the reporter's independence. Because the reporter mediates between audiences and sources, he is pulled in two directions: serving the interests of the source and the interests of the audience, interests which are rarely identical. Often, if not usually, the reporter develops contempt for both parties he serves: the audience because it is so often apathetic and uninterested, the source because it is so often dishonest. Resolution of the strain in the reporting process normally supports the interests of the source rather than that of the audience.[3]

Awareness of journalism's failings has not led to overnight reform. The seeds of objective reporting were sown more than a hundred years ago and have grown deep roots. The strident personal journalism of the early nineteenth-century American press, which sought to persuade rather than inform, gradually gave way to an objectivity spawned by two forces. One was a profound change in the ownership pattern of newspapers, with the editor–publisher replaced by corporate owners more interested in profit than politics. As early as midcentury, owners discovered that factual reporting of public affairs was attracting broad reading audiences. The other force was the growth of the wire services and syndicates, which served the same news material to clients of varying biases. The press associations served to standardize style at the expense of individualized reporting. The result was an objectivity so narrow that it removed all context from news stories. It was the dominant reporting form by World War I.[4]

Challenges to blind objectivity began to appear in the 1930s, in book form,[5] but the first substantial public criticism of this approach was expressed in 1947 by the privately funded Commission on Freedom of the Press. It called on newspapers to give the public "a truthful, comprehensive and intelligent account of the day's events *in a context which gives them meaning.*"[6]

The commission, however, was composed of laymen distinguished in fields other than journalism. Its chairman was educator Robert M. Hutchins. Editors and reporters are not renowned for sitting at the feet of those who have "never met a deadline," and the press establishment reacted predictably to the commission's recommendations: it ridiculed them and then ignored them. It wasn't long, however, before prominent voices within the profession began espousing the cause of news interpretation. One was Erwin D. Canham, editor of the *Christian Science Monitor,* who challenged convention by contending that "the balancing fact should be attached directly to the misleading assertion." Another was philosopher–critic Harry S. Ashmore, who, while editor of the *Little Rock* (Ark.)

Gazette, summed up the growing sentiment for interpretive reporting this way:

> It remains journalism's unfulfilled responsibility to somehow provide per-spective and continuity . . . to add the "why" to the "what". . . . I think we have got to get over the notion that objectivity is achieved by giving a sinner equal space with a saint—and above all of paying the greatest attention to those who shout the loudest. We've got to learn that a set of indisputable facts does not necessarily add up to the whole truth.[7]

A turning point came in the early 1950s, when Senator Joseph R. McCarthy of Wisconsin capitalized on the media's slavish devotion to objec-tivity and became a national figure in the process.[8] His unsubstantiated charges of treason, subversion, and communism in federal government were reported as "straight" news by the media. Thus his accusations of one day stood alone on the front pages, whereas the denial followed later, if at all, on the inside pages. The flaw in the process was eventually recognized by most journalists. The prevailing culture of journalism, which held objec-tivity as its central tenet, was jarred into a new era. It is an irony of sorts that a principal legacy of McCarthyism has been a beneficial effect on a press system that the senator used and abused.

The move from one-dimensional objectivity was by no means univer-sal or consistent. Ground rules for the use of interpretive reporting are selective, and the public figure today can still manipulate the objective tradition to his advantage. Washington correspondent Peter Lisagor ob-served this potential in the 1972 reelection campaign of Richard Nixon. "The rules of objectivity are such," he said, "that a man can make political capital out of them in the way he presents a particular issue."[9] Lisagor was referring to Nixon's practice of including a sensational, if suspect, charge in his speeches. The objective tradition persuaded reporters to use the accusation as the lead of their stories. Time for rebuttal or denial was not available because Nixon knew not only what made a good headline and lead but also the deadlines for Eastern papers and networks.

Timothy Crouse, in his intimate portrait of presidential campaign reporters, *The Boys on the Bus,* concluded that a strict anti-interpretation rule was imposed on most journalists. Whereas the reporter covering the town council might add context to her story, the campaign reporters were confined to conduit status. Said Crouse, "If the candidate spouted fullsome bullshit all day, the formula made it hard for the reporter to say so di-rectly—he would have to pretend that "informed sources" had said so. . . . A reporter was not allowed to make even the simplest judgments; nor was he expected to verify the candidate's claims."[10]

Yet the evolution from rigid objective reporting has come far in the decades since McCarthy. Journalism has moved into two modes of reporting. One is straight news, the conventional journalism that despairs of reporting anything but occurrences. The other is interpretive, which attempts to explain change and relate events to each other. Strangely, they coexist in many newspapers, and this dual approach is perhaps the prevailing method for reporting public affairs today. The principal effort is still devoted to the coverage of events. A small percentage of these stories lead to subsequent interpretive stories, variously labeled in professional jargon as backgrounders, situationers, interpretives, news analyses, think pieces, or, derisively, "thumb-suckers."

The assumption in this schizoid approach to reporting public affairs is that fact-gathering and interpretation are separable reporting functions. Many would argue, however, that they are indivisible for the same reasons that objectivity is unattainable: The very selection (and rejection) of facts, their order of presentation, and other matters of reportorial judgment are, in effect, elements of interpretation. For these and other reasons, the cutting edge in public affairs reporting today is moving toward adequate interpretation in each story produced. The thrust in more progressive newsrooms is toward the full-dimensional story, one in which the reader gets both an accurate account of an event or situation *and* enough additional information to assure understanding. The reporter, to use a medical metaphor, is being allowed to both take the X-ray and read the film.[11]

WHAT IS "NEWS?"

If there is consensus in the newsrooms regarding the inadequacy of classical objectivity and the need for interpretation, are we then on the threshold of a journalistic utopia where the news media will adequately fulfill their obligations to society? Few serious observers of the press take so sanguine a view. The reasons are several. Today, editors talk more of fairness than of objectivity and subscribe to the need for interpretive reporting. Yet the implementation of these convictions is often spotty or half-hearted. Habits die hard; rituals persist. Changing the genes of the journalistic process may be as difficult as restructuring the DNA molecule; those who rely on a hopeful Darwinism in which change will come in due time are perhaps more patient than realistic.

The conventions of journalism, the very structure of news organizations with their reliance on generations-old systems of news-gathering (such as the rigid "beat" system with its arbitrary divisions along lines of geography or subject matter and the often excessive emphasis placed on timeliness and proximity) are factors that are now seen as hindering effective reporting. Most important, perhaps, is the realization that the objectivity versus interpretation debate was just a preliminary bout in a related but much more basic battle: the redefinition of news.

Interpretive reporting and the definition of news are related to each other as an arm is to a wrist, a switch to a lamp, a turntable to a record. Confront one and you confront the other. Success in fulfilling journalism's appointed role depends as much or more on the subject matter selected for attention as on the method of presentation. The problem then becomes a question of emphasis: is the more basic concern substance, or process?

In Chapter 1 the editors of the four hypothetical newspapers justified the story assignments they made by citing their importance to readers or to the community at large. Many editors would invoke similar notions in attempting to define news. But it was also suggested in Chapter 1 that there was really only one workable, all-embracing definition of news: that which appears in the newspaper or on the newscast. Acknowledging this reality averts a good deal of semantic quibbling and goes directly to the underlying question: What *should be* in the newspaper or on the newscast? The "what" in the question doesn't limit the answer to choices among discrete subjects. News has never been selected on the basis of categorical classification alone. One speech is covered, another ignored; one meeting gets front page treatment, a similar meeting goes unnoticed—a tree falling in the forest. It has always been thus in the news business. Factors other than topic influence the choice of events and situations that are made into news.

What, then, are these factors? As noted in Chapter 1, the Bauers considered two factors as determinants of news: a distinct event and recency.[12]

The Commission on Freedom of the Press concluded thirty years ago that the journalist's definition of news, in an operational sense, is something that happened within the last few hours and which will attract the interest of customers. The criteria of "interest," the commission observed, are recency, proximity, combat, human interest, and novelty. Notable for their absence in the list are considerations of significance or pertinence. Critics of the press since that time haven't improved on the commission's observations. The criteria usually lead journalists to report on single events (recency) in their cities of publication (proximity) which contain elements of drama or conflict (combat) or of pathos (human interest) or oddity (novelty). These criteria could lead one to conclude that the ideal story might be about a local beauty queen who mugged the mayor in front of a brothel last night so that she could get enough money to pay for a heart operation for her critically ill younger brother.

Such exaggeration may be unfair, but the inescapable observation is that most news is event-centered. It is typically about a recent happening and is generally uninterpreted, with minimal context, unrelated to other situations and events. This aspect contrasts with what has been termed process-centered news—interpretive presentations of conditions and situations in society that are related in broad context and over time.[13] This latter category is not an academic invention, an ideological improbability nurtured in the ivy tower. It is an approach increasingly occupying the public affairs reporter, fostered by progressive news organizations, large and small.

The central notion fueling this new journalism of public affairs is the obligation of the journalist to act rather than react, to initiate coverage rather than wait for events. The press can monitor, evaluate, prod, question, or review the operations of officials, agencies, and programs. It isn't limited to agendas set by others, which would place it strictly in a reactive role.

Process-centered news is appearing regularly on op-ed pages, front pages, Sunday feature sections, and as special reports on radio and television. Sometimes it is written by nonjournalists with expertise in the subject. More frequently, editors assign staff reporters to this type of story. Newspapers such as the *Wall Street Journal* and the *Christian Science Monitor* were pioneers of the movement toward full-dimensional treatment of subjects that transcend specific events. As the interpretive approach gained acceptance throughout the 1970s, other major newspapers invested in staff and space to pursue regularly beneath-the-surface explorations of nonevents: evaluating the performance of a federal regulatory agency, probing the implications to farmers and consumers of an extended drought, assessing the social and economic impacts of fads in clothing fashions.

Some newspapers, propelled by the shift toward interpretive reporting, have deemphasized spot news coverage and started to produce what might be called a daily news magazine. Perhaps the most extreme example was the *Minneapolis Star,* which in 1982 merged with its sister paper, the *Minneapolis Tribune,* to become the *Star and Tribune.* Even though the *Star's* experiment ended after only four years, many other newspapers have moved in the direction of team reporting and magazine content. This approach eliminates most fixed beats and assigns reporters to teams responsible for broad subject areas—such as social issues or politics and government. Spurred by an emphasis on audience-oriented interpretive reporting, the new arrangement frees reporters to examine news situations without the mental blinders of fixed beat boundaries.

The shift to process-centered reporting is not limited to metropolitan newspapers. The medium-sized *Riverside* (Calif.) *Press-Enterprise,* to name just one, devotes a section-opening page each day to subjects ranging from the growth of fundamentalist religious groups to the backyard impact of inflation and recession. Five reporters are assigned full time to this task. Other small- and medium-sized dailies are also attempting the process-centered approach, within the limits of staff availability. Some weeklies are also attempting to treat important local issues in depth.

These examples, however, are exceptions to the norm. The norm is still covering the mayor's speech, the school board vote, the street demonstration, the unusual crime. The norm in journalism does not yet include discovering the mayor's thoughts and plans when he is publicly silent, or probing the cross-currents of educational thought that never surface before the school board, or exploring the viewpoints and conditions of disadvantaged groups before there are demonstrations, or examining the culture of crime rather than its spectacular artifacts. The reporter and her editor might ask,

[Does racism exist only when there is a riot?

[Is there a problem in education only when parents protest at a public
[hearing?

[Are there public concerns about zoning, garbage disposal, or park facilities
[only when they appear on the city council agenda?

The answers are obvious, but the notion that a topic is not newsworthy until something "happens" has been pervasive. By restricting the definition of news to events, significant phenomena fall outside the reporter's vision, and less significant events, often contrived, get attention. By this criterion, the public doesn't learn of important forces in society until they erupt suddenly, and often traumatically, in events. The recent past is filled with such examples. It required sit-ins, marches, and riots to bring out the state of mind and living conditions of blacks in the 1960s. It required a comic-opera burglary at Watergate to expose the moral poverty of a national administration in the 1970s.

Why is the press so often a prisoner of this dysfunctional definition of news? Press critics and professionals offer a variety of explanations, some harsh, some empathetic. Critic Max Ways blames the situation on the media's decision to focus on governmental decisions as well as on the "event trap."

> Journalism still clings to the legislative act and the presidential decision because they are relatively easy to get into focus. By contrast, such gradual and multicentered changes as the lessening of parental authority or the increase of consumer credit or public acceptance of a new technology are more difficult to pinpoint. They are not events. They did not happen "yesterday" or "today" or even "last week." They do not fit the journalist's cherished notions of a "story." Yet their consequences and implications are far more potent than an isolated legislative act or presidential decision which gets the attention of reporters and space or time in the media.[14]

Journalism critic Donald McDonald also regards the "event mentality" as the most pernicious cause of editorial anemia. But he suggests that other journalistic conventions—the penchant for oversimplification, the preference for the bizarre, the addiction to speed—combine to hamper process-centered reporting. On the question of reducing public issues to a two-sided scenario, McDonald points out that simplification "often destroys the opportunity for understanding, for if anything is characteristic of public affairs, it is complexity."[15] Regarding the rush to get today's news into print or on the air immediately, he observes that it "is axiomatic that the more serious and consequential the public affairs, the untidier they will be and the more unmanageable they will be by any of the metronomic standards set by the print and electronic media."[16]

Sociologist Gaye Tuchman, in her detailed field studies of the professional behavior of journalists, adds yet another explanation for the normative definitions of news. What McDonald termed conventions, she described as "strategic rituals" that are followed more from habit than reason.[17] The rituals are used defensively to validate the reporter's performance. Objectivity is one such defense. Tuchman also views the organizational and operational structure of the news media as a chief determinant of what is considered news.[18] "The way something happens" thus often defines news. If an event occurs on a recognized beat, it has legitimacy and therefore will appear in print. A similar event occurring elsewhere may be rejected or pass unnoticed—an accident of geography.

Clearly, the question of news definition isn't easily answered. Reporters and editors struggle with it daily, as they do with the difficult choice between straight and interpretive treatment. The four story situations in Chapter 1 illustrate these alternatives. Two were spot news treatments, two interpretive. Depending on circumstance, each might have been treated in either mode. Moreover, interpretive stories could have been developed *before* the events in some cases.

Tom Greene's coverage of the zoning meeting was in straight news style. He told what happened at the meeting. It could have been reported in broader context, however. What are the implications of a major pumping station at that location? Is it an indicator of change in developmental patterns? Of transit problems? What significance does it hold for those who didn't attend the meeting but who may be affected by the decision? Is the development a sign of general neighborhood deterioration, signaling a more profound problem?

Chester Bond's series about the mentally retarded could have been treated as a brief announcement of a new state program and left at that. Similarly, if there were no such program—no "event"—Bond could have developed an interpretive story on the possible need for one.

Harold Copeland's investigation of corruption is the type of story that may itself produce an event, in this case a criminal charge or a recall by voters. The digging by Copeland could have been done by an official such as the county attorney, with the result that spot news stories would follow. It was the combination of press and official investigations that distinguished the long Watergate burglary probe and its aftermath, with segments of the press doing much more than covering court appearances.

Susan Kahn led her story with the disclosures of the alleged cover-up by bank officials, a predictable spot news treatment. In future stories, she would be likely to write about other developments in the embezzlement trial. But the disclosures may suggest stories of much greater import than the trial itself. How often do business executives attempt to paper over crime in their own establishments to protect their images with the public? What is the extent of white-collar crime in relation to more sensational and publicized misbehavior? These and similar questions are worth exploring, whether or not an embezzlement case is in progress.

Decisions of the types demanded by these stories go a long way toward determining whether a newspaper is predictable and dull or stimulating and relevant for the reader.

THE BROADCAST DILEMMA

If the structure and heritage of the news system often turn the print reporter toward shallow treatment, the broadcast reporter is almost forced into that mold. The strictures of time and the assumptions of audience interest make radio and television news programs a bulletin board of recent events. News items are rarely allotted more than a minute or two, with the length of those on television frequently dictated by the availability of film. Broadcast reporters, in an effort to capsulize and simplify, tend to use few sources for a given story. Constraints of time, complicated for television by the processing, editing, and transmission of film, are even more severe for the broadcast than for the print reporter.

The generally acknowledged communication effectiveness of television, therefore, isn't exploited on regular news programs to give the viewer a full account of the forces in society. Despite these limitations, broadcast journalists have often produced interpretive essays of exceptional quality. Their opportunity to do so depends on the availability of staff, money, and air time for documentaries and other special news programs. This opportunity varies with the station and the network, although the advent of new technology and inexpensive videotape may soon ease this stricture at many stations.

Network devotion to the documentary has been episodic. The trend, however, is away from regularly scheduled documentaries in prime time (7:30 to 11:00 P.M.), and toward late-night magazine-format shows that offer briefer interpretations of several subjects.[19] The amount of network prime time devoted to public affairs on a regularly scheduled basis averaged 2 percent at the start of the 1970s.[20] Prime time is obviously the preserve of fantasy, not reality. Still, network journalists are producing programs of merit with increasing regularity. A sample of memorable documentaries would include "The Selling of the Pentagon," a critical examination by CBS of the Defense Department's propaganda operations; "The Blue Collar Trap," an Emmy winner by NBC, which probed job dissatisfaction in an age of affluence; and "Close-Up," a series in prime time on ABC of special investigative reports on issues such as the energy crisis and world famine.

Expansion of network news programs from thirty minutes to an hour has been discussed for years, promising greater opportunities for interpretive reporting. Local affiliates, however, object strenuously to relinquishing more of their time to less profitable network programming. Despite the opposition, CBS in late 1981 announced plans to expand its nightly news to an hour. Rising public acceptance of news programming, heralded by the success of shows such as CBS's "60 Minutes" and ABC's "Nightline," promise a changing pattern of television news programming in the 1980s.

Noncommercial public television, chiefly educational stations, devotes more time to public affairs programming than either the networks or local commercial stations. Limited funds, however, restrict these efforts at most stations. The Corporation for Public Broadcasting (CPB), chartered and financed by Congress, distributes some funds to local stations and to the Public Broadcasting Service (PBS). Through PBS and similar special production services funded by CPB and private foundations, high-quality documentaries are shared by hundreds of public stations. But PBS, subject to political pressures and budget control by Congress, has wavered in its support of the public affairs documentary. Several regularly scheduled programs, including the award-winning "Great American Dream Machine," were abandoned in the early 1970s.

Local commercial stations provide the largest potential outlet for interpretive reporting. The amount of such programming varies widely, but as the networks and the PBS have reduced their efforts, local stations seem to be expanding theirs. Stations such as KNXT and KNBC in Los Angeles, KING in Seattle, WCCO in Minneapolis, and WABC in New York are noted for their extensive public affairs programming. Others across the nation react promptly to examine in depth a highly salient local issue when it surfaces, such as busing for school integration. Some local investigative documentaries are change-producing vehicles; an outstanding example is "Willowbrook, the Last Great Disgrace," by WABC-TV in New York. This exposé of conditions at a state hospital for the retarded won a host of prizes for the station and reporter Geraldo Rivera as well as corrective action by the state. Such efforts aren't restricted to the largest stations: Salt Lake City's KUTV won kudos for "Warrior without a Weapon," a documentary on the plight of the Gosiute Indians. Local stations have labored mightily to fill the gap through local fund-raising and foundation support. Much of the effort in the late 1970s, however, went into improved entertainment and feature programs. Other than the well-received "MacNeil/Lehrer Report," current events still make up a small portion of noncommercial television content. Severe cutbacks in federal appropriations starting in 1982 also affect documentary production on public television.

Despite these efforts, documentaries don't constitute a major fraction of programming time or budget. The news special is typically relegated to daytime or late-night hours, when viewing is light. The vast majority of interpretive news available to the public is still found in newspapers and magazines, not on the airwaves.

THE AUDIENCE CONNECTION

Any doubts about the lack of effectiveness of conventional public affairs reporting are erased by studies which show that public knowledge of current events is extremely limited.[21] For example, most citizens can't remember the names of their congressmen, let alone the substance of the legislation with which they deal. Social observers and journalists alike are prone to cluck their tongues in dismay and place the blame for this ignorance on the citizens. They are variously regarded as lazy or alienated or lacking the intellectual ability to become informed about important public matters. For this deficiency, the public affairs reporter typically accepts no responsibility and sees no cure.

There is, however, an alternative and equally plausible explanation for the low level of public affairs knowledge. It holds that people don't score well on tests of current events because such tests are drawn from information appearing in the press. If people conclude that such information—events, names, places—doesn't hold much personal relevance, why should they attend to it? This explanation places the onus for an "ignorant" public squarely on the news media, which have absolute discretion to define news and the form in which it is presented. If the fault lies with the press and not the public, then the press *can* do something about it. Sterile, ritualistic, redundant, irrelevant treatment of public affairs can give way to coverage in which the reader can recognize self-interest. Relevance can be achieved through choice of subject matter and manner of presentation. The reader-centered interpretive article, the humanistic newswriting style, the emphasis on consumer orientation are examples of what some segments of the press are doing to meet this challenge.

It is here that communication research can be particularly helpful to the journalist. Unfortunately, reporters of the trenchcoat-and-felt-hat breed tend to sneer at scientific research, particularly when applied to their own craft. Those who do attempt to use research findings are often misled by the circular nature of conventional readership studies. In these studies, readers are shown copies of newspapers or lists of news items and asked to state their content preferences. Naturally, the range of these preferences is limited to precisely what the newspapers already contain. The result is that editors assume that people want more of what they've been getting, and readers assume that a newspaper is supposed to look like the product that editors have been giving them.

Audience analyst John P. Robinson of Cleveland State University's research center suggests that a more rational approach would start with an inventory of people's perceptions about their own information practices.[22] This inquiry would disclose what people want to know more about, what they think they know and do not know, and what might be a desirable mixture of the two. Actually, a substantial amount of knowledge about how people use news media and other sources of information is already accumulated, waiting for practical interpretation by journalists.[23]

This observation isn't intended to imply that journalists should simply pander to public tastes in the selection of subject matter. Rather, the point is that an understanding of audience behavior may help reporters to design their stories so they will be read as well as printed. Much of the conventional wisdom of the newsroom runs counter to what is already known about when, how, and why people seek information. One such bit of folklore is the once dominant belief in the existence of a mass audience for the media. There is none, in the sense of a diverse aggregation of people "out there," isolated from one another but all connected to the media.[24] Many audiences are out there, some big and some small, and they will vary from topic to topic. The audience for a story on a new zoning plan may differ significantly in size and composition from that for a story in the next column on a proposed art center. More troublesome, each of the stories may have several subaudiences, each with different levels of understanding and needs for information. Recognizing these differences and attempting to provide suitable information for the subaudiences is the reporter's challenge.

Another myth that needs shaking is that the chief function of the media is to transmit information. The late Harold Lasswell, a political scientist who had pioneered research in mass communication, suggested that the media's function consists of (1) surveillance of the environment, (2) correlation (interpretation) of the parts of society, and (3) transmission of the social heritage from generation to generation.[25] The evidence of other studies, however, points to the media's various types of entertainment functions as those most used by most people.[26] Public affairs reporters must be realistic about the purposes as well as the composition of their audiences. One interpretation that could be drawn from the accumulated research is that most people are pragmatic and rational about their reading and viewing. If public affairs subject matter is presented to them in a fashion that clearly shows its personal relevance and value, they will pay attention to it.

IMPLICATIONS FOR
REPORTERS

Objectivity versus interpretation.
Event-centered reporting versus process-centered news.
The dynamics of audiences.

Where does this leave the public affairs reporters of today—and tomorrow? How can they cope with the stresses of a profession in flux and the demands of a society beset by overnight change? Public affairs reporters today are better trained and more highly skilled, collectively, than ever. Yet there is widespread agreement among editors and educators that even more is needed in the way of talent and training. There's more to good journalism than the ability to write a summary lead.

Attributes desired in the ideal public affairs reporter would vary considerably with the source consulted, but a composite list of advice to the reporter-in-training would probably contain many of these suggestions:

Great writing is often a variation of the conventional. The reporter should master the techniques of event-centered straight reporting, with its attendant devotion to accuracy, brevity, and clarity. This is still the criterion in the news business, despite the growth of interpretation. Reporters will have to cover speeches, meetings, and disasters for a long time to come, and they'll be judged on their abilities to follow the standard model, with speed.

Reporters can't expect to function as independent entities, free to shape their own roles. They work, in varying degrees, under supervision and subject to pressure from colleagues and news sources. They should learn something about the care and feeding of editors and recognize that editors will often have superior news judgment. This awareness will help them to cope successfully (if not with equanimity) with the contrasts in journalistic philosophy that are bound to confront them. An appreciation of an editor's values and standards enables reporters to work through them to serve their own interests and helps to avoid fruitless confrontations. The sociology of the newsroom shapes both opportunities and limitations. Equally important but perhaps more intractable are the conflicts that arise between reporters and their sources. The source sees the reporter as a needed ally or a valuable conduit. The reporter sees the source as a vital lifeline. These perceptions and their implications collide with the reporters' own role perception as objective observers, as well as the role expectations of editors and the public. How they walk this delicate line is the measure of their professionalism.[27]

Interpretive reporting requires basic intellectual skills and an understanding of the social forces, power systems, and patterns of group behavior that have shaped our world. The reporter should also develop specialized knowledge in an area that is likely to be valued by news organizations. The choices may range from public administration to home economics. The long-term trend in the newsroom is toward specialization.

News professionals are discovering that a little theory makes the practice of journalism, like sex, more interesting, more understandable, and less dangerous. More and more, they are looking to communication research and theory for a better understanding of how people use information. Increasingly, this knowledge is helping to shape news decisions.[28]

Journalism today, both print and broadcast, is largely a business of communicating with an urban audience. More than 80 percent of the U.S. population is in urban centers. Public affairs reporters, therefore, should become familiar with the dynamics of urban living and the particular traits of their own communities and regions. Communication researcher Jack Lyle suggests these areas of knowledge as useful to all reporters:[29]

Demographics   The characteristics of people differ markedly from city to city, even neighborhood to neighborhood. Reporters will want to know the attributes and distinctions of their audiences—major occupational groupings, income and educational levels, recreation and leisure practices, religious preferences, value systems. Much of this information is available from census data.

Community organization   Patterns of formal organization in their community are reporters' road maps. They should learn the structure of organizations, both public and private, and their interrelationships.

Communication systems   Each city and region develops its own communications complex, serving special informational needs beyond the reach of mass circulation newspapers and television. These subsystems range from school newsletters to the underground press. They can tell reporters much about their audiences and their information practices.

These suggestions have a common thread. They imply that the reporter should guard against insularity, both in the newsroom and in dealing with the relative handful of news sources to which many newspapers restrict themselves. It is the danger of this type of parochialism that Philadelphia newspaper editor William B. Dickinson may have had in mind when he told a gathering of editors,

> We have become accustomed to covering certain beats: police and fire, the city hall, the courts, the Chamber of Commerce, and so on. We are not yet accustomed to covering the new beats, the very people who are transforming our world—the scientists, the physicians, the economists, the engineers, the architects, the educators, the management elite, the planners, the thinkers.[30]

Clearly, to meet Dickinson's challenge, public affairs reporters face demands that were unheard of in a simpler journalistic age. To succeed, they will need talent and training, and journalism will need to agree on a new definition of news.

NOTES

[1]Derick Daniels, "The World of Multi-Media," *The Quill* 58 (July 1970), 8.

[2]Herbert Brucker, "What's Wrong with Objectivity?" *Saturday Review* 52 (October 11, 1969), 77.

[3]James W. Carey, "The Communications Revolution and the Professional Communicator," *Sociological Review,* monograph 13 (Keele, Staffordshire, U.K.: University of Keele, 1969), 33–34. For convenience, English spellings have been changed to the American form.

[4]See Edwin Emery, *The Press and America,* 3rd ed. (Englewood Cliffs, N.J.: Prentice-Hall, 1972), pp. 465ff.; Curtis D. MacDougall, *Interpretative Reporting,* 6th ed. (New York: Macmillan, 1972), pp. 12–16; and William L. Rivers and Wilbur Schramm, *Responsibility in Mass Communication* (New York: Harper & Row, 1969), pp. 150–51.

[5]For one such critique, see Herbert Brucker, *The Changing American Newspaper* (New York: Columbia University Press, 1937).

[6]Commission on Freedom of the Press, *A Free and Responsible Press* (Chicago: University of Chicago Press, 1947), p. 20.

[7]Harry Ashmore, "The Untold Story Behind Little Rock," *Harper's* 232 (June 1958), 19.

[8]A description of Senator McCarthy's demagoguery can be found in Samuel Eliot Morison, *The Oxford History of the American People* (New York: Oxford University Press, 1965), pp. 1074ff.

[9]Quoted in Timothy Crouse, *The Boys on the Bus* (New York: Random House, 1973), p. 256.

[10]Ibid, pp. 323–24.

[11]The X-ray analogy is taken from Alan Pritchard, "The Newspaper Responsibility," *The Quill* 54 (August 1966), 26.

[12]Raymond A. Bauer and Alice H. Bauer, "America, 'Mass Society' and Mass Media," *Journal of Social Issues* 16 (July 1960), 50–51.

[13]The concept of process-centered news is developed in Todd Hunt, "Beyond the Journalistic Event: The Changing Concept of News," *Mass Comm. Review* 1 (April 1974), 23–30.

[14]Max Ways, "What's Wrong With the News? It Isn't New Enough," *Fortune* 36 (October 1969), 110.

[15]Donald McDonald, "Is Objectivity Possible?" *Center Magazine* 4 (September–October 1971), 29–42.

[16]Ibid.

[17]Gaye Tuchman, "Objectivity as Strategic Ritual: An Examination of Newsmen's Notions of Objectivity," *American Journal of Sociology* 77 (January 1972), 660–79.

[18]Gaye Tuchman, "Making News by Doing Work: Routinizing the Unexpected," *American Journal of Sociology* 79 (July 1973), 110–31.

[19]Marvin Barrett, ed., *Survey of Broadcast Journalism 1971–1972* (New York: Thomas Y. Crowell Co., 1973), pp. 9–38.

[20]Marvin Barrett, ed., *Survey of Broadcast Journalism 1970–1971* (New York: Grosset & Dunlap, 1971), p. 13.

[21]Wilbur Schramm and Serena Wade, *Knowledge and the Public Mind* (Stanford, Calif.: Institute for Communication Research, Stanford University Press. 1967), pp. 27ff.

[22]John P. Robinson, "Mass Communication and Information Diffusion," in ed. F. Gerald Kline and Phillip J. Tichenor, *Current Perspectives in Mass Communication Research* (Beverly Hills, Calif.: Sage Publications, 1972), pp. 71–93.

[23]Some current perspectives on media audiences may be found in Maxwell E. McCombs and Lee B. Becker, *Using Mass Communication Theory* (Englewood Cliffs, N.J.: Prentice-Hall, 1979). See also Raymond A. Bauer, "The Audience," in *Handbook of Communication*, ed. Ithiel de Sola Pool *et al.* (Chicago: Rand McNally, 1973), pp. 141–52.

[24]Eliot Friedson, "Communications Research and the Concept of the Mass," *American Sociological Review* 18 (June 1953), 313–17.

[25]Harold D. Lasswell, "The Structure and Function of Communication in Society," in ed. Lyman Bryson, *The Communication of Ideas* (New York: Institute for Religious and Social Studies, 1948), pp. 37–52.

[26]Examined in Jack M. McLeod and Garrett J. O'Keefe, Jr., "The Socialization Perspective and Communication Behavior," in ed. F. Gerald Kline and Phillip J. Tichenor, *Current Perspectives in Mass Communication Research* (Beverly Hills, Calif.: Sage Publications, 1972), p. 134.

[27]For a discussion of reporter role conflicts, see Leon V. Sigal, *Reporters and Officials: The Organization and Politics of Newsmaking* (Lexington, Mass.: D. C. Heath, 1973); and Walter Geiber, "Two Communicators of the News: A study of the Roles of Sources and Reporters," *Social Forces* 39 (1960–1961), 76–83.

[28]Arnold H. Ismach. "Journalism Research: Its Use and Non-use by Newspapers," M. A. thesis, University of California at Los Angeles, 1970. For sources of journalism research, see the following suggested readings.

[29]Jack Lyle, "Study of Urban Life," in *Education for Newspaper Journalists in the Seventies and Beyond* (Reston, Va.: American Newspaper Publishers Association, 1973), pp. 213–26. See also Chapters 13 and 14 in Everette E. Dennis and Arnold H. Ismach, *Reporting Processes and Practices* (Belmont, Calif.: Wadsworth Publishing Co., 1981) for techniques that reporters may use to stay in touch with their audiences.

[30]William B. Dickinson, executive editor (ret.) the *Philadelphia Evening Bulletin* and *Sunday Bulletin*, President's Message to the annual convention of the Associated Press Managing Editors Association, San Diego, Calif., November 15, 1966.

SUGGESTED READINGS

AMERICAN NEWSPAPER PUBLISHERS ASSOCIATION. *ANPA News Research Reports*. Reston, Va.: ANPA. This series offers current research with particular relevance to newspaper editorial concerns. See also *News Research for Better Newspapers*, vols. 1–6, also published by ANPA from 1966–1973. They provide useful summaries of studies from a wide variety of sources.

BAGDIKIAN, BEN H. *The Information Machines.* New York: Harper & Row, 1971. Useful discussions of media roles (Chap. 1) and audiences (Chap. 3) in this early examination of the technological revolution in mass communication.

McCOMBS, MAXWELL E., AND LEE B. BECKER. *Using Mass Communication Theory.* Englewood Cliffs, N.J.: Prentice-Hall, 1979. Relates the findings of communication theory and research to the work of the reporter.

ROSHCO, BERNARD. *Newsmaking.* Chicago: University of Chicago Press, 1975. Useful perspectives on how society influences the news media and their definitions of news.

SMITH, ANTHONY. *Goodbye Gutenberg: The Newspaper Revolution of the 1980s.* New York: Oxford University Press, 1980. Examination of the newer communication technologies and how they are likely to affect the news product.

TUCHMAN, GAYE. *Making News.* New York: Free Press, 1978. Analysis of journalism from the perspective of news organization structure, conventions, and policies.

3

New Perspectives for Public Affairs Reporting

I really have so much fun [as a reporter], I ought to be arrested.

I. F. Stone

"Christ! Maybe someday I'll write a book myself—about all the poor hams I've known in the game who were going to write a book—and never did. What a life!"

Theodore Willis, a reporter,
in Gentlemen of the Press *by Thomas Wolfe*

Public affairs reporters in the 1980s are beset by so many changes in their news organizations that they sometimes find it difficult to comprehend them all. Like everything else in the world, the nature of journalism and journalistic practice change in both quiet and noisy ways. In the late 1970s, critics began talking about the rise of the "use paper" and the "marketing approach to news," two ideas that signaled great changes in the packaging and promotion of the American newspaper. Within a few months many American newspapers introduced new sections that compartmentalized news and feature material about "lifestyles," "entertainment," "shelter," "neighborhoods," and others. Papers from the *New York Times* to the *Albuquerque Journal* offered their readers the new special sections in order to attract more readers. They not only wanted to increase their circulations overall but also pitched the new material in such a way that it would intrigue new audiences, including the so-called "youth market." The changes in format, brought about mainly as a result of the feverish attempt of the print media to compete successfully with television news, which was siphoning off part of the audience, also meant changes in content, style of presentation, and the news organization itself. The material that filled the columns of the new sections was organized in a different fashion from the traditional public affairs story. Rather than aiming just to help readers understand what was going on, it urged them to "use" their communities more effectively. In addition, the old news forms shifted as a less formal, more relaxed style of writing became more common. Naturally, all these changes did not occur in the old hierarchical newsroom with its autocratic structure. Some papers reorganized themselves along topical lines and team reporting gained new adherents. (See the following chart for an example of how such changes affected the organizational structure of one newspaper, the *Minneapolis Star.*[1])

Figure 1-1   *Organizational chart for the Minneapolis Star's news department.* This organization represents an emerging form in which local reporters are grouped in broad subject-matter teams rather than assigned to more traditional beats—such as city hall, statehouse, federal building, police—and reporting individually to a city editor. The Star's experiment was short-lived. With circulation falling, the newspaper's owners merged the evening *Star* with the morning *Tribune* in 1982. But the *Star's* newsroom structure for the preceding four years stands as a model of the shift toward team reporting. Reprinted by permission of the Minneapolis Star and Tribune Co.

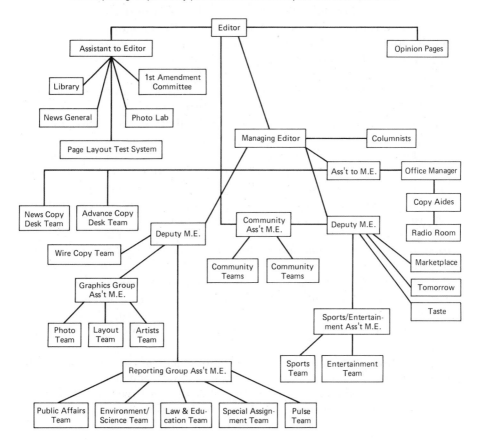

Earlier in the decade, investigative reporting, which has a tradition stretching back at least to the period of the muckrakers, seemed to get a new infusion of energy. In the early 1970s, two investigative reporters at the *Washington Post* helped bring down a president with their revelatory reports. They recounted their story in a book, *All the President's Men,* and the book became the basis for a movie of the same name in which the reporters were played by superstars Robert Redford and Dustin Hoffman. Other movies and television programs like "Lou Grant" helped establish reporters as modern folk heroes. In the journalistic community, interest in investigative reporting heightened. An organization, Investigative Reporters and Editors (IRE), was established and helped promote the concept through regional and national meetings. This group even sponsored a controversial "group journalism" project and led a team of reporters to Arizona where they probed issues and events that had led to the murder of an *Arizona Republic* reporter a few months earlier. Investigative reporting as a kind of journalistic movement attracted considerable attention among media critics and others who debated its place and purpose. Some said all reporting was (or should be) investigative, but the kind of investigative reporting that attracted so much comment was really *adversarial reporting,* reporting that ferreted out corruption and wrongdoing in government and the private sector. As Bob Porterfield, a Pulitzer prize-winning reporter who works in this tradition, puts it, "My job is to take names and kick ass." Fundamentally, though, investigative reporting or adversarial journalism was an elaboration of methods of news-gathering, especially a highly charged use of public records and other documents.

The journalistic movement that preceded investigative reporting was more concerned with style and mode of presentation than with the methods of gathering information. This was the controversial and much debated *New Journalism,* a literary-journalistic movement in which newspaper reporters and magazine writers championed the use of literary devices— dialogue, interior monologue, extensive description, dramatic episode—in their reports. They maintained that they were telling their stories more vividly by means of imaginative literary and journalistic techniques. Although this approach was introduced in magazines like *Esquire* and *New York* and spread to *Rolling Stone,* it eventually had an impact on news writing generally. It helped soften the once hard-and-fast rules about news stories and led to more extensive feature treatment and more interpretation.

Another journalistic trend was *precision journalism,* the use of social science methods, such as surveys, content analysis, and field experiments, by reporters in their news-gathering. Precision journalism is treated in greater detail later in this book. It was born during the race riots of the 1960s when the impressionistic methods of traditional reporting seemed inadequate to probe community attitudes effectively. Precision journalism developed in remarkable ways during the 1970s and 1980s as newspapers and broadcast stations made greater use of opinion research in covering difficult news stories.[2]

Debates among leaders of the news industry about "use paper" journalism, investigative reporting, or the New Journalism often seem quite distant from the realities of the individual reporter in the newsroom. In a sense they are. Trends and debates on the national scene eventually help shape journalistic practice locally, but changes are slow and subtle, sometimes not even recognized by people caught up in day-to-day journalism.

The "use paper" idea or marketing approach to news, however, was quite dramatic. Newspapers established special sections and became deeply involved in readership studies that eventually helped shape news decision making. Still, there were reporters who denied that anything was happening and were genuinely oblivious to it.

Investigative reporting caught the nation's fancy, but many reporters and editors thought it was a lot of hype and denied that the flurry of comment represented any trend. Similarly, precision journalism was often decried as impractical and improbable for most newsrooms even as its use became more common. As with the other trends, the New Journalism was sometimes denounced as the ego-child of eccentric New York writers having little relevance in the hinterlands. Some editors and reporters gave a strange mixed message, saying both "we don't do it" and "there is nothing new about it." The New Journalism seemed to challenge traditional ideas of objectivity, which distressed many in the news business who found objectivity a worthy goal.

The point is that national trends and various reportorial controversies do have an impact, but one sometimes has to look closely to see just what it is. However, without question, public affairs reporting is a turbulent and changing field. There is also more media criticism than ever from a public that has higher standards for the media than it once did. For example, when the American hostages returned from Iran in 1981, there was considerable criticism of reporters for excessive zeal in interviewing hostages and their families.

As a result of changes in the news business and of heightened public awareness, reporters covering public events need to be more introspective, more thoughtful in knowing and understanding their own work and work patterns. Journalistic fashions and fancies do not supersede or negate the need for solid news-gathering, competent writing, and good relations with editors. These are at the base of all reporting of quality, fads and trends notwithstanding. The ferment stimulated by internal and external critics of the media had consequences for public affairs reporters. It provided them with new perspectives.

CASE STUDIES REVISITED

Chapter 1 introduced four reporters and their stories. Tom Greene covered a zoning hearing; Susan Kahn, an embezzlement trial; Harold Copeland, conflict of interest in local government; and Chester Bond, programs for retarded children. These stories were selected because they typify the work of the public affairs reporter who operates as an observer of public decision making, as an investigator of stories not readily apparent on the surface, and as a synthesizer of information that has utility for the public.

On the basis of some of the media criticism, mentioned earlier, it would be easy to find fault with the work of Greene, Kahn, Copeland, and Bond. Some of their work might be characterized as routine or lacking in imagination. Similarly, the writing quality might vary from interesting and competent to downright dull and poorly written. "Why didn't they investigate more, find more sources?" one might ask. "The stories seem so parochial. Couldn't they have provided a more national context?" another could inquire. Does Greene seem like a conveyor belt for information from city hall? Is Copeland a troublemaker in stirring up the local community over the land conflicts of the county commissioners? Have they thought about the effect their stories might have on other people? These and many other questions might be raised about the four stories and the reporters who produced them.

Although there are some general standards for reporting, substantive understanding, and writing (discussed in some detail in Chapter 4), there are also constraints and situational contingencies that must be taken into account in evaluating a reporter's performance. These factors often have considerable control over the final outcome of a reporter's efforts. Here in broad outlines we will sketch some of these contingencies and constraints, recognizing of course that all these factors are endlessly complex. First is the *paper* itself. Its size, nature, morale, staffing patterns, and economic resources can influence the kind of work the reporter does and is able to do. Second, there is the amount of *time* the reporter has to work on the story. Finally, there are the *tools* he chooses to work with—or to put it another way, the method he is allowed to use by his editors. These factors guide, although they do not completely control, the final product: the finished story.

THE PAPER ITSELF

Frequency of publication, circulation size, and locale have a good deal to do with the reporter's work. American newspapers are incredibly diverse, ranging from metropolitan dailies with one-million-plus circulation to rural weeklies with a few hundred. Considerable variation exists even within the standard categories, but one usually thinks of newspapers as falling into the following groupings: the large metropolitan dailies, the medium and small dailies, the suburban papers, and the community weeklies. Some metropolitan dailies—the *New York Times, Washington Post, Los Angeles Times, Toronto Globe and Mail*—have a national character with a staff and resultant content that covers the nation. Other metropolitan dailies have strong regional influence. Regionals that are *the* state paper and have an impact in nearby states include the *Louisville Courier-Journal, Milwaukee Journal, Kansas City Star,* and *Des Moines Register.* Other papers in the metro category are more closely bound to their cities with little attempt to provide outstate coverage. The *Wichita Beacon* exemplifies this subcategory.

The circulation figures and staffing patterns of the medium and small dailies relate to the population of the city they serve. These range from papers like the *Toledo Blade* to the *Burlington* (Iowa) *Hawk Eye.* Similarly, the suburban press, sometimes daily, sometimes semi- or triweekly, is yet another type of newspaper. In many instances these papers tend to supplement other newspapers, assuming that their readers also read the major metropolitan dailies of the nearby city. Thus, their stories amplify and localize national, state, and regional trends and may focus more carefully on the local scene, covering schools, health, and other suburban issues (for example, the quality of life) with some vigor.

The backbone of the grass-roots press is the community weekly. It more often than not has a small staff and is preoccupied with local subjects. Its style is usually less formal, and the paper and its staff are indeed "closer" to the community. "It can't help but affect your writing when you meet your sources on the street the next day," one community editor has said.

As for the paper itself, its ownership can also be an influential factor. It can make a difference whether the paper is an independent, locally owned publication with the owner–publisher having an office in the building or whether it is a paper owned by an absentee entrepreneur who directs it from a distance. It may also be part of a newspaper group—a chain. The chains themselves vary from small ones of two or more papers to those with national holdings of fifty or more. Some papers are part of media conglomerates with diverse newspaper, magazine, and broadcasting interests. Without attempting a treatise on the sociology of media ownership, circulation size, or frequency of publication, one might ask how these factors affect the reporters of public affairs in their work. Here are some of the constraining—and liberating—influences broken down into craft attitudes and staffing patterns:

Craft Attitudes

Craft attitudes of public affairs reporters, the result of internal and external pressures, influence the way in which the journalist works. Within the newsroom, these attitudes about the newspaper organization and how it produces news can be caused by the reporters' interaction with editors, by subtle pressures from the publisher, and by other socializing influences. The internal dynamics of the newsroom (as we have indicated earlier) have a large role in determining what is news. In a classic sociological study of the newsroom, Warren Breed found that its social, economic, and psychological pressures push the reporter toward conformity.[3] This trend toward conformity has also been observed in the television newsroom.[4] Craft attitudes toward writing style, definitions of news, and what sources to contact are also influenced by external community pressures. Public affairs reporters should maintain an awareness of the factors that influence their performance by reviewing the ever proliferating literature that communications researchers are generating.[5]

Staffing Patterns

The size of the staff and its composition have a large influence in determining what the final news product will be. Larger publications tend to have a greater degree of specialization. They may have, for example, an urban affairs writer or an environmental reporter. Specialized reporters may have received specific training, such as science writing, or they may be self-taught; in any event, they spend more time keeping up with their field and cultivating their sources. Specialization is often determined by the nature of the local community. For example, the San José (Calif.) Mercury-News keeps a close watch on the electronics industry, which has major firms in its area; the Topeka (Kan.) Capital-Journal gives detailed coverage to mental health issues as it surveys the famed Menninger Foundation and other psychiatric facilities located there; the Seattle Times takes a keen interest in the environment, a topic of much concern in the Pacific Northwest.

A key factor in staffing patterns is obviously how much money is spent on the editorial product. This amount depends somewhat on the profits of the paper but more on the attitudes of the publisher and other managerial personnel. Some papers, the Jackson (Miss.) Clarion-Ledger among them, go in for group journalism—team reporting. In 1980, reporters at the Clarion-Ledger, after weeks of investigation, produced a tabloid-pullout section on Mississippi's jails. It was a solid and comprehensive piece of reporting that probably could not have been done as well by a single reporter.

When complex news situations involve distinct fields of knowledge, newspapers with staff resources that permit it will assign several specialists to work jointly. An example of this team approach was the response of the Los Angeles Times to the energy crisis. After months of piecemeal and conflicting news reports, the Times sought to sift fact from myth. It assigned six reporters to the job, including specialists in the environment, finance, energy, and federal government. The result: eight articles on aspects of the energy crisis ranging from oil industry profits to the government's role in creating the shortage.

Team journalism is more often the rule at major metropolitan newspapers, although cooperative efforts do occur on smaller papers as well. What are important are the resources allocated. Whether the paper provides ample travel money, telephone expenses, and other items is vital. One newspaper with a reputation for investing in its editorial product is the *Eugene* (Ore.) *Register-Guard*. Investigative reporter Jerry Uhrhammer of that paper meticulously mines public records and documents "following the paper trail" in pursuit of a story that may take weeks or months. His work has paid off with revelations about the wrongdoing of public officials that could not have been determined without a great investment of time. Similarly, the small, struggling *San Francisco Bay Guardian* made a comprehensive study of San Francisco politics by involving journalism students and other volunteers. The result was as follows:

> *The Guardian* unleashed a pack of 40 investigative reporters last summer on the most powerful—and least understood public and private institutions in San Francisco. . . . A small paper like the *Guardian* couldn't possibly publish all the information gathered by 40 volunteer reporters working an entire summer. Most of the material goes into our files and helps form the basis of our continuing editorial surveillance of San Francisco and Bay Area power centers. A good part of it is being worked up into a "Citizen's Guide to San Francisco Politics" due next year. One advantage of operating a small, independent paper in a city dominated by monopoly journalism is that an abundant supply of good stories is out there waiting to be mined—if you can get at them.[6]

A previous *Bay Guardian* summer project resulted in a book on urban growth, architecture, and building codes entitled *The Ultimate High Rise*. In some states rather massive election coverage has been the result of team efforts with paid help and volunteers.

THE TIME FACTOR

Closely related to the staffing pattern as a factor in the reporter's performance is the amount of time allowed the reporter to work on the story. The time allotment determines in large part the scope and detail of the writing, the amount of checking and rechecking of facts, and often the depth of the reporter's understanding of the subject matter. For example, Joel Greenberg, formerly a science writer for the *Miami Herald* and now with *Science News*, demonstrated how the time investment can pay off in a series on a Florida mental hospital. The paper allowed him to spend a week in the hospital, working as an aide so that he could observe the hospital from inside. Time to observe, think about his story, and do background research resulted in a graphic presentation that began,

> "Watch this," Charlotte, the psychiatric aide, smiled slyly and winked at me. "Byron? Byron, how you feel today?" A slight man with a veiny nose and shock of gray hair, Byron did not break stride as he walked briskly down the 100-foot corridor in his bare feet.
> "Awful dammit. O I feel awful," his shaky voice faded like a railroad train in the distance. We all burst into loud laughter. "Damn," we said, "if he don't always feel 'awful, dammit, just awful.'"[7]

Greenberg's story, after providing some humanistic lead-ins, discussed modes of treatment, staff personnel, and types of psychiatric problems in a detailed, sensitive story. Its empathetic view of patients and those who care for them reflected considerable thought and was a refreshing departure from the commonplace exposé stories that so often sensationalize prison, mental hospital, and other institutional conditions.

Sometimes reporting can be a tedious and frustrating task. The tiny *Point Reyes Light's* pursuit of the Synanon story is an example. For three years the editors of this California weekly (along with a Berkeley sociologist) devoted themselves to the investigation of a locally based corrupt corporation whose crimes were ignored by local law enforcement officers. Their work did not show tangible results until 1978 when their revelations about the Synanon organization attracted national attention. In 1979, the paper won the Pulitzer Prize for meritorious public service. The investment of time didn't stop there, though. The paper had to defend itself against several lawsuits brought by Synanon.[8]

Massive investment of time does not always result in a payoff for the reporter. In a story in the now defunct New York journalism review, (*More*), Brit Hume told how Denny Walsh, a reporter for the *New York Times,* spent several months investigating a story regarding former San Francisco Mayor Joseph Alioto's testimony some years earlier about alleged Mafia connections. Hume described Walsh's experience as follows:

> During his three-month investigation, Walsh returned several times to Washington, where he is based, to visit his family and, on one occasion to obtain what he considered a crucial piece of documentation. He also made trips to Los Angeles and San Diego. Most of his time, however, was spent in San Francisco poring over the voluminous record of the libel case [Alioto v. *Look* Magazine] and seeking documentation for instances where his sources had raised questions about the mayor's testimony. He accumulated a massive amount of material. . . .[9]

The *Times,* for reasons questioned sharply by Hume, refused to run the story, due in part to potential litigation.

Time constrains the reporter in many ways. It determines how many sources can be interviewed, how much background research can be done, how much planning can go into the story, and how much attention can be given to improving the prose and revising it. For many reporters, a fast-breaking story at deadline may have to be written in a matter of minutes. Other stories, like those of long, extended trials, may be planned precisely with ample time for special sidebar features and interviews with peripheral sources that would not get into a one-day-only deadline story.

Sometimes background knowledge about the person to be interviewed and a minimum of research can result in a brightly written story with considerable informational value. For example, Ruth Heckathorn of the *Decatur* (Ill.) *Daily Review* wrote this about naturalist Euell Gibbons:

> The man that members of the Federated Women's Clubs of Delaware voted they'd most like to be lost in the woods with came to Decatur yesterday afternoon.
> "It's not all that much of a compliment," insists writer and wild food gatherer Euell Gibbons. "Obviously, they were more interested in the food rather than the man." Many more people are intrigued by the Texas-born Quaker who strode into the public spotlight after reworking a fanciful novel about a school teacher into a back-to-nature book.[10]

The Gibbons story could have been prepared partly in advance by reading his books and checking standard biographical sources.

Within constraints of time, one must consider how facile a writer the reporter is and how much background knowledge he or she has. Either of these factors can affect even a fairly constrained deadline. For example, Roy Reed of the *New York Times* wrote an imaginative story after the trial of a Louisiana Ku Klux Klan leader. Having covered the trial and absorbed days of testimony, the reporter was able to select an interesting posttrial angle to construct a story headlined "How Beckwith Was Cleared in Bomb Case." Reed set the scene for his story as follows:

> Byron De La Beckwith's ideal Christian republic would have no Jews, Orientals or Negroes and would place very little trust in Roman Catholics.
> Imagine his consternation then, when he found himself in this polyglot city, 300 miles from his home in the Mississippi Delta, being arraigned by two Federal magistrates—the first a Negro and the second an Oriental—defended by a court-appointed lawyer who was a Roman Catholic, and tried before a jury that included a black man as a regular juror and another as an alternate, on the charge of possessing a time bomb that, according to contentions by the police outside the courtroom, was being carried into the city to blow up the home of a Jew.
> If ever a man was delivered into the hands of his enemies, Mr. Beckwith said to his friends, that man was he.[11]

What followed was a story that discussed Beckwith's defense, the jurors' response, and the government's case. Of course, such a story would have taken a reporter without Reed's background, derived from covering the trial, days to research.

APPLICATION TO THE CASE STUDIES

How would time, staffing patterns, and the newspaper itself have altered the four stories in Chapter 1? In the instance of the zoning story, a larger newspaper might not have given the story as much play; a smaller one might have given it more. Additional staff might have allowed for more background prior to the meeting and a possible follow-up story several days later.

Similarly, the embezzlement trial story wouldn't have been greatly affected. The reporter was working for a paper with specialists and she was the specialist in charge of court reporting. A general assignment reporter might not have had enough expertise in covering events of this kind and might have required more time to write it.

The story that involved the search of county land records could have been done faster and more extensively if there had been more staff. Indeed, in this instance, a small weekly was doing an extraordinary job of investigative reporting. Larger papers might do this kind of reporting more often, and many small dailies would simply not want to invest the resources unless the chances for a real payoff in terms of a story were assured.

The exceptional children story was motivated in part by the personal interest of the writer and the publisher's wife. A generalized topic of this kind might be covered by a small daily but probably not by a rural weekly. It is more often the kind of story that is particularly attractive to the metro daily and the suburban newspaper. The reporter had ample time for his work, although he might have been assisted by another reporter. Perhaps the result would have been better.

THE REPORTER'S TOOLS

The impact of media criticism, mentioned earlier, has been felt in the nation's newsrooms, where various methods of reporting and writing have been challenged. Four methods to emerge from the discussion—although they are used in varying degrees and in some instances not at all—are investigative reporting, precision journalism, reportage (sometimes called the New Journalism), and the marketing approach to news. None of these approaches to writing is new per se, but each has been given an added impetus in the last few years.

Investigative Journalism

This method is simply an intensification of journalism's traditional way of assembling information. It involves a more concerted effort to gather exhaustive information and make comparisons with checks for consistency. It probably stems from Lincoln Steffens' legendary muckraking exposés (*The Shame of the Cities*) at the turn of the century. Investigative reporting may have a reformist bent, seeking to reveal corruption in government, business, or labor, for example. We have already mentioned Bob Woodward and Carl Bernstein and their doggedly determined investigation of the Watergate break-in. Their work was thorough and involved checking and rechecking sources as well as creatively seeking new information from old and new sources. Woodward's celebrated meetings with an unnamed source called "Deep Throat" were carried out in a clandestine atmosphere. As writer Aaron Latham put it,

> Woodward would arrive at a dark garage and park outside. He would go inside the echoing building, where he would walk down ramp after ramp, deeper and deeper into a subterranean world which seemed like a metaphor for the twisting, convoluted, shadowy plots he was uncovering. Two stories beneath ground level, Woodward says, a man would appear out of the shadows. The reporter and his wary informant would huddle between empty cars and talk about political espionage. The stories which the reporter would later write would in a literal sense be Notes from the Underground.[12]

Investigative reporting is not often as exciting and glamorous as that of Woodward and Bernstein. More often it involves laborious checking of public records, finding documentation for the story. Usually investigative reporting in the public sector centers on misuse of funds, mismanagement, or outright corruption. Some newspapers take their investigative reporting so seriously that they even hire accountants, lawyers, and private investigators to help with the gathering of sensitive information. One example is the *Montgomery* (Ala.) *Advertiser*, which has won national recognition for its exposés of corruption. Investigative reporting involves a considerable investment in time and human resources for the papers that engage in it. Often stories require concerted efforts over several months. Investigative stories are often rather adversarial in nature, stating a suspicion and then following it with documentation. They are also moralistic in tone, sometimes taking a holier than thou stance. One of the nation's chief journalistic moralizers, for example, is columnist Jack Anderson, who describes himself as an investigative reporter.

Perhaps the most visible investigative reporting nationally is seen on the CBS News show "60 Minutes," which has uncovered fraud in the public sector and exposed unscrupulous business practices in the private sector. Sometimes the work of this news show takes a slightly different course. In 1979, for example, "60 Minutes" reporters learned about a black man who had been a candidate for public office, but when polls showed he might win, he was suddenly accused of a crime. Not only did the man lose the election, but he also got a thirty-year jail sentence.

"Our original investigation centered not upon whether the man was guilty," said Leslie Edwards and Dan Rather, who did the report, "but upon whether the sentence represented equal justice under the law."[13] The investigation took the better part of a year. "The more we probed, the more questions were raised about the man's guilt. Eventually, we found officials who came forward and said that Hackett [the accused] may have been prosecuted for political reasons. And we also turned up a key witness who local prosecutors had doubted even existed; this witness attested to the imprisoned man's innocence."[14] After serving eight months, Hackett was paroled but was refused a pardon. The television report won a Robert F. Kennedy Journalism Award.

Precision Journalism

This term is most often associated with the work of Philip Meyer, a national affairs correspondent for the Knight–Ridder newspaper group. Meyer pioneered the use of social science methods in the newsroom in follow-up studies of the Detroit riots of the late 1960s. His work was hailed by the National Commission on Civil Disorders as exemplary journalism, which gave encouragement to his later efforts, including a study of Miami's black community and a series on Berkeley's rebels several years after the campus unrest in 1964. Meyer believes that journalism should use social science methods—especially the survey, field experiment, and content analysis—in gathering the news. This view goes well beyond the pioneering efforts of such newspaper opinion polls as the *Minneapolis Tribune's* Minnesota Poll. Meyer, a former science writer who was trained in social science methods and computer applications while a Nieman Fellow at Harvard, put his thoughts into a book entitled *Precision Journalism*.[15]

Precision journalism, which is a break with journalism's usual impressionistic standard, differs from the standard polls and articles about survey data in a number of ways. Meyer says reporters should learn to use the social science tools themselves, rather than rely on others. Further, the tools should be used for news-gathering purposes, not for sociological sidebars. Others who advocate the use of these methods also suggest that editors and reporters should be better trained to utilize survey and other empirical data already available to them. Meyer, for example, has said that the census should be one of the major stories of the day because it is the most complete and precise index of the American people. Precision journalism also involves a blending of survey data with personal interviews and humanistic examples. But the person interviewed is always cast in the context of the survey data. In 1970, the *Philadelphia Inquirer* launched a seven-month study of court records that resulted in a series on the breakdown in criminal justice—"the jailing of the innocent, freeing of the guilty." As the *Inquirer* explained it, "the study, a sophisticated computer analysis of the way violent crimes are handled in the courts, was based on the cases of 1,034 persons indicted during [the period studied] for murder, rape, aggravated robbery, and aggravated assault and battery."[16] The first story in the series began,

> Soft judges . . . a tough district attorney . . . crowded courtrooms . . . light sentences. These are the catch phrases used today to describe what is happening in many big city criminal justice systems. But how soft are the judges? Is the district attorney really tough? Are courtrooms crowded by necessity? How light are the sentences? For seven months, a *Philadelphia Inquirer* investigative reporting team sought the answers to these questions and scores of others during an intensive probe into the administration of justice in this—the nation's fourth largest city. . . . The findings [ranged] from the existence of broad patterns of discrimination on the part of judges to extreme sentencing disparity and the jailing of innocent persons. . . .[17]

The point is that precision journalists with computer assistance can go well beyond myth and rumor, finding instead hard data to back up their assumptions. And what they do with the social science tools and the computer is either impossible without them or so time-consuming that it would never be attempted.

Notable precision journalism projects have included:

> Surveys on the attitudes of burglary and robbery victims in the *Milwaukee Journal;*
> Surveys on people's attitudes toward the quality of life in the *Chicago Tribune;*
> an analysis of the content of local television news programs in the *Van Nuys* (Calif.) *News;*
> A computer probe of the sources of election campaign contributions in the *Roanoke* (Va.) *Times and World News.*[18]

Precision journalism is not confined exclusively to big cities. The *Dubuque Telegraph-Herald,* for example, is using its business machines to help with reportorial tasks. Reporter John McCormick studied public records to determine why and where traffic accidents happen in that city. The same paper also questioned a sample of doctors in rural Iowa and developed a startling profile of an aging, overworked medical force. Neither of these stories would have been likely for this paper without precision journalism methods. (Precision journalism is discussed in more detail in Chapter 5.)

Reportage, or the New Journalism

No doubt the most controversial of the new methods open to reporters is what is called reportage, or the New Journalism. There is considerable disagreement about what it is—how it is defined—but from the criticism come some clear notions. Reportage is an ancient form of writing that goes back at least 250 years to Defoe's *Journal of the Plague Year.* It is simply the application of such methods of fiction as dialogue, interior monologue, and extended description to the practice of journalism. It usually involves a bombardment of detail for the reader and extensive description. The work of Tom Wolfe, Gay Talese, and Truman Capote is probably the New Journalism in its pure form. Variations on the theme are found in the writing of Hunter S. Thompson and Gail Sheehy, among others.

Those who defend the New Journalism contend that its practitioners do not fictionalize but simply use fiction methods. Talese, for example, says that he asks persons he is interviewing, "What did you think when that happened?" Thus he says he gets the sources' thoughts as well as their words.

Much of the New Journalism is appropriate to the magazine rather than the newspaper, and it is most often found in such publications as *New York*, *Esquire*, and *New Times*. Its virtue is that it breaks out of the traditional journalistic form and provides the writer with new freedom. New Journalists are often participatory journalists. They more than observe from the sidelines—they are frequently involved in the action. Sometimes unconventional interviews result. As Sheehy wrote in *Hustling*, a book describing prostitution in New York City (expanded from articles in *New York* magazine),

> We arrived at David's [a pimp] penthouse in full dress but without a scrap of paper or a pencil between us. Every fifteen minutes I had to excuse myself and dash for the bathroom to make notes with an eyebrow pencil on the back of a checkbook. (Without access to other people's bathrooms, writers would be nowhere.) To stay out of the reader's way, in the story I took the disguise of "the actress."[19]

Sheehy's celebrated story, "Redpants and Sugarman," for *New York* aroused the ire of the *Wall Street Journal*, which learned that the prostitute she wrote about was a composite character. Actually, Sheehy had originally cautioned readers about this in her story, but her qualification was omitted by a magazine editor.

Critics of the New Journalism say it is subjective and dwells too much on details and trivia—clothing, furniture, facial expressions. Dwight Macdonald has called the new form "parajournalism" or a bastard form, one that is neither journalism nor literature.

The critics aside, one must admit that many of the features of reportage do enhance journalism and the once lifeless form of the inverted-pyramid style. There is also evidence that, increasingly, newspaper writers are adopting some of the magazine conventions. Description of people, once commonplace but later nearly taboo in newspapers, is returning, as this story about Lee Radziwill indicates:

> "For the first time, I really feel true to myself," she said, in her throaty, well-modulated voice, as she put one of her navy shod feet on the coffee table in front of her. "I think there's nothing that makes you happier than to be really involved in something. I can't imagine a totally idle life."[20]

The description, along with Radziwill's words, paints a more complete picture and sets the tone without editorializing.

At the very least, the devices that the New Journalists find so captivating should be considered by public affairs reporters. The use of dialogue, extended description, interior monologue, and the hectoring narrator can prove useful. Dialogue can set the tone of a story, humanize the source. Interior monologue, which involves reporting the source's thoughts, is especially important in relating the activities of persons who are not particularly adept at verbal communication. The hectoring narrator, a more controversial practice, usually amounts to having the writer heap invective on some nonexistent person to set a scene or create a mood. Although not always practical for day-to-day journalism, or fast-breaking news, the New Journalism forms can be useful in background pieces and have the advantage of showing the reader the utility of information in a vivid, exciting way.

A cautionary note: Many, if not most, of the New Journalists mastered the standard journalistic form, and their variation is done deliberately and for a purpose. A writer like Tom Wolfe liberated his style after a long apprenticeship on newspapers and magazines. Effective use of New Journalism techniques takes an exceptionally bright and creative journalist and they are not advised for everyone. A second caution is that many copy desks simply will not accept material written in this style, although increasingly it is being included, especially in feature stories and in long background pieces.

The Marketing Approach

By the early 1980s, journalistic trend-watchers and media critics were calling the marketing approach to news or so-called use paper journalism "the next kind of journalism." The implications of special sections, ranging from entertainment and lifestyle to shelter and youth, were not always abundantly clear to reporters. To begin with, the marketing approach to news was originally a packaging idea. It was simply a way to attract readers by providing new sections of the newspaper. Often these new sections fell into a magazine format, though, and required a somewhat altered style of journalistic presentation.

For the most part, marketing approach stories were designed to help readers make better "use" of their communities. Reporters began producing what might be called "service journalism." Stories included "downtown at night" features, wherein reporters provided inventories along with some critical evaluation, of things to do. Articles explained how to choose a psychiatrist; others sorted out diet centers and other weight-loss programs. Fairly often, these stories were concerned with matters of health, interpersonal relations, consumer issues, and financial problems.

There is not yet a distinctive marketing approach style in writing. The stories are usually humanistic, written from the point of view of the reader. They tend to focus on the ordinary rather than the unusual. For example, stories that will interest the greatest number of readers—the quality of fast-food restaurants—will probably get priority over stories about more exotic or obscure places—an expensive, out-of-the-way restaurant with five tables.

Marketing approach stories might use investigative reporting techniques, as in consumer reporting; or they might try to catch the reader's fancy with New Journalistic writing. Some marketing approach stories make use of precision journalism methods.

Often, though, marketing approach stories make comparisons. For example, when the *Boston Globe* published a series called "The Wiring of Boston," reporter Benjamin Taylor explained that eight cable companies were competing for that city's coveted cable franchise. Taylor introduced each of the firms in a sketch report, compared the services they would offer, and explained that the decision about who got the lucrative bid would be largely political. For that reason, he began his series as follows:

> Coming soon, in neighborhoods from Charlestown to Beacon Hill, from Roxbury to Hyde Park, is a new high-stakes television called Cable Comes to Boston.
> It will star Mayor Hagan White in perhaps his biggest role, followed in supporting roles by eight cable companies, including some of the largest media conglomerates in the United States. The plot's a mystery about who will bring cable to Boston's 242,000 households and win what one executive calls the country's "No. 1 prestige franchise of 1981."[21]

Here the writer helps the potential consumer of cable services understand the political scenario that will later unfold. It is accomplished first by mentioning some neighborhoods that will be affected, linking these to political intrigue, and eventually, later in the story, sorting out the nuts and bolts of comparative information. Whether the marketing approach to news will survive depends on whether it helps struggling newspapers gain circulation in the face of competition from television and other sources of information. If it does help, it will no doubt develop further, perhaps even taking on a special character of its own, leading to a distinctive marketing approach in writing style. If it does not work, does not help to boost sagging circulations, then it is likely that editors and reporters will be fashioning another approach.

What is the relevance for public affairs reporters of such journalistic trends as investigative reporting, the New Journalism, precision journalism, and the marketing approach? If we return to the stories introduced in Chapter 1 and referred to again in this chapter we can see some connections.

For example, the marketing approach might lead to an imaginative story on "What Zoning Changes Mean for You," in the case of Tom

Greene's story. The marketing approach wouldn't help much in trial coverage per se but might lead a reporter like Susan Kahn to do a feature on "Using the Courts Before They Use You." Clearly Chester Bond's story has implications for reporters wanting to use the marketing approach if one imagines a story on "How to Find a Day School for Your Retarded Child."

Could the New Journalism have been useful to any of the reporters in our original case studies? The zoning story might have been enhanced with more description and dialogue. The embezzlement trial story probably would not have benefited from reportage techniques. The public records story might have been brighter and more interesting with New Journalism techniques as long as they did not get in the way of the hard information being offered. The exceptional children series, however, definitely would have been improved with stylistic innovation. Imaginative ways of helping readers understand the plight of the retarded child would have enhanced its presentation.

Would the approaches of precision journalism also have been intriguing for our four reporters? Perhaps already existing data could have pointed up something to Tom Greene about the community where the zoning was to take place. The character of a neighborhood cannot always be "eyeballed." Hard data, from the census for example, might have been helpful, if not in the initial news story, certainly in background work. Susan Kahn, working on the embezzlement trial, might be interested to know of the *Philadelphia Inquirer* work because it points up aspects of the legal system that a perceptive reporter should know and could use in coverage. Similarly, Harold Copeland's job might have been made easier with all those dusty records if he had had the aid of a computer—even a very simple one. If he weren't knowledgeable in this area, he could have called on a social scientist at a nearby college. Chester Bond's series might also have been enlarged and perhaps greatly influenced by hard data, such as precision journalism yields. He wrote about exceptional children by talking with authoritative sources, but their comments were impressionistic and they might have been brought into question after a thorough analysis of data.

Thorough investigative methods were used by Harold Copeland and to a lesser degree by Chester Bond. They might have been applied subsequently to Tom Greene's work on zoning as well as to the subject of white-collar crime suggested by Susan Kahn's coverage of the embezzlement trial.

SUMMARY AND CONCLUSION

The means and methods of seeking new perspectives for public affairs reporting mentioned in this chapter are only a few of the avenues open to reporters. What is most important is that reporters be aware of their opportunities and limitations in covering the public arena. Some techniques simply aren't feasible because of time, money, or other resources. Some methods of writing will work in some stories and under some circumstances and others will fail, but at the very least reporters and students of public affairs reporting should keep pace with the future by maintaining an awareness of modes and methods in reporting and their potential application to their own work.

NOTES

[1]For a useful and early discussion of the "Marketing Approach," see Fergus M. Bordewich, "Supermarketing the Newspaper," *Columbia Journalism Review*, September/October 1977, pp. 24–30; and Philip Meyer, "In Defense of the Marketing Approach," *Columbia Journalism Review*, January/February 1978, pp. 60–62. Implications of this trend for reporters are found in Everette E. Dennis and Arnold H. Ismach, *Reporting Processes and Practices: News Writing for Today's Readers* (Belmont, Calif.: Wadsworth Publishing Co., 1981), especially Chap. 1, pp. 3–25.

[2]There are a number of books chronicling journalistic fads and fashions, and many of these trends are summarized in Melvin L. DeFleur and Everette E. Dennis, *Understanding Mass Communication* (Boston: Houghton-Mifflin, 1981), especially Chap. 12, pp. 417–45.

[3]Warren Breed, "Social Control in the Newsroom," *Social Forces* 33 (May 1955), 326–35.

[4]Daniel Garvey, "Social Control in the Television Newsroom," Ph.D. diss. Stanford University, 1972.

[5]See, for example, Herbert Gans, *Deciding What's News* (New York: Pantheon, 1979); and Gaye Tuchman, *Making News, A Study in the Construction of Reality* (New York: Free Press, 1978); and many articles on the subject in journalism, communication, and sociology journals.

[6]"Findings of the Guardian's Second Annual Investigative Project," *San Francisco Bay Guardian*, November 1, 1972, p. 13.

[7]Joel Greenberg, "One Week in a Mental Ward," *Miami Herald*, November 25, 1973, p. 1-F.

[8]For a book on the subject, see David and Cathy Mitchell and Richard Ofshe, *The Light on Synanon* (New York: Seaview Books, 1981).

[9]Brit Hume, "The Mayor, the Times and the Lawyers," *(More)* 2 (August 1974), 1.

[10]Ruth Heckathorn, "The Sport of Food Foraging," *Decatur Daily Review*, October 23, 1973, p. 1, sect. 2.

[11]Roy Reed, "How Beckwith Was Cleared in Bomb Case," *New York Times*, January 21, 1974, p. 10.

[12]Aaron Latham, "How The Washington Post Gave Nixon Hell," *New York*, May 14, 1973, pp. 49–55. See also Bob Woodward and Carl Bernstein, *All the President's Men* (New York: Simon & Schuster, 1974).

[13]*The Twelfth Annual Robert F. Kennedy Awards*, booklet published in Washington D.C., 1980, p. 21.

[14]Ibid.

[15]Philip Meyer, *Precision Journalism: A Reporter's Introduction to Social Science Methods*, 2nd ed. (Bloomington: Indiana University Press, 1978).

[16]"Crime and Justice," republished series from the *Philadelphia Inquirer*.

[17]Ibid.

[18]Arnold H. Ismach, "Precision Journalism: Coming of Age," *ANPA News Research Report*, No. 18 (March 9, 1979), 1, 7–9.

[19]Gail Sheehy, *Hustling: Prostitution in Our Wide-Open Society* (New York: Dell, 1973).

[20]Judy Klemesrud, "For Lee Radziwill, Budding Careers and New Life in New York," *New York Times*, September 1, 1974, p. 42.

[21]Benjamin Taylor, "Courting White for Cable Pact," *Boston Globe*, February 2, 1981, pp. 1, 15. Part I of a series, "The Wiring of Boston."

SUGGESTED READINGS

DENNIS, EVERETTE, AND ARNOLD H. ISMACH. *Reporting Processes and Practices.* Belmont, Calif.: Wadsworth Publishing Co., 1981. An introductory text with newswriting, news-gathering, and news-processing sections. Includes discussion of marketing approach and survival kit for reporters.

FEDLER, FRED. *Reporting and Writing for the Print Media,* 3rd ed. New York: Harcourt-Brace-Jovanovich, 1981. Practical exercises and examples of reporting and newswriting.

HOLLOWELL, JOHN. *Fact and Fiction: The New Journalism and the Nonfiction Novel.* Chapel Hill: University of North Carolina Press, 1977. A good discussion of the literary devices used by New Journalists.

HOUGH, GEORGE, III. *News Writing,* 2nd ed. Boston: Houghton-Mifflin Co., 1980. A readable, straightforward text that focuses strictly on the writing aspects of reporting.

HYNDS, ERNEST. *American Newspapers in the 1980s.* New York: Hastings House, 1980. A good analysis of newspaper trends and conditions at the beginning of the decade. An update of Hynds' excellent book on the 1970s.

LOVELL, RONALD. *The Newspaper, An Introduction to Newswriting and Reporting.* Belmont, Calif.: Wadsworth Publishing Co., 1980. An introductory text that is briskly written with "you-are-there" reporting examples. Well-integrated case studies of three newspapers—*Topeka* (Kan.) *Capital-Journal; Corvallis* (Ore.) *Gazette Times,* and *Washington Star.*

METZLER, KEN. *Newsgathering.* Englewood Cliffs, N.J.: Prentice-Hall, 1979. A general reporting text with strong treatment of interviewing and other news-gathering methods.

SMITH, ZAY N., AND PAMELA ZEKMAN. *The Mirage.* New York: Random House, 1979. A case study of investigative reporting. Tells how the *Chicago Sun Times* bought a bar and exposed political corruption.

WEBER, RONALD. *The Literature of Fact.* Athens: Ohio University Press, 1980. A thoughtful analysis of the New Journalism.

WILLIAMS, PAUL. *Investigative Reporting.* Englewood Cliffs, N.J.: Prentice-Hall, 1976. An investigative text written by a Pulitzer Prize-winning editor. Useful case examples.

4

Investigation and Other Strategies for Reporting Public Affairs

Public service reporting is what, in America's myriad city rooms, we used to call hard-nosed reporting: asking the impolite question, demanding to see a certain government file instead of having it read to us, refusing to accept words and platitudes as a substitute for facts, checking the veracity of statements and claims before we commit them to print. . . .

Public service reporting is also investigative reporting: the uncovering of facts which people or groups are consciously trying to keep secret.

IRE President Robert W. Greene
*1977 Winner, John Peter Zenger Award for Freedom of the Press**

On the morning of June 5, 1976, a new 300-foot-high dam on the Teton River in Idaho split open and the huge reservoir behind it thundered onto the rich farming valley below. A mass of water estimated at 80 billion gallons—the entire contents of a 17-mile-long lake—surged across 7 miles of farms in depths up to 15 feet and at speeds of up to 60 miles an hour. By the time its force dissipated 75 miles downstream, 11 people were dead and 13,000 head of livestock were lost. Thousands of acres of agricultural land were gone and with them the dreams, sweat, and decades of labor of hundreds of Idaho farming families.

Two days later, Gaylord Shaw, a tough veteran reporter of the Washington, D.C., bureau of the *Los Angeles Times,* was on the telephone to the dam's builder, the U.S. Bureau of Reclamation, asking for "any reports . . . from the field during the Teton Dam's construction."[1] He was rebuffed again and again until one engineer tipped him that such reports, known as L-29s, were filed monthly. Shaw dug deeper and by the end of

*Reprinted by permission of the IRE Journal.

July had pieced together an exhaustive autopsy of the Teton Dam's failure.[2]

But he didn't stop there. Digging deeper into the bureaucracy of the federal and state governments, Shaw pursued an examination of dam safety all across America. How many Teton Dams lurked among the 50,000 dams in the United States, he wondered? "We are flirting with disaster," he wrote in a memo to his editors. "One of these days a catastrophe far greater than Teton will rivet attention on the problem. It may happen tomorrow, or it may not happen for 20 years. But it will happen."[3]

By March 1977, he had uncovered dozens of serious problems in large dams across America and reported that at least twenty major structures would not withstand severe flooding. Smaller, private dams were even worse time bombs, he concluded, for they were rarely if ever inspected.[4] He found officials reluctant to take responsibility and records difficult to obtain. But he persisted despite the inert response of a sluggish bureaucracy and an uninterested Congress.

Then on July 20, disaster struck again, this time in Pennsylvania, near Johnstown. The Laurel Run Dam, following a massive downpour of a dozen inches, burst, and another huge wall of water thundered down a narrow valley. Fifty-five people died. Again, Shaw reported the disaster and the ticking danger of dam safety.[5] Again, there was little response. It took a third disaster, one which killed thirty-nine people in Georgia, for the government to finally release inspection funds allocated five years before.[6]

One reporter; one newspaper; hard work; hours of searching records; dozens of interviews and personal inspections; more hours of reading engineering reports, technical data, geologic findings; more interviews and inspections; then story after story. Finally, a bureaucracy stirred into action, and perhaps another tragedy averted. Gaylord Shaw's reporting on dam safety won him the Pulitzer Prize for national reporting in 1978.

At the outset of this chapter, investigative reporter Robert W. Greene compared investigative reporting to public service reporting and what used to be called "hard-nosed" reporting. Whether it is a journalistic innovation or only a more intensive application of standard reporting procedures continues to be debated in some newsrooms. In any case, the investigative reporter shares with other news-gatherers at least three of the basic techniques for getting information: direct and indirect observation of the news situation, interviewing, and search of documents. Because all these techniques are fundamental to the reporting process, we will examine them in detail as they apply to public affairs coverage generally before narrowing our focus to their more refined and intensive application to investigative reporting.

Most often, public affairs reporters get their information by direct observation, watching an event as it occurs—a speech, a city council meeting, a legislative session. In this kind of coverage, the reporter rarely intervenes, and his story is often limited to what he passively observes.

At other times, getting the information requires the reporter to move outside the boundaries of the event. This may involve something as simple as leafing through clippings from the morgue or as complex as contacting a number of secondary sources for confirmation, reaction, or explanation. And there are times when getting the information involves participation by the reporter. She creates an event by asking questions. The press conference, the person-on-the-street poll, the investigative story are common examples of reporters themselves "making" news.

The framework in which most public affairs reporters work, however, puts constraints on many of these techniques. That framework is the traditional information-gathering structure employed by almost all news organizations—the "beat" system. This system makes reporters responsible for a particular area of news, usually an echelon of government. That's their beat, at once their horizon and their anchor.

The news media, perhaps the last bastion of the generalist in an age of increasing specialization, have employed the beat system for decades. This may be partly a gesture to the virtues of specialization and partly a statement about the importance of certain aspects of society that are given beat status. Today, we find an accelerating trend toward the establishment of new beats and reporting specialties.

Once the police station, city hall, courts, statehouse, and federal building made up the universe of beats. The list is now three or four times that length in many newsrooms. It will vary, of course, with the size of the news organization. Some specialties come and go with the whims of news fashion. The civil-rights beats of the 1960s, for example, are largely abandoned, but big on today's scene are environmental specialists.

Broadcast news operations typically have fewer beats and specialties. At medium or large dailies, however, many of these beats are apt to be found: politics, business, education, agriculture, labor, science, urban affairs, religion, medicine, consumer news. Some newspapers, because of unique developments in their circulation areas, will employ unusual specialists. The *Oak Ridge* (Tenn.) *Oak Ridger*, for example, has an atomic energy writer, a specialty few metropolitan newspapers find necessary. And some newspapers, attempting to overcome barriers inherent in a balkanized beat system, have moved toward consolidation of related beats. The criminal justice specialty, combining police, courts, and correction systems, is an example.

The bulk of what we have defined as public affairs news is produced on the governmental beats found in the smallest and largest news organizations—police and courts and city, county, state, and federal governments. Their universality testifies to the journalistic norms of news value: drama, involving individuals, emanating from the police and courts, which enforce the laws, and significance emanating from government agencies, which levy taxes and write and administer laws. In addition to their focus on government, these beats have another common characteristic. Each is usually contained within a single building, enabling the reporters to gather most of their news at one location. These characteristics endow the beat system with some of its strengths—and weaknesses.

Before examining these, let's look at how beats are covered and how they often shape the reporter's strategies. The odds are high that as a reporter you'll be assigned to a beat early in your career. Let's say it's city hall. Again, our description of the beat may vary considerably with the size of the organization, but in all likelihood you'll spend most of your working day on your beat.

Your day may start with a visit to city hall. You'll greet the receptionist in the lobby and then perhaps check in with the city manager. As often as not, she'll be busy, so you'll speak to an aide instead, or a secretary. Part of your job—a big part—is developing and maintaining friendly relations with city employees. You'll spend seemingly unproductive time with them, engaging in small talk, sharing their problems and interests. You'll want to learn their eccentricities, their habits, their personalities, which will help you determine how you deal with them and they with you. They're important to you, and their friendly cooperation is your lifeblood—access to information.

On some days, you'll have a specific story you're following or one that requires more information to complete. It may be in the planning department or the license bureau or any of a dozen other city departments. You'll visit them with specific sources and specific questions in mind. Or you may just visit, passing the time of day with department heads, assistants, public information specialists, clerks, and secretaries. If you work in a large city, there will probably be a press room in city hall, and you'll drop in there to chat with reporters from other media. It's there where you'll probably write your stories, telephoning or teletyping them back to your city desk.

Perhaps the most frequent demand on your time will be attendance at meetings. In a large city, these go on morning, afternoon, and evening, five days a week. You pick and choose among them, rationing your time to the most significant (very often "significant events" can be translated as those your city editor wants covered or those that competing media are covering). You may find yourself covering many meetings by telephone, a hazardous practice forced on you by your work load. A wide acquaintance with city officials may enable you to use them as surrogate reporters. It's a common practice, although the dangers of allowing error and bias to creep into your stories demands confirmation from others when relying on secondhand observation.

The most important city hall meeting is usually the council meeting, weekly or biweekly in smaller cities, daily in the metropolis. In truth, council meetings are often routine in large cities, because the debate and decisions occurred earlier in committee meetings. Nevertheless, your newspaper may want you to sit through every minute of every council meeting; or you may just pop in and out, attending only when those items about which you plan to write are being discussed. You decided on those items in advance by studying the agenda, which you received in the mail or picked up from a clerk.

The same procedure is repeated with the meetings of any of a number of council committees, city commissions, and agencies. The result: After your early round of hellos, you spend the day at one or more meetings. You leave only to write your stories.

The routine is somewhat different if you are a broadcast reporter who covers government news. You'll probably be assigned to several levels of government, not just city hall. You'll be more selective in the events you decide to cover—the quantity of broadcast news is a fraction of that found in a daily newspaper. Your choices will usually be made on the basis of the overriding broadcast news values: conflict, drama, and in the case of television, visual possibilities.[7]

Newspaper reporters should be alert to what broadcast reporters are covering, and not solely because of competition. They know that, increasingly, people are learning about spot news events first from radio or television. The newspaper function on the same story then becomes that of providing the background and interpretation that limited broadcast coverage doesn't provide. Media watchers and critics complain that newspapers often neglect this function. It will become even more important as electronic communication systems, such as cable television, expand.[8]

How do you get the news in the hypothetical city hall beat just described? Partly through direct observation and partly through interviewing sources. You'd find yourself operating in much the same way at the courthouse, the federal building, the legislature, and the police and sheriff's offices. Some conditions will vary. There are few meetings at the police station, for example, and direct observation falls off markedly. You'll rely more on personal contacts and relationships. Still, the strategies of beat reporting and the principles guiding them vary little from building to building and agency to agency.

What are the strengths of the system? They are few, but significant.

Sources   The development of sources may be the chief advantage. Daily contact can lead to friendship, trust, and cooperation from news sources. Personal contact is as important with the mayor's aide as with the mayor himself, for the reporter needs tips, fast help in getting information, and quick access to top officials.

Continuity   Reporters who follow the same story day after day, who deal with the same people month after month, develop insight and expertise that help produce accurate, complete stories. They are less likely to miss an angle or find an important door closed to them. Continuity, in other words, is a major benefit.

Surveillance   The regularity of beat coverage also helps the reporter to perform one of the principal functions of journalism, surveillance of the environment.[9] It's an efficient way to monitor activity in those areas of the social environment that regularly yield news.

"Outside" reporters who break into a beat for a specific news event find themselves handicapped on these counts. They often don't know whom to contact for information. Those they do contact may not know them—or trust them. Rather than cheerful help, they may be confronted with guarded answers or obstructionism from bureaucrats who have learned to fear the potential damage of the printed word.

But outside reporters also bring assets to the task, which can best be seen by examining some of the pitfalls of beat reporting, which include

Cronyism   Beat reporters value their sources, sometimes to the extreme. They eventually tend to protect them from damaging stories, adopting the rationale that they'll need their goodwill another day on another story.

Bias   There's a tendency—the social scientists call it socialization—to acquire the beliefs and values of people with whom you work. This undercuts what many editors consider the first principle of reporting: objectivity. Beat reporters who talk to police officers all day, who go on coffee breaks with them, who may meet them after work for a friendly drink, not only develop good sources. They also begin to think like a cop. If you doubt it, ask defense lawyers: they'll never accept a police reporter on a criminal jury.

Myopia   Beat reporters tend to lose perspective about the relative importance of the subjects they cover. What may seem trivial to their editors appears significant to the reporters. Their beat is their world, and they sometimes fail to see the world as viewed by anonymous observers and readers.

Ego   They may come to view their beat as their personal property. They may resent other reporters stepping in to cover stories on *their* turf. By the same token, they're reluctant to move into someone else's beat to follow a story that naturally leads there. They lose sight of the fact that beats are inventions, arbitrary boundaries that news situations may not follow.

Narrowness This pitfall is an extension of the one involving the ego. It leads to stories that are parochial because beat boundaries become psychological walls, blocking the reporter from adequately developing the story. Consider the court reporter who attends a sanity hearing. He listens to testimony about dismal conditions at a mental hospital. The more important story might come from an investigation of conditions at the hospital. But the mental and physical blinders of the beat system may well convince the reporter to limit his efforts to the statements made in court. Of course, editors can and do assign follow-up stories or bring in other reporters. Truncated coverage produced by the beat approach abounds, however, and these remedies are restricted by the limits of time, personnel, and vision.

Dilution There is a tendency for beat reporters to try to cover everything in the building. The outsider may be more objective and parcel out energy where it counts most. Beat reporters see and hear *too* much, and tend to equalize rather than separate information. By dividing their time among the trivial and the important, they have less time available to work on the more significant stories. A principal effect of this self-imposed time constraint is shallowness. There's no time to check with secondary sources or to do the background research necessary for a complex story. The cure is a willingness by reporters and editors to invest time in the surveillance function, without expecting a payoff for each hour on the job. In practice, however, there's a tendency to expect production from any major effort. Thus, if a television film crew spends a couple of hours at a political rally, some of that film is likely to be aired even if the event itself turns out to be a dud.

The competent reporter, naturally enough, is aware of these pitfalls, and attempts to avoid them. Editors, although devoted to the efficiency of the beat system, also attempt to overcome its limitations. One way is periodic rotation of beats among different reporters, to minimize the perils of cronyism, bias, and myopia. Another is the use of other reporters or teams of reporters in news situations too broad for proper handling by the beat reporter. A more difficult trap to avoid in covering public affairs, however, is one not unique to the beat approach: a tendency to rely almost wholly on direct observation for some stories.

DIRECT AND INDIRECT OBSERVATION

As a strategy for gathering information, direct observation is sometimes invested with an almost mystical authority. Newspaper lore puts great stock in the eyewitness account, citing both accuracy and vividness as products.

When the eyewitness and reporter are one, this belief holds, conditions approach the ideal. Who, What, Where, When, Why, and How will be served, and the prose will throb with color and fidelity.

In some ways, on some occasions, the pure, direct observation model will satisfy these expectations: the delivery of a speech—if all we need to know are the words of the speaker; the report of a ball game—if the reporter also knows the scores of past games and the number of those still to be played; the description of a natural disaster—if the reporter's field of vision includes the entire scene. This is the old mirror-image school of journalism, one that the conventional wisdom heralded as the path of objectivity. Report what you see and hear, the injunction went, and truth will out.

This simplistic hope of the direct observation approach has come under increasing attack since the 1940s and 1950s.[10] Restricting the reporter to direct observation (or, as is often the case, the reports of other direct observers) produces its own distortions. Consider these limitations:

Reporters are restricted to writing about events. If nothing *happens*, there is nothing to report. We can all see, however, that often situations are more important than isolated events. Sometimes the fact that *nothing* has happened is newsworthy. Consider police reporters who spend their days writing about crimes and fatal traffic accidents. If a month goes by without a traffic death, or a year without a murder, news value is the outcome of a nonevent. Which is more worthy of a reporter's—and reader's—time: an account of a fire or an investigative story that deals with fire hazards in retail stores and enforcement policies of building and fire inspectors?

A preference for direct observation pushes journalists into writing about lesser events, when the audience's interest and needs would be better served by developing stories about general situations and collections of events. Scattered coverage of a dozen medical malpractice trials over a year may be a less worthy accomplishment than an investigation of the "why" of malpractice litigation and the characteristics of doctors who are involved.

The inclination to report on events, because by definition they are news, leads reporters to amplify pseudoevents. News manipulators stage events—a press conference, a demonstration, a contest, a speech, a meeting—because they know that this type of activity attracts media attention. A reporter should make a practice of casting a skeptical eye at events to assess their intrinsic worth and the motivation underlying them.

The news values that result in an emphasis on events and direct observation often work to restrict the number of sources available to the reporter. The delegation that speaks at a city council meeting has its viewpoint reported. Affected groups and individuals not present at the meeting don't get exposure to the public. This skewed source emphasis not only introduces bias but also blocks from view important dimensions. Consider the housing authority meeting at which plans for a high-rise development are discussed with builders. Not present at the meeting are representatives of a nearby airport whose operations would be affected by the building, nor are small businessmen, police officials, school administrators, and others whose activities might be affected by the high-rise. In cases like this one—and they are common—the reporter must supplement direct observation with efforts to uncover these other dimensions. They are best presented in the initial story, but they can be done in follow-up stories. Too often, these follow-up stories depend on the initiative and awareness of affected individuals, a tenuous condition, or on the alertness of the reporter and editor.

Time is another victim of heavy reliance on direct observation. Reporters who devote their working hours to events are governed by those events. They are unable to pursue other information more essential to their story. Nevertheless, public affairs reporting is about events and happenings. Journalistic norms specify it, and the audience has been conditioned to expect it. The reporter, then, must develop methods of observation to supplement direct observation and minimize its limitations. These indirect information-gathering strategies can be categorized as preevent and postevent procedures.

The term *preevent observation* sounds like a contradiction. How, after all, can you observe an event before it happens? What the term implies, however, is getting information needed for intelligent coverage of the event, whether it's a meeting, a speech, an interview, or a backgrounder. The procedure starts with anticipating the story, deciding on its probable audience, its significance, its dimensions. This preparation leads to questions that should be asked and answered and points toward the required preevent research.

Often it starts with a search of the newspaper's morgue to gain both historical perspective and a beginning set of facts. If your own morgue doesn't include information on the subject, consider other available sources, such as the *New York Times Index.* One word of caution about morgue clippings: They may contain errors of fact that can easily be perpetuated. The best practice is to read the entire file for later correction stories.

Other preevent research might include background information about individuals. Many biographical directories are available. If the person is an author or specialist in some field, you may want to become familiar with his or her published work. You should also consider contacting other authorities in that field for an assessment of the person's work and some potential questions.

Contacting experts in advance is useful in preparing for any complex subject. Let's say you're going to a press conference about a claimed breakthrough in solar heating for residential housing. You could find someone knowledgeable in this field at a local college or university who will be able to direct you to published material as well as suggest questions for the press conference.

Public records are another strategic weapon in the reporter's observational arsenal. Is it a story about a proposed housing development? Tax and land records can tell a lot about ownership and prices. Does the story concern a mass transit system? Census reports provide accurate information about population densities and commuter patterns. Does the subject concern a legal matter? Many court records are open for inspection. Checking records, before and after the event, is laborious but profitable. A separate section of this chapter offers detailed advice on how to go about it.

By going through these preliminaries, you'll arrive at the event prepared to do something more than passively take notes. You'll have made a preliminary evaluation of the situation, organized the story in your mind, and devised some informed questions to ask. You'll also have facts against which you can measure what you see and hear.

But observation doesn't stop with the end of the event. If the news is complex and involves several categories of people (directly or potentially), you'll want to represent all of them in your story, whether or not they appeared at the event. An unfortunate maxim of the news business is the injunction to get "both sides" of the story. It traps us into thinking that there are only two sides to an issue, when often there are three, four, or more. If the event offered only two, you must seek out the others afterward. On the high-rise apartment story, for example, representatives of groups not present—the police, the zoning board, the school board, the airlines, the control tower—should be contacted to produce a rounded story.

Sometimes independent sources, who can verify or contradict suspicious claims made at an event, should be called on. For the solar heating press conference, an independent source may be the same expert you contacted before leaving the office. A word of caution is in order about this type of source, however. People, reporters included, tend to place great faith in specialists, particularly scientists. You must remember that experts can and do disagree. One engineer may hold a belief about solar heating that another rejects out of hand. If you contact just one, you may not discover the conflict or the truth. Worse, neither will your readers. One way to overcome this danger is to ask your source if there are differing opinions on the subject; most professionals are sufficiently honest to tell you if there are. Another approach is to contact several experts on the same subject. Here, numbers alone are likely to protect the story against bias or distortion. This multiple-source approach also lends credibility to the story.

The technique of direct observation in getting information for a public affairs story, then, may have a number of variations, and these may have varying degrees of complexity. Some of the variations, as we have noted, draw on interviewing, a technique that requires its own set of guideposts.

THE INTERVIEW PROCESS

Interviewing in public affairs reporting is not a simple art, nor is it simply explained. There are as many interview styles as there are individual personalities of interviewers—and they conjure up vivid images:

> With a wide-eyed gaze as direct as her question, Oriana Fallaci inquires of Archbishop Makarios: "Isn't it true you are very fond of women?"
>
> Lacing his language with superlatives, Johnny Carson of NBC's "Tonight Show" turns to an aging trouper and asks a question designed to get a laugh.
>
> Empathy is evident in his eyes and his voice as radio interviewer Studs Terkel queries a factory worker about his inflation-riddled income.
>
> Becoming an actual participant in the event, an unclothed Gay Talese manages a massage parlor, "interviewing" customers in preparation for a book on sex in America.

These are only a few examples of the diversity one finds in the journalistic interview. To be sure, journalists are not the only professionals who use the interview as a tool of their trade. Doctors, lawyers, social workers, social science researchers, and many others are also interviewers.

Because so many people are interested in interviewing, the literature on the subject is expanding rapidly. This growing interest suggests that interviewing is something to which the journalist should devote considerable thought and study. Interviewing is not something one learns and then pursues mindlessly. Instead, it is a purposeful process that requires continual reassessment and readjustment.

All interviews involve verbal interaction between two or more persons, but they are usually initiated for a specific purpose and they usually focus on a specific matter. In this way an interview differs from a casual conversation between friends. The interviewer's objective is always to keep the subject on the point, dealing with relevant information. The interview requires an element of *control*. Just how the interviewer gains that control is sometimes a dilemma. Journalistic interviewers normally try to maintain control regardless of their mode of interviewing: (1) the face-to-face personal interview or (2) the telephone interview. A few sources, among them former popes and some heads of state, required submission of written interrogatories. Press conferences have some of the elements of the interview, but they are usually too unstructured and uncontrolled in content to be termed an "interview" in the sense that we are considering it here. Obviously the reporter has greatest control in the private interview.

When a reporter decides that an interview is appropriate for gathering information for a particular story, time and distance usually dictate the method. Telephone interviewing offers a major advantage if the reporter has only a short time to gather information—or if the person to be interviewed is not personally available. Major disadvantages of the telephone interview stem from the lack of interpersonal contact and the interviewer's inability to exercise persuasion by his or her presence in coaxing out more information than the source would be likely to give over the phone—especially to a stranger. For persons who already have rapport, the telephone interview can be a quite acceptable device.

Although knowing and understanding the interview process is helpful to the reporter, so is an examination of the interview's components. In the next few pages those steps—preparation, setting, questioning techniques, recording and evaluating information, and writing the story—are examined.

Preparation

Good interviewing requires planning—planning who should be interviewed and obtaining background information about the person and the subject. Here the thoughtful reporter should consider a number of questions: Who should be interviewed? Is this person a knowledgeable and appropriate source? What is the extent of her competence? When is he clearly outside his field of expertise? Some sources are willing to speak out on any and all subjects—and every reporter knows such persons, whether they be public officials or self-proclaimed commentators on the state of the world. Often a reporter tends to rely on the most available source, who may not be the best one. Sometimes an agreeable and cooperative source may not necessarily be the right source either.

Securing background information about the topic is also important. Many an interview has gone sour because the reporter squandered precious time asking questions that could be answered by a quick search through the morgue or by consulting a standard reference like *Who's Who in America*. The knowledgeable reporter-interviewer who is well briefed is better able to achieve depth and real substance in an interview. Minneapolis television interviewer Henry Wolfe, who was the host of a local talk show, was usually so well read and backgrounded that he made a strong positive impression on his guests. "It shows them that you care enough about them and their subject to have done some work in advance," Wolfe says. Questions that reflect poor preparation can have a disastrous effect on an interview. If, for example, you are interviewing an author and haven't read her latest book, you can offend her. Or uncertainty about the source's background can arouse doubts in his mind about the interviewer's competence—which can lead quickly to distrust.

Setting

Before making arrangements for the interview, some thought should be given to the place where it will be conducted. What setting will give the reporter the best understanding of the person? At work—an office, factory, or laboratory? Or at home where the interviewee is seen with family members in a relaxed atmosphere? Usually, the location is dependent on the type of information desired. In an interview that requires frank questioning—perhaps of a somewhat unwilling source—a psychologically neutral environment should be found, such as an empty room, an intimate restaurant, or an airport lobby.

For the person who is likely to be interrupted by frequent telephone calls, an interview in a car may be appropriate. Grady Clay of the *Louisville Courier-Journal* is a devotee of the automobile interview. Of course, it has obvious problems for the recording of information—particularly if the car is moving. Friendly feature interviews are sometimes conducted in the source's home or in a neighborhood bar with a convivial atmosphere. Naturally, not all interviews can be conducted under ideal conditions, and many are so impromptu that the setting cannot be planned at all. They occur on the spur of the moment in a courthouse corridor or on a street corner.

Television news interviewers like Mike Wallace of CBS have a singular psychological advantage because the source is usually surrounded by cameras and other apparatus. Under such conditions, some interviewees must feel a sense of entrapment as the inquisitory, slightly hostile Wallace zeros in with one question after another. Wallace is clearly in control, and his style has yielded formidable results as sources blurt out information, often embarrassing to themselves.

Murray Fisher of *Playboy*, who is responsible for the highly successful "Playboy Interview," says that the "hostile interview gives you a feeling of dancing across a bed of coals. Our most successful interviews are those that make the source feel completely relaxed and comfortable—and sort of coax them into a level of trust that opens them up."[11] Thus, the *Playboy* interviews are conducted in settings that enhance this objective.

Questioning Techniques

Questioning techniques differ considerably with the personal style of the interviewer. Even so, most journalists agree that advance planning is useful. A list of questions might be prepared, for example, although they should not be followed so rigidly that they keep interviewees from expressing themselves. Yet planning the questions is helpful in maintaining control over the interview, steering it on the intended course. The tone and substance of questions are adjusted to the interviewer's purpose. They can range from direct, frontal attack—like the questions of Mike Wallace—to a meandering reinforcement technique used by the conservative columnist and television interviewer William Buckley. Buckley is a master of the technique developed by psychologist Carl Rogers wherein sentence endings are repeated as a device to keep the interviewer talking. "Well, it's not very much like that," the interviewee says. "Not very much like that?"

repeats the interviewer. This technique encourages the source to elaborate and expand without having the interviewer phrase another question.

Experienced interviewers advise against questions that can be answered with a simple yes or no. As Robert Maurer of NBC News put it, "If you say to your guest [interviewee], 'When the accident happened were you walking along the lake?' the person can reply in one word—'Yes.' But if you say, 'When the accident happened, what were you doing?' the subject will have to give you a more detailed answer."[12]

Another television interviewer once demonstrated the exhibitionist question, the kind of question that shows off the interviewer's superior knowledge without leaving anything for the interviewee to say. For example,

> Q. Buddy Rogers, you and your wife, Mary Pickford, live in one of Hollywood's great showplaces, "Pickfair." It has been described as a great, big, white country English manor house right in the middle of Beverly Hills, with a great winding driveway, with a big, sprawling lawn, with three floors filled with great antiques and a unique collection of Chinese pieces, and you've entertained celebrities from all over the world as well as the Hollywood greats. Isn't that so, Buddy?

As the interviewer commented later, a better way to have asked the question would have been to say, "Buddy Rogers, you and your wife, Mary Pickford, live in Hollywood's great showplace, 'Pickfair.' Would you describe it for us."[13]

Stanford communications researchers Eleanor and Nathan Maccoby suggest six guidelines for clarity in interviewing:

1. Avoid words with a double meaning.
2. Avoid long questions.
3. Specify exactly the time, place and context which you want the respondent to assume.
4. Either make explicit all the alternatives which the respondent should have in mind when he answers, or make none of them explicit.
5. When the interview concerns a subject with which the respondent may not be very familiar, or one in which he may not have the necessary technical vocabulary, it is sometimes desirable to preface questions with an explanatory statement or an illustration which will set the stage for the question the interviewer wants to ask.
6. It is often helpful to ask questions in terms of the respondent's own immediate (and recent experience), rather than in terms of generalities.[14]

Of course, in addition to the actual wording of questions, the manner of the interviewer in asking them is important. Good eye contact is usually desirable, as is psychological reinforcement for the person being interviewed. It is important for the interviewee to know that the interviewer appreciates the information being imparted. Occasionally nodding or making verbal reinforcements—*uh-huh, right, yes*—can be helpful. Some persons become particularly conscious of the method being used to record the information and slow down their usual speech pattern as the interviewer takes notes. Others get nervous when a recorder is used.

Researchers have found that people speak at a more rapid rate when they are particularly anxious. And sometimes anxious people leave sentences unfinished. According to Eugene J. Webb and Jerry R. Salancik, "Breaking into an ongoing sentence with a new thought, repeating words or phrases, stuttering, using 'I don't know' not as a reply but as an interjection, and shifts of the loudness of voice were all related to the amount of anxiety present in the situation."[15]

At times the interviewer is confronted with an uncooperative source, one who simply refuses to talk or who answers questions evasively. In such a situation the first task of the interviewer is to determine *why* the source is uncooperative. Some understanding of this uncooperative behavior will determine the interviewing strategies needed. Sources can be uncooperative because they have something to hide or fear that too much discussion of the subject will cast them in an unfavorable light. Or they are not used to being interviewed and therefore are shy and uncomfortable. Still others can be blasé—tired of being interviewed, of being asked the same questions. This apathy is notably true of celebrities, like entertainers.

There are a number of different ways in which to conduct an interview with an uncooperative source. When the source is uncomfortable, special care must be taken to establish rapport. One such method is *identifying* with the interviewee. You might explain that you understand and empathize with the individual's plight. Studs Terkel, who has produced three extraordinary books of interviews with the "little people,"[16] says he "reveals his own vulnerability" to the source. Thus Terkel, a middle-aged, upper-middle-class white man, is able to establish lively discussions with people in very different social circumstances. The Terkel technique is particularly useful with those who are reluctant to talk. He is able to convince people who normally do not get interviewed that their views are worth hearing.

For the source who has something to hide or is otherwise unwilling to speak to the press, interviewers must be well prepared. They may want to confront the source with someone's charges or with evidence that suggests a particular explanation of an event. This approach may jolt the uncooperative source into cooperating. Sometimes the uncooperative source can be won over if reporters frankly and fully explain the nature of the story they are doing or offer a specific rationale for why the person's help is needed. At other times a tough interview style, using accusatory questions (based always on evidence the reporter has gathered), may be appropriate. Some reporters use various bluffing techniques suggesting to the source that they know more than they do. Although this device may work on occasion, it is fraught with ethical problems and ought to be employed rarely—and with great care.

Lewis A. Dexter, an authority on elite and specialized interviewing, has suggested that the difficult-to-interview celebrity or public figure is often willing to help the interviewer shape the questions, thus eliminating irrelevant, routine inquiries. Dexter says that the interviewer who enlists the source's aid in exploring questions often gets a better story. Dick Cavett of PBS often asks unusual questions of his guests, eliciting the response, "Nobody ever asked me that before." A fresh question, probing a new subject or looking at an old one in a different way, can be challenging and intriguing to the blasé person who is tired of trite questions.

Recording Information

Facing the reporter is the problem of recording information accurately and in detail without inhibiting the interviewee. Tom Wolfe and Truman Capote, who have both been called New Journalists, represent two extremes of the information-recording spectrum. Wolfe takes meticulous Gregg shorthand, whereas Capote has developed an aural memory system in which he attempts to memorize all the elements of the conversation. Most reporters use neither method. It is common for the note-taking reporter to develop a personal "briefhand" system so that the essence of the conversation and other information can be ascertained. Other reporters use tape recorders and are thus able to spend more time observing physical phenomena—the appearance of the subject, the furniture in the room, and so forth. An obvious disadvantage to tape recorders is the difficulty in transcribing recorded material. In a study of journalists' interview techniques, journalism professor Jim R. Morris found that about 75 percent of the metropolitan news reporters he interviewed were negative about using tape recorders. In the same study, Morris offered some helpful hints about note-taking:

1. Be as inconspicuous as possible. A flashy notebook can be inhibiting to the interviewee. If you sense that he objects to notetaking, don't do it. "The important thing is to get a person to say something."
2. If you don't take formal shorthand develop your own style. A form of speed writing used by most reporters consists of omitting vowels and endings by abbreviating whenever possible.
3. Notes should be taken simply to jog the memory later. Writing down key words and phrases probably will suffice for this. Get to a typewriter as soon as possible to fill in the gaps.
4. Don't shortcut where names, dates and places are concerned. Take a few minutes at the conclusion of the interview to check your notes for accuracy. It saves a lot of time and embarrassment later on.
5. Treat each interview situation differently. Notetaking might be inhibiting to one person, but you might impress the next with your thoroughness and concern for accuracy.[17]

Much of the emphasis on recording information centers on the words that pass from the mouth of the person being interviewed. Other behavior in an interview can be observed, however. The growing intellectual infatuation with "body language" and other nonverbal physical cues in an interview is worthy of consideration, but great caution should be taken in noting physical behavior in order to avoid sweeping interpretations. Does a man scratch his head because he is excessively nervous or thoughtful—or simply because his head itches?

A number of nonverbal cues surfaced in television critic Jack Gould's classic account of underworld figure Frank Costello as he appeared before a congressional committee:

> As he [Costello] sparred with Rudolph Halley, the committee's counsel, the movement of his fingers told their own emotional story. When the questions got rough, Costello crumpled a handkerchief in his fingers. Or he grasped a half-filled glass of water. Or he beat a silent tattoo on the table top. Or he rolled a little ball of paper between his thumb and index finger. Or he stroked the side piece of his glasses lying on the table. His was video's first ballet of the hands.[18]

Evaluating Information

Just how valid is the information collected in an interview? Reporters usually take most of what they get at face value unless there is a clear indication that something is wrong with the information. But reporters would do well to remember that human beings are prone to selective recall and that memory often erodes at an alarming rate. By the same token, psychological studies indicate that people have selective perception; that is, they "note only parts of an event, and the notings are conditional on what we expect and what we are."[19]

Much research remains to be done before interviewers can be very certain about the recall of their sources. Webb and Salancik, in their study of interviewing, suggest two lines of checking: "The first centers on *consistency*—the internal analysis of a source's statements over time or within a single interview on the same topic. The second is *corroboration*, or the verification of a source's statement by comparing it with external evidence—the statements of others or some definitive record."[20] Could the event have happened the way the police officer said it did? Was it possible for the murder suspect to have been in the victim's home at 8:30 P.M. and across town twenty minutes later? Does the story as it was told to you make sense? Is it consistent? Thoroughgoing news coverage also requires corroboration of details and circumstances. Ben Bradlee, executive editor of the *Washington Post,* points out that his paper demanded corroboration of each detail from at least two sources in its celebrated coverage of the Watergate scandals. A single accusation was not enough—there had to be hard evidence acquired through checking and rechecking the material.

Writing the Story

Most interview stories are written to blend quotes into a traditional news-story narrative. A blend of quotes and paraphrase plus some description of the interviewee are typical of the form.

In recent years, however, many newspapers and magazines have become enamored of the "Playboy Interview" approach—a simple question-and-answer technique. Often an interview is tape-recorded, then with modest editing it is reprinted verbatim. A lengthy editor's note, usually preceding the Q-A interview, sets the scene and indicates something about the background of interviewee and interviewer. However, this method is frequently ineffective because few people are articulate enough for their words to be transferred to a written form. The "Playboy Interview" is not such a product but rather a result of heavy editing, rewriting, and rechecking with the interviewee.

The importance of the journalistic interview as a means of gathering information cannot be underestimated. And the interview, because of its strong linkage with other fields and disciplines, is likely to be the source of continued study and interest. For this reason much more will be learned about the interview in the next few years. Public affairs reporters should be ready to make the interview an aspect of journalism requiring continuing reassessment and change. But in the final analysis, the interview is a highly personal tool to be adjusted to both the personality and the personal style of interviewer and interviewee.

A Note on Ethics

Although a concern for accuracy is rooted in all phases of journalism, it is particularly paramount with interview material. Fairness dictates that both the words and intent of a subject be passed along to readers without distortion. Reporters disagree on the amount of leeway permissible in handling quotes. Some insist that the writer should go no further than correcting inadvertent or nonsignificant lapses of good grammar. Others argue that "honing" of quotes is acceptable if the meaning is not changed. But nearly all would agree on the need for substantial agreement between what the subject actually said and what is reported. The New Journalism techniques of interior monologue and scene-setting often run counter to that aspect of professional ethics. When the reporter isn't present to record dialogue, yet wishes to reconstruct a scene from unattributed sources, is it ethical to use direct quotation? Debate over that technique has occupied journalists for years. As a bottom line, most journalists would probably require disclosure of the method at the point the method is employed. Troubling for similar reasons is the presentation of a composite character as a real entity. More than a decade ago, writer Gail Sheehy developed a sensational study for *New York* magazine of a prostitute named "Redpants."

Only later was it discovered that Redpants was a composite character, crafted from interviews with several prostitutes. Again, disclosure of the method is demanded in cases where composites are employed. Journalists have no trouble, however, in demanding that a bold line be drawn between fact and fiction. That standard was highlighted by the Janet Cooke case in 1981. Cooke, a reporter for the *Washington Post*, wrote a story about an eight-year-old heroin addict identified only as "Jimmy." The disclosure triggered an avalanche of concern from the public and law enforcement authorities. When the story was later awarded a Pulitzer Prize, doubts about its authenticity led to the discovery that Jimmy was the product of Cooke's imagination, not the streets of the capital. The revelation shocked the nation and the press establishment, and the reexamination of the boundaries of journalistic truth that followed affirmed the professional ethic: Fabrication is forbidden. Reporters, even in the postobjective age of greater stylistic freedom, are expected to base their accounts on reality. Even in stories where the identity of subjects must be disguised and information can't be attributed, editors are expected to demand full disclosure and verification in the editor-reporter relationship.

Because it is so personal, and therefore subject to human frailties, the interview should be buttressed, whenever possible, with less subjective evidence. Such solid information comes from a variety of public records that are available sources of news and information.

USING PUBLIC RECORDS

In the early 1970s, a weekly newspaper in Omaha became interested in the financial affairs of Boys Town, Nebraska, and the promotion techniques used by the famous home for boys to solicit money from the American public. The paper knew that under revised tax laws the tax records of tax-exempt organizations like Boys Town were available to the public from the Internal Revenue Service.

So the *Sun Newspapers* queried the IRS and obtained Boys Town's tax return, showing the home had assets of more than $190 million. Using the tax records as a starting point, the paper launched an investigation that exposed the home's financial affairs. Published in March 1972, the articles won the paper a Pulitzer Prize.

The *Sun's* investigation is still frequently cited as an example of tenacious reporting by a small paper on a huge subject. It also shows the importance of knowing about public records and how to use them; and although most public records probably won't bring a Pulitzer Prize, all public affairs reporters ought to be familiar with the important public documents in the areas they cover. The court reporter, for example, should be familiar with court filings, suits, liens, judgments, and injunctions. The business reporter should know about incorporation papers. The city hall reporter should know how to find out who holds a liquor license for a local tavern. Indeed, the ability to use public records is a quality honed particularly by investigative journalists. They begin by finding out what records are likely to be open to inspection.

Open Records Legislation

Many states have open records laws that require officials to maintain records of their official duties and that usually allow anyone to examine such records under reasonable conditions. Indeed, records of some government agencies must be certified as "true and correct" if a citizen so demands. Land records, deeds, wills, and other court records often fall into this category.

The investigative reporter usually has a thorough understanding of open records laws, of what materials are available under them, and of what is specifically excluded. Though open records laws may appear, on first reading, to be blank checks to examine documents, most such laws have specific exclusions. For example, juvenile criminal records, private tax returns, and medical records are normally considered confidential, both by statute and court rulings.

Open records laws and court rulings on the issue usually distinguish between "public records," which are the official documents an official must keep and make available, and "working papers," such as letters, notes, memoranda, and internal reports, which an official may be required to keep but which are often considered confidential. In a way, then, the official record is only the tip of the iceberg below which lie supporting documents. Police arrest reports and offense reports, for example, are often available to the public affairs reporter, but "supplementary reports," in which police detectives provide many details of cases, are not public. A school board may have to give the reporter the text of a contract between the board and the teachers union, but it may not have to reveal the negotiating "position papers" on which the contract is based.

Good public affairs reporters, then, should first be familiar with their state's open records law and its interpretation in court rulings. Then, if denied access to a particular record, reporters can ask for a specific reason from the official who refuses to release a document. Under firm but pleasant questioning, reporters will often get to see records that are considered open, but they must first know what their legal grounds are. (See Appendix D for additional information.)

Following are some of the common records normally helpful in covering public affairs. It is by no means a comprehensive list, and we have omitted specific details that may vary from state to state and county to county. Nonetheless, the records here are usually organized in a clear fashion, and you should find them quickly and efficiently in your community.

Chapter 6 deals with questions of libel and privilege, but it is important to note here that a public document is neither necessarily true nor privileged—that is, immune from liability for libel because of its contribution to public discourse. Sworn testimony in court may be privileged, for example, but an affidavit by a police officer alleging that an individual has a criminal history may not be privileged if it has not been presented in court. Although a document may state a fact, the reporter should not assume that the statement is true. Obviously, documents should be used in concert with careful interviewing, checking other sources, and common sense.

Land Records

Let's say you want to determine who owns a particular piece of land. The place to go is the county register of deeds office in the county in which the land is located. But before you do, you'll need to know how land is mapped and surveyed. Almost all land in America is surveyed and divided into identifiable parcels. Rural land is usually arranged according to *township, range,* and *section.* A township is a piece of land six miles square, or very close. It may have a proper name or be identified only by coordinate numbers; for example, Township 28 North, Range 18 West, T. 28 N., R. 18 W., is the normal way in which this township would be designated by coordinates. In this case, the piece of land has a name, Kinnickinnic Township. It is located in western Wisconsin, about forty miles east of Minneapolis, Minnesota, but it is typical of townships all across America.

Each township has thirty-six sections, each one square mile, or very close, on a side. If you have ever flown over the Midwest, perhaps you have noticed how the land appears to be "squared off." This is because roads were often built along the section dividing lines. Each section is numbered, so that, for example, section 11 of T. 28 N., R. 18 W., refers to a one-mile-square parcel of land in Kinnickinnic Township. Within the section, the land may be halved or quartered or both. For instance, one small piece of land in this section is described on a deed as being located in "the NE¼ of the NW¼ of section 11. . . ." That means that if the section is divided into quarters, and each quarter is divided into quarters, the land would be in the northeast quarter of the northwest quarter. (See Figure 4-1.)

In urban areas, land often is identified by *addition, block,* and *lot* in legal descriptions. Additions are tracts of land added to real estate developments, and they normally have given names. The block and lot numbers will identify only one piece of land in any particular addition.

Now let's trace the owner of a piece of land. In Minneapolis, Minnesota, on East Calhoun Boulevard, there is a large green house overlook-

Figure 4-1 Kinnickinnic Township, Wisconsin

ing Lake Calhoun. Its number is 3347. Taking this address to the register of deeds office, you can ask to see the overlay map that correlates street address with legal description. You find that the legal description of the property is "Lot 13, Block 3, McCrory's Rearrangement of parts of Block 48 and 49, Calhoun Park Addition." Taking the legal description to the *tract index,* you can find every filed legal transaction on that piece of land going back several decades. You find that a *warranty deed* was filed on the property in 1969, and the entry provides a document number. You ask for the document by number, and the clerk produces a copy of a deed between Gladys S. MacLean, a widow, and Robert C. Hentges and Judith L. Hentges, husband and wife. (See Figure 4-2.)

Warranty Deed
Individual to Joint Tenants

Form No. 5-M
3802196

Miller-Davis Co., Minneapolis
Minnesota Uniform Conveyancing Blanks (1931)

This Indenture, *Made this* 29th *day of* October *, 19*60 *,*

between Gladys M. MacLean, a widow and not remarried,

of the County of Hennepin *and State of* Minnesota *, party*
of the first part, and Robert C. Hentges and Judith L. Hentges,
husband and wife,
, of the County of
Hennepin *and State of* Minnesota *, parties of the second part,*

Witnesseth, *That the said part* y *of the first part, in consideration of the sum of* One Dollar
($1.00) and other good and valuable consideration ------------------------*DOLLARS,*
to her *in hand paid by the said parties of the second part, the receipt whereof is hereby acknowl-*
edged, do es *hereby Grant, Bargain, Sell, and Convey unto the said parties of the second part as joint*
tenants and not as tenants in common, their assigns, the survivor of said parties, and the heirs and
assigns of the survivor, Forever, all the tract___ or parcel___ of land lying and being in the County of
Hennepin *and State of Minnesota, described as follows, to-wit:*

Lot Thirteen (13), Block Three (3), McCrory's Rearrangement of parts of
Blocks Forty-eight (48) and Forty-nine (49), Calhoun Park, including any
portion of any street, alley, other city property, transportation right of
way, or other right of way, adjacent thereto, vacated or to be vacated,
together with all rights, privileges, easements and appurtenances thereto
attached or belonging, according to the recorded plat thereof on file and
of record in the office of the Register of Deeds in and for said Hennepin
County. Together with the parcels described on the rider attached hereto
and made a part hereof.

State Deed Tax due hereon: $ 71.50

STATE OF
Minnesota
DEED
STAMP
TAX

10-31-69 DEPT. OF
TAXATION

71.50

To Have and to Hold the Same, *Together with all the hereditaments and appurtenances there-*
unto belonging or in anywise appertaining, to the said parties of the second part, their assigns, the sur-
vivor of said parties, and the heirs and assigns of the survivor, Forever, the said parties of the second part
taking as joint tenants and not as tenants in common.
And the said Gladys M. MacLean, a widow and not remarried

part y *of the first part, for* herself, her *heirs, executors and administrators do* es
covenant with the said parties of the second part, their assigns, the survivor of said parties, and the heirs
and assigns of the survivor, that she is *well seized in fee of the lands and premises aforesaid and*
ha s *good right to sell and convey the same in manner and form aforesaid, and that the same are*
free from all incumbrances, except easements, reservations and restrictions of record, if any.

And the above bargained and granted lands and premises, in the quiet and peaceable possession of the
said parties of the second part, their assigns, the survivor of said parties, and the heirs and assigns of the
survivor, against all persons lawfully claiming or to claim the whole or any part thereof, subject to
incumbrances, if any, hereinbefore mentioned, the said part y___ *of the first part will Warrant and*
Defend.

In Testimony Whereof, *The said part* y = *of the first part has___ hereunto set* her
hand___ the day and year first above written.

In Presence of

Gladys M. MacLean, by her mark

Figure 4-2 Warranty Deed

You can also locate the deed if you know the name of either the seller (called the *grantor*) or the buyer (called the *grantee*). Deed offices file land transactions by both grantor and grantee, and you can thus determine all the land in a particular county held by an individual under one name. There may be, of course, other names under which a person may own a piece of land. The deed tells you that Mrs. MacLean conveyed the property to the Hentges, and it appears to say that the selling price was for "One dollar and other good and valuable consideration." Do not be misled at this point into thinking that the Hentges bought the property for one dollar. They did not. In Minnesota, as in other states, the one dollar is merely a conveyance symbol.

So how much did the property sell for? Look for the *deed stamps* on the deed. The stamps on this deed total $71.50. Other states have different rates, but in Minnesota, deed stamp taxes are figured at a rate of $2.20 per $1,000 in transfer value. Knowing that formula, you can quickly figure that the property was sold for $32,500, although that amount is not stated on the deed.

Because the last entry in the tract index for this property is the warranty deed, you can state that the Hentges are the "owners of record" of the property. But you cannot be certain that they still hold the title. In Minnesota, as in other states, property may be purchased on a *contract for deed,* a document that buyer and seller agree to privately and that will convey the property to the buyer once the full purchase price is paid, often years later. Until that time, when a deed would be filed, the contract for deed need not be recorded or filed.

Zoning   In many urban areas, and in some rural ones as well, land is zoned, meaning that once its use has been specified by zone—industrial, commercial, residential, and so forth—the land may be used for that purpose only, unless an exception is granted. For example, a commercial building may not be built on land zoned residential. It is common, however, for zoning changes to be made, usually upon request of the owner. If the applicant seeks a change in the zone classification, the petition is called a *zoning amendment.* If the request is for an exception to a zone requirement, the request is called a *variance.* In either case, zoning matters are heard by a municipal zoning board or planning commission and then referred to the city council for final action.

Building Inspection

You can find out whether a particular building is below acceptable living standards by going to the building inspection office in the municipality in which the property is located. Many states now have uniform building codes that specify electrical, heating, plumbing, and general construction requirements. Many municipalities also have similar codes. The inspection office of the municipality maintains records of when a particular building has been repaired, what improvements have been made, and whether the owner has failed to comply with violation tags issued by inspectors. The records of the municipal inspection offices are generally organized according to street address, and these records are often a good source to determine who owns a building. Although all inspection records may not be public, they will give you leads if you are checking on slum property in your community.

Taxes

Tax records are normally considered nonpublic. Nevertheless, certain types are often available for inspection. One is the property tax assessment record, normally kept by the city or county assessor's office. This record can provide a reliable indication of ownership because it is unlikely that someone without an interest in a piece of property will be paying the taxes on it. The assessment record is often organized by *plat* and *parcel* numbers, which correspond to legal descriptions and street addresses. The record will give the *estimated market value* of the property, that is, the dollar amount it might bring if sold. Normally, the estimated market value of land is a bit less than its true value, probably because assessors do not always get around frequently enough to reflect increased value. The record will also give the *assessed valuation,* the figure on which taxes are computed. The formula for computing tax rates varies from state to state and county to county, and you will have to find out the formula used in your community. The assessment record will also break down the tax paid on the land, buildings, and sometimes the physical assets on the property, such as machinery. The record should indicate whether the taxpayer lives on the property, in which case the tax is computed at a *homestead* rate. It may also indicate whether the taxpayer is entitled to any special credit because of blindness or other disability.

Individual tax returns are confidential, but if the state or federal government files a *lien* against the taxpayer, this tax record may become part of the public record in a court filing. In asking a court for a tax lien, the government alleges that taxes are owed but have not been paid. A lien, if granted, places a "hold" on a person's property, such as real estate. It allows the government to sell the property to recover the taxes owed. Normally, tax liens are filed with either the clerk of court in the county in which the individual lives or with the register of deeds or recorder's office.

We have already mentioned the Pulitzer Prize-winning story developed by the Sun Newspapers on the tax returns of a tax-exempt organization. Other tax-exempt foundations and corporations file similar returns, and as the case illustrates, these documents may indeed lead to important news stories.

Campaigns and Disclosure

There seems to be a trend in American politics toward greater disclosure by public officials of their financial assets and of the contributors to their campaigns. Many states, in recent years, have enacted campaign reform laws that require political candidates to reveal who contributes to their election campaigns. Some also require public officials to disclose their interests in financial ventures. Even when disclosure is not required, the politician who refuses to reveal either contributors or assets is risking defeat.

There are numerous records dealing with disclosure, and they may be found in a variety of state and county offices. Statewide election candidates normally file such information with the state secretary of state. County officials generally file with the county auditor, and municipal officials with the municipal clerk. Federal candidates, such as U.S. congressmen and senators, also file such statements, usually with their state's secretary of state's office.

Let's say you examine the disclosure of a state senator and find that he owns stock in several mining companies. Your next job would be to examine carefully his voting record, as well as the bills he has introduced in the legislature, to see whether there has been an apparent conflict of interest. In the case of an administrative official, you would have to examine her administrative decrees to determine whether she gave special treatment to the requests of campaign contributors. Again, a word of caution is necessary here. Once you have determined a politician's financial assets or campaign contributors, you have nothing more than a circumstantial case. To round out the story, you would have to conduct interviews and compare the answers with what is shown in public documents. As with other public records, the use of campaign records requires discretion. Nothing destroys the credibility of a public affairs reporter faster than making unsubstantiated charges that are later refuted.

Corporations

One of the most difficult tasks for the investigative reporter is investigating a corporation and determining its holdings, officers, and assets. The task is made more difficult by laws in many states that allow companies to operate pretty much in secret, particularly if the company's stock is held privately and not traded on the open market.

Corporations are generally required to file—with the state secretary of state, and often with the county register of deeds where they do business—articles of incorporation that set forth the purposes of the company. If you are checking on a company, the *incorporation papers* should be your first stop. In many cases, these will tell you who the owners and directors are or were at the time of incorporation. A word of warning here, too: In some states, the law allows attorneys to incorporate companies for private clients and then turn over the control to those clients. So if you see an attorney's name as an incorporator, be cautious. The attorney may be an owner, but more likely he or she is acting for a private client.

If the company is publicly owned, meaning that its stock is traded on a stock exchange, you will be able to learn more about it. A good source is the office of securities, normally in an agency like your state's department of commerce. Companies that sell stock must be registered, and often the securities office will have summaries of the company, including stock circulars and prospectuses. These give a substantial amount of information, often including the background of the individual incorporators and how much stock they hold. Publicly owned corporations also file annual reports with the federal Securities and Exchange Commission. These reports, which disclose financial condition and other important data, are open to the public.

Figure 4-3 Bank Charter

The applicants' background and business interests and their involvement in community affairs are as follows:

> (a) *J. Kimball Whitney:* age 45, is married and currently resides with his wife at 559 Harrington Road, Wayzata, Minnesota. He graduated from Phillips Academy, Andover, Massachusetts and attended Williams College, Williamstown, Massachusetts, graduating with BA degree in economics in 1950. He was in the U.S. Army, Qtr. Master Corps. from 1950–1952. From 1954–1964 he was a private school bus operator and president and chairman of the board of Minnesota Transit Lines, Inc. in Excelsior, Minnesota. From 1957–1967 and from January, 1971 to the present time he has been president of the Whitney Land Company of Minneapolis, Minnesota. From 1967–1971 he was commissioner of the Minnesota Department of Economic Development for the State of Minnesota in St. Paul, Minnesota. From 1971 to the present he has been the director of commercial development for Cedar-Riverside Associates, Inc., Minneapolis, Minnesota. He owns 1/9 of the stock in the Whitney Land Company; less than 1% of the stock in Cedar-Riverside Associates, Inc., Minneapolis, Minnesota; and less than 1% of the stock in Jonathan Development Corp., Chaska, Minnesota. He is the director of the North American Corp., Columbus, Ohio owning less than 1% of the stock. He is the trustee for three separate trusts. He is a member of the Wayzata Community Church; Vice President of the Woodhill Country Club; member of the board of governors of the Minneapolis Club; member of the National Executive Board of the Boy Scouts of America; treasurer of the Children's Home Society of Minnesota; director of the Northwest Growth Fund, Inc.; for 1½ years he was director of the North Shore State Bank, Wayzata, Minnesota.

An often overlooked source of information is the stock brokerage firm. Many investigative reporters own a small amount of stock through a major firm and thereby can have access to the brokerage house's research. All you have to do is call your broker, and the brokerage firm will often send you information on a company.

There are a number of other sources for tracing a company. One is *Moody's Industrial Manual,* which lists American companies and provides histories, activities, officers, directors, and balance sheets. Others are the directories of major industries. A good indication of who controls or has an interest in a company is gained by checking court records on a company to see if it has even been a defendant or plaintiff in a civil suit. If so, the file may reveal who appeared in court to represent the firm. A similar source is the zoning variance application. Often, a company seeking a zoning variance will file an application with the municipal council, which will indicate who is behind the company.

One good rule of thumb is to ask yourself if the company is regulated by the state or the federal government. Many businesses, such as banks, financial loan companies, power companies, trucking firms, and warehouses, are regulated by the state, and the files of various state agencies may contain eye-opening information on them. For example, five individuals applied for a bank charter for a new bank in Minnesota in 1973, and the application gave each individual's net worth and a picture of his financial interests. One of the applicants was J. Kimball Whitney, a former state official. The file on this case contains a summary of Whitney's financial assets at the time of the bank application, including his stock holdings in other companies. (See Figure 4-3.)

Individuals

One of the most common questions asked by news reporters is "Who?" Many sources are available to the public affairs reporter who wants information about a person and family, assets, politics, and financial debts. Here are a few of those sources, and we again remind you of the cautions suggested earlier about the verification of information from public records.

Bankruptcy   When individuals file for bankruptcy, the public affairs reporter can get a complete financial picture of them at the time of the filing, including assets and debts. Bankruptcy files are kept by the clerk of the U.S. district court in the district in which the individual resides. Corporations may also file for bankruptcy, and usually do so in the district where their principal office is located.

Births, deaths, marriages, and divorces   All these records are kept in the clerk of court's office for the county in which the action occurred or—as in the case of a marriage—was applied for. In addition, birth and death records are usually maintained by the state division of vital statistics, which is most often a division of the state health department. Birth and death records will provide a record of true names, birth dates, and parentage, although many states specifically consider records of illegitimate births and adoptions to be confidential. Marriage records will indicate the date of the marriage, as well as the names of both parties, including the maiden name of the woman. Divorce records often contain a careful tabulation of assets held by both parties which are divided at the time of the divorce. Thus, the public affairs reporter may learn whether a person kept a home in a divorce settlement or whether there was a cash settlement or alimony, and if so, in what amount.

Wills and judicial commitments   Again, a will often can provide an inside look at an individual's assets. If you are interested in the financial situation of a person who is forty or fifty years old, one or both of whose parents are dead, be sure to check for a will for one or both of the parents. Because of life expectancy patterns, it is common to find individuals named as beneficiaries of wills who are at the peak of their political or business careers.

Figure 4-4   Portion of a Will, Showing Mineral Rights

Additional real estate—St. Louis County, Minnesota			
Description	*Section*	*Township*	*Range*
Und. 1/20th of SW¼ (Pioneer Mine) except a portion of the surface thereof as conveyed by Document No. 89165 and filed for record on December 6, 1967.	27	63	12
Und. 1/30th of Lot 2 except 2 acres for road	28	63	12
Und. 1/10th of Lot 5	32	63	12
Und. 7/160ths of SE¼ of NE¼, except 2 acres for road	32	63	12
Und. 7/160ths of SW¼ of NW¼, except 2 acres for road	33	63	12
Und. 1/120th of NE¼ of SW¼	25	63	13
Und. 1/120th of SW¼ of SW¼	25	63	13
Und. 1/120th of SE¼ of SW¼	25	63	13
Und. 1/120th of NW¼ of SE¼	25	63	13
Minerals only—St. Louis County			
Und. 1/30th of Lot 2	27	63	12
Und. 1/10th of Lot 4	28	63	12
Und. 1/10th of NE¼ of SE¼	33	63	12
Und. 1/10th of SE¼ of NE¼	33	63	12
Und. 1/10th of NW¼ of SE¼	33	63	12
Und. 1/10th of SW¼ of SE¼	33	63	12

The portion of the will shown in Figure 4-4 is that of the mother of a former state senator from Minnesota. Upon her death, she left her heirs several parcels of land mineral rights, including a portion of an iron mine. Notice in the example how the land is located by legal description.

Both wills and judicial commitments are filed in the probate court of the county in which the individual died or lived. Judicial commitments are filed when a person is committed to a mental institution, and a record of the commitment may contain medical information that normally would be considered confidential.

Voter registration   Records filed with the municipal clerk where individuals live may disclose full names, addresses, and telephone numbers, even if unlisted. Voter registration records will also tell you if persons are citizens and in what elections they have voted.

Military discharges   The armed forces recommend that servicemen and women file their discharge papers with the county register of deeds office in the county in which they are planning to live or have lived before entering the service. These records provide a person's military history and reason for discharge. Under the category of reason for discharge, you will often find an "SPN" (Separation Program Number). By checking the number given against military regulations, available in many libraries, you can determine the reason for the discharge. It may be for a number of reasons, including psychiatric. Again, a word of caution is important here. It would be irresponsible indeed to write that an individual had a history of mental illness on the basis of a military discharge record alone.

Criminal records   If there is one area where the warnings about unverified information apply, it is to the use of criminal records. It is libelous to accuse someone falsely of a crime, and summary arrest records, such as the type kept by the Federal Bureau of Investigation (FBI), are notoriously incomplete. Often, these records contain an initial entry at the time of arrest or inquiry but do not indicate disposition. A person may be questioned by police and released, but that latter fact may not be recorded.

The best source for criminal records is the court of the district—state or federal, depending on the nature of the crime—in which the action occurred or the charge was filed. There you will find a complete file, showing the specific charge and the disposition of the case. Misdemeanors and other petty offenses are normally recorded by the municipal court or court of limited jurisdiction. Felonies and gross misdemeanors are recorded by the district or superior court of the state system, and federal violations are recorded by the U.S. district court.

State departments of motor vehicles keep lists of driving violations, and some of these, contrary to general belief, are often available. The same is true of motor vehicle registrations. Trailer, boat, and recreational vehicle registrations also may be kept by the state department of natural resources.

Licenses Municipalities and states often require the licensing of certain businesses and professions, ranging from taverns and automobile-towing companies to doctors and attorneys. Normally, the fact that an individual holds a license to engage in a particular business or profession is a public record. Thus, reporters can find, by checking with a state board of medical examiners, whether a particular physician is licensed to practice in that state. They can also determine, by checking with the municipal clerk's office, who holds the license of a particular tavern.

Determining whether or not there have been complaints against a professional person may be much harder. Normally, the disciplinary action taken will be public, but the allegations on which that action is taken may not be. You may learn that a particular attorney has been disbarred, but you may not be allowed to examine the hearing transcript. The same is true for a doctor whose license has been suspended or revoked. The best way to proceed here is on a case-by-case basis. If you are interested in the reputation of a particular attorney, check court files to see if he or she has been sued for shady practices. Check also with the state bar association, although this source may not reveal much. Check also with the state supreme court, which takes final action in such cases.

If the business or profession operates under a state-granted charter or license, check with the office which regulates that business or profession. Some states, for example, now regulate debt prorate firms, which for a fee will help debtors pay their obligations. The state regulatory agency files may well provide important information on the firm's business practices.

Other public agencies are to be checked as well. For instance, many states now are establishing offices of consumer affairs to protect consumers against shoddy business practices. In some states, these agencies are connected with the state attorney general's office.

Audits The financial affairs of state, county, municipal, and other public agencies are audited, normally, by a state unit called the public examiner's office, the state auditor, or the state department of administration. Regardless of what the division is called, it may be a particularly valuable source if you suspect financial discrepancies in the books of a public agency.

Census Data

The records described so far are normally used to obtain information about individuals or organizations. But there is another category of record that provides information about entire populations. Demographic data and similar summary statistics are collected, compiled, and published by many local, state, and federal agencies. Private foundations and institutions also gather information about populations in specialized fields, as do corporate, labor, and trade organizations. The Insurance Institute, for example, publishes an annual guide containing data on accident rates, claims, actuarial tables, and similar information. These statistical records are immensely valuable to the public affairs reporter. They can add precision and dimension to stories, suggest important new angles for exploration, and serve as a check on the validity of assertions by news sources.

The list of agencies providing summary statistics is as varied as government itself—city planning departments, court administrators, law enforcement units, health departments. The federal government is a major originator of statistical materials, with almost every major agency serving as compiler and disseminator. The FBI gathers crime data at the local and national levels. The National Center for Health Statistics is a funnel for information from the states. But the biggest numbers game in town is operated by the Bureau of the Census, a branch of the Commerce Department.

The bureau produces a vast storehouse of information, from periodic news releases on its frequent special surveys (for example, the fertility of American women, energy use by manufacturing plants, and per capita expenditures of local governments) to the massive census of the population of the United States. The latter, mandated by the Constitution, will be conducted every five years, starting in 1985, rather than using the ten-year cycle it has followed up to now. The bureau also conducts a monthly study, the Current Population Survey, based on a survey of more than 60,000 households.

Reporters who monitor census publications can develop stories on the reports themselves or use them as starting points for further investigation. Consider this example, by William Dunn of the *Detroit News:*

> America, long a bastion of white, Anglo Saxon Protestantism, is becoming increasingly less so.
> Changing immigration patterns and a birthrate that varies widely among racial and ethnic groups have been teaming up to rearrange the pieces in the ethnic-religious jigsaw puzzle that is America.
> The results:
> * America in recent years has been slowly but surely growing more Spanish and Catholic and darker-skinned.
> * At the same time, the size of the American Jewish community has levelled off and may actually be getting smaller.
> *It's not clear yet, but birth-immigration trends may also go a long way toward altering American foreign policy, reviving parochial schools and re-populating the cities.[21]

Dunn, who specializes in the interpretation of social statistics, pieced that story together from government surveys and interviews, giving readers of the *News* an early insight into trends that signal change for society.

The use of census data by reporters isn't limited to interpretive features; it is useful in routine situations as well. Let's say you are covering a legislative hearing on mass transit for a metropolitan region. The debate centers on alternative routes for the proposed transit system, but none of those testifying offers information about the present number of commuters in each suburb and their destinations, occupations, or means of transportation—all relevant to the choice of routes. You have two alternatives: to forget about these factors and deprive readers of important information or to get the information yourself. And information about commuting patterns is available from census reports.

Opportunities for enterprising reporting based on census data are almost endless. Is the increasing proportion of elderly in the population a grey time bomb, leading to economic crisis for the nation? How are birthrates and educational patterns influencing training and deployment policies in the armed forces? What effects are changing family patterns and lifestyles likely to have on the economy? Are the higher than average rates of disease and violent death in the black population leading to other changes? These are the kinds of questions that population statistics can help answer.

Population data are available in libraries and from the Bureau of Census itself. The data are presented in separate volumes, by state, and on microfiche and computer tapes. The tapes permit manipulation by the user of variables in combinations not provided in printed form. Some data can be organized by small geographic units—census tracts of about 4,000 residents or even city blocks—enabling you to build units of your own choosing, such as a central business district. The national census also presents separately collections of housing data that contain information on how people live, for example, the availability of appliances in homes and the amount of space per capita.

Reporters can learn to use census materials from the governmental document divisions at major libraries, from university sources such as urban planners and sociologists, from local government units that use the data for their own analyses, and from the hundreds of manuals, guides, and other publications of the Bureau of the Census. For an overview of the journalistic possibilities in census materials, one of the better guides is *Census '80: Continuing the Factfinder Tradition,* by Charles P. Kaplan and Thomas L. Van Valey. A road map for navigating the voluminous 1980 census landscape is provided by the *1980 Census Users Guide,* which locates materials by subject and source. The *1980 Census Indexes* and the *Bureau of the Census Catalog* are also useful sources. The bureau publishes a monthly newsletter, *Data User News,* which monitors new reports and projects. It also publishes the *Monthly Product Announcement,* listing new publications. Other useful statistical summaries published by the bureau include *Social Indicators* (revised every four years), *Statistical Abstract of the United States* (an almanac-type book published annually), and the *County and City Data Book* (issued every five years). All bureau publications are available through the

Superintendent of Documents, U.S. Government Printing Office, Washington, D.C.

Directories

There are hundreds, perhaps thousands, of professional directories available in America. Many of these are municipal directories, such as the Polk directories for many communities. Others are published by state agencies, professional and business associations, and municipal governments. Most contain names, addresses, titles, brief biographical sketches, professional awards, education, and family information.

Directories are important to the reporter of public affairs in at least two ways. First, they can be used to provide leads. For example, you want to know something about the background of a major political figure, say a state senator, and the legislative manual will provide a brief biographical sketch. Directories can also be used to cross-check information from public records. Let's say you find a John Smith who is married to a Mary Smith. You need to be sure you are looking at the right John Smith, so you check a directory that contains Smith's name. It tells you that Smith's wife's name is Joan. A bell ought to go off in your head at this point. Perhaps there has been a second marriage, or perhaps not. In either case, you should be aware now that there may be another John Smith who might be confused with the first one.

Many directories gather information on a voluntary basis. Such information, therefore, is not likely to be incriminating, at least on the surface. A contractor you suspect of making payoffs to a city official is not going to list himself in a contractor's directory as a briber. On the other hand, you may well determine more details about the business, its location, and other facts.

The point to remember here is that using public records is a slow, cumulative process. Rarely are reporters going to find a single document to pull a particular investigation together by itself. Usually, they'll need a number of sources, including public documents, interviews, directories, and perhaps statistical data. But by using these sources together, reporters can often provide a focus for the story or the inquiry.

At the end of this chapter, a number of important directories are listed. The list is not exhaustive, and you should check your own library to see what's available locally.

THE INVESTIGATIVE MODE

Earlier we noted that the techniques of observation, interviewing, and documentary search were fundamental to public affairs coverage generally, and we suggested that the same techniques, refined and intensified, were essential to investigative reporting. Now that we have considered them in detail, let us see how these techniques are adapted to the investigative mode in the practice of a number of journalists who report in depth.

Investigative reporting has a history at least a century old. In the 1880s, *New York World* reporter Nellie Bly posed as a mental patient to expose the wretched conditions in New York's insane asylums. Two decades later, investigative reporters turned up abuse after abuse in American industries and institutions, including race relations, patent medicines, politics, finance, insurance, railroads, prisons, and meat packing. In the last area, Upton Sinclair's *The Jungle* described widespread filth and squalor in the food industry and led directly to the passage of the Pure Food and Drug Act of 1907. "I aimed at the public's heart, and by accident I hit it in the stomach," Sinclair later wrote.[22] Theodore Roosevelt assailed "the man with the muckrake" but succeeded only in giving investigative reporting a name which has stuck.[23] In the 1960s and 1970s, aggressive, enterprising reporting was on the cutting edge of American journalism, helping in the exposure of the My Lai massacre and the Watergate scandal.[24] Actors Robert Redford and Dustin Hoffman helped make *Washington Post* reporters Carl Bernstein and Bob Woodward into national figures through the movie version of *All the President's Men,* which had already added the secret source Deep Throat to American journalism history. Not incidentally, the courageous reporting by the *Post* and other papers polished journalism's surface and probably helped swell the ranks of college journalism classes in depth and investigative reporting.[25]

Although most investigative reporting is directed at the exposure of wrongdoing, its techniques can be applied to many situations that involve neither sin nor corruption. Many conditions in society deserve thorough examination, yet don't get it in routine press coverage because of their complexity or the absence of readily available information. Subjects such as the impact of electronic technology on business firms and their employees, the distribution of tax burdens and government benefits among social classes, the financial standing and internal operations of nonprofit organizations, and dozens of other significant topics are within reach of reporters—and their readers—only through investigative techniques. They are subjects for which sources are unlikely to volunteer information but which will yield valuable insights to resourcefulness, energy, and persistence.

How do investigative reporters work? What techniques do they use? Approaches vary from story to story, but most investigative reporting uses at least one of the following tactics, and often several in the same investigation:

Diligent, thorough record-searching.   Records, both public and private, are the factual base of many investigative efforts. No reporter gets very far into an investigative subject without a detailed search of many records. Some reporters rely on records extensively, using them to lead the way to inconsistencies that might be missed in interviews and to a sense of the scope of an inquiry. Jack Taylor of *The Daily Oklahoman,* for example, has filed so many federal Freedom of Information suits that his journalistic colleagues call him an "FOI junkie." But his persistence has turned up story after story. With the help of records he squeezed from the Bureau of Indian Affairs through FOI actions, Taylor learned that the federal funds available to American Indians totaled $3.7 billion in 1979, enough "to run Oklahoma City's budget at its current level for 32 years."[26]

Appropriate interviewing.   Joe Murray, editor of the *Lufkin* (Texas) *News,* tells a story of how reporter Ken Herman had to interview a huge Marine recruiter as part of the paper's investigation into the death of a young Marine. "He didn't start out asking a bunch of insulting questions," but "sat down and started talking to him in a nice respectful way." A reporter's first job, says Murray, is to "get the story." "Now sometimes you have to be tough. And sometimes you have to be determined. But don't ever forget that sometimes you just have to be nice," he advises. The tactic helped bring the *News,* circulation 14,000, a 1977 Pulitzer Prize for public service for its reporting on the Marine's death.[27]

Statistical analysis.   Precision journalism—the use of computers, polls, and other scientific data-gathering techniques—has developed dramatically in American journalism in the past decade. The *Philadelphia Inquirer's* James Steele and Don Barlett pioneered the technique in the early 1970s along with Philip Meyer, whose seminal book, *Precision Journalism,* popularized the name. We discuss precision journalism in detail in Chapter 5, but the techniques are often used by the investigative reporter to wade through stacks of documents, generate original data, or analyze statistics by looking for obscure patterns. Systematic counting techniques for such work are invaluable. "Under the systematic approach," Steele says, "the reporter is no longer wholly dependent on the data or viewpoint of others."[28]

The criminal justice system is one area where the use of precision journalism has mined important data. Barlett and Steele examined the Philadelphia criminal justice system, coded their information on almost 10,000 cards, ran them through a computer, and analyzed nearly 4,000 pages of printouts.[29] A smaller but more recent study by the *Fort Lauderdale* (Fla.) *News,* using the same techniques, reached a similar conclusion: that the assumption of equal justice in the local court system was a myth. Justice, the *News* found, "favors whites. It favors those with the money to hire private lawyers. It favors drug suspects. And it favors those facing sex charges."[30]

The undercover sting.   One technique which has both intrigued and chilled investigative reporters and their editors is the undercover operation in which reporters conceal (or at least do not volunteer) their identities in order to mix less conspicuously in the activities they are investigating. The approach often brings charges of entrapment, and in the case of the *Chicago Sun-Times'* widely acclaimed 1978 articles on the Mirage Bar, probably cost the paper a Pulitzer Prize. In that operation, a team of reporters went into the tavern business in Chicago to document how payoffs and kickbacks permeated the city's bar inspection system. "I've heard people say, 'Gee, we ought to try that in our community,'" says the *Sun-Times'* Pam Zeckman who headed the project. "I advise you to plan it very carefully," she continues, "because it can blow up in your face."[31]

Yet such stories can produce dramatic results and generally have high readership. The *Sun-Times* examined the accident-swindle racket in Chicago in 1980, with reporters faking injuries in phony accidents to document how lawyers, doctors, clinics, and hospitals skim off benefits and "stick it to the insurance companies." At one point, a reporter with a phony injury was admitted to a hospital which created records so inaccurate that a doctor referred to him as a "black male" although he is white.[32] Undercover work can produce dramatic stories for the local reporter as well. At the *Anniston* (Ala.) *Star,* reporter Pam Sohn spent two days in a home for delinquent teenagers to probe the boredom and pitiful lack of educational opportunities there.[33]

Is it deceptive to assume such a role? And if it is, can the deception be justified? Investigative journalists are divided on these questions. "The standard view," writes John Simon of the University of Missouri, who conducted a survey on the subject, "is that deception should be used only when all other methods have been exhausted and only when the information to be gathered is a matter of overriding public concern." In his study, Simon found reporters assuming roles as salesman, buyer of illegal goods such as drugs, student applicant at a career school, nursing home resident, wino, john, migrant, and deputy sheriff.[34] One scholar, Paul Williams, concludes that the ethics of the investigative reporter are, by nature, "situational" and subject to change to fit the conditions of the inquiry. "If the reporter is going to find out something that people less moral than himself are trying to conceal, he must use imagination, guts, guile, and, yes, sometimes deception, to do it," writes the late Paul Williams. But he adds quickly that the investigative journalist must avoid self-righteousness. "He must be a passive observer, not a provocateur or a modifier of what he is observing."[35]

That is not to say investigative reporters should not have goals in mind when they start a project. Perhaps the most important trait is their ability to synthesize information, to keep their sights on the objective, to work within reasonable time frames, and to accomplish the task with a reasonable but not inordinate amount of effort. Investigative reporters and their editors are often geared toward results, and that means a story produced on time. Nothing sours an editor on an investigative project quicker than having it drag on endlessly without conclusion. The best investigative reporters, therefore, work often from carefully defined but flexible plans. Typically, a project will start with a study of the investigation's feasibility, based on available resources, time, experience of the reporter, and nature of the investigation. A good idea is a feasibility study of perhaps several single-spaced pages with the following topics covered thoroughly: the concept and its corollaries, the sources and their reliability, what questions need to be asked, what resources can be brought to bear, and how long the project might take. Such an outline forces the reporter to sharpen the concept and strengthen its weak points. It gives an editor a working document rather than a vague concept to start with.

The feasibility study is most often followed by a stage Williams calls "planning and base building" in which the reporter maps out the project, task by task, and assigns times to each. This step is followed by research, both interviews and record-searching, and very likely, a redefinition of goals and purposes. Finally, the project moves to "key interviews" with key subjects, which may mean reevaluation of the project. Writing and publication, which many beginning reporters see as the most difficult phases, are normally derived directly from the earlier research, and for many experienced reporters, are easier to accomplish.[36]

Although every investigative project has its own restrictions, the following tips should make sense, particularly to the beginning investigative reporter:

Stick close to your editor.   Most local editors have a solid sense of their community and where its most worthy projects lie. Start by talking with the editor about several ideas you have; then follow up your talk with crisp feasibility studies. Demonstrate follow-through immediately, a step that gets you started right with editors who are used to seeing and hearing only grandiose plans from young reporters. Be realistic about what you think the project should take in the way of time and resources. Start with a project you are sure you can complete in a week or two; then do it in close to that time. You'll gain confidence in yourself, and as important, your editor's confidence. Respect the publisher's money and watch your costs. Don't run up huge bills.

Master the basics.   An investigative reporter who makes factual errors and mistakes in quotes has a very short life as the paper's detached, roving specialist. Nothing hurts the credibility of an investigative effort quicker than a correction in the next day's paper. Be sure your report is fair, balanced, and comprehensive. Make an extra effort to see the perspective of the other side. Watch your tendency to crusade in a cause you're certain is right.

Bite off only what you can chew.   If you're on a small paper near Boston, you probably won't be able to investigate Montana wheat futures. Recognize that distance, time, and economic resources are as important as your own energy and as limiting. The more complex the topic and the weaker your own knowledge of the field, the more study, planning, and research you'll need to do. That's particularly true in scientific fields where precision is critical and jargon reigns. If you're not willing to start out by spending hours in a library, consider the project—and your own commitment to it—once again.

Remember that investigative reporting is mostly just plain hard work. If you never liked studying a new topic in school, this journalistic specialty isn't likely to be your strongest.

Weigh tips carefully.   Remember that tips often come from sources with axes to grind, enemies to skewer, and careers to wreck. Ask yourself if the person giving the information is in a position to know. If your answer is yes, check out the tip. Listen for the ring of authenticity in every story you hear. Ask yourself what the possible explanations are for what happened. Ask for documentation from the sources. Get specific dates, times, places, persons. Without that kind of confirmation, your investigation may soon wallow in rumors chased but never caught.

Learn to use public records.   Solid investigative reporting often depends on an impressive paper trail. Learn the access laws in your state and area of inquiry and how they've been interpreted legally. Study the loopholes used by officials to close records. Become familiar with the federal Freedom of Information Act and how it can be used (see Appendix D).

Watch other investigative reporters work.   Join several professional organizations in journalism and go to regional and national conferences when it's feasible and you can afford to. Groups like Investigative Reporters & Editors, based at the University of Missouri's Journalism School, Columbia, Mo., 65211, hold regional workshops in several parts of the country each year. These are good opportunities to hear seasoned professionals on a wide range of practical information on specific topics and more general subjects like interviewing, computers, and using records.

Read all you can in the field.   When you spot an announcement of an award to a paper or reporter, write for a copy. Most papers will supply such examples free. If you're working on a specialized topic, find out who else in the country has worked on the same topic. Make professional contacts and share your own work. The *IRE Journal* is considered by working investigative reporters as one of the best sources for ideas and tips, and the group maintains a growing resource library. Watch trends in the law carefully, particularly in the areas of libel, access to records, and privacy. Spend some time at your law library. All these sources can help the beginning investigative reporter through contacts, similar investigations, and just plain moral support from professional comrades. Investigative reporting is often a lonely, singular calling in which the hours are very demanding and the rewards often slim. For many, the greatest satisfaction comes through small achievements and victories they have worked hard to obtain.

THE WRITING PROCESS

For both the investigative reporter and his or her colleague on the public affairs beat, at some point data-gathering must come to an end and the writing begin. Even for the most facile writer, preparing the final product can be an agonizing process. After determining that the data are complete, that all bases have been covered—or at least as many as time and circumstances allow—hard decisions must be made about emphasis and style, about what to retain from the mass of notes and other material the writer has assembled. With the writing process, reporters must shift gears, thinking in a more direct sense than they have before of editor and audience. Here is the result of one reporter's journey from a story assignment to finished product.

The assignment was routine: coverage of a Sunday afternoon meeting of laymen representing the conservative faction in a doctrinal dispute that threatened the unity of the second-largest synod of the Lutheran Church.

The reporter was Peg Meier, twenty-seven-years old, a wispy but hard-headed journalism school graduate with five years' experience on general assignment, the first two on a small daily, the last three on the *Minneapolis Tribune.*

She made the customary preparation: checked the fat morgue file on the Missouri Synod, Lutheran Church; phoned the local office of the synod to confirm the meeting's time and place; checked with the photographer assigned to accompany her; interviewed by phone a minister identified with the moderate faction.

Her report of the meeting opened this way:

Mayer, Minn.—When Edwin C. Weber was studying for the Lutheran ministry in 1935, his professors warned that no church body in history had survived more than 100 years without a major dispute over beliefs.

"They told us to be on guard so when the time came we would stand up for the doctrine we believed in," he said. "Now is the time."

The Rev. Dr. Weber, now first vice president of the 127-year-old Lutheran Church's Missouri Synod, one of the most conservative synods of the church, continued: "Trouble has been brewing for the last 25 years. Now it's out there in the open and the laymen are getting concerned."

More than 1,200 laymen were concerned enough Sunday to turn out for an afternoon meeting about the synod's problems—problems that threaten to split their congregations. The meeting was sponsored by the conservative element of the synod.[37]

"I had trouble with that story," Meier said afterward. "I must have fiddled with the lead for a full half hour. The desk wanted me to try for a local angle because the meeting had been out of town, but there was no way."

A more traditional lead might have read: "The first vice president of the Lutheran Church's Missouri Synod yesterday told more than 1,200 laymen that "now is the time" to stand for the doctrine they believe in. The Rev. Dr. Edwin C. Weber addressed a meeting sponsored by the synod's conservative wing to air the doctrinal dispute that threatens the synod's unity."

The element that makes Meier's lead an inspired departure from tradition is its unexpressed reference to the root of the controversy: suspension of the president of the synod's seminary for favoring a "liberal" interpretation of the Bible—the background that most readers could be expected to know.

Offbeat or traditional, public affairs reporters can follow their bent in reporting public affairs on more and more newspapers today. But their bent must never violate the standards of effective communication, and the most important of these are accuracy, clarity, economy, vigor, and specificity.

You have already survived the rigors of a basic reporting or journalistic writing course. You are, as a consequence, alert to the necessity for verification of such essentials as dates, addresses, titles, place names, ages, and correct spelling of proper names. These are only the start of the discipline. In reporting public affairs, you move into a world where the complexities of procedure lay snares for the reporter who is too shy or too sloppy to ask the questions that minimize the chance of inaccuracy. Does the appeals court's decision to remand mean a decision in favor of the appellant? Does the planning commission's recommendation of a variance mean a change of zoning? Does a filing in bankruptcy justify use of the term *bankrupt?* Failure to understand procedure, readiness to assume that appearances are reliable, reluctance to seek the verifying or clarifying answer—all these are marks of the undisciplined reporter. The road to inaccuracy is paved with misunderstandings and faulty assumptions.

Nonetheless, we assume that basic training has instilled in you a passion for lucid expression, like precise diction: that you don't use *continually* when you mean *continuously, comprise* when you mean *compose, uninterested* when you mean *disinterested, imply* when you mean *infer;* and like well-ordered sentence structure: that related words should not be separated, that modifiers belong as close as possible to the word they modify, and that coordinate ideas demand parallel construction. Reporting public affairs demands that these writing rules, among others, be adhered to. The world of public affairs can be a jungle of jargon for the unguided reader. Legalese lurks behind every bench. If, for the sake of precision, you must use such terms as *writ of certiorari, codicil, quitclaim deed, subornation of perjury, bench warrant, peremptory challenge,* or *deposition,* you should translate, or at the least, provide the context that permits understanding.

How, you may ask, can writing on such subjects be both clear and economical? It's not easy; good writing seldom is. But clarity and economy march in lockstep by avoiding such redundancies as "the reason is because," "he personally," and "period of time," as well as by pruning all words and phrases that do not contribute to meaning: "the fact that," "needless to say," "he made a speech," "they held a meeting," "the delegate made a motion," "the judge handed down a decision," "the senator put the bill in the hopper."

Many of these verbal excesses are the clichés of public affairs reporting, and as such, they rob writing of vigor. (Less windy but almost as tedious are last year's *viable,* this year's *thrust* and *machismo,* and that barbarism of an entire decade, the free-floating *hopefully.*) Let a few of these creep into writing that is tranquilized by passive verbs and nonstop sentences and you have encouraged the lassitude with which too many readers yawn through news of government.

Involvement, not indifference, is the attitude public affairs reporters should seek to encourage in their readers. We wonder how much alienation, how much of the pervasive you-can't-fight-city-hall defeatism, can be attributed to inadequate reporting and dull writing about public affairs.

How much can you involve your reader? You don't need to be an advocate; the desired involvement is the reader's, not the reporter's. This is where specificity comes in: concreteness, humanizing. The *Wall Street Journal* has been showing the way for years with its "trend" stories. Consider this one describing a trend among colleges to award scholarships on merit rather than need. The lead loses no time in particularizing a generalization: "To many American families, the problem Alan Weiss faced last year sounds only too familiar." Alan's problem, the reader learns, is that his parents' income boosts them out of the needy class but not into the affluent class that can afford college without strain. No matter. Alan, like an increasing number of his contemporaries, got a scholarship on merit, the *Journal* notes.[38]

Or consider the *Journal's* exposition of an increasingly numerous character in the business world: the corporate, or in-house, economist. The article provides a lot of general information about this new breed: estimates of their numbers range from 3,500 to 5,000; they are "largely a phenomenon of the last 20 years"; "their jobs are becoming harder"; their problems include "the persistence of inflation," shortages of energy and materials, "the growing involvement of many companies in international markets." The article quotes a number of such economists, along with a professor of economics. But the story's interest, and the reader's involvement through empathy, are heightened by its focus on a specific example,

Stanley V. Malcuit, chief economist at Alcoa. "On his desk one recent day: a request from a sales executive for information for a speech . . . about the 1974 outlook; a request from the public relations department to review the script for a state-of-the-company movie Alcoa is making for hourly workers: a request from the Federal Trade Commission for information that will help it sharpen its definition of industries." And to help in labor negotiations, Stan (he is Stan by this time) had to "figure out how much the consumer price index might rise over the life of the contract." The reader learns more about Stan through comment by other corporate economists to whom he is "something of a crusader." He sounds like a crusader when he tells the reporter, "First of all, I love Alcoa. That's a horrible thing to say, but I almost literally love this company." And the *Journal's* readers can doubtless empathize with Stan as he rides a bus to work, "figuring the time is well-spent in reading" (he's a speed-reader) and returns to his "substantial nine-room house in a fancy Pittsburgh suburb" where a handyman does the yard work because Stan doesn't care much for that sort of puttering.[39]

Obviously, the device is not universally applicable in public affairs reporting. But the principle of specificity, of concreteness, is applicable, and when applied, it lessens the distance between the reader and city hall.

So how do you put it all together? Journalism professor David L. Grey has defined these steps in *The Writing Process:* prewriting (conceptualizing, observing, checking sources, interviewing), writing, rewriting and editing, reaction and reassessment.[40]

Most reporters don't wait to start writing the story until they get to typewriter or telephone. They are already formulating the lead and organizing the body as they leave the interview or scene of the event. What is the essence of the event or the situation? What are its most significant elements, the essential components of the lead? The persons? If so, how are they to be identified? The action? If so, how is it to be defined concisely yet graphically? The place? The time? Or is cause or manner of greater significance? Which of these is going to be of greatest interest to readers? Which can be subordinated? Does the nature of the material demand exposition? Narration? Description? Dialogue?

Reporters, if they are lucky, may be aided in the process by the necessity of a summary oral report to the city desk before beginning to type or dictate. Space limitations set by the desk may determine how tight or how detailed the account is to be. In any case, it must have coherence and unity, whatever the limits of space or pressure of deadline. And that means careful selection and logical organization of significant detail. Marilyn Bender, for example, in an extended piece for the *New York Times* on General Motors' failure to surmount the energy crisis with smaller models, noted deep in her story: "The men who do succeed at GM accept compromise by committee. They govern from the southeastern wing of the 14th floor of corporate headquarters, a grey edifice furnished in faint-hearted modern monotony."[41]

The reporters' problem of organization may be complicated if they have covered a city council meeting or a news conference, at either of which the agenda might encompass a number of unrelated topics of almost equal news value. A good practice to follow in writing such a story, they know, is to devise a summary lead that breaks into item-by-item capsule statements of the various topics, each of which is amplified in turn in the body of the story.

If there is time when they have finished writing and copy editing, they will scan their notes to insure that no needed detail has been overlooked. If there is time, they will read the piece again: Are there holes? Is it clear? Is it balanced? Is it fair?

They may not be sure until they see the piece in print. Or until their telephones ring or the letters to the editor start coming in—from Missouri Synod Lutherans, conservatives and moderates.

NOTES

[1]Covering page, Pulitzer entry, *Los Angeles Times*/Gaylord Shaw, 1978.

[2]Gaylord Shaw and John Kendall, "Collapse of the Teton Dam: A Man-Made Disaster," *Los Angeles Times,* July 18, 1976.

[3]Covering page.

[4]Gaylord Shaw, "Unsafe Dams: Red Tape and Politics Snarl Repairs," *Los Angeles Times,* March 13, 1977; and "Private Dams—A Reservoir of Danger," *Los Angeles Times,* March 14, 1977.

[5]Gaylord Shaw, "Johnstown Dams Called Time Bombs," *Los Angeles Times,* July 23, 1977.

[6]Gaylord Shaw, "Dam Apparently Never Inspected At All," *Los Angeles Times,* November 8, 1977.

[7]See, for example, Don R. Pember, *Mass Media in America* (Chicago: Science Research Associates, 1974), chap. 7, and especially pp. 211–14. Many critics have argued that the desire for film dominates broadcast news decisions.

[8]For a recent exploration of the complementary roles of television and print news, see Ben H. Bagdikian, "Newspapers: Learning (Too Slowly) To Adapt to TV," *Columbia Journalism Review* 12 (November-December 1973), 44–51.

[9]The belief that mass media should perform a surveillance, or scanning, function has been put forth by many communication theorists. The first and fullest exposition of this concept is by Harold D. Lasswell, "The Structure and Function of Communication in Society," in ed. Lyman Bryson, *The Communication of Ideas* (New York: Institute for Religious and Social Studies, 1948).

[10]Useful discussions about reporting objectivity can be found in Donald McDonald, "Is Objectivity Possible?" *Center Magazine,* September-October 1971, pp. 29–42; and in the introduction to Philip Meyer's *Precision Journalism: A Reporter's Introduction to Social Science Methods* (Bloomington: Indiana University Press, 1973).

[11]Murray Fisher, comments at Symposium on the Journalistic Interview (Department of Journalism, Kansas State University, Manhattan, Kansas, April 1972).

[12]Robert Maurer, taped comments on interviewing practices prepared by *Monitor* staff for symposium in note 11.

[13]Ibid.

[14]Eleanor and Nathan Maccoby, "The Interview: A Tool of Social Science," in ed. Gardner Lindzey, *Handbook of Social Psychology*, Vol. 1 (Cambridge: Addison-Wesley, 1954), p. 546.

[15]Eugene J. Webb and Jerry R. Salancik, "The Interview; or, The Only Wheel in Town," *Journalism Monographs* 2 (November 1966), 15.

[16]Terkel's books, which provide excellent case studies of different kinds of interviews, include *Division Street America* (New York: Avon, 1967); *Hard Times: An Oral History of the Depression* (New York: Pantheon, 1970); and *Working: People Talk about What They Do All Day and How They Feel about What They Do* (New York: Pantheon, 1974).

[17]Jim R. Morris, "Newsmen's Interview Techniques and Attitudes Toward Interviewing," *Journalism Quarterly* 50 (Autumn 1973), 540.

[18]"Costello: TV's First Headless Star—Only His Hands Entertain Audience," *New York Times*, March 4, 1951, p. 1.

[19]Webb and Salancik, "The Interview," 4.

[20]Ibid., 6.

[21]*Detroit News*, November 28, 1977, p. 1A.

[22]Upton Sinclair, "What Life Means to Me," *Cosmopolitan*, October 1906.

[23]Roosevelt claimed he never intended to stop journalistic investigations but only to curb abuses. See Arthur and Lila Weinberg, *The Muckrakers* (New York: Capricorn Books, 1964), p. 57.

[24]See Carl Bernstein and Bob Woodward, *All the President's Men* (New York: Simon & Schuster, 1976).

[25]A 1980 unpublished survey by Iowa State Professor William Kunerth found at least twenty-two courses in "investigative, depth or interpretative reporting" in American journalism schools, up from fourteen a decade before.

[26]Jack Taylor, "Legacy of Wounded Knee," *Daily Oklahoman*, June 8, 1980.

[27]Joe Murray, "Walking in the Front Door," speech at the Investigative Reporters & Editors National Conference, June 1977, Columbus, Ohio; and reprinted in "The Best from IRE Conferences: Columbus," published by IRE.

[28]James B. Steele, "Precision Journalism," talk at the 1976 IRE national conference, Indianapolis, Ind.; and reprinted in "The Best from IRE Conferences: Indianapolis," published by IRE.

[29]*Philadelphia Inquirer*, February 18, 1973.

[30]Marion Hale and Dan Lovely, "Courts Favor Whites, The Wealthy," *Ft. Lauderdale* (Fla.) *News;* reprint booklet, 1980, "Broward Courts: Justice Denied."

[31]Pam Zeckman, "Behind The Mirage," speech at the IRE National Conference, 1978, Denver, Colo.; reprinted in "The Best from IRE Conferences: Denver, 1978."

[32]Pam Zeckman and others, "The Accident Swindlers," *Chicago Sun-Times*, reprint series, February 18, 1980.

[33]Pam Sohn, "Detention," *Anniston* (Ala.) *Star*, February 3, 1980.

[34]John Simon, "Use of Deception Debated Among IRE Members," *The IRE Journal*, III, 4 (Fall 1980), 16.

[35]Paul N. Williams, *Investigative Reporting*, (Englewood Cliffs, N.J.: Prentice-Hall, 1978), pp. 95, 96.

[36]Ibid.; see chap. 2, "Thinking About It," for an analysis of planning the investigative story, from which the foregoing is partly adapted.

[37]Peg Meier, "Laymen Come to Grips with Theology," *Minneapolis Tribune*, March 25, 1974, p. 1.

[38]Roger Ricklefs, "More Colleges Grant Scholarships Based on Merit, Not Need," *Wall Street Journal,* March 25, 1974, p. 1.

[39]John V. Conti, "Corporate Economists Give In-House Advice on Future's Course," *Wall Street Journal,* March 26, 1974, p. 1.

[40]David L. Grey, *The Writing Process* (Belmont, Calif.: Wadsworth Publishing, 1972).

[41]Marilyn Bender, "Energy Pinch Has Stunted GM Profits, Sales," *New York Times Service* in *Minneapolis Tribune,* March 28, 1974, p. 8A.

SUGGESTED READINGS

ANDERSON, DAVID, AND PETER BENJAMINSON. *Investigative Reporting.* Bloomington: Indiana University Press, 1976. Anecdotal overview of how investigative reporters work.

COUSINS, NORMAN, ED. *Reflections of America, Commemorating the Statistical Abstract Centennial.* Washington, D.C.: U.S. Government Printing Office, 1980. Collected essays by authors including John Kenneth Galbraith, Walter Heller, and Ben Wattenberg.

DEXTER, LEWIS A. *Elite and Specialized Interviewing.* Evanston, Ill.: Northwestern University Press, 1970. An excellent treatment of the "elite" interview with special implications for political scientists and oral historians that can be adapted by journalists especially with regard to letting the subject help structure the interview.

DOWNIE, LEONARD. *The New Muckrakers.* Washington, D.C.: The New Republic Books Co., 1976. Profiles of a number of investigative reporters.

GILLELAND, LaRUE W. "Simple Formula Proves Helpful to Interviewers." *Journalism Educator* 26 (Summer 1971), 19–20. A journalism educator's method for improving interviewing skills.

HARTGEN, STEPHEN. *A Guide to Public Records in Minnesota.* Minneapolis: Minneapolis Star and Tribune Co., 1975. One of the few books devoted to state and local records.

IRE Journal. published quarterly by Investigative Reporters & Editors, Inc., School of Journalism, University of Missouri, Columbia, Mo., 65211. How-to's and examples of investigative reporting in newspapers, magazines, and broadcast stations.

McCOMBS, MAXWELL, DONALD L. SHAW, AND DAVID GREY. *Handbook of Reporting Methods.* Boston: Houghton-Mifflin, 1976. Techniques for gathering information, with an emphasis on scientific approach.

METZLER, KEN. *Creative Interviewing.* Englewood Cliffs, N.J.: Prentice-Hall, 1977. Helpful and extensive guide to the journalistic interview.

MOLLENHOFF, CLARK. *Investigative Reporting.* New York: Macmillan Publishing Co., 1981. A personal, anecdotal account by a veteran Washington reporter. Includes some good tips.

MURPHY, HARRY J. *Where's What.* New York: Warner Books, 1976. A declassified CIA manual on where to obtain governmental information.

PETROCELLI, WILLIAM. *Low Profile: How to Avoid the Privacy Invaders.* New York: McGraw-Hill, 1981. An attorney suggests ways officials can avoid publicity and thus provokes thinking about countermeasures.

ULLMANN, JOHN, AND STEVEN HONEYMAN. *On the Record: An Investigative Reporting Manual.* New York: St. Martin's Press, 1981. IRE experts discuss many aspects of records.

WEBB, EUGENE J., AND JERRY R. SALANCIK.   "The Interview; or The Only Wheel in Town." *Journalism Monographs* 2 (November 1966), 1–49.
WILLIAMS, PAUL N.   *Investigative Reporting.* Englewood Cliffs, N.J.: Prentice-Hall, 1976. Williams won a Pulitzer Prize in the early 1970s for articles on Boys Town, Neb. A carefully researched, comprehensive classic.

A CHECKLIST OF USEFUL DIRECTORIES FOR THE PUBLIC AFFAIRS REPORTER

The following list includes directories that are generally national in scope. There are many local and regional directories, and public affairs reporters should become familiar with those in their areas.

Architecture. The American Architects Directory lists professional architects and architectural firms in the United States. It is a valuable "first source" on the qualifications and career histories for the reporter checking on buildings and construction projects.

Businesses and Corporations. Moody's Industrial Manual is a guide to industrial corporations and enterprises across the nation. It has a geographic index and provides a brief history of companies, their activities, subsidiaries, officers and directors, and consolidated balance sheets. The *World Bank Directory* lists bank officers and bank holdings. Many states have directories of manufacturing, such as the *Minnesota Directory of Manufacturing.* These are often published by the state and include the size and type of business firms by region or community or both. Chambers of commerce also publish similar directories for their regions. See also the *Standard & Poor's* business directory, which gives more information on business firms and officers.

Consultants. Technical advice in many fields is provided by consultants and consulting organizations. The *Consultants and Consulting Organizations* directory offers a guide to these individuals and associations.

Education. State educational directories list teachers and administrators in various school districts. There are similar guides for colleges and universities.

Engineers and Scientists. Several directories of engineers and scientists have been published. See *Engineers of Distinction, International Engineering Directory, Engineering Consultants, The American Society of Mechanical Engineers Membership Directory, The Institute of Electrical and Electronics Engineers Membership Directory,* and *The Directory of Engineers in Private Practice.*

Government. There are many government directories at the state, local, and federal level. Public affairs reporters should certainly be familiar with their states' *Legislative Manual.* States, counties, and municipalities also publish directories of personnel and guidebooks to their governmental structure. Similar guides are published for federal public officials and employees, and some are organized topically, such as the *Directory of Governmental Occupational Safety and Health Personnel.*

Lawyers and Law Firms. The *Martindale & Hubbell* legal directory lists practicing attorneys in the United States and law firms. It also includes lists of the firms' "representative clients," so the reporter can get an idea of which law firm represents which corporations and businesses.

Medicine. Many medical directories exist, such as those of the *American Association of Endodontists, American Academy of General Practice, Aerospace Medical Association,* and *American Psychoanalytical Association.* See also the directories of the *American College of Surgeons* and the *American College of Physicians* and the *American Medical Directory.*

Newspapers. Editor and Publisher Yearbook lists the editorial staffs and managerial personnel of daily newspapers, along with the names of weekly newspapers and press associations. It also presents statistical information about a newspaper's circulation and advertising rates, as does the *Ayer Directory of Publications.*

Who's Whos. There are many such publications, divided both by region and profession. Some of the more useful ones, which provide biographical sketches on individuals, are the *Who's Who in: College and University Administrators, Engineering, Insurance, Electronics, Securities Industry, Public Relations, Advertising, Railroading, Computers and Data Processing, American Art,* and *American Theater.* Be sure to see the regional who's who for your area, such as *Who's Who in the Midwest.*

5

New Techniques for Monitoring Public Problems

> One of the great tragedies of life is the murder of a beautiful theory by a brutal gang of facts.
>
> *La Rochefoucauld*

On a sultry Saturday in May 1980, an all-white Florida jury acquitted four police officers charged in the slaying of Arthur McDuffie, a black insurance salesman. By nightfall, angry blacks in Liberty City, a Miami suburb, were exchanging gunfire with police. Four died in that night of racial violence, the start of three days of rioting that turned Miami into a city under siege. Before it ended, eighteen were dead, hundreds were injured, and damages approached $200 million.

Why did it happen? Was there something more than rage over the McDuffie verdict? Who were the rioters? And what were the prospects for racial harmony in Miami? Although swarms of reporters covered the rioting, reliable answers to those questions weren't available from traditional news sources. To find out, the news media had to go to primary sources—the black residents of Miami.

Within two weeks of the first gunshots, *Miami Herald* interviewers were on the street in black neighborhoods. Aided by a commercial research organization, the *Herald* questioned 444 black residents about their attitudes toward the riot and the conditions that led to it. They discovered high levels of frustration and bitterness that went beyond outrage over the McDuffie verdict. They found that participation in the riots was more widespread than in past racial disturbances. They also uncovered a long list of perceived grievances, headed by allegations of widespread economic discrimination and police brutality.[1]

The *Herald* survey is an example of precision journalism, the use of social science research methods as a tool for interpretive reporting. It illustrates the capacity of news organizations to accomplish what social scientists rarely can: the systematic examination of significant social events almost as they happen. Philip Meyer of the University of North Carolina, a pioneer in the development of precision journalism, calls it "fire engine research."[2]

Precision journalism isn't limited to breaking news events, of course. Whereas the *Miami Herald* employed a field survey to measure public opinion on a developing situation, the *San Bernardino* (Calif.) *Sun* used content analysis of documents to measure objectively the quality of justice in county courts.[3] As part of a comprehensive study of minorities in San Bernardino County, the newspaper examined 1,000 felony cases over an eighteen-month period. It collected 80,000 pieces of information from police, prosecution, court, and probation records. When the computer analysis was completed in 1980, the newspaper was able to report that black and Hispanic defendants, in contrast to whites, were:

> more likely to serve longer prison terms,
> more frequently held in jail before trial,
> less likely to be released from jail without bond,
> less likely to receive reduced sentences through plea bargaining.

The study showed conclusively that two kinds of justice were being dispensed in San Bernardino County, one for whites, another for minorities. If the newspaper had gone to court officials or defense lawyers for the same information, it would have come away, at best, with self-serving, impressionistic accounts lacking supporting evidence.

Scientific research doesn't necessarily mean dry, statistics-laden stories. Precision journalism makes use of case studies, examples, and focused quotations to make the statistics come alive. The late *Minneapolis Star* spent most of 1980 developing a series of thirty-two stories describing residents of the seven-county metropolitan area it serves. More than 1,100 people were questioned by interviewers from the news staff. The result was a mass of data profiling the people of the Twin Cities: who they are, how they spend their time, how they feel about their jobs, whether they lock their doors when they leave home, and more than 400 other aspects of their lives. If written as statistical summaries, the stories could have put the entire population of Minnesota to sleep. Instead, the *Star's* writers often followed the approach taken in this story by reporter Kay Miller:

> Susan Meyer is stuck in a single-story suburban box with her child and fears she always will be. . . . Looking back, she'd have done things differently, she

says, and it all boils down to one thing: "I would've waited 'til I got my degree to get married and have a family.

But for now, Meyer's a housewife. And she hates it.[4]

Only after humanizing the material with the illustration of Susan Meyer and her regrets does reporter Miller present the survey's findings—the degree of satisfaction with their work expressed by homemakers.

When traditional sources can't produce the information desired by reporters, as in the examples presented, precision journalism techniques can mean the difference between a revealing story and no story at all. In other situations, reporters can use scientific methods to confirm the accuracy of assertions by sources or expand the meaning of limited data. If city officials, for example, say that a new antilitter program has reduced the amount of debris on downtown streets, a simple experiment might be designed to test the assertion. Similarly, if a business group contends that shoppers avoid the downtown district because of inadequate parking, a survey could test the claim.

The growth of precision journalism in the past decade has been dramatic. Many large newspapers, wire services, and television networks are engaged in regular and frequent survey projects. Even medium- and small-sized daily newspapers venture into the field on occasion. More than a third of newspapers responding to a survey in 1978 said they had conducted surveys for use in local stories.[5] But efforts of the scope represented by the Miami and San Bernardino examples require substantial commitments in staff time and funds. Even news organizations dedicated to precision journalism don't undertake field studies on a daily basis.

Short of formal research projects, however, precision journalism techniques are being used to add power to the less elegant methods of information-gathering used by reporters in their daily work. All that is required is an awareness of the principles on which scientific research is conducted. The reporter who systematically checks several sources on one subject rather than relying on a single source has, in effect, committed an act of precision journalism. As an example, the statehouse reporter for a metropolitan daily wants to learn the likelihood of passage of a bill. She has several options. She could question every member of the legislature. She could conduct a formal sample survey, questioning perhaps a fourth of the members, selected randomly. She could search out a handful of legislators, perhaps several from each faction or party, and ask for their estimates of the vote. Or she could seek the answer from just one friendly legislator who is willing to speak, relying on that person's predictive acumen. The four approaches range from the most rigorous (the first) to the most casual of reporting techniques (the last) and testify to a journalistic truth—that reporting, like politics, is the art of the possible. But any move toward precision should be welcomed by journalists, and their critics.

The research described thus far might be classified as "active" uses of precision journalism. Although many news organizations have moved vigorously into research, most have not. The costs in time and money are inhibiting factors, as is the fear that journalists can't be trained to perform adequately as researchers.[6] The principles of quantitative research, however, need not be limited to "active" projects. They can be applied to almost every facet of public affairs reporting on a daily basis. This latter application represents what might be termed the secondary use of precision journalism. The only requirement is knowledge of research methods and statistics. Many reporters may consider these secondary uses more important than the primary uses, simply because of the wide utility of the former and the infrequency of the latter.[7] It's a rare day when the average newspaper doesn't publish several stories that include research-based information. Every time a news source gives reporters the results of an empirical study, the situation calls for familiarity with the techniques used in that study. Indeed, a presentation from a source without benefit of research is often a signal to the reporter to question the information.

Reporters on most beats confront these situations regularly, from the political writer presenting the results of an election poll to the medical writer passing along the findings of an experiment, from the governmental reporter confronted with conflicting conclusions in two feasibility studies to the police reporter trying to find significance in quarterly crime reports. All signify danger to the unwary. Research conducted by investigators with a point of view to defend may be suspect because of bias; research from independent sources may be flawed by methodological or statistical improprieties. The reporters (and their editors) must have at least a minimum knowledge of research methods and analysis in order to recognize these faults. Only then can they interpret the information accurately or be alert to the need for checking with a competent authority. Otherwise, the error is passed along uncritically to a public even less able than the journalists to evaluate the findings. The files of newspapers are filled with examples of this failing.

The case for precision journalism as part of the professional's standard repertory, then, is based on three benefits:

1. Original research to obtain information not available through other sources.
2. More accurate procedures for conventional news-gathering.
3. Interpretation and evaluation of the increasing amount of quantitative research that is flowing across newsroom desks.

Traditional modes of news reporting—direct observation of events, such as covering a trial, or indirect observation of events, such as a press conference—serve well in the appropriate situation. Often, however, they can't meet the demands of a given case. That new models are needed for contemporary journalism is apparent from the criticism of straight reporting as discussed in previous chapters. In the introduction to his seminal work, *Precision Journalism,* Meyer suggests a rationale for the scientific method as a successor to other reporting models. Objectivity of the old-fashioned variety, Meyer writes, presents few problems to the reporter. He merely records, so the myth goes, what he observes. He needs no thoughts of his own about the subject. But the shift to interpretation in news writing requires the reporter to have a reference point, an anchor, on which to base his analysis. Objectivity not only doesn't require a reference point—it prohibits one.

Anchor points for interpretation can be supplied by the reporter's personal convictions, by ideology shared with a group, or by prejudices shaped by consensus. Meyer suggests abandoning these anchor points because they jeopardize the journalist's goal of truth. "Instead of starting from a base of personal conviction, ideology or conventional wisdom," he writes, "we can start with intensive and systematic fact-finding efforts."[8] This approach, he contends, is not a return to the old model of abject objectivity, but is intended "to reduce the size of the leap from fact to interpretation, and to find a more solid basis of fact from which to leap."[9] The effect of such systematic fact-finding can be objective interpretation rather than simplistic objectivity.

Meyer and the *Detroit Free Press* put this conviction into practice with a sample survey of racial attitudes following the 1967 Detroit riot. It was a landmark in the journalistic use of social science research methods—and required only three weeks from conception to newsprint. Some precision journalism efforts predate the Detroit survey, of course. There was a time in newspaper history when enterprising editors sent untrained reporters into the streets to sample the views of the "man on the street." Pulse-taking by reporters, however, may have been limited to a bartender, two taxi drivers, and three people waiting for haircuts. Few well-edited newspapers are guilty of that type of travesty today, although survey research of questionable methodology is still being published.

Most newspaper research is devoted to opinion polls, particularly the voter preference poll. The *Minneapolis Tribune*'s Minnesota Poll, perhaps the oldest, has been conducted since the 1950s. The shift to "in-house" research conducted by the news organization itself, however, is a development of the 1970s. A more common practice is the commissioned poll, conducted for the newspaper by a commercial research organization. That practice dates back to the 1930s, when *Fortune* magazine published a series of essays on national issues, accompanied by the results of opinion polls.

A confluence of factors may account for today's greater sophistication in the journalistic uses of research. The growing acceptance of precision journalism may be an extension of wider press understanding of the social sciences since World War II. It may also originate in what newspaper critic Ben Bagdikian described as "the disappearing antiintellectualism" of the press.[10] Editors are more willing to accept specialized training for their staffs and make use of it in their newspapers. Some impetus for change has undoubtedly come from demands by critics that the media develop better ways to translate complex issues accurately and understandably. And news professionals themselves have testified to the desirability (and inevitability) of precision journalism. In 1973 J. Edward Murray, then president of the American Society of Newspaper Editors, called for a major shift in reporting emphasis toward the use of social indicators, statistical models, and opinion polls.[11] A year later, an association of precision journalists was founded by working newspersons who attended a summer institute in research methods.

Although these developments may herald the oncoming age of precision journalism, prospects for the availability of journalists equal to the task are not so sanguine. Reporters once were expected only to read and write well. Now they are also being asked to count. The untrained reporter can meet the opportunity—and challenge—of precision journalism in two ways. The first is to rely on social scientists for advice. Most cities have colleges rich in authorities who can guide and backstop the journalist. Obviously, there are limits to the extent of this type of help, so it is clear that journalists must themselves come to terms with the business of research and analysis. This means formal training—enough to speak the language of science, to recognize danger areas, and to conduct studies appropriate to the skills acquired. It is not essential for the journalist to match the rigor or sophistication of the professional researcher. As Meyer notes,

> Not all the rules can be observed all the time, but it is important to know them so that you are aware of what you are doing when you break them. There will always be occasions when quick and dirty research is the only kind a newspaper is capable of. If designed with its limitations in mind, such research can still take you closer to the truth than pure intuition or thumb sucking.[12]

For the college student, training is easily obtained. Courses in statistics, research methods, data analysis, and computer operation are offered by several departments at most universities. Some journalism departments also have courses in these subjects, shaped to fit press interests. For the working professional, extension courses are often available, and summer workshops in precision journalism are likely to become more numerous.

This chapter is intended to offer an elementary introduction to some of the concepts and techniques of precision journalism. The sections on statistics and research methods that follow can be considered as curtain raisers; students who plan to develop their own research capability or properly report on the research of others must go on from here to more thorough study.

STATISTICS AND ELEPHANTS

To eat an elephant standing in your path, according to an old African proverb, you must first cut it into small pieces.

Reporters and their publics frequently are confronted with elephants in the form of complex phenomena. What are the reasons for low reading scores among sixth graders? Is there a solution to the conflict between economic development and environmental protection? How can we predict the effects of welfare programs on the components of society? To get at these questions, we usually try to reduce the information to digestible portions.

There are many ways to look at, or analyze, information in the sense of arriving at conclusions. We can rely on experience, common sense, or intuition; we can decide by consensus or voting; we can rely on authority; we can apply logical reasoning; and we can use statistics, if the information is quantifiable. People commonly use the word *statistics* to refer to specific facts or figures. Scientists, however, apply the term *data* to accumulations of information and reserve *statistics* to refer to methods of summarizing, analyzing, and interpreting data.

The use of statistics as an analytical tool dates back to humankind's earliest time, but the field has flowered in this century because of great advances in data-gathering methods, measurement techniques, and electronic computing. Particularly in the social sciences, certain attributes once considered qualitative (for example, intelligence or apathy) are being cast in numerical terms.[13]

Social scientists distinguish between two branches of statistics, *descriptive* and *inferential*.* Descriptive statistics involves measurement or counting of observable objects or their attributes. The compilation of batting averages, weather records, and occupations according to income are examples of descriptive statistics. This statistical approach simplifies masses of data by classifying, comparing, and ordering them. Inferential statistics deals with phenomena that are less easily observed and attempts to explain or predict outcomes on the basis of partial information. Underlying these attempts are the laws of probability, which determine the accuracy (validity) of the predictions. Examples of inferential statistics are those determined by predicting student grades on the basis of previous grades of other students or by isolating the probable causes of juvenile delinquency through an examination of relevant hereditary and environmental factors. Some fundamental scientific concepts and statistical terms will be examined next.

---

*The terms and concepts described in this chapter can be studied in more detail in any of a number of excellent books. Several are listed in the suggested readings at the end of the chapter.

Scientific Method

The minimum goal of reporters is to describe events. Sometimes they also attempt to explain and predict events, which brings them into league with scientists. The scientific method imposes order to the effort of describing, explaining, and predicting events. Typically, the process begins with an informal observation of facts, which leads to beliefs—guesses, if you will—about relationships among these facts.

The reporter who finds inconsistencies in the state's handling of two liquor license applications is at this first stage. If his suspicions carry him beyond that stage, he may begin a systematic examination of the disposition of all license applications for the past year. Such an examination would be the second stage of scientific inquiry—formal observation to confirm an initial guess about the functional relationship among facts. If the relationship is confirmed, a "law" may be established; in this fictional case, the general law may be that liquor licenses are awarded on the basis of political campaign contributions. If our persevering reporter discovers in later investigations that political contributions indeed seem to benefit the giver in a variety of situations, he may arrive at the third stage in the scientific process: developing a theory. A statement that functionally relates at least two sets of laws is a theory.

Journalists, as do other people, invoke theories frequently, except that they don't call them theories. When an editor exhorts a reporter to limit his sentences to fifteen words, she is following the theory that short sentences are more understandable. When a reporter uses the most dramatic element of an event for his lead, he too is applying a theory. Journalists' theories are often passed off as *reasons* for doing things the way they do; they are rarely explicit or testable. Scientists demand that theories be explicit and subject to verification by test. To accomplish this task, scientists follow one of two rigorous courses: field studies or experiments. Field studies are attempts to observe functional relationships among events as they occur in nature—the equivalent of the reporter examining a year's liquor license applications. Experiments use the controlled setting of the laboratory in an effort to avoid the accidents of nature that often contaminate field studies. In the liquor license example, a reporter–experimenter could arrange to submit license applications by persons who did and who did not contribute to the governor's campaign, with all other factors about the applicants being equal. The pattern of license awards would then tend to confirm or disconfirm the theory of political favoritism.

In both field and experimental studies, scientists try to describe their observations in numerical terms. This procedure allows different studies to be compared and permits statistical tests to measure accuracy.

Measurement

Underlying all quantitative analysis is measurement, but all measurement is not the same. In a preelection poll, registered voters may be classified as Republicans, Democrats, or independents. The count of each category is known as *nominal* measurement, the lowest order of scientific measurement. If there are more Democrats than Republicans and more Republicans than independents, arranging the categories in that order is known as *ordinal* measurement, the next level on the precision scale. If the same voters are classified according to how many times they have voted in the past ten years, the result would be *interval* measurement. Each vote is an absolute and equal quantity, qualities required of interval scales. The most refined measure, *ratio,* might be represented by the ages of voters. Ratio measurement requires a scale with a true zero point, a quality possessed by age. The significance of the type of measurement lies in the statistical tests that can be performed. Only weak tests are possible for nominal scales, but stronger tests are possible for ordinal, interval, and ratio scales.

Averages

Most people understand and use averages, but the layperson usually considers only the arithmetic mean—the sum of all values in a group divided by the total number in the group. There are, however, several other "averages" that indicate midpoints in a group of values, each with its own special advantage. The scientist finds it useful to distinguish among these types because some give a better picture of reality in certain situations. The most commonly used measures of centrality are the arithmetic mean, the median, and the mode. The *median* is the point at which a set of values can be cut in half, with an equal number of cases above and below that point. It is preferred to the mean when a distribution has extreme scores on either end or is not symmetrical. An example would be family income in a heterogeneous population. The *mode* is simply the point at which the greatest number of values occur. It is used primarily as an indicator of the most common score, or "the typical case." An example would be an examination of grades. If more students receive C's than any other grade, then C is the modal grade. Sometimes averages don't provide enough information about a set of measurements; they may distort reality, as when two sets of values have the same average but major internal variations. In such cases, measures of *dispersion* provide more useful indicators. These measures show the configuration of individual values within a group. For example, two groups of employees may have the same average salaries, but one group may have several very high salaries and many low salaries, whereas the other group's salaries all hover near the average. The true differences in the groups' incomes can't be seen by looking at their means but can be observed in dispersion statistics, which measure internal variability. The most useful measure of dispersion is the *standard deviation,* which summarizes the differences of all individual values in a set from the mean value of that set. It is a sort of average of individual deviations from the mean. The standard deviation has widespread use in statistical analysis, because it is used to compute correlations between two or more sets of values and to determine the amount of error likely in these computations.

Probability

The ability to make confident predictions from a set of observations is founded on the laws of probability. Everyone is familiar with probability in the form of odds. Most often we estimate probability objectively, by observing a large number of events. Sometimes probability estimates are subjective, such as the degree of confidence a person has about catching a fish. Another person may assign different odds to the same proposition. Probabilities, which are usually expressed as proportions, can be determined for any event by empirical methods. Once determined, they can be applied to future events that are identical to the original in all significant respects.

Sampling

The procedure that makes possible field research, such as opinion polls, is sampling. Samples are based on probability determinations of the number of units of a population required to reflect faithfully some characteristic of all units in the population. They allow predictions to be made about whole populations after studying just a relatively few members of that population. With proper sampling methods, a group as small as 1,000 can reflect, within a known range of accuracy, the characteristics of a population of 100 million. That principle bothers many people, including some journalists, who object that such generalization is impossible. What makes accurate generalization possible is the *probability sample,* in which each unit of the population has an equal or known chance of being selected. Accuracy then depends on the size of the sample, but large samples (above 2,000) don't substantially improve accuracy. There are several types of probability samples, but the most basic is the *simple random sample.* Random does not mean accidental; the researcher must assure that all segments in a population have an equal or known chance of selection. Nonprobability samples, in which a researcher selects population segments with a special purpose in mind, are often used, but these have limited value in prediction because the degree of error can be estimated only with true probability samples.

Analyzing the Data

Data are typically analyzed to see if they are generalizable to a larger population or to discover the possible causes of a condition or happening.

The analysis of quantitative data requires technical knowledge of statistics that is beyond the scope of this book, but which the student can readily obtain from a number of sources suggested at the end of the chapter. The books by Wilhoit and Weaver and by McCombs, Shaw, and Grey are particularly useful for reporters.

The journalist dealing with research material should become familiar with a number of analytical concepts, including correlation, causation, statistical significance, variance, and confidence limits. Correlations and comparisons of data summarized in the form of means and proportions are the modes of analysis that confront reporters most often. Pitfalls await the untrained or unwary reporter, even with those relatively unsophisticated methods.

Correlation, for example, is likely to lead the careless analyst astray in one of two ways: unjustified causal inferences and spurious relationships. A correlation indicates an association between two or more factors, that is, variables. It means simply that they are observed to change at the same time by a known amount. Most measures of correlation show the relationship in a range from -1 to $+1$, with the extremes indicating perfect correlation, and numbers close to zero a weak association.

A positive correlation means that the factors move in the same direction; that is, when one increases, so does the other. A negative correlation means that they move in opposite directions; when one increases, the other decreases. But the fact that each variable changes in relation to the other doesn't mean that one causes the other to move or that their movements are related. A rise in the sale of artichokes accompanied by a corresponding increase in movie attendance is an example of a spurious correlation; there is no likely connection between the two events. Similarly, the fact that newspaper readership has declined at the same time that television viewing has increased does not mean that television has caused the decreased readership.

To claim a causal relationship, three types of evidence are necessary: that other factors are not responsible for the change observed, that the suspected causal variable preceded the other in time, and that the variables change in the way predicted before measurement.[14] It is often impossible to rule out "third variable" explanations, in which some unknown or unmeasured factor may be the true cause of change. In complex social situations, there are often dozens of factors that contribute to an outcome, and it is futile to attempt to attribute cause to one factor. For this reason, cause-and-effect relationships are usually considered beyond the proof available from surveys.[15] The controls possible in experiments, where third variables or extraneous factors can be eliminated, make that approach more suitable for testing causal hypotheses.

FIELD SURVEY METHODS

Sample surveys are the Fords and Chevies of the research business. Journalists are likely to see more of them than any other type of scientific study in the course of their work, and if they do the research themselves, they will probably use a field survey. The qualifier *field* means that the research is conducted not in the laboratory but somewhere in the real world where the subjects of interest reside. The term *sample* means that only a part of the study's universe, or population, is being examined. The field and the population can range from all voters in the United States to homeowners in a defined neighborhood in a city to all members of the county medical society.

Field surveys can be conducted in several ways. One is by direct observation, viewing the behavior of a specific group of people in a systematic manner. To find out how many government cars are parked in restaurant lots after 5:00 P.M. each day, the reporter might resort to direct observation. More typical of survey research is the self-administered questionnaire, in which subjects in a sample respond to a fixed set of written questions. The questionnaire can be mailed to respondents or delivered and retrieved by the researcher. A third method, the most expensive and often considered the most accurate, is the interview, which can be done in person or by telephone. Each method has its advantages and disadvantages.

If surveys differ in method, they also differ in purpose. Some seek only descriptive material about the respondents, such as demographic characteristics or purchasing habits. Food price comparisons are a common use of descriptive surveys by newspapers in this age of consumer consciousness. Other surveys attempt to measure attitudes or predict behavior. These are the types of surveys most frequently found in the news media—the Gallup, Roper, and Harris polls are examples—and the types most likely to be undertaken by journalists.

Public-opinion polls and election polls are merely special cases of field surveys. They are the ones to which the public is exposed most frequently and the ones that have generated both skepticism and criticism of survey research in general. Election polls in particular have been faulted, for allegedly influencing voter decisions on the one hand, and for failing to accurately measure opinion on the other. The first complaint, that polls create "bandwagon" effects favoring the leading candidate or create sympathy votes for underdogs, has been largely dismissed. Witness after witness testifying before a congressional hearing on polling practices in 1972 discounted the existence of either effect.[16] As to the validity of the attitude and opinion measured, most researchers in the field share the public's qualms to some degree. Leo Bogart, one of the leading figures in survey research for a generation, distinguishes between good research and bad (and laments that the media rarely make this distinction). But even the best opinion surveys, he says, fall short of the goal of capturing reality. "There is a vast difference," Bogart writes, "between the reality of public opinion and the polls that measure shadows cast, as in Plato's myth, upon the wall of the cave."[17] One of the reasons for this lack of agreement between opinions held and opinions measured is the intrusiveness of the survey question itself, which often limits the range of responses open to the interviewees or conditions their answers. As Bogart describes it, "The paradox of the scientific method is that we change phenomena by measuring them."[18] Michael Rappeport, an executive of a commercial research organization, points to another weakness of survey methodology: "Before assuming that a poll reflects public opinion, we should find out just what proportion of the adult public has any opinion to reflect . . . substantial minorities or even majorities of people questioned do not have even the barest minimum of factual material on which to base an opinion."[19] Rappeport contends that "don't know" or "no opinion" response categories don't correct for this problem because people prefer to give a specific answer. "It is human nature," he contends, "not to want to admit ignorance."[20]

Despite these fundamental problems and others equally troublesome, sample survey research shows no signs of withering. The challenge to commercial, academic, and journalistic researchers is to follow proper procedures rigorously and to seek better methods. Whatever the purpose and form of the survey, there are a number of steps common to all.

Defining objectives   Decisions about what the survey is attempting to discover must come before anything else. A clear picture of the information desired will help determine the proper survey method, the appropriate population group, and a useful line of questioning.

Sample design   Proper sampling is crucial to accuracy. As discussed in the previous section, probability samples are required if generalizations to a larger population are to be made. The pure random sample, in which every member of the population is in the original pool from which names are drawn, is rarely used in field surveys because of the high cost of locating persons scattered throughout the population. Other probability methods, such as the systematic, stratified, cluster, and sequential samples, enable the researcher to confine the study to convenient geographic areas. Some use census tract maps; others, directories of some kind. All, however, possess the quality of unbiased selection. Nonprobability samples, on the other hand, introduce bias because the researcher's judgment determines the selection of the respondents. Sometimes such a "purposive" sample is appropriate, as when a decision is made about items to be included in a cost of living index. One type of nonprobability sample, however, the convenience, or "accidental," sample, is rarely justified. This type of sample is employed in the discredited newspaper "person-on-the-street" polls.

Sample size The layperson is often surprised by the small numbers involved in sample surveys and therefore becomes skeptical of the results. National polls generally use samples of from 1,200 to 1,600 respondents. Some local surveys use only 600 to 800. Depending on the degree of accuracy desired, the type of data sought, and the size of the population to be surveyed, samples as small as 200 can still be useful. Formulas and tables to help choose sample size are available. If it is randomly drawn, a sample of about 1,200 will provide an error margin of ±3 percent or less for surveys in cities, states, and the nation. Larger samples reduce the error potential only fractionally, and are therefore uneconomic.

Questionnaire construction A large body of literature exists solely on the topic of questionnaires. The potential for error in the wording of questions is obvious. Questions should not "lead" the respondent to a particular answer. They should be easy to understand and unambiguous.

© King Features Syndicate 1973.

Figure 5-1 Forcing survey respondents into a box by limiting their response choices may distort results—just as Hagar's height is distorted in this comic strip.

They should produce answers that speak to the question. It's not a simple task. There are two schools of thought on the subject of style. Some researchers prefer the closed question, in which respondents must choose from a fixed number of specific responses ("Do you approve _____ or disapprove _____ of a special tax for mass transit?" Others believe that the closed question leads to distortion and advocate instead the use of open-ended questions in which respondents provide answers in their own words. ("How do you think funds should be obtained for mass transit systems?") The disagreement is likely to go on for some time.

Pretesting   After the questionnaire is completed, prudence demands that it be tested on a small group to discover flaws, such as ambiguous wording. Pretest subjects should be similar to those who will participate in the larger survey, but not the same respondents, of course.

Data collection   If interviewers are used, they should be thoroughly trained in procedures and techniques. Excellent instructions can be found in a monograph published by the University of Michigan's Institute for Social Research, the *Interviewer's Manual.* Two major cautions for interviewers will help protect the integrity of the survey: The sampling plan should be followed faithfully, and respondents should not be coached on their answers.

Data processing   The final steps in a survey include coding the responses so they can be transferred to computer cards, tabulating by computer, and analyzing the results. Most cities have commercial firms that will prepare computer cards from code sheets supplied by the customer. Computer time is also widely available on a rental basis. The researcher need not be a computer programmer, either. Many data analysis programs, written in nonmathematical language, are available, as are consultants at computer facilities. It is a good idea, however, to study the computer program that will be used *before* designing the questionnaire, so that responses can be coded to conform to the program. The analysis of data may consist simply of counting responses in different categories. If this is the case, and if there are few variables and a small sample, the counter-sorter machine may substitute for the computer.

Reporting results   Although studies differ according to subject matter and findings, certain information should be included in published accounts of all surveys. This information gives the reader a basis for judging the validity of the findings. The National Council on Public Polls suggests seven disclosures that are necessary: sponsorship of the survey, if not evident; dates of data collection, if relevant to interpretation of the poll; method of interviewing (mail, personal interview, phone interview); wording of questions; size of sample; population sampled; and the data base used for the findings if it is less than the total sample. (The last item refers to situations in which only a portion of the sample has responded to a question.) The American Association for Public Opinion Research advocates similar reporting guidelines, with one addition: an indication of the allowance that should be made for sampling error (the "confidence interval").

The foregoing is a skeletonized checklist of procedures followed in most surveys, small or large. It can serve as a starting point for the journalist who plans to undertake a survey, although much more is involved than the steps outlined here. A number of books offer detailed instructions on how to conduct a survey, including Meyer's *Precision Journalism,* Charles Backstrom and Gerald Hursh's *Survey Research,* and others listed at the end of the chapter.

That rigorous surveys are feasible undertakings for news organizations is evident from the increasing number appearing in print and on television. Voter preferences during election campaigns occupy a central place in media polls, but a variety of other subjects is also being examined through surveys. Consider this sampling:

The *Chicago Sun-Times* and television station WMAQ jointly sponsored a series of statewide polls on major issues in 1980. This was the report on one of them:

> A majority of Illinois voters approve of registering women for possible military service, but few would want to see women in combat roles.
>
> The Sun-Times/WMAQ statewide poll found 57 percent of the voters in favor of registering women for the draft, with 38 percent opposed and 5 percent "not sure."[21]

The *New York Times* wanted to gain insight into the feelings of Spanish-speaking immigrants. A sample survey led to four stories by reporter David Vidal that began,

> In neighborhoods throughout New York City, nearly two million people of Hispanic birth or heritage are facing the pull of two cultures—that of their homeland and that of their new country—as millions of immigrants did in the past.
>
> But a six-month study by the *New York Times* involving interviews with 566 Hispanic New Yorkers suggests that most of these newcomers, dismayed by what they consider the attitude of non-Hispanic people toward them, are unwilling to call themselves "Americans" or to let their language, traditions or way of life disappear.[22]

The sample survey in the form of a statistical prediction model was used in this study by reporter Bernie Shellum, formerly of the *Minneapolis Tribune:*

Teachers will play a disproportionately powerful role in the shaping of a Democratic-Farmer-Labor platform and in the party's upcoming endorsement of candidates for the Minnesota House of Representatives. . . .

In caucuses held in thousands of neighborhoods Tuesday night, the teachers, who represent less than 2 per cent of the state's voting age residents, were elected to fill 15 per cent of the DFL's precinct delegate spots. . . .

Projections from the Minneapolis Tribune's 100-precinct model indicate that members of Common Cause, the so-called citizens' lobby for political reform, won 10 per cent of the DFL seats.[23]

These examples demonstrate the role played by precision journalism in obtaining information not available from conventional sources. The list could be expanded with dozens of stories both more and less elaborate than those just described. There is no dearth of available subject matter suitable for inquiry. Every time reporters cover a story that leaves questions unanswered, they have a potential subject for research. Consider these:

Student values   What are the values of high-school students today? An attitude survey might produce findings that run counter to expectations.

The "lemon"   There is always coffee-table conversation about automobile "lemons"—cars that are in the repair shop more often than out. What proportion of new cars are lemons? What do people do about them? A sample survey could provide the answers.

Food prices   Food-market chains advertise prices that apply to all their stores, but what about prices of nonadvertised items? Do these vary from store to store? Is there a relationship between price variation and the economic level of the neighborhood served by the stores? A careful survey could test this hypothesis.

Anyone can make up a list of researchable questions that would interest the public. Some, like the preceding, might be suitable for field surveys. But others may require experiments, and still others the analysis of available records and documents. These methods will be examined next.

THE FIELD EXPERIMENT

Field surveys, it was noted earlier, are limited in their power to identify causes. So many factors operate at once in the real world that isolating one or two to examine alone is virtually impossible. Because of the many unmeasured factors in any survey environment, researchers can rarely be sure that one or more of them isn't causing the phenomenon they are studying, rather than those they have chosen to measure.

A researcher may believe, for example, that voting is a function of the educational level. If a representative sample of voters is examined, it is likely that a relationship between regularity of voting and amount of schooling will be found. Still, the claim that more education leads to faithful voting habits can't be made with confidence; a number of other factors are possibly greater influences on voting (for example, income level, cultural values, occupation, social pressure, distance from the home to polling place). Even if we manage to measure some of these other variables, there is always the possibility of still other variables that haven't been considered. The most likely explanation is that several factors account for voting habits, and the researcher's task is to identify all of them, measure them accurately, and attempt to determine through statistical analysis the relative magnitude of influence for each.

In the search for causes, experiments get around some of these problems. An experiment is a controlled situation in which the relationship between two or more variables can be examined by deliberately changing one and observing whether this change is accompanied by a change in the other.[24] In the jargon of science, the variable that is deliberately changed is known as the *treatment* or the *independent* variable. The one that is examined for effect is known as the *criterion* or the *dependent* variable. The researcher selects the subjects, or experimental groups, through unbiased random procedures. Typically, two groups are used in experiments: One receives the treatment, or suspected causal factor; the other, the control group, does not. Inasmuch as subjects for both groups were chosen randomly from a common population, it is assumed that they are equivalent on all extraneous factors. Many experimental designs are more complex than the one described, but it nonetheless illustrates the advantage of experiments over surveys because it can minimize third-variable explanations.

The procedure is so clean and logical that experiments are the preferred method in much of science, from biology to psychology. Most often they are conducted in laboratories, where conditions can be controlled. Unfortunately, they are more difficult to execute in dealing with social relations. Experiments can be conducted in the field by finding a treatment or independent variable that can be applied selectively to large population groups, but it is a difficult and expensive procedure. People are not easily accessible and manipulable in large numbers for extended periods. For a hypothesis such as the voting-education relationship, it would be impossible to "apply" education to one group, much less withhold it from another.

Even so, the field experiment is an option open to the social researcher and the precision journalist, and it is sometimes used. An example of its use in communications is the testing of different advertisements for a product in different marketing regions to see which has the greatest effect. The news media have rarely employed the field experiment as a reporting tool, but one approach has been widespread in recent years: the consumer protection study in which a product (say an automobile or a television set) is purposely damaged before it is brought to repair shops. News stories then report which shops correctly identified the fault, which padded the bills with unneeded repairs, and the range of prices charged. The studies are sometimes done without proper controls, but they are experiments in a basic sense.

A clever use of the field experiment was demonstrated by the *Miami Herald* in 1973 and 1974. Dade County officials ruled that Spanish would be the county's second official language, requiring all government agencies to deal with the Spanish-speaking population in its native tongue. About a month after the ordinance was passed, the *Herald* selected eighty municipal agencies throughout the county and had a Spanish-speaking reporter call each one and ask for assistance. In only about 8 percent of the cases did the reporter get help in Spanish. The stories that followed the experiment made quite an impact. But a year later when the *Herald* repeated the experiment, it found that the number of public agencies that could respond to a plea for help in Spanish had actually declined. (So much for the power of the press.)

Few news organizations use the experimental method, yet academic research provides many examples that could be adapted by journalists. One such example is offered by Meyer in *Precision Journalism:*

> Stanley Milgram of the City University of New York has reported how his students devised an experiment to test the relative helpfulness and trusting-ness of city dwellers as compared to residents of small towns. Two boys and two girls rang doorbells, told whoever answered that they had lost a friend's address, and asked to use the phone. They did this 100 times in middle-income housing developments in Manhattan and 60 times in small towns in Rockland County, N.Y. Girls had more luck than boys in getting in, regard-less of location, but the city-town distinction was even greater. All four did at least twice as well in gaining entry to the small-town homes as they did in the city.[25]

Another example: A student in a precision journalism class at the University of Minnesota designed an experiment to test for apparent sex bias among employment agency job counselors. She arranged for men and women students to apply for jobs with a randomly selected group of agencies. Each applicant gave the same background description of himself or herself and asked about identical job opportunities. The finding: more women than men were routed toward clerical jobs.

Imagination is the only limit to the range of field experiments possible for journalists, given time and resources. The method requires meticulous attention to detail and careful controls, as well as some knowledge of analysis procedures suitable for experiments. It is worth the journalist's attention both for the opportunity it presents to answer questions that defy other approaches and for understanding the work of professional experimental researchers.

MINING AVAILABLE DATA

Surveys and experiments can be powerful reporting tools in trained hands, but they also have drawbacks. They usually are costly and time-consuming; few can recover information from the past; and they tend to produce biased data (that is, people and their responses are changed by the very act of measuring them). These weaknesses are overcome by another research approach: analysis of public records, documents, and data archives.[26]

The use of records to gather information—from sifting through the daily police log to painstaking examination of property deeds—is a common reporting technique. (Some of these uses were examined in Chapter 4.) Searches of this type, however, are typically focused on a single person, transaction, or subject. Social science objectives in analyzing records have a broader target: aggregate information about larger populations or general topics. As with surveys and experiments, the purpose is to examine the relationship of one category of data to another. Though records can provide purely descriptive information, their greater use is to confirm or disprove beliefs and to uncover trends. The Philadelphia criminal justice study described later in this chapter is an example of the extensive use of court records to test hypotheses.

Court records have, in fact, become a prime source for precision journalists. The range of suitable archival material, however, is much broader. There are police files; voting registers; city, county, and state clerks' records of births, deaths, and much human activity between those extremes; and statistics compiled by governmental agencies at all levels. There are also records of private groups, such as trade associations, that are sometimes available to the reporter. Another source is the data archives gathered by several universities, which often are available to the public. The Survey Research Center at the University of Michigan is one such source, offering data from its lengthy series of national election studies, among other materials. Another depository is the Roper Public Opinion Research Center, which collects data from more than forty commercial and academic survey organizations in the United States and abroad. Usually, these data are available on computer tape, making analysis less expensive and more convenient.

Computers have enabled newspapers to undertake massive examinations of records that were previously beyond the practical reach of journalism. The *Dubuque* (Iowa) *Telegraph Herald* analyzed almost all traffic accidents in the city for a period of one year, with the help of a university computer, and came up with these findings:

> Drivers who cause injury accidents are likely to be charged with fewer violations than drivers causing only property damage.
> Men tend to commit different traffic violations than do women.

The high number of accidents occurring on streets slickened by weather conditions may evolve from a common fallacy: it appears that many drivers don't realize that treacherous road conditions linger hours or days after rain, snow, or sleet has stopped.[27]

In a similar computer-assisted study, reporters with the *Roanoke* (Va.) *Times* examined campaign finances in a state election and discovered that the candidates for governor spent a third of a million dollars more than their principal campaign organizations had reported spending.[28] The data were available under new election spending laws but required 130,000 pieces of information on 13,000 data cards to analyze usefully.

The granddaddy of all records sources is, of course, the U.S. Census. It presents a vast body of information for the reporter with a calculator or computer who wants to analyze the characteristics of any defined geographical unit, from four city blocks to an entire state. For a full examination of the materials available from the Bureau of the Census and other generators of statistics, see Chapter 4.

Sources need not always be formal records. Some of the most useful and accurate information is produced by simple observation or comes from unintended sources. In their monograph, *Unobtrusive Measures*, Eugene Webb and his coauthors describe many ingenious ways researchers have obtained otherwise inaccessible information.[29] How, for example, can whisky consumption be measured in a town that is officially "dry"? One researcher's method was to count empty bottles in trash cans. In another case cited by Webb and his colleagues, the question was raised about the effect of a newspaper strike on retail shopping. An answer was found by examining parking meter revenues before and during the strike.

Whatever the source of the data, systematic methods must be employed in order to assure validity and accuracy. Records involving large numbers of units can be approached with the same random sampling procedures used for surveys. A first step is defining the population to assure consistency—for example, all the Democrats on the voter lists or all the murders and homicides from court records. After that, a unit of analysis must be determined so that the same attribute is measured or counted for each case. If health conditions in restaurants were the subject under study, for example, the unit of analysis might be an employee serving food and the presence or absence of hairnets.

Caution must be exercised in records analysis, as with any other research method. Just because the source is a record does not assure it is accurate. Reporters should determine how the records were compiled and whether they contain built-in biases. They should also tread carefully when making comparisons among records from different sources. Some criminal acts, for instance, are felonies in one state but misdemeanors in another. Unless this fact were known, a study comparing rates of felonies in the two states would be distorted. The danger of making careless causal inferences because of an observed association between two factors is also ever-present. Records can be a gold mine for the alert reporter, a mine field for the unwary.

SOCIAL INDICATORS

One of the growing fields of social science, if not *the* glamor field, has been the development and use of social indicators. A social indicator is a relatively easily obtained measure of a characteristic that permits inferences about another characteristic that can't be measured. The first measure is often a simple counting statistic, such as average income; the second an abstraction, such as happiness. Some might say the higher the average (real) income, the higher the happiness in a community.

Indicators themselves aren't new. Some, like employment rates and school attendance, have been used for decades to tell us something about the state of the economy and the culture. Until fairly recently, however, many indicators weren't sufficiently refined to provide precise predictions or valid representations of current conditions. In the past several years social scientists in several disciplines have turned to the development of new and better indicators. The activity has been so widespread and intense that the Institute for Social Research at the University of Michigan has described the investigations as "a new frontier in social science."[30]

An area of great interest and activity has been in the "quality of life" studies. Indicators have been developed to evaluate important aspects of community life, enabling planners, political leaders, and citizens to be guided in decisions about community needs and priorities. They also permit comparisons between communities and measurement of change over time.

One of the more active organizations in the social indicators field in the United States is the Urban Institute, of Washington, D.C. It began in 1969 to take available measures in many areas of concern (for example, health and crime) and to develop models in order to interpret the indicators in relation to human welfare. One such model measures the state or condition of human well-being in terms of consumption of goods and services.[31] This model has been applied to several areas of social concern, such as housing and neighborhoods and learning and education.

One of the Urban Institute's major works, and one that attracted massive news media attention,[32] was a study comparing eighteen large metropolitan regions on fifteen quality-of-life categories.[33] Each category was measured by one available statistic. For example, health was measured by infant deaths per 1,000 live births; citizen participation by the percentage of the voting-age population that voted in recent presidential elections.

On infant mortality, as one illustration, Minneapolis–St. Paul was rated best among the eighteen cities, Chicago worst.

Some quality-of-life studies are based on discrete behavioral data, such as the Urban Institute's indicators. Others, such as those sponsored by the Institute for Social Research, tend toward psychological indicators, measured through field surveys.[34] An example would be social or political alienation, obtained through tests of sample populations. The psychological measures reflect public perception of the quality of life; the behavioral measures, a more objective assessment of that quality.

Interest in social indicators appears to be high in the news media, judging by their use of reports on the studies. Journalists are going much beyond the mere reporting of formal studies in their use of indicators, however. *Time* magazine examined statistics describing trends in income distribution among blacks in 1972 and discovered a growing schism between blacks who are catching up with the white population in income and those who are falling behind. These income statistics were interpreted by *Time* writers to indicate the creation of two societies within black America—separate and unequal.[35]

Another use of available statistics for indicating social conditions and prospects is demonstrated by this excerpt from an article in the *Washington Monthly:*

> The 1970 census reveals another major demographic fact: that the potential for migration of poor people (mostly Southern blacks) to the cities has sharply declined. . . . The absolute number of blacks outside the metropolitan areas diminished only slightly in the last 10 years. With almost 60 per cent of all blacks now living in the central cities, one of America's historic migrations is coming to an end, at least relatively, and quite possibly in absolute numbers. The lessening of this influx of poor people will reduce the demand on city budgets for public services. This reduced migration, when coupled with declining birth rates for both blacks and whites in the cities, should reduce the pressure for the spread of ghettos.[36]

Of course, much use of social indicators by the news media is not so heavily interpretive. Economic indicators are presented in news columns almost daily, ranging from the familiar stock market price indicators to the cost-of-living index, the wholesale price index, and literally hundreds of other indexes compiled for specialized interests by government, business, and other institutions. The opportunity for journalists to discover and use indicators applying to their own communities—or to develop their own indicators—is new and challenging.

The key to developing indicators is the discovery of suitable available statistics, or the collection of such statistics. Often, social indicators are index numbers (such as the cost-of-living index) that must be constructed with skill and caution. Index numbers sometimes represent simple averages or, more frequently, weighted averages of a series of data. A given average is taken as a base (for example cost of certain goods and services in 1970), and the other averages for the same goods and services in later years are expressed as ratios or percentages in relation to the base. The result is an index number. Usually, index numbers are expressed as a percentage of some base value, which is taken as equal to 100. If the cost of a market basket of goods in the base year was $50, the base becomes 100. If the cost of the same market basket rises to $75 a year later, that would become 150 on the index scale.

Although the development of new indicators is an option open to journalists, most will probably rely on existing measures. Some of the measures used in the Urban Institute study of eighteen cities included[37]

> Social Disintegration: estimated narcotics addiction rates per 10,000 population.
> Mental Health: reported suicides per 100,000 population.
> Racial Equality: ratio between white and nonwhite unemployment rates.
> Community Concern: per capita contributions to United Fund appeals.
> Poverty: percentage of households with incomes less than $3,000 per year.

With these and other established indicators, the news media can monitor the quality of life in a community on a continuing basis. The public would be served with a psychosocial weather report, telling it about its climate of life at one time and providing it with an early-warning system for problems ahead. Used with caution, appropriate advice, and training, social indicators offer the news media another opportunity to bring interesting and useful information to their viewers and readers.

STATISTICS AND BIKINIS

Statistics, a perceptive wag once remarked, are like bikinis. What they reveal is interesting. What they conceal is vital.

Disraeli was more direct. There are, the British statesman said, three kinds of lies: lies, damned lies, and statistics.

© 1974 United Feature Syndicate, Inc.

Figure 5-2

Others are more charitable. Figures, they say, don't lie, but liars figure. Author Darrell Huff capitalized on that belief with what may be the all-time best seller among books dealing with numbers. His irreverent monograph, *How to Lie with Statistics,* has gone through more than twenty printings since it first appeared in 1954.[38]

In applying this aura of pervasive if healthy incredulity about statistics to the field of precision journalism, a double challenge arises. Reporters must conduct their own research in a way that doesn't mislead their audiences. They must also guard against distortion from statistical information that comes through the newsroom door from other sources. Whether the error comes from intent or from honest mistake, the problem remains: When the reporter is gulled, so is the public. The increasing amount of social science and other quantitative research in the news today testifies to the potential of the problem. Two examples, one a report on "outside" research, the other a case of newspaper enterprise, will show the range of the problem.

On November 9, 1965, the greatest power failure in history darkened New York City and most of the Northeast. About 30 million people were without lights, in some areas for more than twelve hours. The impish question on everyone's tongue was, "What did you do when the lights went out?" The implication was that bereft of television and other electrified diversions, people would naturally turn to bed—together. The *New York Times* decided to test this theory nine months later. Its story, picked up by newspapers all over the world, appeared on August 10, 1966: "A startling increase in the birth rate has been reported by hospitals here in the last 36 hours, exactly nine months after the big blackout."[39]

The *Times* based its conclusion on a survey of eight hospitals in New York City. One had twice the normal daily average of births. Five reported slight increases, and two reported no change. The only problem with the conclusion was that it was wrong. The *Times* did not include enough hospitals in its sample, nor were the eight selected randomly. A few days later, after reports from 100 hospitals throughout the city were studied, a different picture emerged. The number of babies conceived on that dark November night was actually slightly lower than normal.[40] Stories correcting the initial error appeared, but myths die hard. Seven years after the baby boomlet was deflated, this item appeared in a national magazine:

> LONDON—Having ordered television off the air by 10:30 P.M. to conserve energy, the British government is now concerned that earlier bedtimes will lead to a baby boom similar to that which occurred in New York nine months after the Northeastern U.S. was blacked out by a massive power failure in 1965.[41]

The *Times* mistake was caused by improper sampling for a rudimentary descriptive survey. Sometimes the journalist must confront much more complex questions. Consider the second example.

"TV Violence Held Unharmful to Youth," read the headline in the *New York Times* of January 11, 1972. Under it, a story by television editor Jack Gould gave details of the U.S. surgeon general's report on the effects of television violence on children.[42] The series of studies on which the report was based, Gould wrote, indicates that there is no compelling evidence that viewing violence leads to aggressive behavior in children.

A week later, hundreds of other newspapers ran headlines similar to this one in the *Seattle Post-Intelligencer:* "Study Links TV Violence to Children, Says Official."[43] The story that followed quoted Surgeon General Jesse L. Steinfeld as saying that research showed for the first time a link between television and real-life violence.

Why the disparity between these two stories (and many others that appeared in the same time period)? Gould based his story on an eighteen-page summary of the research findings that he had obtained a week before the official release date. He was forced to rely on his own interpretation of the findings. When the report was officially released to the press on January 17, Steinfeld backed away from the "no connection" conclusion that appeared in the summary.

Complicating the situation for reporters was a dispute over the meaning of the findings among members of the research teams that had participated in the thirty-month, million-dollar project. Some contended that a link between television and aggression was not definitely established. Others asserted that the connection was proved. Their conflicting claims appeared in a 260-page cover report that accompanied the five volumes of data produced by the study.

The point of this discussion is not which group of scientists was correct but rather the role of journalists in presenting and interpreting complex research. The failure of reporters in properly presenting the television violence report is widely recognized. The public endured weeks of inconsistent stories until the press finally dropped the subject. Many of the researchers blamed the press for the confusion. Asked for their reaction to media coverage, fifteen of twenty-one project investigators responding to a questionnaire said it was, in general, "inaccurate."[44] One of the investigators, Steven H. Chaffee of Stanford University, blamed the inaccuracies on what he described as the media's "scoop mentality" and the fact that few reporters have had training in social research methodology. Said Chaffee in a report to a professional research group two months after the report was released:

> In all, then, we should not be surprised that the first news story on the committee report was written a week before the report was issued, that the article was inaccurate and misleading, that the headline was much more so, and that—since the story appeared in the *New York Times*—it set the tone for subsequent reporting on the committee report.[45]

The problem for journalists was pinpointed by *Newsweek* magazine,[46] which concluded that it would require "an almost total familiarity with sociological parlance" to grasp the significance of conflicting arguments in the cover report. "Such expertise," the *Newsweek* writer allowed, "is not readily available around most newspaper city rooms."

The solution is obvious. Journalists must develop at least a minimum level of sophistication about social research methods. This fiasco might be interesting only from a historical standpoint if similar situations didn't occur with depressing frequency. On the premise that one can learn from the mistakes of others, here is a sample of just a few types of press mishandling of research information.

Crime statistics are a staple item for news organizations. Police and sheriffs' departments, state agencies, and the FBI regularly issue reports on crime rates. Stories developed from these reports are familiar to all:

> Serious crimes in the city went up (or down) 11 percent in the past three months, Police Chief Bruce Stalwart reported yesterday.

or

> The rate of burglaries in Integrityville increased last year, and the rate in Pottstown decreased, according to state crime statistics released today.

The only problem with these stories is that the data on which they are based are notoriously inaccurate. Crime reporting procedures vary markedly from city to city, and even within cities. Residents in some communities report a larger percentage of crimes to police than do residents of other communities. Some police departments manipulate statistics to inflate law enforcement achievements. Different bases for records are often used. These and other flaws in crime statistics are spelled out in a series of studies conducted in 1973 and 1974 for the Law Enforcement Assistance Administration of the U.S. Department of Justice.[47] The message for reporters is clear: Qualify stories about crime statistics and warn readers about their evaluation. One other opportunity is always present. News organizations can conduct their own field surveys, perhaps annually, to serve as a check on police reports of crime rates.

Sampling irregularities account for a major portion of research mistakes, with the self-selected sample a chief offender. A Chicago daily in 1973, for example, asked its readers to "vote" on whether they favored giving reconstruction aid to North Vietnam. About 1,700 responded, with the vote almost 10 to 1 against aid.[48] This percentage was projected to reflect sentiment in Chicago rather than the 1 percent of that newspaper's readers who responded. In a similar case, a national Sunday newspaper supplement, with a circulation of 12 million, published a questionnaire in one issue. It received "more than 25,000 replies," on which it based conclusions about "typical" parental concerns about children's television programs.[49]

That type of reader-participation survey has become popular with magazines in recent years. The large number of responses tends to blur the fact that all the respondents are self-selected, and therefore do not represent an identifiable population. These are much like the familiar surveys of constituents by members of Congress—usually conducted in the months before election. The response rates vary from 10 percent to 20 percent, so even though the gross numbers are large (some as high as 50,000), the results have little meaning as measures of opinion.

Each of these examples involves large samples, certainly as large as, or larger than, those used by commercial pollsters. Yet sample size alone does not guarantee accuracy, unless it approaches 100 percent of the population. More important, as discussed earlier in this chapter, is the quality of randomness. When a survey permits respondents to select themselves as participants, bias must be assumed. All types of people don't answer surveys; studies have found that certain types of people will usually respond, and others will never respond. Those who do participate are hardly representative of the population as a whole.

Comparing findings from two different studies is a particularly dangerous practice. The results of a Gallup poll and a Roper poll on the same subject may differ markedly, despite valid sampling procedures. One reason for the difference may be the timing of the two surveys. If they were done in different weeks, events may have intervened to change public opinion. Another reason is differences in the wording of questions. Subtle differences in language are known to produce different results. Reporters should also look for comparability in the data bases in two surveys. Consider this story distributed by a news service in 1974:

> WASHINGTON, D.C.—Two new studies show that teen-agers are just as likely to run afoul of the law in rural areas as in big cities.
> In rural Oregon, a study by the University of Oregon showed that 25 per cent of the 16- to 18-year-old males in one county had a record with the juvenile department, excluding minor traffic violations.
> In a Philadelphia study . . . 35 per cent of the teen-age boys had a juvenile record, including traffic offenses.[50]

Two sources of invalidity are evident. The age groupings differ, with one including all teenagers, the other covering only three years. One study included traffic offenses; the other didn't. Beyond that, there is no indication that other categories of juvenile crime were recorded similarly in the two regions or that enforcement practices in rural Oregon and urban Philadelphia are comparable.

Another type of journalistic misrepresentation involves the unsupported causal inference. Typically, it appears when a correlation is observed between two possibly related events. The temptation is to assume that one event caused the other, even though the connection may be incidental. An example appeared in 1979 when a national tabloid reported a link between a drug used by pregnant women to control morning sickness and the incidence of birth defects. The writer implied that birth defects were caused by the drug, used at that time by about one-fourth of all pregnant women. One-fourth of all defective children could be expected among these women (since they made up one-fourth of the population) even if they had not been taking the drug. Only if the women taking the drug accounted for significantly more than one-fourth of the defective children born could the drug be implicated as a probable cause of birth defects.

The three classes of potential error just described represent the tip of an iceberg. Dozens of other analytical traps await the unwary—or untrained—reporter. In addition to inadequate samples and inappropriate comparisons, a list of the more common pitfalls would include the following:

Miscounting   Perhaps it isn't surprising, but the most common statistical error is a mistake in computation. Checking addition, subtraction, multiplication, and division should be a reportorial routine.

Correlation   Interpreting a correlation between two factors as evidence of a causal connection is rarely justified. Always look for spurious associations and other variables that may explain the findings.

Percentages   Many people use percentages improperly. A rise in the cost of living from 100 to 150, for example, is a 50 percent increase, not 33 percent. A classic misuse of percentages is in applying them to small numbers. If there are only two copy boys in a city room, and one of them is eventually hired as a reporter, it would be misleading to say that 50 percent of copy boys become reporters.

Charts   Manipulation of the scales on charts or graphs can distort the meaning of the data. Choosing the proper scale is a judgmental matter, with no fixed rules, but critical examination is always wise in order to avoid deception. If a chart doesn't contain a zero point, for example, try to ascertain whether it would make a difference in the configuration of the data. Also, see if representing data in percentages gives a different impression than would the raw figures.

Exaggerated accuracy   Presenting statistical projections to the second decimal point can lead to spurious accuracy. If a health agency is quoted as estimating the number of new cases of tuberculosis at 112,426 next year, compared with 108,079 this year, the precision of the figures themselves claims more accuracy than deserved. These and similar estimates are often based on samples, and rounding the numbers would avoid imparting undeserved confidence in them.

STATISTICS AND STYLE

A central tenet of good reporting is reader identification, demonstrating the relevance of news situations to the individual. Unless readers can see themselves related to the story in some way, they're not likely to go beyond the headline and lead paragraphs.

Helping the reader to identify with content is more difficult with the quantitative approaches of precision journalism. How, after all, can one find oneself in a percentage? Yet the presentation of aggregate data is often essential to an understanding of civic and social problems. Author and journalist Martin Mayer once observed succinctly that "societal as distinguished from individual reality is always statistical." In the journalistic context, his observation means that writing exclusively about individuals can't produce an accurate picture of the larger community. The challenge to reporters, then, is to make the statistically described societal reality palatable by bringing in the individual reality as well.

This approach is illustrated in the following story by Pulitzer Prize-winning reporters Donald L. Barlett and James B. Steele of the *Philadelphia Inquirer:*

> Angus Williams, a 57-year-old laborer, was arrested in November 1971 and charged with the street robbery of a retired North Philadelphia machinist. For five months he sat in jail awaiting trial, unable to post the $3,000 bail.
> In the end, he was acquitted of the charges. As it now turns out, Angus Williams—who never went to school, who cannot read or write, who had never been arrested before—was indeed innocent. Another man committed the robbery.[51]

The story goes on to describe other cases in which judges acted with apparent inconsistency, depicting the uneven quality of justice in Philadelphia courts. Barlett and Steele provide statistics produced by their study, but only after presenting flesh-and-blood humans to illuminate them. The technique of breaking up dry recitations of numbers and percentages by seasoning them with case studies, quotes, and comments from appropriate sources is desirable in all precision journalism projects.

Interviewers conducting surveys can obtain useful quotes for later consideration by writers. In a survey of residents following a speech by President Nixon on the Watergate affair, the *Seattle Post-Intelligencer* found that almost half of the respondents thought the president was not telling the truth. A third said they believed his version of the burglary, and the remainder were uncertain. To illustrate these groupings, newspaper interviewers obtained quotes that added dimension and emotion to the cold statistics:

> "What does he take us for? Idiots?" said one Bellevue resident. "No, I don't believe him."
>
> "I've been standing here cooking dinner, thinking about it," said a resident of southeast Seattle. "I wholeheartedly think he knew nothing about it. I'm shook up, but I still have faith in the president."[52]

Obviously, statistical and individual reality complement each other in this example. The approach is similar to a reporting method known as "humanistic newswriting," in which the focus is placed on the impact of news on the individual. Journalism professors Alex S. Edelstein and William Ames, who coined the term, define humanistic writing this way: "It is individualized and personalized, in the hope that the reader will see common threads of experience between his own life and that of another individual. . . . If the reader can identify with another person's experience, he feels less isolated as a human being. He develops a greater understanding of others and becomes more able to cope with events."[53]

An example of humanistic reporting and its straight news counterpart can be seen in these leads about a rise in real-estate and housing costs. First, the conventional treatment:

> The price of a new single-family house has risen more than twice as fast as the increase in the consumer price index in recent years, according to a report by the National Industrial Conference Board.[54]

The same subject was introduced this way in the *Wall Street Journal:*

> There is this married woman in the East who is in love with this airline pilot in the West. And he is in love with her. So they have made plans to marry.
>
> But they cannot start out on a shoestring. Expenses of a divorce, a wedding, a new home were to have been paid from the pilot's stock portfolio. Until the market dropped. There are other examples:
>
> While the pilot is postponing his marriage, a 73-year-old Cleveland man is postponing his retirement. A Boston man is having second thoughts about buying a $24,000 Mercedes. The backers of a screenplay have pulled out. And a Chicago executive has ordered his wife to serve cheaper cuts of meat.[55]

There is a danger in the case-study approach, of course, that the writer will restrict the story to examples. To be useful, the story must move from the specific to the general. Economist Herbert Stein complains that journalists sometimes resort to this technique, attempting to draw general significance from a few selected cases. "These vignettes really aren't significant unless the people represent some general category," Stein writes. "And we can only tell that from the statistics, however unreliable they may be."[56]

Stein's challenge to reporters is being met today in those news organizations that value fluency in numbers as well as fluency in language. The marriage of precision journalism and humanistic newswriting is fortuitous, stable, and productive.

NOTES

[1]The survey and stories on the Miami riot are reprinted in a special supplement to the *Miami Herald*, "Three Days of Rage." The coverage began in editions of the *Herald* beginning on May 18, 1980.

[2]The descriptive phrase *precision journalism* was suggested to Meyer by Everette E. Dennis, a coauthor of this book. See Meyer, *Precision Journalism: A Reporter's Introduction to Social Science Methods* 2nd ed. (Bloomington: Indiana University Press, 1979).

[3]"Skin Deep, a Study of Minorities," supplement to the *San Bernardino* (Calif.) *Sun*, September 7, 1980.

[4]*Minneapolis Star*, December 9, 1980, p. 1A.

[5]John N. Rippey, "Use of Polls as a Reporting Tool," *Journalism Quarterly* 57 (Winter 1980), 642–46, 721.

[6]Training of journalists in research methods is examined by Philip Meyer, "Social Science Reporting" (pp. 149f), and Jack Lyle, "Study of Urban Life" (pp. 213–26), in *Education for Newspaper Journalists in the Seventies and Beyond* (Reston, Va.: American Newspaper Publishers Foundation, 1973).

[7]Opportunities and problems in newspaper reporting of social science subjects are exhaustively examined in Frederick T. C. Yu, ed., *Behavioral Sciences and the Mass Media* (New York: Russell Sage Foundation, 1968).

[8]Meyer, *Precision Journalism*, p. 13.

[9]Ibid.

[10]Ben Bagdikian, Chapter 3, "A Review of Session One," in *Behavioral Sciences and the Mass Media*, p. 47.

[11]J. Edward Murray, speech to the Georgia Press Institute, Athens, Ga., February 23, 1973.

[12]Meyer, *Precision Journalism*, p. 292.

[13]A brief treatment of the history and uses of statistics can be found in Boris Parl, *Basic Statistics* (Garden City, N.Y.: Doubleday, 1967), pp. 1–4.

[14]Hubert M. Blalock, Jr., *Causal Inferences in Nonexperimental Research* (New York: Norton, 1964) offers a thorough examination of causation in survey research.

[15]Claire Selltiz, Marie Jahoda, Morton Deutsch, and Stuart W. Cook, *Research Methods in Social Relations* (New York: Holt, Rinehart and Winston, 1959), p. 422.

[16]U.S. Congress, House Subcommittee on Library and Memorials, Committee on House Administration, *Public Opinion Polls*, hearings on H.R. 5003, 93rd Cong., 1st sess., 1972 (Washington, D.C.: U.S. Government Printing Office, 1973).

[17]Leo Bogart, *Silent Politics* (New York: Wiley, 1972), p. 17.

[18]Ibid., p. 18.

[19]Michael Rappeport, "The Distinctions the Pollsters Don't Make," *Washington Monthly* 6 (March 1974), 13.

[20]Ibid.

[21]*Chicago Sun-Times*, February 29, 1980, p. 6.

[22]*New York Times*, May 11, 1980, p. 1.

[23]*Minneapolis Tribune*, March 3, 1974, p. 1.

[24]Definition adapted from Barry F. Anderson, *The Psychology Experiment (Belmont, Calif.: Wadsworth Publishing, 1966), p. 21.*

[25]Meyer, *Precision Journalism*, p. 249. Reprinted by permission of Indiana University Press.

[26]See Eugene J. Webb et al., *Unobtrusive Measures: Nonreactive Research in the Social Sciences* (Chicago: Rand McNally, 1966) for exploration of the range of archival material.

[27]*Dubuque* (Iowa) *Telegraph Herald*, December 1, 1974, p. 1.

[28]*Roanoke* (Va.) *Times*, February 10, 1974, p. 1.

[29]Webb et al., *Unobtrusive Measures*.

[30]University of Michigan, Institute for Social Research, *Newsletter* (Summer 1974), p. 3.

[31]Harvey A. Garn, Michael J. Flax, Michael Springer, and Jeremy B. Taylor, "Urban Institute Working Paper 1206–11," Mimeographed (Washington, D.C.: Urban Institute, 1973).

[32]*New York Times*, October 21, 1973, p. 1.

[33]Michael J. Flax, *A Study in Comparative Urban Indicators: Conditions in 18 Large Metropolitan Areas* (Washington, D.C.: Urban Institute, 1972).

[34]University of Michigan, *Newsletter*.

[35]*Time*, September 3, 1973, p. 75.

[36]Michael Rappeport, "The Cities Turn a Corner," *Washington Monthly* 4 (March 1972), 30.

[37]Flax, *Study in Comparative Urban Indicators*.

[38]Darrell Huff, *How to Lie with Statistics* (New York: Norton, 1954).

[39]"Births Up 9 Months After Blackout," *New York Times*, August 10, 1966, p. 1.

[40]Another aspect of the Northeast blackout is reported in an essay by W. Phillips Davison, "The Russell Sage-Columbia Program in Journalism and the Behavioral Sciences," in *Behavioral Sciences and the Mass Media*, p. 221: "During the New York power failure last November, many of the news media reported that, in the face of the shared calamity, New Yorkers became more friendly, more neighborly. A survey conducted by the Columbia Bureau of Applied Social Research during the blackout found that such a reaction was indeed characteristic of those belonging to the higher educational and income groups. Poorer, and more ignorant people, on the other hand, tended to feel more isolated and to show more signs of apprehension. The research thus suggests that journalists assigned to cover popular reactions during similar emergencies might well be advised to seek out representatives of different social classes when making interviews. Indeed, awareness of class structure and of the different reaction patterns of different population strata is probably relevant to a great many news stories. . . ."

[41]*Playboy* 21 (May 1974), 61.

[42]Surgeon General's Report, *Television and Growing Up: The Impact of Televised Violence* (Washington, D.C.: U.S. Government Printing Office, 1972).

[43]*Seattle Post-Intelligencer*, January 18, 1972, p. A1.

[44]Matilda D. Paisley, "Social Policy Research and the Realities of the System: Violence Done to TV Research" (Stanford, Calif.: Institute for Communication Research, Stanford University, March 1972).

[45]Steven H. Chaffee, "Television and Growing Up: Interpreting the Surgeon General's Report," paper presented to the Pacific Chapter, American Association for Public Opinion Research, Asilomar, Calif., March 1972.

[46]*Newsweek*, March 6, 1972, p. 55.

[47]Reports on the National Crime Panel surveys were carried in newspapers of April 15, 1974, and November 28, 1974.

[48]Reported in *Time,* April 9, 1973, p. 10.

[49]*Parade,* March 4, 1973, p. 12.

[50]Newhouse News Service article, published in the *Minneapolis Star,* September 18, 1974, p. 10C.

[51]"Equal Justice for All? . . . It's a Myth," *Philadelphia Inquirer,* February 18, 1973, p. 3.

[52]*Seattle Post-Intelligencer,* May 2, 1973, p. A-1.

[53]Alex S. Edelstein and William E. Ames, "Humanistic Newswriting." *The Quill* 58 (June 1970), 28.

[54]Ibid., 30.

[55]Ibid.

[56]*Newsweek,* July 29, 1974, p. 11.

SUGGESTED READINGS

BABBIE, EARL R. *Survey Research Methods.* Belmont, Calif.: Wadsworth, 1973. One of many excellent general texts on social science research methods.

BUREAU OF THE CENSUS. *1980 Census Users Guide.* Washington, D.C.: U.S. Government Printing Office, 1981. Basic manual for locating and retrieving census data.

———. *Social Indicators III.* Washington, D.C.: U.S. Government Printing Office, 1981. Third in a series of collections of important statistics summarizing the social and economic conditions of the United States.

CANTRIL, ALBERT H., ED. *Polling on the Issues.* Cabin John, Md.: Seven Locks Press, 1980. Collection of twenty-one essays on the role of opinion polls in journalism and politics.

HAACK, DENNIS G. *Statistical Literacy, A Guide to Interpretation.* North Scituate, Mass.: Duxbury Press, 1979. A readable and comprehensive introduction to statistical methods and reasoning.

McCOMBS, MAXWELL E., DONALD L. SHAW, AND DAVID GREY. *Handbook of Reporting Methods.* Boston: Houghton Mifflin, 1976. A practical text for the reporter or student who is new to the field of precision journalism.

WILHOIT, G. CLEVELAND, AND DAVID H. WEAVER. *Newsroom Guide to Polls and Surveys.* Washington, D.C.: American Newspaper Publishers Association, 1980. A handbook for journalists, providing basic concepts and terminology used in surveys.

WILLIAMS, FREDERICK. *Reasoning with Statistics,* 2nd ed. New York: Holt, Rinehart and Winston, 1979. A survey of statistical concepts, with emphasis on communication-related research problems.

6

Understanding
Communication Law

No system of freedom of expression can succeed in the end unless
the ideas which underlie it become part of the life of the people.
There must be a real understanding of the root concepts, a full
acceptance of the guiding principles, and a deep resolve to make the
system work.

Thomas I. Emerson, The System of Freedom of Expression*

The inadvertent turn of a phrase or an accusatory statement may be among
the issues that bring a reporter into a legal conflict. In spite of the absolute
ring of the First Amendment ("Congress shall make no law . . ."), the
rights of the press frequently collide with the rights of individuals, groups,
or even the government. When this happens, litigation involving such issues as libel, privacy, and free press versus a fair trial may result.

It is almost a truism to say that public affairs reporters should maintain an interest in, and knowledge of, the law of mass communication if for
no other reason than self-protection. Schools and departments of journalism usually insist that their students take at least one course in communication law, but beyond this requirement there are few efforts to keep journalistic practitioners aware of legal trends and circumstances.

Yet public affairs reporters who do make an effort to stay current
with communication law can have a real advantage over their colleagues
who may slavishly follow the timid advice of the company lawyer. This is
not to suggest that reporters should second-guess their newspaper's or
broadcast station's attorney, but they should know enough about the law as
it affects them to ask substantive questions. A vigilant reporter who follows

*Reprinted by permission of Random House, Inc. © 1971.

the law with care may know more about libel law, for example, than company lawyers who spend most of their time on financial matters, labor negotiations, and tax problems.

Sometimes thorough investigative reporting requires tough-minded articles that ease toward the ragged-edge of libel. Many of the exposés of government officials' wrongdoing were initially threatened by libel suits. Even the *New York Times* would have averted its celebrated 1971 confrontation with the federal government over the Pentagon Papers had the editors followed the cautious legal advice of the firm representing the newspaper. Sanford Ungar in his account of that case, *The Papers & The Papers*, chronicles the resistance of the *Times*'s lawyers and how they were eventually overruled.[1]

Editors and their bosses, the publishers, are only too aware of the dangers to the balance sheet of troublesome litigation and stinging court judgments. Sometimes, a highly celebrated libel or privacy suit will make editors think twice before approving a critical or controversial piece of reporting. In 1981, when actress Carol Burnett won a $1.6 million libel case against the *National Enquirer* for inaccurate and erroneous statements made about her behavior in a Washington, D.C. restaurant, some editors fretted openly that the award would have a "chilling effect" on the First Amendment and on reporting.

When small newspapers and broadcast stations see how even a large organization like the *New York Times* or CBS News can be stung by multimillion-dollar suits, they worry about the effect local suits might have on them. Naturally, this can lead to quite cautious behavior and a tendency not to print material that might take the paper or station into court.

The widely held belief in the late 1970s and early 1980s that freedom of the press was under attack in the courts, because some large and well-publicized cases were lost by the press, gave credence to the idea of a chilling effect on public affairs reporting. The Reporter's Committee on Freedom of the Press frequently encourages this position in the magazine *Media and the Law*, which catalogues current legal struggles by reporters and their bosses.

Thus, the alert reporter may have to do far more than prepare a competent story to convince editors that there is a sound reason to run it; there must also be a legal basis for defending it should court action be threatened by a source or subject who is displeased.

Journalists covering the complexities of the public arena commonly hear legal threats and thus must be especially careful in their work while maintaining a delicate balance between justifiable caution and appropriate revelation. This chapter attempts to suggest some boundaries for that balance, to mention briefly important areas of communication law, and to chart a direction for the conscientious journalist who wants to keep pace with communication law. No attempt is made here to offer an exhaustive compendium or guide to self-protection. The law is dynamic with frequent contours and changes. Keeping up with it, even in a specialized area, requires an energetic commitment by the journalist.

THE LAW OF LIBEL

State laws of libel, which frequently confront reporters, were "intended to protect the individual against unfair damage to his reputation."[2] Samuel G. Blackman, a general news editor of the Associated Press, says that "from a practical standpoint, the chief causes of libel suits are carelessness, misunderstanding of the law of libel, the extent of the defense of privilege and the extent to which developments may be reported in arrests."[3] Defining libel, communications scholars Harold L. Nelson and Dwight L. Teeter write, "Libel is defamation by written or printed words, by its embodiment in physical form, or by any other form of communication which has the potentially harmful qualities characteristic of written or printed words."[4] Libel, explains legal scholar Thomas I. Emerson, "applies to a communication that subjects a person to ridicule, hatred or contempt in his community or lowers him in the estimation of his fellows."[5] Dean William L. Prosser, a distinguished authority on tort law, suggested that of all laws, defamation law is one of the most complex. Several elements are necessary for a *prima facie* case of libel, which exists when a person suing for libel has enough evidence for the reporter and the reporter's organization to be called to answer it under the law. The traditional *prima facie* case in libel requires that the material (1) be published to a third party—be disseminated in a newspaper or on a newscast, (2) be capable of having defamatory meaning, (3) be understood as referring to the plaintiff (the person libeled), (4) be understood in a sense that it is defamatory to the person libeled, (5) have causation—meaning that the libelous statement be the thing that caused the injury being complained about, (6) cause either direct financial loss or an identifiable damage to reputation that deserves financial redress.[6]

There is no agreement on what precise interests must be damaged in order for libel to exist, but according to Emerson some of them are said to include

1. Injury in one's trade, profession or other economic pursuits.
2. Injury to prestige or standing in the community, which affects one's position as decision-maker or participant in the community.
3. Injury to feelings, arising out of an affront to one's dignity, distortion of one's identity, reflection on one's honor, or lessening of the approval of one's peers.[7]

Naturally, many news stories that reflect negatively on persons might be considered libelous. Communication law scholars Donald M. Gillmor and Jerome A. Barron say it is necessary to determine whether the libel is actionable and what defenses the journalist can offer. They explain that actionable libel requires "(1) defamation, (2) identification, and (3) publication."[8] Thus, there must be an injury to reputation; the injury must be applied to an identifiable person; and the statement must be published or broadcast. (Group libel and criminal libel, which involves the government, are not treated here.) Importantly, the burden of proof in a libel suit must be understood. Gillmor and Barron explain:

> In the first instance, the person bringing a libel action must persuade the court that a defamatory publication has been made concerning him. Ambiguity is for the jury. Since the law presumes that a defamation is false, the publisher then has the burden of pleading an affirmative defense such as truth, good motives, privilege or fair comment. The burden then shifts to the plaintiff to show that a defense of privilege or fair comment has been nullified by malice on the part of the publisher, or that a defense of truth has been lost for want of good motives or justifiable ends.[9]

There are four defenses against libel, including truth, qualified privilege, absolute privilege, and fair comment and criticism. There is "only one complete and unconditional defense to a civil action for libel,"[10] says an Associated Press report on libel: "That defense is that the facts stated are provably true." Note well the word *provably*. Though often repeated, this assumption is not quite accurate. Other unconditional defenses to a libel suit are (1) consent, (2) the statute of limitations, and (3) political broadcasts under the Equal Time provisions of Section 315 of the Federal Communications Act. These are absolute defenses. Furthermore, truth alone is an unconditional defense in only about half of the states.

Privilege is an exemption in the law in which the social good in communicating certain information in the public interest overrides damage to individual reputation. Absolute privilege applies to individuals testifying at official court proceedings or before legislative bodies. As Nelson and Teeter put it, "Anyone who reports proceedings is given an immunity from successful suit for defamation; and for the public at large, 'anyone' ordinarily means the mass media. The protection is ordinarily more limited for the reporter of a proceeding than for the participant in the proceeding. It is thus called 'qualified' (or 'conditional') privilege, and is qualified in that it does not protect malice in reports."[11]

The fourth defense in libel actions—fair comment and criticism—has undergone considerable change in recent years. Originally, it was intended to protect persons (including the press) in assessing public officials, institutions, and other visible public activity. Fair comment and criticism applied as long as there was no malice, but unfortunately for years the courts had a variable standard of malice and no one was ever sure what it was. In 1964 the defense of fair comment and criticism was more fully defined in the landmark Supreme Court case of *New York Times* v. *Sullivan*. In that case the Court ruled that public officials are prohibited from recovering damages for a defamatory falsehood relating to their official conduct unless they prove that the statement was made with "actual malice—that is with knowledge that it was false or with reckless disregard of whether it was false or not."[12] That, in effect, provided the long-needed definition of malice. The *New York Times* doctrine was eventually extended from public officials to public figures ("persons caught up in the vortex of public discussion") in a series of progeny cases. By 1971, when the *Times* malice rule had been extended to purely private persons caught up in public events, some commentators thought that "the law of libel has been all but repealed."[13] Although this assumption did not seem unreasonable at the time, the number of libel suits continuing after this period necessitated abandoning it. In 1974, the Supreme Court pulled back from its liberal standard (as developed further in *Rosenbloom* v. *Metromedia*) in the case of *Gertz* v. *Welch*. The ruling narrowed the conditions under which private persons might be considered public figures, and thus made it easier for private persons to sue successfully. "It is clear," wrote D. Charles Whitney in *The Quill*, "that the ruling destroys musing that libel suits are a thing of the past."[14]

At first commentators thought the *Gertz* case might bring about a redefinition of the term *public figure*, but its most powerful impact was instead a sweeping reaffirmation of the dictum that there can be no such thing as a false idea. If *Gertz* is followed by courts, recovery of damages can be obtained only for statements of *fact* that are proved to be false. Thus statements of *opinion* cannot give rise to successful libel suits, and it becomes irrelevant whether the individual libeled is a public or private figure. Actual malice becomes a factor only if the court requires it to be shown that the speaker actually held the opinion.

Because the *Gertz* rule is a matter of constitutional law, appellate courts must search the record independently and decide whether a statement is protected opinion. The burden on the plaintiff then becomes one of trying to show that the statement actually is factual and therefore not protected as opinion—proof to the degree of "convincing clarity."

The question arises that if this is the rule, is the common law privilege of "fair comment" needed at all? Many courts have said no, although many have also been unwilling to accept fully the general immunity for opinion that is suggested in the *Gertz* case.

As Robert D. Sack has written in his 1980 book, *Libel, Slander and Related Problems*, whether fair comment has expired has yet to be determined. Many courts still use it as a means of dismissing suits, and the U.S. Supreme Court will assume that lower courts have decided a case on non-constitutional grounds if available.[15]

Cases in the U.S. Supreme Court sometimes change the contours of libel law by more fully defining a concept or issue. For example, the 1979 case of *Herbert* v. *Lando* gave courts the right to investigate the manner and motives involved in news-gathering. Although the press saw this as a setback for freedom of expression, it was a natural outgrowth of the *New York Times* malice rule, which was quite vaguely defined in the 1964 Court decision. There is a continuing tug of war between media interests and those of other segments of society. The press is a vigilant advocate for its own rights and interests and sometimes overstates the apparent impact of a Supreme Court decision. The *Gertz* and *Lando* decisions are cases in point. There was a collective gnashing of teeth in the press and the prediction by some commentators that the Court had all but abolished the First Amendment. Of course, this was not the case, and in later instances the press sustained victories in libel cases.

Although celebrated libel cases sometimes result in huge judgments against the press, relatively few of the cases that are originally filed actually come to trial. Most are dropped by the plaintiff, dismissed by the court, or settled before trial. Still, it is useful for reporters to be familiar with the current state of libel law and to have an idea of how lower courts are interpreting constitutional decisions. Sometimes reporters realize that it is not so far from the lofty pronouncements of appellate courts to their own daily work. It is naïve, and indeed dangerous, to assume that freedom of the press means that you can write anything you want. There are definitely legal limits, as courts point out with great vigor in occasional libel decisions.

REPORTERS AND PRIVACY

As with libel, reporters often find that the rights of a free press can collide with the right of individual privacy. Emerson offered this keen observation in distinguishing between privacy and libel:

> Communication that invades the inner core of the personality, assaulting the dignity of the individual by depicting matters of a wholly personal and intimate nature, may be subject to government control. Under existing legal doctrine, if such a communication contained matter that was false and defamatory, it would be governed by the law of libel. If the matter was not false, it would be subject to a privacy action.[16]

For years scholars have spoken of the "law of privacy" as differentiated from the "right of privacy." The right of privacy is implicit in the Constitution and in various social and political rights. The law of privacy, first proposed by two legal scholars in a law review article in 1890,[17] is narrower and more specific. It refers to the specific statutory provisions for the protection of privacy, for the right "to be let alone." Statutes for privacy protection in the United States are relatively recent in origin and vary considerably from state to state. Dean William Prosser, the leading authority on torts, has written that there are four kinds of torts included under privacy:

1. Intrusion on the plaintiff's physical solitude.
2. Publication of private matters violating the ordinary decencies.
3. Putting plaintiff in a false light in the public eye, as by signing his name to a letter attributing to him views he does not hold.
4. Appropriation of some element of plaintiff's personality—his name or likeness—for commercial use.[18]

Privacy scholar Don R. Pember says that courts dealing with press privacy cases must work toward a "desirable compromise":

> In almost every case the problem before the court could be reduced to this simple question: Which is more important, the protection of society by a free and unfettered press, or the individual's claim to personal solitude? When the publication has involved commercial or false material, the court usually has sided with the individual. In this case the public interest involved was not great enough. When the publication has been a truthful or factual account of even private or personal affairs, the court usually has sided with the press. Here society's interest in a free press took precedence.[19]

Usually two defenses are advanced by the press in privacy cases: newsworthiness and consent. In the first instance, courts decide that the publication of the material, even though it invaded a person's privacy, was in the public interest. In the second, the individual simply consented to have the information published, either by signing a release or by seeing the reporter in the first place. Of course, complex arguments can be marshalled in both areas as the adversary process of a trial unfolds.

Suits in which disclosures have been protected because they are of general interest relate especially to involvement of individuals in crime as criminals (arrested, tried, convicted, acquitted, paroled, punished, or pardoned), as victims, or as police officers. Other protected newsworthy events include birth, death, marriage, divorce, old age, personal tragedies, civil suits, interesting accomplishments or behavior, events dealing with race relations, events related to substandard housing, and other intentionally public events.

Rarely is information reported in the press held not to be so protected. These few instances include the name and photo of a woman with an unusual disease, disclosure of a person's debt, photo of a woman whose dress has blown above her waist, and telephone number of a receptionist with a sexy voice.

Not until 1967 did a privacy case reach the Supreme Court of the United States. In *Time Inc.* v. *Hill* the Court extended the *New York Times* malice rule (reckless disregard or knowing falsehood) to privacy cases and ruled that in some instances the First Amendment prohibited state courts from imposing liability upon a publication for an invasion of privacy. Privacy, like libel, is an active area of the law and bears careful observation.

FREE PRESS VERSUS FAIR TRIAL

Another focal point for rights in conflict between the press and the public is in the area of free press versus fair trial, wherein the First Amendment right of a free press runs head-on into the Sixth Amendment "right to a speedy and public trial, by an impartial jury. . . ." Celebrated public trials in which the press offers heavy, detailed, and sometimes sensationalized coverage have led to considerable conflict between the press and the bar. The conflict came to a head in the mid-1960s when the American Bar Association appointed an advisory committee on fair trial and free press headed by Justice Paul C. Reardon of the Supreme Judicial Court of Massachusetts. The Reardon commission, working concurrently with a number of statewide bar and press efforts, recommended some standards for the release of material in criminal trials. The recommendations, however, were generally rejected by the press.

Although the bar and press discussions on reporting restrictions did not have the force of law, the rules they promulgated were generally adopted by many courts and by the U.S. Justice Department.[20] Agreements generally ran along the lines of this press and bar code adopted in the State of Minnesota:

RECOMMENDED GUIDELINES OF THE FAIR TRIAL–FREE PRESS COUNCIL OF MINNESOTA RELATING TO ADULT CRIMINAL PROCEEDINGS:

The following information generally SHOULD be made public at, or immediately following the time of arrest:

1. The accused's name, age, residence, employment, marital status and similar background information.
2. The substance or text of the charge, such as is, or would be contained in a complaint, indictment or information.
3. The identity of the investigating and arresting agency and the length of the investigation.
4. The circumstances immediately surrounding an arrest, including the time and place of arrest, resistance, pursuit, possession and use of weapons, and a description of items seized at the time of arrest.

The following information generally should NOT be made public at, or immediately after, the time of arrest:

1. Statements as to the character or reputation of an accused person.
2. Existence or contents of any confession, admission or statement given by the accused, or his refusal to make a statement.
3. Performance or results of tests, or the refusal of an accused to take such a test.
4. Expected content of testimony, or credibility of prospective witnesses.
5. Possibility of a plea of guilty to the offense charged or to a lesser offense, or other disposition.
6. Other statements relating to the merits, evidence, argument, opinions or theories of the case.

Cooperation among the bar, law enforcement officers, courts, and the press is substantial, especially at the local level, students of free press versus fair trial agree. In numerous cases, however, the potential for prejudicial publicity is high. In fact, one recent study linked prejudicial pretrial publicity to adverse jury verdicts.[21] The heavy press coverage of the Abscam cases made it difficult for the courts to find impartial jurors. The reasoning of courts in proceeding to try cases even in instances of heavy publicity, says Lesley Oelsner of the New York *Times*, is as follows:

> It is impossible in an age of mass communications to find reasonably intelligent jurors who have heard nothing about famous cases; defendants in sensational cases should not be freed before at least an attempt has been made to try them; the courts can often meet the problem of prejudicial pretrial publicity by delaying the trial until the publicity abates, moving the trial to a town where publicity is less extensive, sequestering the jury, ordering lawyers and witnesses not to talk to the press, and interviewing prospective jurors carefully.[22]

Although some agreements have been worked out between the press and the judicial system, the area of free press versus fair trial is by no means settled. Jack C. Landau, Supreme Court reporter for the Newhouse News Service and a trustee of the Reporters Committee for Freedom of the Press, has suggested that a long-term, bitter institutional conflict between press and courts is likely unless so-called "gag orders" by judges are controlled. Gag orders are issued without hearing or explanation when judges forbid coverage of certain proceedings. Four types of gag orders have been detailed by Landau:

> First are direct prior restraints on information obtained out of court. Second are restrictions on access to information in court. These access limitations are mechanical; they limit the numbers of reporters admitted to the courtroom. Third are restrictions on attorneys, police and other officials with responsibilities in a given case. Very frequently the press argues the prosecution has had a terrific advance start on publicity—and the defense wants its point of

view known. Finally, there is the problem of confidential sources—the cases where the attorney is ordered to divulge his source or go to jail.[23]

Fair trial versus free press is one of the liveliest points of debate between the press and the courts. In a 1979 decision (*Gannett v. DePasqualle*), the U.S. Supreme Court seemed to permit closed courtrooms during certain pretrial hearings. Just what this decision meant was unclear. The press generally called it a travesty of press rights, and even the members of the Court did not offer a very spirited defense for their much confused decision. Departing from conventional practice whereby the justices write their opinions and then remain silent, several justices went on the speaking circuit and attempted to explain just what the Court meant in the DePasqualle case. This confused things even more, and the result was that lower courts tended to close some trials. In 1980, the Supreme Court in another case, *Richmond Newspapers v. Commonwealth of Virginia,* offered a stirring defense of open criminal trials and for the first time gave protection to the right of news-gathering. The *Gannett* case ban on pretrial matters still stands, however.

Reporters need to know just what the practices of trial courts are in their individual areas. Although the Supreme Court rules do set a national standard, there are many variations in local areas.

Organizations such as the American Society of Newspaper Editors, Reporters Committee on Freedom of the Press, and American Newspaper Publishers Association have kept a close watch on this issue. In most states there are free press versus fair trial councils and compacts.

OTHER AREAS

The long-standing debate over "shield laws," recognizing the right of reporters to protect confidential sources, has raged in recent years. The heavy use of subpoena power by the Department of Justice in the 1970s, which led to some celebrated court cases, has heightened the interest in shield laws. The result has been a call for a national shield law and the passage of shield laws (some absolute, some qualified) in many states. These cases usually arise in instances when courts cite the press for contempt for refusing to reveal sources. Pointing to practical and conceptual difficulties, the Supreme Court in *Branzburg v. Hayes,* a 1972 case, said that journalists' privilege to refuse to identify sources was defined by the Court as being outside its purview. As Justice Byron White wrote in the majority opinion, "At the Federal level Congress has freedom to determine whether a statutory newsman's privilege is necessary and desirable and to fashion standards and rules as narrow or broad as deemed necessary. . . ."[24] There are occasional instances when reporters are jailed for contempt for refusing to reveal their sources. This is a matter of ethics and conscience for the reporter. Shield laws rarely provide an absolute privilege or full protection.

Of particular interest to public affairs reporters are state statutes for open meetings and open records. Although they differ considerably from state to state, the general idea is that public business should be conducted in full public view. In some instances these laws are called "sunshine" laws. Reporters should familiarize themselves with the open meetings and open records legislation of their state or efforts to obtain such statutes. It is helpful to know whether or not a school board can declare an "executive session" and refuse to admit reporters or whether a city council can have sub-rosa ways of not discussing the public business openly in council meetings. Frequently, the absence, presence, or application of open meetings and open records laws has been the cause of conflict between public officials and the press.

As might be surmised from the foregoing discussion, the application of communication law to the press should be seen in the context of journalistic ethics. The legal protection and subsequent defenses begin in court (sometimes called the court of last resort) when the interpersonal bargaining between the press and individuals or government ceases. Nevertheless, reporters need a good working knowledge of press law. One pathway toward that knowledge is as follows:

1. Take a course in press law or communication law in a college or university or attend a short course or special seminar on the subject.
2. Familiarize yourself with a major treatise on the subject (for example, Nelson and Teeter's *Law of Mass Communications* or Gillmor and Barron's superb casebook, *Mass Communication Law.*
3. Familiarize yourself with the law of your particular state or locality, either through special materials developed by local publisher associations or through Arthur B. Hanson's detailed, three-volume, state-by-state compendium, *Libel and Related Torts*. Robert D. Sack's *Libel, Slander and Related Torts* is also useful.
4. Keep a handy desk reference on press law—either one of the major treatises or a shortened version like Paul B. Ashley's *Say It Safely* or the Associated Press's *The Dangers of Libel*.
5. Follow current press law developments in *The News Media and Law* published by the Reporters Committee on Freedom of the Press; the *FOI Reports*, published by the Freedom of Information Center of the University of Missouri; or such random sources as *Editor & Publisher, Broadcasting*, and the *IRE Journal.*
6. For more detailed knowledge, search law reviews (through the *Index to Legal Periodicals*) and other legal periodicals for the current status of particular cases.
7. Watch the book reviews of such publications as *Journalism Quarterly* for materials of special interest.

The importance of a knowledge of press law in competent journalistic performance cannot be overestimated. Reporters who avoid controversy, fearing litigation unnecessarily, may be doing themselves and their public a disservice.

NOTES

[1]Sanford Ungar, *The Papers & The Papers* (New York: Dutton, 1972).

[2]Thomas I. Emerson, *The System of Freedom of Expression* (New York: Vintage Books, 1971), p. 518.

[3]Associated Press, *The Dangers of Libel*, rev. ed. (New York: AP, 1969), p. 1. See also Paul B. Ashley, *Say It Safely* (Seattle: University of Washington Press, 1966).

[4]Harold I. Nelson and Dwight L. Teeter, *Law of Mass Communications*, 2d ed. (Mineola, N.Y.: Foundation Press, 1973), p. 61.

[5]Emerson, *System of Freedom of Expression*, p. 518.

[6]See Marc A. Franklin, *Torts*, Gilbert Law Summaries, 13th ed. (Gardenia, Calif.: Harcourt, Brace, Jovanovich Legal and Professional Publications, 1978), pp. 155–63.

[7]Emerson, *System of Freedom of Expression*.

[8]Donald M. Gillmor and Jerome A. Barron, *Mass Communication Law: Cases and Comment* (Saint Paul, Minn.: West Publishing, 1974), p. 194.

[9]Ibid., p. 214.

[10]Associated Press, *Dangers of Libel*, p. 3.

[11]Nelson and Teeter, *Law of Mass Communications*, p. 140.

[12]*New York Times* v. *Sullivan*, 376 U.S. 245 (1964).

[13]See Frederic Coonrandt, "The Law of Libel Has Been All But Repealed," *Quill* 60 (February 1972), 16–19.

[14]D. Charles Whitney, "Libel: New Ground Rules for an Old Ball Game," *Quill* 62 (August 1974), 22.

[15]Robert D. Sack, *Libel, Slander and Related Problems* (New York: Practising Law Institute, 1980). For a useful comment on the current state of libel law, see Jonathan Friendly, "Double-Edged Challenge to Press Freedom," *New York Times*, March 27, 1981, p. 17.

[16]Nelson and Teeter, *Law of Mass Communications*, p. 183.

[17]See Samuel D. Warren and Louis D. Brandeis, "The Right of Privacy," *Harvard Law Review* 4 (December 1890), 193–220.

[18]Nelson and Teeter, *Law of Mass Communications*, p. 183.

[19]Don R. Pember, *Privacy and the Press, The Law, the Mass Media, and the First Amendment* (Seattle: University of Washington Press, 1972), p. 249. Pember's contention is supported in two cases: *Cantrell* v. *Forest City Publishing Co.*, 95 S. Ct. 465 (1974): and *Cox Broadcasting Corporation* v. *Cohn*, 95 S. Ct. 1029 (1975).

[20]Gillmor and Barron, *Mass Communication Law*, p. 415.

[21]"Jury Verdicts Linked to News Reports," *New York Times*, October 21, 1973, p. 23.

[22]Lesley Oelsner, "Watergate Jury Quest: Pretrial Publicity Creates a Problem That Many Believe Is Insurmountable," *New York Times*, October 11, 1974, p. 14C.

[23]Jack C. Landau, "Free Press–Fair Trial," *Criminal Law Reporter* 15 (September 4, 1974), 2489.

[24]*Branzburg* v. *Hayes*, 408 U.S. 665, 706 (1972).

7

Covering
the Legal Process

It is one of the press's great—if not greatest—responsibility to provide the essential information regarding the administration of justice,
without which no progress whatever is possible in a democratic
society.

*Curtis D. MacDougall, Covering the Courts**

Public affairs reporting has its historic roots in the coverage of courts. One
of the first collections of newspaper reportage, John Wight's *Mornings at
Bow Street* (1824), provided a moving, human glimpse of English courts. It
is appropriate that law, the legal process, and its consequences shall continue to absorb the attention of journalists in a democracy. "The law is,
among other things, a series of commands about how people in a society
ought to behave,"[1] writes political scientist Jonathan Casper. The legal
process is the mechanism by which disputes are settled when informal
interaction fails. Intensely human and rife with drama, the legal process is
also a stage on which conflict is resolved.

Because the legal process is a highly visible index of society coping
with its problems, it has been standard fare for media coverage. Even so,
"the legal process is one of the most fundamental yet least understood
aspects of American government,"[2] law professor Marc A. Franklin asserts.
In part, this lack of understanding may be due to the fact that the law and
legal process are so rarely treated by reporters in the context of their total
functioning, but rather as individual and unrelated cases. Not without
reason, the legal scholar Morris L. Cohen has written of "the lawless science

*Reprinted by permission of Prentice-Hall, Inc.

146

of our law, that codeless myriad of precedent, that wilderness of single instances."[3] For, as Cohen implies, the law is, in fact, cumulative and dynamic. Operating within the somewhat stable framework of the legal process, individual cases—the results of personal disputes or conflicts between the individual and the state—lead to legal principles and theories of recovery. The tendency for the reporter and for the citizen is to look narrowly at single instances—disputes in a vacuum—without considering the overall context of the legal process. One hears of a settlement in a civil suit or of conflicting testimony in a criminal case, but only as fragments of a larger picture.

THE LEGAL PROCESS DEFINED

To Marc Franklin, the legal process is the distance between the origin of a grievance between individuals (in a civil case)* or between individuals and the government (in a criminal case) and its final resolution in either the trial court or the appellate process. Although there are some variations in procedure between civil and criminal cases, there is much similarity in their movements. The process, using Franklin's explanation, can be described as follows:

1. *A grievance arises.* A dispute between individuals cannot be resolved at the level of personal discussion.

2. *An attorney is retained.* The aggrieved party finds his or her way to an attorney, who advises whether or not the issue should be pressed in a court case.

3. *The attorney identifies the relevant law* by examining the legal consequences of the facts of the case.

4. *The law is researched.* The attorney searches the various sources of law (statutes, constitutions, court opinions) to make a systematic determination about the chances for recovery.

5. *The court system is chosen.* In the United States, there are federal courts and state courts. In both the civil and criminal areas, federal courts deal severally with federal questions arising under the Constitution or federal statutes and with disputes between residents of different states and between states themselves. Most other matters are first handled in state courts.

6. *The correct court is chosen.* Once the correct court system is determined, the lawyer or, in some instances, law enforcement officers must choose the correct court within that system. The magnitude of the offense (in a criminal case) and the amount of damages or type of relief sought (in a civil case) will determine the court in which the case will be tried initially.

*See Appendix A, "The Guide to Legalese."

Minor cases (traffic violations, misdemeanors, small claims) are assigned to municipal or local courts, whereas more serious criminal charges, larger money claims, divorces, and real estate claims are resolved by district or circuit courts, which are ordinarily courts of first instance in most jurisdictions. The money sought or the extent of punishment that the court may render determine the choice of the correct court. All state "blue books," or governmental directories, describe the functioning of courts and the appropriate names for the particular location. Courts, their names and responsibilities, differ considerably among the various states, and reporters must learn the idiosyncracies and nuances of their own area.*

7. *The action commences.* A legal action begins when the plaintiff's attorney does two things: "(1) starts the 'pleading' stage by putting in writing the plaintiff's 'complaint' and what he wants from the defendant; and (2) takes steps to bring this 'complaint' to the defendant's attention."[4] In a criminal case, the state issues a formal charge or presents an indictment.

8. *The complaint is served.* The defendant (or party against whom an action is brought) is served with a formal complaint, itemizing the charges or grievance against him or her.

9. *The defendant's turn comes.* Once notified that he or she is to be a party in a legal dispute, the defendant also seeks an attorney who follows many of the procedures indicated earlier.

10. *A defense is chosen.* A defense is decided on by the attorney and client, and the attorney drafts an "answer" to the original complaint. The complaint and the answer are called *pleadings.* These are public records, open to the press (and public) for inspection. In a criminal case, the first stage of the defense is the entry of a plea. In a civil case, Franklin says, "almost always the defendant asserts that there are mistakes or inaccuracies in the plaintiff's case in one or more of four categories: (1) technical objections unrelated to the merits of the case; (2) disputes about the underlying legal rules implicit in the plaintiff's complaint; (3) claims that the plaintiff's fact allegations are not true or that he has omitted some vital facts; and (4) claims that the damages sought are too high."[5]

11. *Pretrial activities occur.* These are in several areas, including (a) *judgment on the pleading:* "The party making the motion asserts that with all the pleadings filed, no fact disputes remain so that there is no reason for a trial and the judge should decide the case now".[6] (b) *Discovery:* Through written interrogatories, oral depositions and by providing documents and other physical evidence, both sides share information about the case to narrow the dispute. Discovery is more extensive in civil cases than in criminal, but it is a process that virtually prevents the kind of unrealistic courtroom confessions that take place in television dramas and also makes unlikely the appearance of surprise witnesses. (c) *Conferences:* factual disputes

*See Appendix B, "Federal and State Court Structure."

are narrowed and exhibits marked by pretrial agreements and discussions.

12. *A jury is selected and the trial begins.* Although some parties may waive jury trials, jury selection is often a vital part of the case. Lawyers try to get juries that will favor their clients.

13. *The trial takes place.* The trial consists of the plaintiff's case, the defendant's case, including direct and cross-examinations, and occasional rulings by the judge on objections and motions by attorneys. Eventually, the case goes to the jury, and under the American system of justice, juries decide questions of *fact,* not questions of *law.* That is, the jury decides whether a car ran a red light at a particular time, not whether running the red light should be actionable. The jury eventually renders a verdict and the judge can accept it or grant a posttrial motion brought by the losing party.

14. *Posttrial motions are made.* These include "judgments n.o.v.," which are judgments notwithstanding the verdict. The judge rules here that the jury came to an "impossible" decision (one contrary to the evidence or the law) and renders a judgment for the other party.

15. *A judgment order is made.* In a civil case the judge concludes that the jury was correct and directs by judgment that payment of civil damages be made. In a criminal case a sentence is pronounced.

16. *Appeals are made.* Making claims that there were errors in the trial, the losing party might ask for an appeal to a higher court. Appeals in state cases go to intermediate appeals courts (in California and New York) or to the state supreme court or its equivalent. There is also an appeals structure in the federal system from district courts to circuit courts of appeal to the U.S. Supreme Court.

17. *The appeal is decided.* A decision based on briefs presented by the opposing parties is eventually rendered by the appeals court if the case is accepted for consideration.

Each phase of the legal process as sketchily outlined here is worthy of considerable study. Unfortunately, much of its dynamic nature is hidden from the public and is rarely treated by the news media. Such issues as how people find attorneys, the nature of legal fees, and pretrial conferences are largely ignored.

Although Franklin's description of the legal process as the movement from an initial grievance to the appeal structure is useful to the reporter in considering the context of most legal disputes, the term *administration of justice* has come to have more discrete meanings. Here the emphasis is on the various components of the legal system rather than on the process itself. For example, the system is seen as having three components: law enforcement agencies, or police; adjudicatory agencies, including courts and bar associations; and corrections, including jails, prisons, and facilities for forensic psychiatry. It is on these components of the system that most media coverage focuses.

Efforts to improve the quality of criminal justice in the United States during the 1970s often added a fourth component: crime prevention. It was aimed at reducing crime through preventive programs prior to police intervention or through rehabilitation programs at intermediate stages between courts and prisons.

LEGAL PROCESS COVERAGE

The complexity and scope of the legal process may work against comprehensive analytical reporting. A cursory examination of most newspapers and newscasts indicates that there is more news about crime, police activities, individual trials, and prison riots than interpretive reporting of legal trends, law firms, performance of judges, or penology. Of course, this coverage is in line with conventional news standards and news judgment.

The 1966 Reardon commission (on fair trial versus free press) report found considerable cooperation between reporters and those charged with the administration of justice. That cooperation has found expression in many ways. In its 1978 revision of the Fair Trial and Free Press Standards, the American Bar Association approved a less restrictive standard on how much attorneys could say to the press without endangering the right of a defendant to a fair trial. "Any threat to trial fairness is a matter of degree that will vary with the nature of the information disclosed and the circumstances under which the extrajudicial statement is made," the association said.[7] More recently, the changing technology of photography has helped relax restrictions on taking pictures in courtrooms by both television and still cameras. Some of those restrictions went back to the 1930s and the Lindbergh case, regarded now as a media circus.[8]

But the journalist covering the legal system is often an "outsider" treated with a cold correctness. Legal sociologist Abraham S. Blumberg says that personnel throughout the legal system "are deeply suspicious of—almost hostile to any effort to unearth embarrassing material."[9] In his daily activity, a member of this system soon learns, says Blumberg, "that too often the fact that he 'talked too much' meant conviction for an accused person." Blumberg continues, "This virtually hostile attitude toward 'outsiders' is in large measure a psychological defense against the inherent deficiencies of assembly-line justice, so characteristic of our major criminal courts. Intolerably large case loads, which must be handled with limited resources and personnel, potentially subject the participants in the court community to harsh scrutiny from appellate courts and other public and private sources of condemnation."[10]

News media sources in law enforcement, courts, and corrections, as well as others interested in legal problems, promote different images of the legal process. In a study of the criminal justice system from a defendant's perspective, Jonathan Casper suggests three images of reality:

> (1) On television we see a dramatic, carefully controlled process, in which each side is represented by committed, often brilliant attorneys jealously guarding and defending the rights of their clients. Mistakes may be made, but truth and justice generally triumph: the guilty are convicted and punished, and the innocent are vindicated and set free. We see the adversary process at its finest, operating to protect the rights of defendants and to arrive at a judgment conforming to absolute truth.
> (2) If, on the other hand, we listen to professional prosecutors, police officers and critics of recent Supreme Court decisions, a somewhat different picture emerges. We see a victimized majority and hamstrung police and prosecutors, unable to deal effectively with those who violate the law. We see a scale balanced unevenly in favor of the criminal defendant. These critics conjure up the image of the crazed bad man—the mugger, the rapist, the junkie—free to pursue his heinous activities because of procedural protections that hamper his capture, conviction, and punishment.
> (3) If, finally, we examine the growing body of reformist literature dealing with the criminal justice system, we find the image of an assembly line. The system is a machine which begins with raw material consisting of those arrested. They are processed and emerge as a product; the convicted criminal, sentenced to prison or released on probation. Between arrest and disposition are a series of points on the assembly line. . . .[11]

Naturally, these points of view are fostered by different, but equally self-serving, sources for the reporter. Yet too often, coverage of law enforcement agencies, the courts, and the corrections system today has serious flaws. As journalism professor David L. Grey points out,

> The press often handles such complex fields as law by preoccupation with personalities, drama, action and other often-superficial issues. *Time* magazine is the institution, of course, which has probably most glamorized news about names; but skimming or scanning most daily newspaper front pages or television newscasts shows perhaps even more preoccupation with who-just-did-what-to-whom rather than the more substantive issues of what-is-going-on-and-why.[12]

With the antagonism between police and press in the 1960s, particularly during the demonstrations and riots, has come criticism of the press's role in covering such events. A study team, reporting to the National Commission on the Causes and Prevention of Violence, found that some police complaints about press coverage were justified:

> There is some explanation for the media-directed violence. Camera crews on at least two occasions did stage violence and fake injuries. Demonstrators did sometimes step up their activities for the benefit of TV cameras. Newsmen and photographers' blinding lights did get in the way of police clearing

streets, sweeping the park and dispersing demonstrators. Newsmen did, on occasion, disobey legitimate police orders to 'move' or 'clear the streets.' News reporting of events did seem to the police to be anti-Chicago and anti-police.[13]

Other observers have found that coverage of police news suffers because of attitudes and methods police reporters bring with them. "Too soon," writes Police Lieutenant James Robertson in the *Twin Cities Journalism Review*, "the eager young reporter attempts to flex his journalistic muscle, and rather than develop rapport—at least an avenue of sound communication—he attempts to demonstrate to his superiors how adept he is in dealing with the police. Soon, there is a head-on confrontation with the police, and the reporter's effectiveness is soon diminished substantially, if not completely."[14]

Coverage of corrections institutions—prisons, lockups, and work-houses—has only recently begun to deal with substantive issues. "For the most part," writes attorney William J. vanden Heuvel, "the press has accepted arbitrary and ridiculous regulations that keep it from reporting the true nature of our institutional tragedies. It has been content to report events such as prison riots."[15] He explains,

> The responsibility of the news media is to lift the veil of secrecy surrounding the nation's prisons to give voice to both the victims of crime and of the criminal justice system, and to reveal the incredible waste that our jails and penitentiaries represent. . . . The simple conclusion is that the reporting of criminal justice has been grossly inadequate to the country's need. Billions of dollars are being spent on a system that does not work. Vigilant observation of the exercise of governmental power is a basic need in a democracy. Yet large sectors of the criminal justice system—from police power through procedures of the courts into the walled recesses of the prisons—operate practically without objective scrutiny and evaluation.[16]

Some corrections officials also see the need for more complete press coverage of penal institutions and issues. In evaluating press coverage during his administration, David Fogel, former commissioner of corrections in Minnesota, writes,

> It is my belief that public information is vital to correcting corrections. The cost of an "open access to the media" philosophy can sometimes be burdensome, but I believe necessary. I would have liked more analysis than was present. Sometimes the individual parts do not make up the whole. Programs or incidents taken serially were not well connected to indicate the real issue. For example, an escape, a runaway, a lockup for a non-violent demonstration all seem, as individual acts, to show "chaos" in the prison—the press very infrequently "put it all together."[17]

Part of the problem is the reactive nature of much of public affairs reporting. Typically, journalists wait for "events" to lead them and their news organizations toward coverage. It is not unusual, for example, for a crowded county jail to languish for months, barely noted except in items on the county commission budget. But let one prisoner die or a riot erupt and the jail and its problems suddenly become more visible in the local media. The same pattern emerges in the coverage of state and federal penal institutions. A bloody riot focuses attention on a crowded prison in a way that few other dramatic events can. Yet quality reporting can often follow the event. Two months after thirty-three inmates were murdered in a devastating riot at the New Mexico state penitentiary in 1980, a team of reporters from the *Albuquerque Journal* sifted through the series of blunders and mistakes which fueled the riot. "The state didn't lose control of its penitentiary; it never had control," the report concluded. "For decades, the state turned its back on the prison system. Officials ignored the telltale signs of impending disaster: overcrowding, understaffing, inadequate funding and repeated inmate disturbances."[18]

REPORTING FUNCTIONS
AND THE LEGAL PROCESS

A heightened awareness of the importance of legal process and criminal justice stories has been evident as thoroughly researched stories about the quality of judges, police performance, specific crimes (such as rape), and court procedures have had generous treatment by various publications and broadcast outlets. The *Minneapolis Tribune,* for example, assigned three reporters in 1974 to examine the quality of juvenile justice. They wrote a seventeen-part series that included careful examination of juvenile court cases and extensive interviews with juvenile offenders, corrections officials, and judges.[19]

These articles, and others like them, indicate a widening role of the reporter covering police, courts, and corrections. What should be the objectives of the reporter in these areas? Several come to mind:

Helping to control and prevent crime. Although reporters are not police auxiliaries, and ought not to function as a publicity arm for police departments, one of the hoped-for effects of thorough coverage of crime is to prevent it.

Helping to provide due process. By considering the administration of justice from the standpoint of the defendant in both civil and criminal cases, the press can help prevent maladministration by police, judges, and others. This approach can also give readers and viewers an empathetic view of "what it is like to be arrested, go to court, be convicted and perhaps be sent to prison."[20]

Critical surveillance of the legal process.   By exposing activities and practices not in the public interest, the press can help the legal system function in the best interests of all. Reporters who take this role seriously have exposed police corruption, helped unfairly convicted defendants prove their innocence, and promoted, as a side effect, legislation to improve the legal process.

Making sense out of single cases.   Interpretive reporting can help the public understand what the fragmented single instances mean. Often, crimes are reported as single incidents. In many large newspapers, only major crimes are reported in any detail. By examining single cases in context, and as a group, the reporter can help make sense of the process. The *Minneapolis Star*, for example, summarized twenty-five murders in the city in a six-month period.[21] The articles included a breakdown of the victims and suspects by age, race, and sex, as well as by location of the murders; the stories also drew comparisons between Minneapolis homicides and national patterns. "The fact remains that nearly 360 people were killed with handguns in three years," wrote *Atlanta Journal* reporter Hank Ezell in 1981 following a similar study. "Most rated two or three paragraphs in the newspapers and some of them didn't even get that. The squibs that did appear had a monotonous, business-as-usual feel to them, even to casual newspaper readers. But if one looks at a few individual cases, they are not all routine." Ezell found that handguns were used in more than 60 percent of the cases, that victims and suspects often knew each other, and that both were often poor.[22]

In all these functions, reporters should "humanize" their stories, by making them understandable to laypersons. Most citizens have only an occasional brush with the legal system, usually in the form of a court appearance for a minor traffic violation, a minor civil claim against another person, or a common legal matter such as a divorce or legal title search on a piece of property. Most citizens never become defendants in a criminal felony case nor become entangled in a complex civil suit nor find themselves indicted by a grand jury. Most people's exposure to the trial process, for example, may come from television shows such as "Perry Mason," but such "trials" bear little resemblance to reality. The reporter, aware of the reader's lack of knowledge, should be careful to provide information that is understandable.

This inside-the-system view can sometimes be accomplished with compelling power. Consider these examples:

New York Times writer Barbara Basler profiled twenty-year-old Harvel Wilder, a street-hardened criminal with eleven arrests and five convictions who had avoided prison. He would stalk the streets of Manhattan with a revolver "in search of people who had money. He made it clear that while the city feared him, he had very little fear of the city or the massive system it had set up to deter, try and punish him."[23]

In a series of articles on how the criminal justice system works in Broward County, *Fort Lauderdale* (Fla.) *News* reporters Marion Hale and Dan Lovely looked at the inequities of race, the nature of the crime, and whether the defendant could afford a private attorney. They used actual cases, comparing differences point by point:

> For stabbing another 14-year-old boy three times and leaving him bleeding on a Wilton Manors street corner, Matt Thompson was placed on 10 years' probation and sent off to a camp for juvenile delinquents for a year.
>
> For shooting his girlfriend in the back during a quarrel at Hallandale High School, William Preston Sands was sentenced by a different judge to 10 years in the Florida State Prison at Starke.
>
> Both Thompson and Sands had spent time in mental hospitals. Both were teen-agers when they were convicted of aggravated battery. But that is where the similarities end.
>
> William Sands entered the Broward court system at the age of 17 with one strike against him—he's black. From the moment of his arrest, he was more likely to be convicted than Thompson, who is white, and more likely to end up in prison.[24]

Every story should offer the reader enough information to understand the case fully. One obvious task for the reporter, therefore, is to translate technical legal jargon into understandable English. To do that, the reporter should have a clear understanding of legal principles and terms. (Legal research is discussed later in this chapter.) This necessity does not mean that the public affairs reporter must be an attorney, although an increasing number of reporters, such as attorney–reporter Fred Graham, who covers the U.S. Supreme Court for CBS News, are trained in the law.

COVERING CIVIL AND CRIMINAL ACTIONS

Writing about civil and criminal cases requires different investigative, research, and writing strategies. Civil law cases generally, but not always, require more legal research by the reporter. Precedents and legal interpretations are cited more often in civil cases. In legal research, the reporter learns how the specific cases relate to trends and developments in the law. By research of cases on racial integration, for instance, the reporter can grasp important changes that led up to, and followed, the U.S. Supreme Court's landmark desegregation case, *Brown* v. *Board of Education* (1954). Since civil suits often involve several plaintiffs and defendants, the reporter should be careful to understand the legal position of each and to weight them fairly and accurately in news stories. In interpretive reports, such as an examination of divorce law, the reporter needs to interview plaintiffs and defendants as well as authorities on the issue who are not parties to the cases.

Accuracy is vital in reporting all types of public affairs, and it is particularly important in criminal court cases. Criminal statutes are specific, and to identify incorrectly the crime of which a person is accused is as serious an error as a false accusation of crime. Auto theft, for example, differs in some states from "unauthorized use of a motor vehicle," although both may be felonies. The reporter who assumes one is the other without checking the statute is simply being careless. It is the kind of carelessness for which reporters and their publications may have to pay libel damages.

Criminal cases generally don't require the extensive legal research of civil cases, but the writing techniques are just as rigorous. Every effort must be made to place the trial, arrest, hearing, or other criminal proceeding in context. This effort could well involve extensive interviewing. Because prosecution officials—district attorneys, police, investigators—may be more accessible to the court reporter assigned to cover the courthouse, there is a tendency for the reporter not to interview the defendant. At the very least, the reporter should attempt to contact the defendant's attorney, particularly if the case appears to be one worthy of extended coverage.

All of this discussion indicates an approach to legal reporting that goes beyond the superficial. "The trouble is," writes one jurist, "too many newspapermen and perhaps too many lawyers and judges *act* too often, again, at least on a day-to-day basis, *as if* these things were neither important nor interesting, and scarcely worth our time." He cites specifics:

> We can improve our techniques. We can cover the ball game, the trial itself, and the real evidence in court—not the before, through the eyes of a self-serving sheriff, or the after, through the eyes of the winner or loser. We can use more discretion and acuteness. We can check both sides. We can describe and report the physical facts, even help gather them; but we should not take sides in conclusions. Lawyers and judges and juries are occasionally wrong—how do newsmen get to be so cocksure? On sources, we can ask ourselves the questions: is he in a position to find out? is he smart enough to find out? did he find out the truth? does he have any reason to lie? would he lie if he did have a reason? has he told me the truth?[25]

Most criminal trials begin with a police investigation, followed by the filing of a formal complaint by a prosecutor or indictment by a grand jury. The reporter who wants to cover such legal actions accurately must have a firm understanding of the police investigations that precede the courtroom activity.

COVERING POLICE AND LAW
ENFORCEMENT AGENCIES

Police reporters must be able to write accurately and concisely on fast-breaking news stories such as crimes, traffic accidents, fires, and natural disasters. They must be able to convey human emotions accurately and sympathetically without being maudlin, for every crime and tragedy has one or more victims. They must be able to convey police attitudes without being either "copper-hearted" or overly critical. In short, they must be effective interviewers and writers with considerable energy and enthusiasm for journalism, since the police beat is a demanding one.

The relationship between police and press is often strained. As Professor Arthur Niederhoffer, a former New York City police officer, explains: "Distrust and suspicion, so deeply imbued in policemen, often alienate those agencies upon whom they depend: the press and the courts. The police need the support of the press in order to clarify their attitudes for the public. They need the cooperation of the courts because police arrests must be validated by conviction in court. Yet the police often take pains to offend journalists and judges by impugning their motives."[26] When Niederhoffer surveyed 220 police officers, he found that 72 percent believed that newspapers in general "seem to enjoy giving an unfavorable slant to news concerning the police, and prominently play up police misdeeds rather than virtues." For police officers with between two and twelve years' experience, the figure was 95 percent.[27] As a report to the National Commission on the Causes and Prevention of Violence suggests, police–press relations are particularly strained during civil disorders. The *Report of the National Commission on Civil Disorders,* which studied the causes of riots in the 1960s, found that

> A recurrent problem in the coverage of last summer's disorders was friction and lack of cooperation between police officers and working reporters. Many experienced and capable journalists complained that policemen and their commanding officers were at best apathetic and at worst overtly hostile toward reporters attempting to cover a disturbance. Policemen, on the other hand, charged that many reporters seemed to forget that the task of the police is to restore order.[28]

The experienced police reporter recognizes the importance of maintaining trustworthy police contacts. Although some officers are especially critical of the news media, probably every police department has some persons who get along well with the Fourth Estate. These may be officers intent on being promoted or on running for election as county sheriff, or they may simply be dedicated police officers who recognize that the press, as well as the police, has duties to perform. Such officers may be found at every rank, and the reporter who does not seek them out may miss many important news stories. Many officers do not want publicity themselves, but will "tip off" a trusted reporter to a particularly interesting story. Many such stories will be "events," but such police contacts may help the public affairs reporter "get beneath" that kind of story and probe important issues in law enforcement, criminal justice, and corrections.

There is a line here, obviously, that the experienced reporter soon learns not to cross. A reporter on any beat can become too chummy with the news sources, and in police reporting, that may lead to special problems. The reporter who has become a close friend of a policeman may find it difficult to write about corruption in the department. The lines of cooperation and adversarial combat are sometimes particularly elastic in practice. "There is virtual unanimity within journalism . . . that the primary obligation of the press in reporting about criminal activity is to serve, both in fact and in public perception, as an instrument of public information, not as an arm of law enforcement," writes the National News Council. "But the consensus on keeping this precept paramount leaves latitude for wide differences on where, if at all, to fix the boundary. . . ."[29]

ORGANIZATION OF POLICE DEPARTMENTS

There are many types of law enforcement agencies in the United States, and reporters assigned to cover them in their localities should familiarize themselves with structures, overlapping duties, and jurisdictions. Typically, police agencies have structured chains of command, and the department is usually headed by a chief or a public safety director. Depending on the department's size, there may be one or several deputy chiefs, and beneath them in authority, various divisions, typically headed by captains and lieutenants. These divisions often include traffic, homicide, theft and burglary, juvenile, planning and research, and license inspection. If the department is in a large city, patrol officers will generally be assigned by precincts, each headed by a captain or lieutenant. Large cities may have specialized divisions as well, such as morals and vice and narcotics. The reporter is likely to find several types of law enforcement agencies, including:

Municipal police departments   Most cities, towns, and villages have these departments. Generally, they handle traffic control and criminal apprehensions.

Sheriffs   Sheriffs are elected officials generally, and their jurisdiction is normally countywide. Along with traffic patrol and other law enforcement functions, sheriffs and their deputies often maintain jails and lockups, provide court bailiffs, and in some areas, collect taxes and serve legal papers such as subpoenas.

Highway patrols and state police Some states have state police with crime-investigation powers. Others have patrols whose principal duties are the surveillance of state highways. In a few states, bureaus of criminal apprehension buttress local and county law enforcement agencies.

Federal agencies The FBI, U.S. marshals, Internal Revenue Service agents, U.S. customs officers, postal inspectors, and other federal law enforcement officers are found in many large cities. These groups have differing jurisdictions, and they vary from press-shy to publicity-seeking.

POLICE INFORMATION

Police departments, like other governmental agencies, have made important changes in recent years in their records-keeping systems. In some departments, the reporter may find information being logged on offense reports and arrest reports. In other departments, arrest and offense information may be in computerized form. Whatever the form, the police reporter will find that for day-to-day news items, these two types of reports will be most helpful. Offense reports are made out for all crimes and generally include the type of offense, the victim, and other details. They are also made out for noncriminal activities, such as accidents and lost children. Arrest reports, sometimes called "show ups" or "booking sheets," identify arrested suspects, normally by name, age, and address. They usually include a brief statement of probable cause for the arrest and the statute or ordinance number under which the arrest was made. Departments keep other types of records, such as suspect photographs, supplemental reports on serious crimes, and reports on alleged criminal activities, such as gambling.

Normally, the police reporter will have access to offense and arrest reports, but this is by no means standard. "Moreover," writes communications researcher Michael J. Petrick, "police may refuse access to the police blotter [arrest reports] as a form of 'punishment' for a non-cooperative newsman, or for other reasons of self-interest."[30] In most states, he concludes, control of police arrest information is in the hands of local police authorities. "Occasionally, these decisions [about access] come in the form of municipal legislation and municipal court decisions. More often, however, they are administrative instruments in the form of departmental regulations, unwritten rules or 'working agreements' between the police and press."[31] Police officials tend to guard reports carefully, and the reporter who wants access may have to be careful not to offend police officials needlessly. This doesn't mean that the critical story should never be written; indeed, sometimes it is essential and is welcomed by police officials who are interested in the furtherance of police professionalism. Nonetheless, reporters who write a critical story short on facts and long on unsupported allegations will find themselves faced with an immediate and extensive stone wall. Other types of police reports are normally not available to reporters until they have "proven" themselves to the police to be "trustworthy." Many experienced police reporters maintain a few close contacts in the department who will sometimes provide such information on a "background" basis only.

HANDLING POLICE NEWS: SOME CAUTIONS

Accuracy

Regardless of the type of police record, the reporter must exercise a high degree of caution in using police information. It is not unusual to find a wrong name, age, or address in a police report, and the reporter who accepts police information without question will soon be making mistakes. The best rule of thumb for reporters is to check the facts themselves.

Fairness

Occasionally, police arrest a suspect and later release him or her without formal charge. Some editors and educators believe the ethical course is to wait for the charge—in the form of a criminal complaint or indictment—to be issued before identifying a suspect. Some publications routinely ignore this rule of thumb. In highly newsworthy situations, most reporters and editors would not hesitate to report the arrest, say, of the mayor on an armed robbery charge before the formal complaint is issued.

Crime Statistics

Reporters should be particularly skeptical of the "crime statistics" press release. At regular intervals, law enforcement agencies issue crime statistics, and whether crime goes up or down, the reports normally get considerable media coverage. But the reporter should be aware that the statistics are often misleading. Police departments are not above showing a "crime increase" if they are seeking a budget increase; nor are they above showing a "crime decrease" to give the public the impression they are doing their job well. Crime statistics are based on "reported crime," not on all crime. Too often, a reporter raps out a lead like "Crime was up 10 percent in the county in 1981 compared with 1980." Because only a fraction of actual crime is reported to law enforcement agencies, it is misleading to imply that the statistics represent the full picture of criminal activity. The proportion of crimes reported fluctuates widely from community to community and sometimes within the same community from year to year.

Police and Politics

At election time, police reporters may find their duties similar to the public affairs reporter who is covering politics. Although certainly not the general rule, some police and sheriff's offices insist that the chief or sheriff announce the solving of crimes. And it is not a coincidence that such releases become more common during campaigns or when the city's police budget needs public support. In short, the astute police reporter will question whether such "news stories" are legitimate.

WRITING THE POLICE STORY

How could the public affairs reporter, using techniques and strategies mapped out in the first part of this book, research, investigate, and write stories about law enforcement that go beneath the "event"? What tactics might be used? Obviously, the approach to any one story may depend, in part, on the nature of the topic itself, and the guidelines suggested here are not meant to be prescriptive. But let's take a hypothetical example:

The legal process reporter for a metropolitan newspaper writes several short stories during a several-month period about individuals killed or injured in high-speed chases with police. Perhaps, the reporter wonders, police are not being adequately trained in driving techniques under stress. Perhaps there need to be revisions in the state law that allows a police officer to pursue a fleeing suspect. On this story, the reporter might begin by building a careful statistical base. What is the rate of traffic accidents for police officers? How many officers have been injured in such accidents in the past five years? How many innocent bystanders or suspects have been hurt in crashes resulting from high-speed chases? These questions could be answered by careful examination of records from, say, the state department of motor vehicles, the highway patrol, and local law enforcement agencies. The reporter might also examine the training program for officers. How many hours of driving training are included in the police training program? Who does the training? Is that person qualified? Here the reporter might examine the training programs in other states, pulling information from police professional journals or magazines. The interviewing on such a story might be extensive, including interviews with the captain of the city police traffic division or patrol division, an academic professional with the local university's criminal justice studies department, the training personnel at the state police academy, attorneys, and legislators. Professional organizations, such as the state chiefs of police association, might also be able to provide useful information. To round out the story, interviews might be conducted with hospital and medical personnel, the victims of such chases, and of course, some police officers who have been involved in high-speed chases. The reporter might want to use direct observation here, as well, by riding along in a police vehicle on emergency runs. At the writing stage, the story might contain a main story and several sidebars, and perhaps some statistical tables, carefully explained. Because the issue is a complex one, the story might well discuss contrasting views. A similar approach might be adapted to other stories involving police training, such as gun training and arrest techniques.

If the story had involved allegations against police, such as an investigation of police brutality, the reporter might have broadened the research base further. Careful, specific statements by alleged victims would be needed, and to be doubly safe, the reporter might seek signed affidavits from interview subjects.

Whatever the subject or approach, the reporter covering the law enforcement part of the criminal justice system quickly learns to place events in context carefully. In its comprehensive report on blacks in Detroit, the *Detroit Free Press* devoted considerable space to reviewing what it called "a past of racism" on the part of Detroit police. It also traced the increasing numbers of black officers on the force and the appointment of a black police chief in 1976. But the paper was careful also to review the career of one tough black detective who was respected but feared in the black community.[32] The *St. Petersburg Times* took a similar comprehensive view in a series of articles on how blacks in that city live. The paper conducted interviews with nearly 900 residents for an opinion survey, then followed up with interviews of reporters and analysis. The result was a survey, but one with strong touches of the personal:

> Though black residents believe they receive unequal treatment from police in St. Petersburg, they want more police patrols in their neighborhoods.
> Ask 58-year-old Katherine Bivens. She lives in a ground-floor apartment on 22nd Street S, on the fringe of the highest crime zone in the city.
> She welcomes the presence of police officers, expresses admiration for their work and believes the community does not appreciate them enough.
> "They're human beings too," Mrs. Bivens says, sweeping the dust from the front porch of her ground-floor apartment. "They're taking an awful chance with their lives out there."[33]

Handling such sensitive matters as an ongoing police investigation or corruption within a police department can be particularly touchy and difficult. The reporter must develop good sources but must be careful not to fall into their control.

COVERING THE COURTS

Earlier in this chapter, it was suggested that there is a widening role for the public affairs reporter in covering the legal process. Several objectives were suggested: helping to control and prevent crime, helping to assure due process, critical surveillance of the legal process, and making sense out of single cases. How can the reporter meet these objectives?

One way is to see courts as an integral part of the system of justice which includes police, corrections, the legal profession, and citizen groups. In covering these diverse groups, the reporter needs to have some sense of the "big picture" to avoid falling into the limited day-to-day coverage of trials, arraignments, hearings, and motions that make up the daily court calendar and provide the bulk of court news for American newspapers. "So, in analyzing press coverage of the courts and the law," writes Professor Grey, "there are many reasons for doubting the 'educational value' of such actual news leads and headlines as: 'Supreme Court Convicts Martin Luther King' and 'Supreme Court Frees Tim Leary' or 'Court Denies Protest by (Chicago 7) (Manson) (Angela).' Such emphasis is usually not inaccurate or 'wrong'; it is instead simply stressing too much the actors and the action at the expense of such important legal questions as rights of dissent and of the accused."[34]

The need for writing news stories in which news is seen as a process, in which systemic issues are dealt with, is suggested by other critics of the press's coverage of public affairs. Professor Todd Hunt writes that "if the self-reflexiveness of event-centered reporting is to be avoided, news media will have to nurture a whole new breed of information gatherers. They will have to be people who are capable of going into a situation . . . and studying the event at a generic level. 'What's going on here? What are these people doing? How are they using this event? Are they all using it in the same way; if not, what differences and variations are there?'"[35] Court news, traditionally, has been oriented toward events. Arraignments, trials, pleas, motions, arguments—all appear on court calendars on specific days, and the reporter who covers courts may be tempted to "scan the calendar" looking for "interesting" news stories on a day-to-day basis. Recent articles on police reporting suggest that coverage is generally focused toward "covering the crime." "Police reporters," writes one observer, "have become specialists in the art of listening to police radios and using the telephone. Communications are so rapid and thorough that *a reporter need only lift up a telephone receiver, make a few calls, and a story is virtually complete.*"[36]

But an increasing number of observers recognize that this approach to crime and court news is not adequate. "Urban courts are a disaster area," writes Professor David B. Sachsman. "They are understaffed and poorly managed. And while some court reporters have clearly documented the problems of the judicial system, most are too busy with day-to-day coverage."[37] Illinois Circuit Judge James O. Monroe, Jr., concludes that on some topics, there is too much coverage, but on other topics, the coverage has been inadequate.

> Delay in court, the pileup of cases, the appalling bad habits of lawyers and judges, the simple remedies that are ignored—these have scarcely been touched except in petulance and periodic squawks. In every court, state and federal, and in all divisions in local courts, there are serious stories in the statistics of cases on file (the inventory), cases being filed (the input), and cases disposed of (dispositions or pace). Law reviews and bench and bar reports provide over-all studies and viewpoints. Trends in civil torts and criminal case disposition represent major philosophic developments of importance. On the dockets of all courts, we ought to know what cases are *not* called, which are reduced, which are lost or ignored or conveniently forgotten. Yet there continues to be too little coverage of all these things.[38]

Covering the courts as part of the legal process, these writers suggest, means being able to stand back from day-to-day reporting and to look for systemic issues. Process-centered news is not necessarily current.

The reporter might examine the grand jury system, as did the *Los Angeles Times*. It discussed the grand jury's strengths and weaknesses, cited current thinking of legal scholars, and provided historical perspective on how grand juries originated. The reports included interviews with members of the grand jury, together with suggestions for changes and modification of the grand jury system.[39] Or the reporter might use new social science techniques, discussed in detail by Meyer in *Precision Journalism* (see Chapter 5), to examine criminal justice in a court system, as did the *Fort Lauderdale* (Fla.) *News* in a 1980 series. As these and other stories indicate, reporters assigned to cover courts need not restrict themselves to day-to-day events.*

DIFFERENT COURTS, DIFFERENT STRATEGIES

Within the court component of the legal system, there are different courts, of varying complexity and remoteness from the local scene, and these may require different reporting strategies. In local courts, the reporter may be able to become quite friendly with individual judges, attorneys, and law enforcement officials. Normally, these courts are rather informal, and the reporter sometimes needs to work closely with court officials and personnel.

District courts, or courts of original jurisdiction or of "first instance," normally have complex rules of procedure, particularly on such matters as

---

*See Appendix C, "Criminal Justice and Criminal Trial Process."

the presentation of evidence and the taking of testimony. Few cases go to trial. In the typical civil case the parties agree to an out-of-court settlement, and in the typical criminal case the defendant pleads guilty to a lesser offense. But some cases do, of course, go to trial, and it is there, in the courtroom, that the reporter's abilities are most severely tested. Reporters must weigh hours of testimony, and perhaps piles of evidence, and from that mass select the most important items for their news story. They must judge the continuing questions of excessive publicity, yet provide readers with accurate and complete accounts of the trial proceedings. This task becomes particularly difficult during the taking of testimony. One witness may contradict another, and the purpose of calling a particular witness may not be clearly stated but only implied. Reporters must take special care to balance their reports: a too-heavy emphasis on either the prosecution or defense risks distortion. At the same time reporters must watch out for grandstanding, behavior and remarks by attorneys intended as much for the press as for the jury. Beyond the obvious need for accuracy, reporters should try to catch the flavor of an important or interesting trial, and yet do so in a way that is neither sensational nor maudlin. And as if that weren't enough, reporters must stand back from the trial as an "event" and ask themselves questions about the administration of justice, due process, and the quality of justice as suggested by the trial. In short, they must see the trial as part of, but not the whole, legal process.

At the district court level, the reporter is also likely to run into other components of the system, such as the grand jury. Rather than simply covering the indictments and "no bills" that are routine, the reporter might well attempt to examine the components in context, providing the reader with perspective. And this objective can be accomplished in writing that is both dramatic and informative. *Los Angeles Times* reporter Gene Blake, in a 1974 report on the grand jury system, for example, began his story this way:

> Twenty-three pairs of eyes—seemingly cold and distrusting but perhaps merely bored and apathetic—stare at a lone witness seated in a somber chamber behind a locked and closely guarded door.
>
> He fidgets and glances nervously about. There is the man asking him the probing question—the prosecuting attorney. There is the steno-typist, carefully taking down every word for possible future use.
>
> And there are the men and women behind the 23 pairs of eyes—all his fellow citizens—holding in their hands the fearsome power known as "indictment."
>
> There is no lawyer to sit beside the witness, to give him advice and perhaps ask additional questions of him and other witnesses who may precede or follow. There is no judge to referee. There is no audience to pierce the veil of secrecy.
>
> This is the grand jury.
>
> It is a venerable institution, with roots going back to 12th century and ingrained by the American founding fathers in the Bill of Rights.

It has been called a "protective bulwark standing solidly between the ordinary citizen and an overzealous prosecutor"—which, at one point in its evolution, it was.

But hardly anyone believes the grand jury is serving that function today.[40]

Seeing the components of the legal system in context becomes particularly important when the reporter covers federal courts, for rulings here often affect state court decisions and the functioning of state and local agencies. From obscenity and the death penalty to abortion, reapportionment, and busing to achieve racial integration, federal court rulings in recent years have had an important impact at the state and local level. Though most public affairs reporters will never cover a case before the U.S. Supreme Court, the Court's decisions are often very important to the reporter at the local or state level. Local judges, in their rulings, often cite Supreme Court rulings, and the reporter who hopes to cover these issues well should be familiar with the cases that are relevant. Perhaps reporters cannot read every federal court ruling, but they should at least read summaries and excerpts.

The court reporter must also humanize the legal process. Too often, the law is presented as a complex monster defeatable only by lawyers and judges and others who know its terms, scope, applications, and quirks. One task of the reporter in this field is to make legal institutions intelligible. That function serves a high philosophical purpose of affirming the rule of law in a democratic society, but in more immediate terms, it forms the basis of solid, interpretive reporting. "First, learn the process," admonishes reporter Dick Krantz of the *Louisville Times*. "Learn how cases are disposed. Learn what the shorthand on the docket means. It's very confusing. The docket is your key to the lower courts. . . ." Adds the late Gerald White of the *Cincinnati Enquirer*, "Part of investigating the court system is breaking down the hypocrisy. There is more hypocrisy per square inch in the courts than in any other place in the world. . . . Get the law. Find out what is supposed to be done. Then go and see what actually is being done."[41]

LEGAL RESEARCH

Unless they wish to rely entirely on personal sources, many of them self-serving, in covering the legal process, public affairs reporters must gain some knowledge of legal research methods. The legal research resources available to the reporter may vary from one community to another, ranging from a large university law library to a lawyer's private, working collection. In between there are legal libraries and collections in courthouses, city halls, community libraries, and law firms. No community is without some rudimentary collection of legal materials.

Learning something about legal research is useful to the reporter in several ways. It can provide context and background for various legal process stories, ranging from individual cases to legal trends. It can also help the reporter ferret out stories that are not immediately evident in a superficial observation of the procedures followed by courts, law enforcement, or corrections. Ideally, reporters should search legal materials on their own, but they should also consult attorneys and others schooled in the law for help in interpretation. Without some formal training, reporters should not second-guess trained attorneys, but legal research will help them formulate better questions and should result in more understandable and knowledgeable stories.

The public affairs reporter may want to make use of some of the following materials:

Research guides   Several research guidebooks list major sources of American law and help the reader find them. They include such works as Morris L. Cohen, *Legal Research in a Nutshell* (West, 1978), Miles O. Price and Harry Bitner, *Effective Legal Research* (Little Brown, 1969), J. Myron Jacobstein and Ray M. Mersky, *Fundamentals of Legal Research* (Foundation Press, 1977), James A. Sprowl, *A Manual for Computer-Assisted Legal Research* (American Bar Foundation, 1976). These are essentially guidebooks to law libraries and collections of legal materials, and they explain how to search out information. Also essential is a copy of *A Uniform System of Citation*, published by the Harvard Law Review Association. This pamphlet identifies various abbreviations and other legal shorthand and helps in the use of court opinions, statutes, law reviews, and other materials.

Dictionaries and encyclopedias   The search for legal definitions and brief mentions of cases in which legal principles were decided is assisted by consulting a legal dictionary. The best-known are *Black's Law Dictionary*, *Ballentine's*, and *Bouvier's*. For more detailed treatment of legal issues, consult legal encyclopedias such as *Corpus Juris Secundum*, published by the West Publishing Co., and *American Jurisprudence 2d*, published by the Lawyer's Co-operative Publishing Co. Also useful to the reporter are various directories of practicing attorneys. The most comprehensive directory is *Martindale-Hubbell*, which provides a listing of lawyers by state and includes most cities and towns. In listing law firms, the directory gives an indication of who are some of the firm's clients.

Legal periodicals   Keeping pace with the law and legal developments is aided considerably by a number of legal periodicals. *U.S. Law Week* covers the Supreme Court, the federal courts, and major state cases. Law reviews, published by bar associations, university law schools, and various legal organizations, present scholarly comment on recent cases and articles about legal trends and concepts. Reading a law review article, which usually offers a nearly exhaustive search of relevant materials, can be particularly useful to the reporter and may save considerable work in the law library, although it should be noted that these articles are often adversarial by nature and push a particular legal view. Finding articles of interest in legal periodicals is assisted by the *Index to Legal Periodicals*. A "reader's guide" for legal materials, and the *Current Law Index*, a larger microfilm version of the latter is the *Legal Resource Index*. There are also *The Index to Periodical Articles Related to Law* (in nonlegal publications) and an *Index to Foreign Legal Periodicals and Collections of Essays*.

Although these materials are useful secondary sources for legal research, the major sources of law are found in court opinions and statutes. Here law libraries have vast holdings that are easy to use, once you learn about citation.

Court Decisions

Decisions of the U.S. Supreme Court are found in *United States Reports*, *The Supreme Court Reporter*, and the *Lawyer's Edition of the Supreme Court Reporter*. Federal circuit courts of appeal are covered in the *Federal Reporter*, and decisions of district courts can be found in *Federal Supplement*.

State appeals court decisions are given in officially published reports (for example, *Nevada Reporter*) but are also brought together in a regional reporter that is a part of the West Publishing Co.'s *National Reporter System*. This system divides the country into seven regions, and the decisions of appellate courts in the states in each region are collected into series of volumes. Separate series are also published for New York and California (*New York Supplement* and *California Reporter*), the two most litigious states. The West system is particularly important because a number of states have stopped publishing their own official reports and rely on the regional reporters.

In using federal or state reports, a case citation is needed. For example, 354 U.S. 449 (1957) is the citation for *Mallory* v. *United States*, a Supreme Court case. The citation is read as follows:

<u>volume</u> <u>source (U.S. Reports)</u> <u>page number</u>
354   U.S.   449

Citations are obtained from various sources, including briefs in an appeals case, in case digests, and in other materials.

Statutory and Related Materials

Statutes of the federal and state governments are another important source of law. These are usually laws passed by legislative bodies. Legal sources in addition to statutory law include constitutions, resolutions and acts of legislative bodies, treaties, interstate compacts, reorganization plans (executive decrees and administrative regulations, court rules, and local laws and ordinances). Federal public laws in the United States are published regularly in the *U.S. Code Congressional and Administrative News* shortly after enactment, and later, in *Statutes at Large* (the official publication) as well as in the *U.S. Code* and the *Federal Code Annotated*. State laws are also codified. Similarly, some cities publish compilations of their ordinances. Uniformity in state laws, part of a growing legal trend, are found in *Uniform Laws Annotated* or in specialized codes, such as the *Uniform Commercial Code*. Statutory citations are similar to case citations. For example, 18 U.S.C. 641 refers to

chapter number	source (U.S. Code)	section number
18	U.S.C.	641

This simple citation leads the searcher to the exact place in the statutes where the official law is found.

There are, of course, hundreds of other sources of information in law libraries. This discussion was designed to deal briefly with a few of them, with the understanding that serious public affairs reporters will become knowledgeable users of law libraries, whether massive ones or small collections.

THE ACTORS: LAWYERS, JUDGES, JURIES, CLERKS— AS SOURCES, HOW MUCH CAN THEY SAY?

At the beginning of this chapter, it was pointed out that the journalist covering the legal system is viewed, generally, as an "outsider" and that personnel in the legal system are often suspicious of efforts to "unearth embarrassing material." Though civil servants and bureaucrats generally may regard the press with suspicion, there are legal constraints in the legal system that inhibit the reporter in the search for news. In most states and jurisdictions, for example, grand jurors are prohibited by law from commenting on cases before them. Legal canons of ethics warn lawyers about making statements in public that might influence the outcome of pending cases. Some judges have imposed "gag" orders on the press, prohibiting the reporting of certain cases under pain of a contempt citation.

Few journalists or lawyers, however, naïvely believe that violations of such rules and laws do not occur. The "leak" from a grand jury or from a legal investigating agency has become routine. Such leaks may and do prejudice cases, but the "calculated leaks are a highly exaggerated tool of

investigative reporting," Bob Kuttner wrote in (More).[42] The motives behind the leak from a prosecutor, defense attorney, judge, or juror should
be carefully considered by the reporter. Most such leaks carry a built-in
bias; that is, the material leaked is often selective. Journalistic standards
about using leaked material vary from paper to paper and from case to
case. The reporter should consider the public interest of the material, as
well as the potential to invade a person's privacy and prejudice public
opinion against him or her. Few editors would tell a reporter to ignore
leaked materials, but many would urge the reporter to exercise great caution in weighing the newsworthiness of the leak against the potential harm
to the defendant. Journalist Walter Pincus suggests that newswriters ought
to be less willing to take leaked material and more careful to consider the
source's motives:

> While I believe newsmen should—must—use confidential sources, I also
> think the time has come for journalism as a profession to come to grips with
> one fact—the press is being manipulated more and more by sources whose
> motives for providing sensational "facts" may be newsworthy, even more
> newsworthy, than the information given. Newsmen, eager for scoops or want-
> ing just to keep up with the competition, by design or through ignorance,
> prefer to overlook the important question of *why* the information is being
> given to them.[43]

So the reporter covering the legal system, then, needs to be particularly careful about sources. Discussing a case with a juror while the case is
being heard, for example, could be grounds for a mistrial. But this doesn't
mean that the reporter should assume all avenues are closed. Some judges
will discuss cases on a not-for-attribution basis. Many lawyers will do the
same, although the reporter should be aware that such comments may be
self-serving. Generally, the reporter needs to establish the trust and confidence of court officials and personnel, and the best way to do that is to act
in a professional manner. A quote given "not for attribution" that later
shows up in the paper with a named source is likely to get the reporter very
little from that source again. Similarly, a reporter who "sneaks a peek" at
legal documents that are not part of the public record is likely to find
attorneys and judges reluctant to discuss cases frankly in the future. Usually, legal personnel are more apt to discuss a case after it has been decided
in court, and reporters may, in the meantime, have to forego some day-to-
day stories and keep their eyes on the "big" story when the case is concluded. Although some important stories may be missed, reporters may
have the perspective in the future to write a more valuable story dealing
with how the legal system functions. The Los Angeles Times's reports on the
grand jury, for instance, included interviews with former grand jury members who spoke candidly about their roles and how they believed the grand
jury functioned as an institution.[44] In his article on New York judges,

reporter Jack Newfield relied on off-the-record interviews with both attorneys and judges:

> No agency regularly monitors the courts—the press can go all out on one trial or another, but it is notoriously indifferent to the trial *system*—and no agency retains records of judicial dispositions. The Bar Association's files of formal complaints against sitting judges are closed to the public. For fear of reprisal, if not out of respect for the code of ethics, no lawyer I spoke to would let himself be quoted about a specific judge. And the mystique of respect that allows us to criticize poets, fighters, generals and Presidents, but not judges, silenced some of those who know the inner workings of the courts best.
>
> Nevertheless, enough people, especially several good judges anxious to redeem their own profession, did talk off the record, so that a consensus of the worst judges, reinforced by personal observation, finally did emerge.[45]

These articles illustrate that the well-timed, and sometimes off-the-record, interview can be a valuable tool to the reporter who deals with press-shy court officials and personnel.

What strategies and tactics can the reporter use in covering courts as part of the legal process? Again, without being prescriptive, let's take a hypothetical example. The court system of a small city has a procedure called pretrial diversion, in which a defendant is diverted from the criminal court process and given rehabilitative job and educational training. The purpose of the program, which is supported by a state crime commission grant, is to prevent crimes against property by giving potential thieves training so that they will be able to earn an income and not have to steal. How well, the public affairs reporter asks, does the system work? Does it really rehabilitate? Do defendants in the diversion project receive job and educational training that really helps them?

This is a multisource story for which the reporter will need to tap different types of resource material, interview a range of authorities, and employ various techniques. To define the perimeters of the story, the reporter might begin by examining the program's grant. What does the grant say the project will do? Then, the reporter might examine how the program's staff evaluates itself, keeping in mind that any such examination could be highly self-serving. Are the evaluation methods reasonable? How have other courts handled such projects? What statistical base is there for saying such-and-such a percentage of the defendants complete the job and educational training? The reporter might then turn to some of those involved with the project and interview probation officers, judges, court and corrections workers, and police. The reporter might examine police records to see whether the defendants are arrested any less often. The reporter might also ask some defendants, past and present, for their evaluation of the program and also talk with employers. As with the story on police training, some academic opinions from criminal justice experts would add dimension to the story. This investigation would reach across the traditional police–court–corrections beat lines by examining a problem that is centered in the court system, but which has law enforcement and correction elements, too.

COVERING THE PENAL SYSTEM

The corrections component of the legal system in America is perhaps the most difficult to cover. Unlike courts and police departments, prisons are generally closed to the public and the press, and even news dealing with a prison "event" is difficult to obtain. "The peculiar nature of covering a prison riot," writes journalist John Linstead, "is the ability of officials to control almost totally the flow of information. In an urban street riot, you can drive through the area, watch what the police are doing, talk to residents and rioters. In a college takeover or street demonstration, you can find leaders who may condescend to talk to you. But whom do you talk to in a prison riot?"[46] All the same, reporters need not restrict themselves to "official" accounts of what is going on inside prisons. Nor need they restrict themselves to covering prison "events" such as riots, murders, escapes, and suicides, all of which are fairly common. There are other ways to handle news from corrections. At the Attica (N.Y.) prison riot, reporters soon learned to tap other sources for their stories. Says Linstead,

> We talked to so many families of hostages, camped outside the gates, that they grew sick of reporters walking up with tape machine or pencil ready. The nearby residents told us their life stories in the first few days. Local barflies soon learned to shut up when an obvious reporter type walked in. Doctors, priests, and negotiators who had been inside the prison for hours without sleep knew they'd have to answer hundreds of questions before they could get to bed. Reporters who managed to get into the prison in pools during the days before the attack grew weary of repeating to us what they had seen, heard and smelled. And a short-wave radio tuned to the police band provided a running account of police moves during the attack.[47]

"Prison riots," writes vanden Heuvel, "like cowboy movies, have a quick audience because the 'good guys' and the 'bad guys' are identifiable and they meet in violent confrontation. But as reporter Nat Hentoff has pointed out, 'Except for brief public interest during a prison rebellion, what happens inside these institutions remains unreported and, therefore, unexamined.'"[48]

Part of the problem is that covering complex issues behind the walls of a restricted institution like a prison is difficult. A journalist must gain access, win trust, and move within a prison under its rules, not those of the more free-wheeling world outside.

Many stories need to be written about prisons, and the reporter needs to see corrections as part of the legal system. On a good number of newspapers, beats are divided into "police," and "courts," but few newspapers designate a reporter to cover corrections. Furthermore, a tendency prevails among reporters to think that once a police investigation of a crime and a trial of the defendant have been completed, the story's over. Sending a defendant to prison after a trial often means the end of coverage by the press, unless the defendant returns to the court system to file an appeal. Such appeals are covered routinely as they come up in the day-to-day court news. This approach, however, leaves important stories untouched. Vanden Heuvel suggests thirty assignments that would "revolutionize our awareness" about corrections, including

> Live TV coverage of a prison council such as in the Women's Prison of New York City, where elected prisoner delegates meet regularly with correctional personnel to discuss institutional grievances.
>
> A study of the correction officer, including an analysis of how he is chosen, his responsibility, training, and personal attitude toward his work.
>
> A feature story on prison chaplains, including prisoner reactions to organized religion and the clergy.
>
> A visit to the court pens where prisoners await court appearances—and an analysis on any given day of the disposition of the cases on the court calendar.
>
> A review of the prison commissary system and an accounting of the monies involved.
>
> A profile of solitary confinement with a review of the procedures by which prisoners are sent to such quarters.
>
> A story about the consequences to a family when the father is sentenced to prison.
>
> An evaluation of the rehabilitation programs in any prison.
>
> A productivity audit and itemized analysis of a correctional budget so that an average citizen can understand it.
>
> A story about what happens to children whose mother is sentenced to prison.
>
> An in-depth interview with an adolescent prisoner at the beginning of his sentence and when he leaves the prison.[49]

Let's follow vanden Heuvel's last suggestion to see how it might be approached by the public affairs reporter. Most likely, the reporter would want to pick out an individual who is going to prison for the first time. She could make such a selection by examining court records, including presentence investigation reports, which are normally confidential but which a reporter can see if she is careful to explain her purpose to court officials and the sentencing judge. There is a commonly held belief that prisons, rather than reforming young offenders, merely educate them in the sophisticated ways of crime by putting them in contact with older, more experienced prisoners. In addition to interviewing the prisoner, the reporter might want to find out more about him than court records and a talk with him permit. Interviews with his family, friends, and schoolmates, as well as with victims of his crime, would help here. To get perspective on the issue of prison reform, the reporter might examine statistics on recidivism rates, how they are measured, and what they show and don't show. While the individual is in prison, the reporter might interview him frequently, getting him to talk about the changes he perceives in himself as a result of prison. Such material could be self-serving in the extreme, but the reporter could also talk with other prisoners, prison officials, and employees and psychiatrists. When the individual is released, the reporter might do a lengthy interview, then follow it up six months later. Obviously, the reporter would have to keep a careful interview and records file on the individual so that, at the writing stage, she could show his transformation, or at least what effect prison has had on him.

By intensive research, carefully arranged questions, and a real empathy with the prisoner, the reporter might develop real insight into what it's like to go to prison for the first time. The lack of a deadline would remove the necessity of "rushing into print" with the story. But would not the final stories, if well written, say more about prisons than the typical news story that emphasizes the escape of a certain "hardened criminal"?

Stories like this have already been done, but others of vanden Heuvel's suggestions have not. One problem is that reporters don't take advantage of access to prisons, which is, in some institutions, replacing secrecy and control. "Despite our liberal inmate interview policy," says former New York City Corrections Commissioner Benjamin Malcolm, "the press has not stampeded to the cellblocks to interview inmates. Most reporters have not availed themselves of the opportunity as often as we thought when we first relaxed the rules. Most interviews granted have been with a small selected group of highly vocal individuals whose cases have received front page treatment. There have been few interviews concerning the pathetic cases of inmates who may have been trapped in the judicial whirlpool."[50] The interview with an inmate or ex-convict can provide reporters with new insights into how the criminal justice system works from a perspective that is normally different from their own. Two months after fights between black and white inmates at Minnesota's Saint Cloud State Reformatory, student reporter Greg Breining went to the prison to interview inmates. He wrote the following:

> But if the reformatory approximates a small society because of the occupations of its residents and the politics of its administration, then it is also a small shadow of the outside in that society's problems are accentuated by the close, intense living conditions and a population perhaps more volatile than normal. . . .
>
> Since April, tensions seem to have mellowed. Some staff members and inmates attribute this to optimism over the upcoming talks [between inmates and staff]. Others say that fewer problems arise because the inmates are separated into smaller groups in trouble spots like the ball diamond and the

lunchroom. Others say that for the first time, white inmates are unified like the blacks and a balance of power exists. Other inmates, particularly blacks, say that the racial tension still exists as pervasively, and only needs a catalyst.[51]

Interviews need not be limited to inmates. "There are few things more necessary than for the public to understand the strain of the correction officer's work and the alienation he feels because of the hostility directed toward him," writes vanden Heuvel.[52]

Whatever the sources, the reporter should attempt to research and write stories that give the reader different perspectives on the problems of corrections. Fortunately, some of these attempts are already being made, for as vanden Heuvel says, "unless the media can translate these [prisoner's] grievances into public understanding, there is little hope for prison reform. The quality of justice must be measured periodically by the press. . . . How can a prison be free of anger and grievance when an inmate convicted of selling 1/73 of an ounce of heroin receives a sentence of thirty years, while another defendant in another court guilty of the same crime is sentenced to three months?"[53] By approaching corrections issues as "events" (the riot, escape, murder, suicide), reporters limit themselves greatly. By seeing corrections issues as part of the generally unreported legal system, reporters can begin to make sense of single incidents. There will probably always be a need to cover the prison riot or to investigate and write the story by which an innocent person is freed from a prison. But these stories do not, in themselves, deal with root social problems and issues.

There are many types of corrections facilities, and though the reporter needs to cover them all from broad perspectives, special investigating problems emerge with each one.

Local Lockups

The county and municipal jails and workhouses are probably the most ignored component of corrections facilities. Usually small, and carefully tucked under the wing of a county sheriff or local police department, these facilities range from adequate to poor. Some conditions border on the inhumane. Here, the reporter will need to deal with local sources in the pursuit of stories: not only lawyers and local branches of civil liberties unions and other groups interested in corrections reform, but also law enforcement officials and the prisoners themselves. With enough persistence, the reporter can sometimes find a sympathetic judge, lawyer, or other official to provide information. Then comes the writing, like this moving excerpt from a story on local jails by Newfield, originally published in the *Village Voice:*

A few facts to meditate on. Almost all the inmates of the Kew Gardens jail, of the Tombs, and of the Long Island City jail have *not* been convicted of a crime. According to the Constitution, they are innocent until proven guilty, by a jury. These institutions are detention facilities, not punishment prisons. The men are detained there usually because they could not raise the $500 or $1,000 bail on the single phone call they are allowed. Most of them have been in these dungeons for six and twelve months *waiting for their trials to begin,* 25 percent on bail of $500 or less. Under any name this is preventive detention. They rot in these Cancer Wards because they are poor, and because some criminal court judges are political hacks who work only five hours a day. Most of these judges are opposed to the penal reform supported by Chief Justice Burger and Mayor Lindsay, and already adopted by the State of California, the reform that places a sixty-day legal limit on the time between arrest and trial.[54]

In some places, the attention of the press on local jails and lockups is infrequent and incomplete. Too often, local press attention is focused elsewhere as prisoners languish in cramped, ill-kept, and underfinanced facilities. A spotlight of attention on such matters may win the local press few friends among the jail's custodians, but it is likely to at least focus attention on a long-neglected area of American criminal justice. In Cherokee County, Alabama, for example, *Anniston Star* reporters Laura Freeman and Robin MacDonald chronicled jail conditions in a series of articles through 1980 and 1981. They pinpointed safety and health violations and traced an investigation by the FBI into violations of prisoners' civil rights.[55]

State Facilities

In some states, penal institutions harbor dozens of suspicious officials who are reluctant to give the reporter any assistance in developing complex and important stories. The reporter often needs the help of other sources, such as court records, but can sometimes, through careful interviewing of officials, present processes or abuses clearly. For instance, reporter Robert Pearman, writing in *The Nation* in 1966, followed up the Arkansas state penitentiary's policy change that allowed prisoners to be whipped:

After O. E. Bishop, superintendent of the Arkansas state penitentiary, has sentenced a man to be whipped, he sits at his desk and waits until the punishment is carried out. If the door is open, he can hear the sounds of the strap falling in a room just down the hall, but Captain Bishop (in Arkansas all wardens are called "Cap'n") never watches the whippings. He has no stomach for such things. "I'd just rather see anything other than that," says the superintendent, who took over his present job last January, after seventeen years as sheriff of Union County. "I know you have to have some means to cope with the things that happen here. That's why I want to build the facilities for solitary confinement. I just think it would work better."[56]

There is a continuous need for follow-up stories. In 1968, three mutilated bodies were found at the Cummins Prison Farm in Arkansas. "The state's two largest newspapers," writes *Los Angeles Times* reporter Nicholas C. Chriss, "have repeatedly lambasted the prison officials over the past years. Nevertheless, the horror stories continue to emerge."[57] In the South, *New York Times* writer Wendell Rawls, Jr., examined the state prison system in Alabama eighteen months after a federal judge had ordered improvements and found some had been made. His follow-up report sketched positive changes in the state but also pinpointed additional needs.[58]

Juvenile Facilities

Juvenile justice stories are also difficult for the reporter to get because of various state laws that prohibit the release of information about juvenile offenders. Often, the reporter will have to work with sympathetic judges, lawyers, and corrections officials, as well as the juveniles themselves, to unearth these stories. The *Minneapolis Tribune's* series on juvenile justice, for example, concluded as follows:

> The delinquent encounters a large number of competent, well-meaning adult workers as he wends his way through the system. But the sum total of the adults' efforts remains a mystery. . . . The question is: What does all the work accomplish? The answer is: Nobody knows. Oh, there are success stories. . . . But overall, there is no evidence that the juvenile justice system is effective— no evidence that it rehabilitates youthful offenders.[59]

Sometimes, a reporter can go undercover in such facilities. *Anniston* (Ala.) *Star* reporter Pam Sohn posed as a teenager and spent two days as an inmate of a juvenile detention facility.[60] Sometimes a reporter needs to work through agencies directly. In Hot Springs, Arkansas, *Sentinel-Record* reporter Lisa Godwin examined state juvenile detention records to sketch the effects of poverty on juvenile crime.[61] As with the other aspects of the legal system, the quality of the reporting in juvenile corrections is not determined as much by the size of the news-gathering institution as by the imagination and tenacity of the reporter. From the *New York Times* to the *Hot Springs Sentinel-Record*, legal institutions and issues are worth searching reports by journalists.

Institutions for the Criminally Insane

These institutions exist in every state but are little covered, at least in detail, by the press. Furthermore, few reporters probably know much about forensic psychiatry or the tests applied legally to determine if a person is criminally insane or competent to stand trial. Traditionally, such matters are covered as they come up in court hearings, but occasionally, defense and prosecuting attorneys will parade conflicting expert witnesses who present opposite findings. Psychiatrists are more commonly seen as witnesses in court, and the psychiatrist's relationship to criminal law is one that needs more attention by the public affairs reporter covering the legal process.[62] The reporter here might consider preparing articles on the quality of care for emotionally disturbed prisoners, on the commitment process, and on the legal rights of a criminally insane person.

Community Corrections

In recent years, corrections has moved out of—at least in part—the isolated, maximum-security institution and into neighborhoods. Halfway houses, which include education and employment programs for ex-convicts, need more examination by the press, as do pretrial diversion projects, which take nonviolent offenders out of the criminal justice system and provide them with vocational training. Traditionally, the press's interest in such programs has been centered on the reaction (often disapproval) of neighborhood groups to plans to locate a drug rehabilitation center or halfway house in a neighborhood. But these programs, many of them funded by state and federal crime-prevention grants, are in need of serious evaluation by the press. The reporter will have to deal here with opponents, proponents, and academic scholars, all of whom have theories on whether such programs work. He will have to examine funding and granting documents and perhaps do considerable research in professional and academic journals of sociology and criminology. As with other fields in public affairs reporting, there are dozens of stories in this area at the local level.

BROADER PERSPECTIVES
ON CRIMINAL JUSTICE

State and federal governmental agencies have taken an increasingly broader role in various aspects of the criminal justice system. In 1968 Congress passed the Safe Streets Act, which provides federal funds to the states to improve court systems, initiate crime-prevention programs, and improve the quality of police services. These funds are administered by the Law Enforcement Assistance Administration (LEAA), a division of the U.S. Department of Justice. In every state, crime commissions review grants and disburse the funds. Traditionally, the media have covered these organizations at the state level as another state agency, and the typical story has been one that announces the awarding of major grants to various local law enforcement groups. Relatively little has been reported on the effectiveness of individual programs, and there has been little media investigation of the procedures by which funds are expended. These, as well as detailed analyses of various programs, should be more thoroughly covered by reporters in their pursuit of stories that examine the total legal process. For example, the reporter might ask whether a small police department needs sophisticated riot-control equipment, whether a program to hire ex-convicts is working, whether computer technology to speed processing of criminal court cases improves the quality of justice, or whether a pretrial diversion program reduces crime by raising the job skills of nonviolent criminals. There are dozens of such programs in every state, and the reporter who wants to give a broader perspective to the legal system should not ignore them.

In addition to these state and federal initiatives, local "task forces" and "commissions" have become increasingly involved in various aspects of the criminal justice system. Bar associations, associations of judges and prosecutors, and citizen groups have all begun to evaluate seriously their roles in reducing crime and making the criminal justice system more equitable. As with the LEAA programs, the media have tended to cover these developments on a one-shot basis, reporting the findings of a commission or task force but rarely following up, perhaps months later, to see whether improvements have been initiated and whether they are working. For example, if a state bar association recommends changes in the state's rules of criminal procedure, the reporter might examine what the proposed changes would accomplish, then follow up the story with a look at the implementation phase. These types of stories obviously require informed investigation and interpretation, and a broad perspective on the legal process and its components.

NOTES

[1]Jonathan D. Casper, *American Criminal Justice, The Defendant's Perspective* (Englewood Cliffs, N.J.: Prentice-Hall, 1972), p. 145.

[2]Marc A. Franklin, *The Dynamics of American Law, Courts, the Legal Process and Freedom of Expression* (Mineola, N.Y.: Foundation Press, 1968), p. v.

[3]Morris L. Cohen, *Legal Research in a Nutshell* (Saint Paul, Minn.: West Publishing, 1971), p. 228.

[4]Franklin, *Dynamics of American Law*, pp. 26–27.

[5]Ibid., p. 36.

[6]Ibid., p. 41.

[7]The American Bar Association, *Fair Trial and Free Press*, (Chicago: American Bar Association, 1978), p. 3.

[8]The "cameras-in-the-courtroom" issue is discussed in many sources. See, for example, William E. Francois, *Mass Media Law and Regulation* (Columbus, Ohio: Grid, Inc., 1978), pp. 305–12. The U.S. Supreme Court has recently ruled that cameras in the courtroom do not inherently violate a defendant's right to a fair trial. (See *Chandler* v. *Florida*, Jan. 26, 1981). The ruling is expected to further camera access in state court systems.

[9]Abraham S. Blumberg, *Criminal Justice* (Chicago: Quadrangle Books, 1967), pp. x–xi.

[10]Ibid., p. xi.

[11]Casper, *American Criminal Justice*, pp. 1–2.

[12]David L. Grey, "Covering the Courts: Problems of Specialization," *Nieman Reports* 26 (March 1972), 17.

[13]Daniel Walker, *Rights in Conflict: The Chicago Police Riot"* (New York: Signet, 1968), p. xxv.

[14]James C. Robertson, "Cooperation Needed in Police-Press Relations," *Twin Cities Journalism Review* 2 (March–April 1974), 16.

[15]William J. vanden Heuvel, "The Press and the Prisons," *Columbia Journalism Review* 11 (May–June 1972), 35.

[16]Ibid., 35, 39.

[17]David Fogel, "David Fogel Talks Back," *Twin Cities Journalism Review* 1 (March–April 1973), 12.

[18]"Prison Perspective," *Albuquerque Journal* March 30, 1980, p. 1.

[19]Frank Premack, Doug Stone, and Peter Vanderpoel, "Juvenile Justice: A Defective System," *Minneapolis Tribune,* August 4–20, 1974.

[20]Casper, *American Criminal Justice,* p. 1.

[21]Stephen Hartgen, "Murder in Minneapolis," *Minneapolis Star,* December 11–13, 1972.

[22]Hank Ezell, "Portrait of Handgun Murder," *Atlanta Journal-Constitution,* May 17, 1981, p. 1.

[23]Barbara Basler, "Mugger's Tale: He Prowled Without Fear Through a Fearful City," *New York Times,* November 17, 1980, p. 18.

[24]Marion Hale, "In the Courts, a Suspect's Color Counts," *Broward Courts: Justice Denied, Fort Lauderdale News* reprint booklet, 1980.

[25]James O. Monroe, Jr., "Press Coverage of the Courts," *Quill* 61 (March 1973), 24.

[26]Arthur Niederhoffer, *Behind the Shield: The Police in Urban Society* (New York: Anchor Books, 1969), pp. 121–22.

[27]Ibid., p. 234.

[28]*Report of the National Advisory Commission on Civil Disorders* (New York: Bantam, 1968), p. 378.

[29]National News Council, *"Covering Crime: How Much Press-Police Cooperation? How Little?"* 1981.

[30]Michael J. Petrick, "The Press, the Police Blotter and Public Policy," *Journalism Quarterly* 46 (Autumn 1969), 475.

[31]Ibid., 477.

[32]"Blacks in Detroit," *Detroit Free Press* reprint booklet, December 1980, pp. 70–74.

[33]John Harwood and Marcia A. Slacum, "Blacks See Unequal Treatment from Police but Want More Patrols," in "To Be Black and to Live in St. Petersburg," *St. Petersburg Times* reprint booklet, 1980, p. 45.

[34]Grey, "Covering the Courts," 17.

[35]Todd Hunt, "Beyond the Journalistic Event: The Changing Concept of News," *Mass Comm Review* 1 (April 1974), 28.

[36]Mark H. Litke, "Police Beat: Still the Place There's Fast-Breaking News," *Editor & Publisher* 105 (January 1, 1972), 15. Emphasis added.

[37]David B. Sachsman, "Mass Media and the Urban Environment," *Mass Comm Review* 1 (July 1974), 5.

[38]Monroe, "Press Coverage," p. 23.

[39]Gene Blake, "Grand Jury: 'Bulwark of Liberties' or Aid to Prosecution," *Los Angeles Times,* November 3, 1974, section 2, p. 1.

[40]Ibid.

[41]Dick Krantz and Gerald White, panelists, "Investigating the Courts," in "The Best from IRE Conferences: Columbus," 1976, pp. 9–11.

[42]Bob Kuttner, "The Politics of Leaksmanship," (MORE) 3 (November 1973), 1, 15.

[43]Walter Pincus, "The Usable Press," *The New Republic*, October 20, 1972, pp. 17–18.

[44]*Los Angeles Times*, November 3, 1974.

[45]Jack Newfield, "The Ten Worst Judges in New York," *New York*, 5 (October 16, 1972), 33.

[46]John Linstead, "Attica: Where Media Went Wrong," *Chicago Journalism Review* 4 (November 1971), 9.

[47]Ibid.

[48]vanden Heuvel, "Press and the Prison," 35.

[49]Ibid., 39–40.

[50]Quoted in Edward M. Swietnicki, "Gaps in Crime Reporting Are Noted at Symposium," *Editor & Publisher* 106 (June 9, 1973), 14.

[51]Greg Breining, "St. Cloud Reformatory," *Minnesota Daily*, July 17, 1974, pp. 8–10.

[52]vanden Heuvel, "Press and the Prisons," 38.

[53]Ibid., 39.

[54]Jack Newfield, "The Law Is an Outlaw," in *Bread and Roses Too* (New York: E. P. Dutton, 1971), p. 342.

[55]Laura Ann Freeman, "Cherokee Jail in Controversy," *Anniston* (Ala.) *Star*, September 28, 1980; and R. Robin MacDonald, "Jails Called Overcrowded and Unsafe," *Anniston* (Ala.) *Star*, March 5, 1981.

[56]Robert Pearman, "The Whip Pays Off," *The Nation* 203 (December 26, 1966), 701.

[57]Nicholas C. Chriss, "New Chapter in Horror," *The Nation* 214 (January 10, 1972), 50.

[58]Wendell Rawls, Jr., "Alabama Racing to Avert Order Freeing Prisoners," *New York Times*, May 4, 1981, p. 10.

[59]*Minneapolis Tribune*, August 4, 1974, p. 9.

[60]Pam Sohn, "Detention," *Anniston* (Ala.) *Star*, February 3, 1980.

[61]Lisa Godwin, "State Juvenile Justice System Devours Youths from Impoverished Families," in reprint, "Children of Poverty in the Land of Opportunity," *Hot Springs* (Ark.) *Sentinel-Record*, October 7, 1980.

[62]See Richard C. Allen, Elyce C. Ferster, and Jesse G. Rubin, eds., *Readings in Law and Psychiatry* (Baltimore, Md.: Johns Hopkins University Press, 1968).

SUGGESTED READINGS

BURGETT, CLAUDE, ET AL. "Editorially Speaking," a symposium on police reporting, *Gannetteer* 30 (June 1975), 1–8.

COHEN, STANLEY, AND JOCK YOUNG, EDS. *The Manufacture of News*. Beverly Hills, Calif.: Sage Publications, 1978.

DENISTON, LYLE W. *The Reporter and the Law*. New York: Hastings House, 1980.

FRIENDLY, ALFRED, AND RONALD L. GOLDFARB. *Crime and Publicity: The Impact of News on the Administration of Justice*. New York: Twentieth-Century Fund, 1967.

WICKER, TOM. *A Time to Die*. New York: Quadrangle-The New York Times Book Company, 1975. A personal account of the Attica prison riot that provides useful ideas on covering penal institutions.

8

Covering Government Agencies and Services

The media generally do not value state government news very highly.

John Burns, The Sometime Governments

At all levels of government in the United States, executive departments, commissions, boards, and agencies are organized to deliver governmental services to people. Guided by legislative intent and checked by the courts, agencies are administered by the executive branch of government whether at the federal, state, or local level. The executive function of government as it applies to the delivery of services is vast and complex. And these activities are administered by executives who have a number of things in common, as political scientist John C. Ries has observed:

> Whatever their titles, they share many common characteristics. They are expected to take the lead in initiating new policies. They are called upon to define public problems and to come up with solutions for them. They are required to manage the financial, procedural, and practical aspects of government. They occupy the highest offices in the vast complex of agencies through which the government operates. Because they are viewed as solely responsible for the "execution" or the carrying out of the activities of government, we call them executives.[1]

The responsibility of executive agencies may involve monitoring agricultural standards, providing civil defense protection, administering prisons and mental hospitals, dispensing welfare and public health payments, building highways, and planning for future growth. Some services are direct; some indirect. Both must be reported on, interpreted, and analyzed within the context of important dimensions of executive roles.

For the reporter covering government agencies and activities of the executive branch, it is important to understand that government is both stable and changing. As Ries has pointed out, there are the stable demands to which government responds—which explains why Governor Jerry Brown of California conducts many of the affairs of that state in much the same way as did his predecessor, his father.

Some governmental functions and activities go on in much the same fashion from generation to generation. But there are also important changes. There are changing demands on government dictated by public attitudes, for example. "Some of these changes," writes Ries, "reflect changes in political ideology on the part of the electorate. Some of them result in advances in technology. . . . Finally there is the personality and political ideology of the incumbent. . . ."[2]

In the early 1980s, on the wave of conservative political victories that put Ronald Reagan in the White House and gave the Republicans control of the U.S. Senate, there was a dramatic effort at cutting the budget and reducing governmental expenditures. Yet, any changes had to be accomplished within the existing governmental structure and framework, and even as some programs got a meat axe, others continued to operate much as they always had. This discrepancy is explained in part by what one wag has called "the Newtonian law of systems inertia," which posits that "A system that performs a certain function or operates in a certain way will continue to operate in that way regardless of the need or of changed conditions."[3]

Coverage of the executive functions of government would be less difficult if it could be assumed that all agencies and departments within a single system were directly responsible to a single executive. Then, one would contact governors, mayors, and county executives. As early as 1835, the French writer Alexis de Tocqueville used words that are apt today: "The executive power of the state is represented by the governor . . . although he enjoys but a portion of its rights."[4] Municipal governments range from highly centralized "strong mayor" systems to those that are decentralized with interrelated and overlapping checks and balances. In some states, governors appoint members of their cabinets to supervise state agencies; in others, some cabinet members are elected directly by the people. In some states, a governor or mayor will have thousands of political patronage appointments to make; in others, a tightly organized civil service will fill almost all jobs by competitive examination.

The work of the public affairs reporter is made even more complex by the interdependence of the executive agencies. No agency or department can ever be viewed as an independent entity. It must be seen in its relationship to other units in the executive bureaucracy, to the legislature which provides its budget, and to the courts which monitor its policy. Political scientist Morton Grodzins has rightly observed that one cannot even make simplistic observations about "layers" of government. Indeed, writes Grodzins, the American system of government is more like a marble cake with federal, state, and local functions interrelated and intermingled.[5] Thus, there is the context of intergovernmental relations whereby an agency may blend federal, state, and local funds in its allocations mix.

COVERING THE EXECUTIVE PROCESS

Although the importance of the executive process in terms of public services or monitoring nongovernmental activities for the public interest is self-evident, government agencies and departments do not attract much attention in the media. Preoccupied with coverage of the seemingly more newsworthy activities of legislatures, courts, and chief executives, the municipal, state, and federal bureaucracies often escape the scrutiny of the press. John Burns's lament that the press does "not value state government news very highly" might even be understated, though Burns himself admitted that "such news usually ranks a poor third behind national and local news."[6]

Paul Simon, former lieutenant governor of Illinois and a journalist, has urged editors "to help destroy the attitude on the part of reporters that an assignment to Springfield (or any other capital) is an assignment to purgatory. Too often good reporters view the state capital as an unhappy stopping place on the way to Washington or some other assignment.[7]

To Simon and other critics of the noncoverage of government departments and agencies, partial blame can be laid to a tendency of the media not to follow through on a story. A new program for drug abuse may, for example, be announced with fanfare by a government or mayor and move through the legislature or city council with conflict and argumentation. All this is covered with lively flair by the press. When the program moves to the implementation stage, however, to the state or municipal agency, it seems to lack news appeal. It drops out of the press's vision. Yet, whether the new program succeeds or fails may be the most important aspect of the story.

Some municipal governments get more coverage of agencies and services than do state governments—due partly to the beat system whereby a reporter covers city hall on a regular basis. But even at the municipal level the emphasis is on the day-to-day views of executives and lawmakers. Part of the problem is that many agencies and departments are covered only as they collide with the executive or legislative authorities. A health commissioner argues about a program before a city council, a county commission, or a legislative committee; a highway department director openly criticizes the governor; state employees decide to strike in defiance of the courts. These activities get coverage, whereas the major part of the agency's activity, the organization and delivery of services, is ignored. One reason for this lack of systematic coverage is the exodus of reporters from a state capital once the legislature recesses. In many states there are dozens of regular legislative correspondents, but few reporters are given responsibility for covering state agencies on a regular basis. Increasingly, some of the functions of agencies are being covered by such specialists as environmental writers and medical writers. The specialist, however, covers the agency only as it relates to his particular story, making no attempt to examine systematically all the services provided. Thus, with the infrequent coverage by legislative correspondents and the highly selected coverage by specialists, the treatment of government agencies and institutions is necessarily fragmented.

Attempting to reverse this pattern of noncoverage are groups such as the Council of State Governments. The council has organized a national task force to stimulate coverage of governmental services. Ralph Nader and other consumer advocates have offered vivid illustrations of the vital role state agencies and departments play in the lives of people. Schools of journalism are also now urging improvement in public affairs reporting on the state level.

REPORTING FUNCTIONS
AND GOVERNMENT AGENCIES

There are no doubt hundreds of reasons why the press should cover government agencies and services. Three that stand out in bold relief, though, are these:

The watchdog role.   As a watchdog, the press keeps an eye on the activities of government, looking for conflict of interest or other improper conduct. In this function, the press is an adversary of government, demanding that it serve the public interest through an ethical delivery of services.

The performance-monitor role.   In this function, the press is not necessarily adversarial, but more neutral. It looks for standards by which the work of an agency can be evaluated, judged for what it is worth on neither a positive nor negative basis.

The service-utilization role.   Here the press attempts to help people utilize effectively the services to which they are entitled. Sometimes the roles overlap in the same story, of course, but the model of three roles is helpful in directing the reporter toward more thoughtful coverage.

In the spotty coverage of agencies and services, the watchdog story is most common. Winners of Pulitzer Prizes for community service often engage in watchdog journalism. A notable example was George Thiem's series in the *Chicago Daily News* some years ago that proved improper fiscal management and embezzlement on the part of the Illinois state auditor. Also in this genre are the traditional exposé stories that reveal corruption in government. The exposé traces its origins to the journalism of Nelly Bly, who wrote a sensational series on life in the "madhouse" for the *New York World*. The exposé often involves subterfuge on the part of the reporter who poses as a prisoner or mental patient and then reveals a firsthand account of the horrors observed. The result of many exposés has been the scapegoating of particular public officials (for example, a warden) and collective legislative clucking. The exposé sometimes helps stimulate legislation, improve funding, and change conditions. However, this form, with its attendant sensationalism, has mostly passed out of fashion. Exposés require relatively simple targets and simple, easily understood conditions. The growing recognition that social conditions are extremely complex has reduced the tendency to indulge in exposés. One notable exception has been the continuous coverage of the Willowbrook State School, an institution for the mentally retarded, on Staten Island, New York, which has been under fire for more than twenty years. Newspapers and television news shows, in a reformist bent, are still pointing to overcrowded, subhuman conditions at Willowbrook and demanding change.

Watchdogging has long been a hallmark of journalism on the national scene. As Richard Strout of the *Christian Science Monitor* has observed, "There is a major scandal in American political life every 50 years: Grant's in 1873, Teapot Dome in 1923, Watergate in 1973. Nail down your seats for 2023."[8]

In recent years more subtle watchdogging has been apparent in the press. Questions about agency functions are raised. Instead of searching for overt incompetence or corruption, reporters look for conditions caused not by individuals per se but by sluggish bureaucracies and inappropriate governmental structures. This story about the Chicago transit situation is an example:

> There is a model train on display at the offices of the Chicago Transit Authority. It's painted the regulation green and white. At the side of the tracks, switches flash their lights. Plastic commuters stand on the platform and wait. The train rarely gets to them. It's too slow, it stalls and nobody pays attention to it. Neglect plagues the CTA itself, with its 1,329 real subway cars, 3,300 buses, and a very real $30 million it may lose this year. It is just starting to get attention now, because its 800,000 daily riders are not plastic people, but real people who can scream and vote.[9]

A series of articles that examined the operations and practices of the Boston transit system won the *Boston Globe* a Pulitzer Prize in 1980. The *Globe*'s team of reporters found featherbedding union practices and whole-sale waste in their detailed investigative reports.

Closely related to the watchdog story is the performance story. Inher-ently less sensational than stories of corruption, this story centers on the question of how well the agency is doing its job. The reporter asks about the agency's function, its interaction with other agencies, and its relative power in the governmental arena. Here the reporter must learn to dissect and analyze programs and to ask the right questions. The reporter's job is quite difficult because government officials like to talk about success, not failure. They try to accentuate programs that are highly visible and that make them look good. Programs that are less than successful are often not discussed. The information on agencies that makes news usually flows from official press releases, news conferences, and interviews with officials. The government is seldom averse to announcing new programs, but it is not nearly so zealous about following up on old ones. Status stories are released, but usually they are quite self-serving.

This article by Trudy Lieberman in the *Detroit Free Press* illustrates the subtleties of monitoring agency activity:

> The consumer press has frequently castigated government agencies for not releasing information deemed to be in the interests of consumers.
>
> But in an ironic switch, the usually zealous consumer press can be partly blamed for the elimination by the Federal Trade Commission (FTC) of press releases on flammable fabrics. For it was press indifference coupled with some well-applied pressure by the carpet industry's trade association that led the agency to announce on Nov. 9 that it was killing its release program on flammable fabrics.[10]

INSIDE THE AGENCY

Reporters rarely look single-mindedly at one agency but instead at a whole array of agencies. From them they must choose those that will be useful sources of news. The agencies that usually get the most attention are the ones that (1) are developing new programs or making major changes; (2) are building new facilities, selecting sites for new hospitals, colleges, experi-ment stations; (3) affect the greatest number of people; (4) fit in with topical issues of interest at the time; or (5) are deemed to be important in terms of public policy.

Agency bureaucrats usually prefer to see stories in the press on their own terms. It is the responsibility of the reporter, however, to translate the activities of the agency into pertinent information for the reader. One function of agency stories only recently recognized is the service-utilization role. A typical story about a new health center might focus on and quote a physician, using his or her language to explain the function of the center. It does the public little good to hear about "innovative programs," "broad panoplies of service," "crisis intervention programs," and "comprehensive modalities of treatment" without knowing what this bureaucratic jargon means specifically. The reporter must be able to translate these terms into information that makes sense to readers who are also potential users of these services. In a story aimed at helping the disadvantaged use the services to which they were entitled, Margaret Kuehlthau of the *Tucson Daily Citizen* wrote the following:

> Are the minority groups in Tucson, the needy and those just on the borderline of poverty, using to any great degree many agencies ready to assist them?
> The answer is a loud resounding, "No!"
> A *Tucson Daily Citizen* survey indicates that most tend to use only governmental health and welfare agencies. Spokesmen for many charitable and social agencies gave this almost unanimous response: "We could help many more poor people but they do not seem to be aware of the services which we have to offer. If they do, seemingly they do not care to use our services."[11]

In some instances it is important that citizens know the distinction among different kinds of services to save themselves long trips and long waits. Although government agencies have become more concerned about providing adequate information to the public about human services, there is still no central location for such information and the press must continue to serve this vital function.

To some reporters there is little excitement in helping people use services. They see this function as a glorified bulletin board. It need not be. The kind of reporting of services that is needed should be discerning and questioning. Here the reporter is the eyes and ears of the public, attempting to ask the questions that a consumer of services would want to know: Can I use it? Am I eligible? How good is it? How does it differ from what was available before? How do I get there? Falling into the agency bureaucrat's jargon, thus obscuring a clear view of the services, does just the opposite of what is needed.

AGENCY NEWS SOURCES

Reporters covering an agency need to understand bureaucracy and how bureaucrats operate. They need to know how the agency is organized, who does what, and what's in a title. Often stories about government agencies refer to the source as an assistant commissioner or community liaison officer without any indication of what the person does, who he or she speaks for, and the person's degree of expertise. All too frequently the reporter deals with a governmental information officer who is sometimes "an underling whose only aim is to get the boss's name in print,"[12] writes an editorialist in the *Delaware Valley News* of Frenchtown, N.J. So many information officers these days are well-trained writer–publicists who are among the strategists trying to inspire confidence in the agency they represent. They usually provide honest, rapid information when asked but otherwise spend their time attempting to get favorable publicity for programs and projects. Usually busy people with more responsibilities than they can carry out, they can both aid and mislead the reporter. One of the most misleading practices (and sometimes it is unconscious) of governmental information officers and officials generally is to fail to distinguish between *planning* and *implementation*. A cautionary note: It is always important to find out the exact status of a program. Sometimes such a determination is not easy to make from an interview without asking specific questions: Is the program actually operating now, or is it just in the planning stage? When will people be able to take advantage of the service? Questions like these often lead to qualifications and a little clearer explanation—that, for example, it may be seven years before the new recreation center for teenagers opens its doors. Usually there are announcements by various legislative bodies, the agency itself, and others long before the new facility is completed. One of the functions of the press is to provide the public with an awareness of what stages projects and programs are in—a kind of status table. Such reporting will furnish the public with the kind of information it needs to hold the government accountable for its activity—or inactivity.

Also important for the reporter in covering governmental services is to recognize the distance between central office rhetoric and field office activity. Sometimes the programs perceived by supervisors in the state capital as operating are only on the drawing board in the field. Similarly, there is often a misunderstanding between the managerial personnel at the state or regional level and those who implement programs at the grass roots. These differences can make for interesting copy. For example, federal law enforcement initiatives should be viewed not only from the state and regional offices of the LEEA but also from the project-level firing line. The federal government's objective may call for better preventive measures. The state, with federal assistance, may have funded a halfway house supervised by a regional state crime committee. But the day-to-day problems of this halfway house—and its battles with a middle-class community that wants no part of it—may make a much more vital story than a dull interview with the state commissioner of corrections. It may also be more useful to the reader to get a broader view of several halfway house projects rather than a single case.

The presence since the 1970s of federal revenue-sharing funds also complicates the local picture with less clearly defined lines of authority between local and state agencies. This growing tendency for shared funding at several governmental levels leads to interesting stories about how funds are being used and for what purpose.

The relationship among local, state, and federal agencies can sometimes be complex and difficult to trace. The lines of authority and responsibility are by no means clear in all instances. In the early 1980s, the administration in Washington attempted to shift many funding burdens from the federal to the state governments, a move away from a pattern of revenue sharing prevalent in the 1970s. For reporters this change means watching not only the dramatic decisions to shut down a federal program or slash its budget substantially but also the consequences of this action on state and local communities. In 1981, when the federal administration proposed sweeping cuts in federal arts and humanities programs, the CBS news show "Sunday Morning" examined the possible effect of such budgetary cuts on arts programs in Mississippi. The presentation looked at current federal-state relationships that were responsible for local arts programs, and it then tried to assess the possible impact of budget cuts on these activities. The story involved interviews with officials and citizens at both levels (state and federal) as well as sources who could engage in some creative (and knowledgeable) speculation.

Making sense out of the complex web of governmental activity, however, is a singularly difficult assignment. Yet its importance at all levels is pointed up by Joe Pierson of the *Binghamton* (N.Y.) *Evening Sun,* a county reporter, who described his job as follows: "Perhaps a task of equal difficulty (equal to getting governments to cooperate) is transcribing in readable, if not lyrical, form the decisions, actions, details, intricacies and personalities that make the governments click or falter. In other words, the job of reporting the government's activities in depth."[13] In jocular fashion, Pierson urged reporters of governmental services to develop these attributes:

> The curiosity of a 4-year-old. (Government officials love to be questioned by reporters.)
>
> The patience of a fly fisherman. (Those same officials always seem to be busiest when the reporter wants them the most.)
>
> The mathematical genius of an Einstein. (To interpret those budgets and allocation formulas.)
>
> A law degree. (To interpret legal papers, especially reapportionment suits.)
>
> A diploma from a Dale Carnegie course. (To make friends and influence sources.)[14]

Reporters who look beyond their local assignments can find useful assistance on topical and agency subjects in a variety of places. The League of Municipalities and the Council of State Governments, among others, have active publications and programs to disseminate information. There are also citizen groups, such as the League of Women Voters, that monitor and report on governmental activities. Sometimes citizen and governmental task forces also supply this information. At the state level useful information can be found in the state's "blue book," sometimes called a "red book," or state directory. These volumes usually have factual information about state agencies, state laws, and state constitutional requirements. Some cities also have public affairs directories which list the names of municipal agencies and their officers and explain interrelationships between intra- and intergovernmental units.

AGENCIES THROUGH THE EXECUTIVE

At the policy-making level, an agency is often perceived differently by its chief executive (mayor or governor) than it is by those inside the administrative apparatus of the department itself. This difference can be observed in the kind of information that comes from official messages to the legislature, from staff papers, and from interviews. Covering an agency that is a particular favorite of a governor, for example, can prove especially interesting to the reporter. In fact, knowing in what esteem the agency is held by the executive or his or her staff is usually a good indicator of its relative power. Those who followed the career of New York's master builder Robert Moses were always aware of his relationship with governors, mayors, and members of Congress. These relationships—whether warm or heated—invariably reflected the amount of support—and money—Moses was likely to get from the legislature or city hall.

Reporters also must know what involvement the executive has with a particular agency. Is there an official in the executive's office who monitors the agency's activities? Does the commissioner or director report directly to the governor or the mayor? Here the structural and organizational questions of who reports to whom and with what effect can be vital indicators of stories to come. Certainly it is useful to view the agency from the standpoint of the chief executive and his or her program.

BUDGETS AND SERVICES

No reporter can have a full understanding of a government agency without some knowledge of public finances. Excluding the legislative body, which usually grants the funds, organizations for fiscal management include the following:

1. Agencies in the executive branch that must have money in order to carry out their programs.

2. Agencies organized primarily to implement the acquisition of funds and oversee their expenditure.

3. Agencies created to check on the fidelity and legality of disbursements after they have been made.[15]

The specific function and power of chief executive officers, treasurers, budget officers, comptrollers, auditors, and purchasing agents must be known by the public affairs reporter. The titles—and relative position and authority—of these officials differ from one jurisdiction to another. But whatever they are called, they are important in tracing the budget process. A budget, according to public administrators Russell Maddox and Robert Fuquay, is "a comprehensive plan, expressed in financial terms, by which an operating program is effective for a given period of time. It includes estimates of (a) the services, activities and projects comprising the program; (b) the resultant expenditure requirements; and (c) the resources usable for their support."[16] Tracing an agency's budget to evaluate its effectiveness is difficult but not impossible. Budget planning usually begins in the agency, proceeds to an intermediate budget office, and eventually is taken into consideration by the chief executive's fiscal advisers. The steps along the way, differing from state to state and city to city, are fascinating adventures in priorities and in the decision-making process. Eventually, the product of this negotiation becomes part of an official legislative request and often is best considered from the legislative hearing room where agency officials go to testify. Indeed, the style of these legislative presentations may be yet another clue to an agency's plight or situation. Some presentations are flamboyant and are accompanied by visual aids; others are quieter and more measured. Legislative budget hearings also offer lawmakers the opportunity to support certain officials on certain projects and to denounce others with whom they disagree. Thus, governmental budget hearings can make good news copy.

For most reporters, understanding the budget is difficult, and they have too little time in which to thoroughly analyze it and translate it into terms the public can grasp. Reporters tend to become preoccupied with how much larger—or smaller—the budget is than the previous one. Some newspapers now hire accountants and tax attorneys to assist in the complex job of making city and state budgets intelligible. Such governmental units as school boards and airport commissions are also coming in for this kind of scrutiny. In this way the annual budget story becomes comprehensible. More and more reporters are also humanizing the budget by translating it into personal terms.

The *Chicago Tribune* conducted a three-month investigation in which reporters scrutinized the city's budget requests to determine whether they were justified or bloated. This is how the *Tribune* report began:

A burned out light bulb on the Michigan Avenue bridge is guaranteed to draw a crowd—of city payrollers.

Changing that bulb requires:

A city electrician to climb up and remove the outer globe.

Another electrician to unscrew and replace the bulb.

A third to hold the scaffold and shoo away pedestrians.

A fourth to stand by in case his coworkers need tools.

A city foreman to supervise the four.

The half hour job observed October 30 cost Chicago taxpayers $24.33 based on the salaries of city electricians.

Is it any wonder, then, that Chicago has to pay an average of $37.43 a year to maintain each of the city's 230,000 street lights with crews ranging from three to five men while Milwaukee, for example, gets by with two-man crews at half the cost?

The changing of the bulb is a graphic example of waste totalling more than $91 million uncovered by the Tribune Task Force and the Better Government Association in Chicago's first billion dollar budget. The investigation dealt with just nine bureaus of three major city departments.[17]

In a six-part series, the *Tribune* used examples that almost everyone could grasp and laced its reports with comparative statistics from other cities and government agencies.

Whereas public officials tend to immerse themselves in the minutiae of budget detail, readers usually care more about what a proposed budget means to them and their pocketbooks. Because for the public governmental activity translates into taxes, many budget stories can be presented in terms of tax costs rather than services. This can be done gracefully in a manner that means something to the reader. Consider the following leads for a city budget story:

An operating budget of $3.4 million for the 1982–83 fiscal year was proposed today by the Windswept mayor's budget office. The budget is almost 10 percent greater than last year's but is less than the mayor's original proposal made last month.

The new budget will mean a property tax rate of $7.25 next year, up from $6.60 last year.

Another approach changes the focus, taking it from city hall to the individual's home:

Windswept home owners will pay 9 percent more in property taxes next year, if the budget proposed by the mayor's budget office today is adopted. The 1982–83 budget proposals will require a tax rate of $7.25 per $1,000 of assessed property value, 65 cents more than last year.

That means the owner of a house assessed at $50,000 will pay $362 in city taxes. The owner of a $75,000 house will pay $543, and a $100,000 house will be taxed $725.

Although the first lead provides interesting overall budget figures, the material has little meaning for the average reader. Clearly, the numbers in the second lead have consequences for readers who will be directly affected, namely homeowners. With either approach, the reporter would go on to explain the details contained in both leads. But the second lead is clearly designed to help the reader identify quickly with the subject; it answers the most important question first. Still another way to convey personal impact to the reader involves an emphasis on services rather than taxes:

Streets will be swept less often next year, municipal swimming pools will close earlier, and police cars will have only one officer in them.

Those are the major effects Windswept residents will be likely to see as a result of an austerity budget adopted by the mayor's budget office today. The $4.3 million budget will keep property tax rates the same as last year's, but city services will be cut back.

Stories about government finance and budgets should always include definitions of important technical terms and procedures. Many readers won't know the difference between an *operating* budget (everyday costs of running government, such as salaries and office supplies) and a *capital improvements* budget (long-term expenditures, such as new buildings and sewers). Nor are many readers likely to know the difference between *general obligation* bonds (borrowing that is backed by the taxing power of the governmental entity) and *revenue* bonds (borrowing that is repaid solely by the income from a specific project that the bonds finance, such as a sports arena).

Bonds are one source of money for city, county, or state governments. Others are property taxes, license fees, sales taxes, parking meter revenue, court fines, and grants from higher levels of government. Some or all of these sources are used to pay expenses described in a budget. Although we hear most about property taxes, they often account for half or less of budget expenditures. However, because property taxes are the only major source of revenue that legislators can adjust to balance a budget, they receive a great deal of public attention.

Property tax rates are determined by the portion of the budget that must be financed by local sources. Legislators typically will first estimate all other sources of revenue, then calculate a tax rate that will cover the balance of the budget. Determining the tax rate is fairly simple. By dividing the total value of assessed property in the city or county (most states do not levy property taxes) into the budget amount that property taxes must cover, a figure is obtained that represents the tax cost against each dollar of property value. For example, let's say $5 million must be raised through property taxes, and the assessed value of all taxable property in a city is $100 million. Dividing $5 million by $100 million gives a dividend of 5 cents, the tax rate per dollar of assessed value.

Tax rates are usually expressed as so many dollars per $1,000 of assessed value. Five cents per dollar, from the example just given, would mean a tax rate of $50 per $1,000 in assessed value. Many states designate tax rates in *mills*—a thousandth of a dollar. The mill rate is levied against each dollar of assessed property value, so a tax rate of 50 mills would produce the same amount of revenue as a rate of $50 per $1,000.

In reporting tax rates, the reporter should point out that assessed (taxable) value is often less than market value, or the price a home would bring if it were sold. In most states, assessed value is a fixed proportion of market value. If a $60,000 home were assessed at 40 percent of market value, the owner would pay taxes on $24,000. If the tax rate were $50 per $1,000, the tax bill for the owner would be $1,200. Some states have more complicated formulas for calculating assessments and taxes, so reporters should become thoroughly familiar with them before attempting to write budget and tax stories.

Too often, journalists look upon the budget story as a once-a-year occurrence, dictated by the government's agenda. The *Chicago Tribune* series shows that a follow-up, after-the-fact report can also be a powerful and compelling piece. The budget process is not a once-a-year activity to be announced by a mayor or governor but a year-round activity. Departments and agencies often start preparing the following year's budget request as soon as the preceding year's is adopted. Reporters can cut into the process at any point: when planning is going on for the next year, when expenditures are being made under an existing budget, and when legislative bodies act on new requests.

Whatever type of story is planned, reporters can look at the subject in terms of people and services as well as dollars. Appropriated funds usually translate into employees and programs. Reporters should ask what the addition of more employees will mean in terms of expansion of services or improvements in their quality. Similarly, when budget cutbacks are proposed, the story should focus on the effect of those cuts on services as well as on tax dollars. By examining budgets for major departments (such as police, fire, and street departments in a city) as they are developed, readers will be better prepared to assess budget proposals at the time of legislative hearings.

Once budgets reach the stage of legislative hearings, a useful technique is translation of big numbers into human terms to describe budget effects on individuals or classes of people. The case-study approach, mentioned earlier, is one such technique. A similar method is illustrated in the following story by Associated Press writer Evans Witt:

> *Washington D.C.:* President Carter's final budget proposal calls for spending $739 billion, but if you have trouble dealing with figures longer than your ZIP code, try this nickel-and-dime approach:
>   *Traveling later this year? If you drive, the Carter proposal envisions having you pay a dime more for every gallon of gasoline. If you want to spend your vacation on the Riviera, the Carter budget would have you shell out an additional $16 for a passport.
>   *Sick and tired of taxes? Too bad. Your Social Security tax would go up under Carter's budget. His proposal still calls for a tax credit that could cut federal income taxes, but he wants to defer the effective date of this credit from what he had proposed previously.
>   *If you're on the receiving end of Social Security or if you get veterans' benefits or federal pensions, the Carter budget plans to continue increases designed to keep pace with inflation. But the proposal would require the increases to be smaller than in the past and they would come less often.[18]

COVERING LEVELS
OF GOVERNMENT

There are many fine examples of how a newspaper can use local resources to cover a story of national significance. One way is to cover federal programs from the standpoint of their impact on the local area. Most cities have a federal building that houses the regional offices of federal agencies, ranging from the office of the U.S. attorney, who represents the Department of Justice, to the Weather Information Service. In the regional offices, the reporter is dealing with middle-level bureaucrats who have limited contact with Washington. But finding out just how much contact they have with their federal department is important. In the early 1970s some federal offices at the regional level, partly because of revenue sharing, were given certain autonomous powers by Washington. Local federal offices can be used to present the local angle on a national story or to get information in order to present the national background on a local story. Reporters can also get assistance on information about national programs from the staffs of senators and members of congress, who usually have offices in the local federal building. Agencies are often more responsive to elected officials than to reporters; therefore, this avenue of prying loose information should be used. The Federal Freedom of Information Act, designed to make government information available to the public, can also be used as leverage to gain information from local federal offices.*

---

*For information about how the FOI Act can be used by the press see Appendix D.

State government can be covered from the state capital, where many departments are headquartered, or in some states from the largest city, where important state functions are carried out. Of course, most state governments have some presence in almost every local community and can be covered in a manner similar to that suggested for the federal government.

Although many of the examples presented in this chapter refer to state, city, and metropolitan government, they have wider application. Agencies and services exist, of course, at every level of government from the large federal bureaucracy to villages, townships, boroughs, counties, and other political jurisdictions. There are thousands of units of government in the United States, many overlapping and interrelated. But the general assumptions about the executive process presented earlier in this chapter apply.

The tendency toward decentralization of government has also affected municipalities, which have fanned out their services to local neighborhoods in an unprecedented manner. Covering city hall may now mean getting a more thorough knowledge of local community areas. County governments, which also operate agencies and services responsible to the county board of commissioners or its administrator, have also extended their services. The growing tendency toward metropolitan government is another phenomenon that deserves the attention of the public affairs reporter. Metro governments have varying degrees of authority, but they do serve as useful sources of information about the delivery of services to an entire metropolitan area. Metro government administrators and their staffs can supply valuable insights about the interlocking and interrelated nature of various government agencies, thus saving the reporter much time. Similarly, many interstate compacts and other intergovernmental relationships are important in understanding how policies are conceived and how services are delivered to the public.

All these visibly interrelated workings of government may presage more broadly based coverage by the media of government and its services. The present practice of covering the city hall, the metropolitan offices, the state capitol, or the federal building should be replaced by topical coverage that looks at problems and programs of interest to people with wider vision and that draws generously from many sources for news regardless of arbitrary beat boundaries. Stories about land use or health or mass transit should not be developed by limiting contact to one or two agencies. They should be based on many sources of information.

Public affairs reporters who prepare for coverage of public agencies and services—potentially the most important governmental story of the future as people become increasingly consumer-oriented and as government continues to play a greater and greater role in their lives—must prepare themselves by studying state and local government, taxation, and urban politics. They must also keep abreast of developments in these fields. In this connection, more and more university journalism programs are being organized to assist the reporter already on the job. During 1974, for example, there was a special conference for public affairs reporters covering law enforcement. In the final analysis, the coverage of agencies and services must be seen in human terms and within the complex interplay of the executive process.

NOTES

[1]John C. Ries, *Executives in the American Political System* (Belmont, Calif.: Dickenson, 1969), p. 2.

[2]Ibid., p. 3.

[3]John Gall in *Systematics,* as reported in Harold Faber, *The Book of Laws* (New York: Times Books, 1979), p. 24.

[4]Alexis de Tocqueville, *Democracy in America,* 2 vols. (New York: Vintage Books, 1954), vol. 1, p. 88.

[5]Morton Grodzins, *The American System: A New View of Government in the United States* (New York: Random House, 1966).

[6]Ralph Whitehead, Jr., and Howard M. Ziff, "Statehouse Coverage: Lobbyists Outlast Journalists," *Columbia Journalism Review* 12 (1974), 11.

[7]Paul Simon, "Improving Statehouse Coverage," *Columbia Journalism Review* 11 (September–October 1973), 51.

[8]Richard Strout, reported in *Time,* March 27, 1978. Gall, *Systematics,* p. 73.

[9]Ralph Whitehead, Jr., "The CTA: Does Anybody Give a Damn?" *Chicago Journalism Review* 3 (April 1970), 9.

[10]Trudy Lieberman, "Press Indifference and Manufacturer Vigilance Kill FTC's Flammability Releases," *Media & Consumer* 1 (April 1972), 24; reprinted from the Detroit *Free Press,* November 9, 1971.

[11]Margaret Kuehlthau, "Big Gap Exists in Use of Agencies," *Tucson Daily Citizen,* April 29, 1968, special supplement, p. 14.

[12]"The Press Release," *Grassroots Editor* 12 (November–December 1971), 32; reprinted from *Delaware Valley News,* Frenchtown, N.J.

[13]Joe Pierson, "The Recurring Problem of Reapportionment," *The Gannetteer,* December 1965, p. 27.

[14]Ibid.

[15]Russell W. Maddox and Robert F. Fuquay, *State and Local Government* (Princeton, N.J.: D. Van Nostrand, 1966), p. 389.

[16]Ibid., pp. 393–94. For another useful treatment of fiscal administration and budgets, see James W. Fesler, ed., *The Fifty States and Their Local Governments* (New York: Knopf, 1967); and Charles R. Adrian, *Governing Our Fifty States and Their Communities* (New York: McGraw-Hill, 1972).

[17]"Padding Found in Budget," *Chicago Tribune,* November 24, 1974, p. 1.

[18]Associated Press wire, January 16, 1981.

SUGGESTED READINGS

ADRIAN, CHARLES R.   *State and Local Governments,* 4th ed. New York: McGraw-Hill, 1976; paperback ed. 1978. A standard text on state and local governmental issues and problems. Especially strong on governmental structure.

BERKLEY, GEORGE E., AND DOUGLAS M. FOX. *80,000 Governments: The Politics of Subnational America.* Boston: Allyn & Bacon, 1978. A book that points up the complexity of local governmental units in the United States.

HILLS, WILLIAM G., ET AL. *Conducting the People's Business: The Framework and Functions of Public Administration.* Norman: University of Oklahoma Press, 1973. Useful commentary and readings growing out of research, consultation, training, and administration of human service agencies.

NATIONAL JOURNAL. A magnificent publication that covers national and state issues, published in Washington, D.C. Look at this journal in a library as it is prohibitively expensive.

PEIRCE, NEAL R. This writer's coverage of state and metropolitan issues in *Congressional Quarterly* and *National Journal* has been exemplary and provides models for superb public affairs coverage. See Peirce's excellent books on the people, politics, and power of the American states in *The Border States* (1975), *The Deep South States* (1974), *The Great Plains States* (1973), *The Megastates of America*—ten largest—(1972), *The Mid-Atlantic States* (1977), *The Mountain States* (1972), *The New England States* (1976), and *The Pacific States* (1972). (New York: Norton).

STATE GOVERNMENT. A journal of state affairs published by the Council of State Governments, Lexington, Kentucky, 40505. Articles by state officials, researchers, and others on governmental problems and issues. Published quarterly.

WILDAVSKY, AARON. *The Politics of the Budgetary Process,* 3d ed. Boston: Little, Brown, 1979. An analysis of the political aspects of budget-making. Many examples from the federal government but useful at all levels of executive decision making. Also see Aaron Wildavsky. *Budgeting: A Comparative Theory of Budgeting.* Boston: Little, Brown, 1974.

9

Covering Politics
and Elections

If you were to generalize—probably outrageously—and say you
know what really is at the root of so much of the discontent with
political institutions in this country, I think you would suppose it is the
feeling that seems to be so widespread, and it goes from the ghetto
to the affluent suburb, that events are taking place and decisions are
being made in this political process without the meaningful understanding and participation of the people who are affected by those
decisions. This is really an indictment of the press and the politician
equally.

David S. Broder*

The shortcomings of both press and politician in fulfilling the democratic
process have often been remarked by less qualified observers than the
Washington Post's political columnist David Broder. And it is small comfort
to devotees of the press that the indictments of the media have been figura-
tive, whereas those of some politicians in recent times have been literal.
The press—despite the credit reflected on it by the *Post*'s dogged disclosures of Watergate corruption—shares with politicians a low regard by
the public that ranges from indifference to distrust.

The public's low regard for both may perhaps best be seen in the low
voter turnout that characterizes elections in the United States—despite the
inevitable urgings by media and politicians for citizens to do their duty.
The extent to which the press is responsible for voter apathy is a subject for
conjecture, but the shortcomings of the media in covering politics have
been documented again and again by responsible critics. These shortcomings range from superficiality to outright bias and include, more specifically, reliance on handouts, dependence on events, too-rigid adherence to an
idealized objectivity, herd instinct, and misuse of polls. They also include
the failure to dig: for the facts of campaign financing, for the authenticity

*Reprinted by permission of Harper & Row.

of organizations and endorsements, and for what people—the apathetic and the not-so-apathetic—are thinking about the issues that concern them.

The criticism has come in bursts—at two- and four-year intervals, much of it being directed at coverage of congressional and presidential campaigns and elections. But politics is a continuing activity, locally as well as nationally, and apprentice reporters, whether or not their goal is a Washington assignment, need to be aware of its ramifications. The contest for power that is politics may underlie a grand jury's report criticizing administration of a state mental hospital if the jury's foreman happens to be an ardent Democrat and the board of hospital supervisors happens to be dominated by a Republican committeewoman. It should not pass unseen by reporters covering the courts simply because their focus is too narrowly on the judicial process. Reporters assigned to education are myopic indeed if they fail to note that the newest appointee to the state commission on higher education was a heavy contributor to the campaign of the governor who makes the appointment. Politics, then, pervades most of the action in the public arena; it is not merely a biennial or quadrennial contest culminating at the polls. Public affairs reporters, whatever their beat, need to recognize the maneuvers and identify the players. A reporter who shows the inclination and aptitude may move up to regular coverage of politics; it is a coveted assignment on most newspaper staffs, gained, traditionally, via city hall and statehouse experience. If the reporter's first job is on a small daily or weekly, initiation in coverage of political events may come in an assignment to report on a county convention. Or on a larger daily, it may come in monitoring a number of precinct polling places or the county auditor's offices on election night when the entire staff is mobilized for the harvest of election returns. The county convention may seem like ritualized tedium, relieved, if at all, by committee reports and occasional balloting; and the election night, a vigil protracted by an auditor's inefficiency in reporting results in a crucial county. But as these isolated events come to be perceived in the context of the political process, the fascination of watching the exercise and pursuit of power takes hold.

THE REPORTER
AND POLITICAL REALITY

Politicians, political scientists, opinion analysts, and just plain observers have long debated the extent of the influence of the mass media on elections. Those who minimized the influence of editorial page endorsements invariably have pointed to Franklin D. Roosevelt's heavy reelection majorities in the face of overwhelming newspaper opposition. Yet communications researcher John P. Robinson, directing a study for the University of Michigan's Institute for Social Research, concluded that the influence of newspaper endorsements is seriously underestimated; he found that newspaper support "had a significant bearing" on the votes cast for Nixon in both 1968 and 1972.[1] Other factors affecting voter behavior cited by Robinson are those most often noted in other studies: party identification, age, education, region, size of city, ethnicity, economic status.

Whatever the effect of editorial endorsements on election results, there can be no doubt about the importance of the coverage of primaries, conventions, and campaigns in the news columns and on the television screen. As control of selection of presidential candidates has slipped from the national parties, through changes in the nomination process engendered by television itself, that control has moved to the media by default, in the opinion of some careful observers. John Sears, Washington attorney and former campaign manager for Ronald Reagan, affirms that "the news media control the nomination and election of the president today. They did not seek this responsibility. They feel uncomfortable with it. They do not discharge it well. But they have it, and until the politicians change the nomination system, journalists will be the real bosses in American politics."[2] Political scientist James D. Barber similarly concludes that the power of selecting the president has passed to the press. "With the lapse of the parties, the people turn to their newspapers and magazines and television sets for guidance. And it is there, in political journalism, that they find a new elite who, through no conscious conspiracy or neurotic lust for power, have had power thrust upon them. . . . What is new is not mass communication as one of the major forces in politics, but rather its emergence to fill virtually the whole gap in the electoral process left by the default of other independent elites who used to help manage the choice. Their power is all the stronger because it looks, to the casual observer, like no power at all."[3] And another political scientist, Frank Sorauf, citing a Survey Research Center report "that in the 1968 campaign only 22 percent of American adults had been contacted by someone from one of the parties," concludes that "most of the voting electorate, in other words, were reached exclusively, if at all, by the mass media."[4] At the very least, as two other political scientists express it, "Mass communications . . . furnish much of the material from which voters build their mental pictures of political reality."[5]

What are the functions that the political writer must fulfill if the voter's picture of reality is not to become hopelessly skewed, blurred, or incomplete? Those functions can be identified as follows:

Reporting and interpreting events
Defining issues
Portraying personalities
Investigating support

Identifying trends
Checking and analyzing public opinion

These functions are as applicable on the local level as they are on the state and national; the stakes may be higher in Washington, but the interest may be more intense in Goshen or Gallipolis.

Before we look at these functions, some generalizations about the reporter and the political process deserve attention. They apply to the reporter who undertakes any and all of these functions.

If ever the heat of reporters' curiosity needs to be fueled by skepticism, that time is when they are checking with political sources. It's not that the politician necessarily lies—although some do—or creates pseudo events—although many do—or withholds or only partially discloses information—although most do. It's just that the relationship between reporter and politician is essentially adversarial.[6] They need each other, but the politician's need of the reporter is as a channel to the public in the pursuit and retention of power, whereas the reporter's need of the politician is as a source of reliable information. The needs do not regularly balance out in favor of the public interest. The device of the leak, for example, discussed with reference to the legal process in Chapter 7, is used by politicians for their own ends, which may be to provoke action or to undermine an opponent or to test public response to a possible course of action. The leaked information may also be useful to reporters, though not until it has been verified by other sources. Many reporters have been left feeling used—and abused—because their too-ready acceptance of the reliability of a source led them to publish misinformation. Furthermore, of course, some politicians are not above claiming they have been misquoted, so reporters are well advised to retain their notes.

The healthy skepticism of reporters may be compromised in some instances by too close an association with a political source. Reporters may rationalize a chummy relationship with a politician in office on the grounds that it will serve them and their newspaper well by making them privy to "the real inside." But if they enjoy dining at the politician's home and are friends of the family, how likely are they then to ask the really hard questions that may embarrass their sources?

The political reporter is vulnerable enough to charges of bias without that kind of association. In an area of news where merely the publication of a public figure's name is held to be an advantage, contenders for the public's attention are quick to charge favoritism. It would appear that the political reporter whose newspaper endorses candidates is particularly susceptible to bias in favor of those the paper supports. A number of studies have shown that unfortunately a paper's editorial endorsement tends to be reflected in the news columns of the paper.[7] That reflection may lie in space allocations, which are outside the reporter's range of responsibility, but it should not show in the reporter's writing, which is well within it.

One of the most frequently voiced criticisms of political reporting is that it relies heavily on handouts. The promotional mills of political candidates and officeholders grind frequently, and always in self-interest. How much of their output gets published would seem to depend on a newspaper's policy but also on the energy and initiative of the reporter. A study published by the American Institute for Political Communication suggests that dependence on press releases by Washington correspondents varies inversely with the amount of news competition faced by their home papers: The less competition, the more dependence.[8] There is little reason to believe that the finding would not apply as well to the use of campaign publicity at every level of government. One of the troubles with the release, of course, is that it tends to put a barrier between the candidate or officeholder and the reporter; it is the information that the originator wants the public to have, and unless the reporter probes beyond it or rejects it out of hand, the picture of political reality suffers further distortion.

REPORTING FUNCTIONS
AND THE POLITICAL PROCESS

Politics—"this striving to win the things one holds desirable"[9]—is limited for the political reporter to the sphere of government and public policy. Although, as we have suggested, its ramifications are not confined to campaigns and elections, "the most critical political decisions are those determining who will hold public office; for by these decisions we decide who will decide all other questions."[10] The process of such determination, then, is the essential political process. That process encompasses institutions (the parties), events (primaries, conventions, campaigns, and elections), issues, personalities, and of course, the electorate on whom the entire process is based. The accuracy of the picture of political reality provided by the media depends on the ability of political reporters to understand and interpret all these components. Such, then, are their functions.

The Institutional Background

Well-educated public affairs reporters come to a political assignment with a background of courses in American government and politics. They are familiar with the recent history of the two major institutions, the political parties. They are aware that social and technological changes of the last couple of decades—the emergence of television among them—have weakened the parties, especially at the national level; that the parties are no longer the major sources of funding, patronage, information, expertise, and organizational support that they once were. Nonetheless, these reporters understand the loose confederation of sectional and state interests in both parties at the national level, the relative autonomy of state parties, and the wide variations in the effectiveness of one or both parties at the local level. They know that the two-party system is represented structurally, with variations among states, by functionaries and committees that tend to correspond to voting districts: from precinct through ward and city (if urban) to county, to state legislative and judicial, to congressional. They know that the party structure, for all its apparent similarity to the public's image of a political machine, is only occasionally, if ever, complete in all its parts and that the locus of power is more often in the city or county than in the state organization.

Because party organizations are regulated, in varying detail, by state statute rather than by federal law, political reporters will be familiar with the relevant statutes of their own states. If, in one state, party auxiliaries of dues-paying voluntary membership clubs have been formed to articulate ideology or simply to circumvent statutory regulations, the reporter is aware of their influence. Reporters are also conscious of the political influence of such nonparty organizations as chambers of commerce, industrial associations, and labor unions. Reporters appreciate the role of the parties in government, their part in organizing and promoting party interests in deliberative bodies from city councils to the national Congress. And they are aware that on the local level, nonpartisan elections of commissioners (in the commission form of government) and councilmen (in the city manager form) do not mean an absence of politics but rather that politics are managed by persons not responsible to party organizations.

Political science courses will also have made the educated newcomer to political reporting familiar with the key events of the political process: the primaries, the conventions, the campaigns, and the elections.

The increase in the number of states holding presidential primaries in recent years has markedly changed the nomination process as well as media coverage of it. Fewer than twenty-five states held presidential primaries in 1972, but by 1980, as a result of a movement to "open up" the nominating process, the number had swelled to thirty-eight. As a consequence, "the number of delegates selected by the party leaders dropped from approximately 70–80 percent in 1968, to about 25 percent in 1980," according to the estimate of one party leader.[11] More significantly, as far as the media are concerned, the proliferation of primaries, combined with the extension of public opinion polling, intensified the horse-race aspect of political coverage. In arguing the importance of the media as a determiner of candidates, political scientist Herbert Asher observes, "The horse race mentality can be very intrusive. Few people would want to bet on a candidate identified in the media as a loser. The interaction among media coverage, poll results, and primary outcomes can generate interpretations and prophecies that assume a life of their own and act to promote the prospects of one candidate over another."[12]

More specifically, with reference to reporting the 1980 presidential primaries, one research team found little improvement over past years, despite acknowledgment of the justice of past criticism. A research team for the *Washington Journalism Review* studied primary campaign coverage of the *Washington Post,* the *New York Times,* and the *Chicago Tribune* from October 1979 through the first week of June 1980. They found the newspapers "provided more of the same reporting as in the past, including: an uncontrollable addiction to forecasting results; a subjugation of stories about issues by stories about pithy speeches, tactics, style, and above all else, who was ahead; a tendency to hype events and manufacture issues; a propensity for grossly over-covering the campaign, resulting in hundreds of non-newsworthy pieces; the cavalier treatment of 'minor' candidates."[13]

Furthermore, the magazine reported, "A random sampling of other newspapers around the country, including the *Boston Globe,* the *Atlanta Journal and Constitution,* the *Baltimore Sun,* the *Los Angeles Times* and the *Cleveland Plain Dealer,* suggest that the coverage in the three papers studied was repeated in varying degrees by most major dailies."[14]

Assuming that novice political writers will not immediately be assigned to cover a national convention, they may nonetheless win spurs at county, district, or state versions of the quadrennial spectacle. Whether the purpose of the convention is to endorse candidates or elect party officials or select delegates to the next higher convention, the procedure is pretty much the same: a keynote speech, reports of committees—credentials, rules, nominating or endorsements, and platform (if any)—and debate and voting on the reports by the delegates. Conventions are usually characterized by factional struggle, much of which goes on in the committee sessions and is prefigured by the composition of the committees. Because conflict is such a traditional staple of news reporting, no reporter needs to be told to look for it. What he does need to look for are the issues, the ideologies, the personalities, and the histories that underlie the conflicts so that his report of the convention can help the reader to understand it in the context of the political process.

Conflict is obviously a staple, as well, of the series of events that constitute political campaigning. In no aspect of the political process have the media come to play a more important role. Television and radio, particularly, have brought about what is often called "the new campaigning," managed by public relations and advertising firms, whose decisions are based on public opinion polling.

It is precisely because these experts know the customs of the media journalists and exploit them to the advantage of their clients that the commonly practiced standard of objectivity is too often a disservice to the reader—and the viewer. Timothy Crouse, whose account of life with the

1972 campaign press corps, *The Boys on the Bus,* is a litany of reproaches against the inadequacy of objectivity, crisp wire service leads, and the herd instinct in reporting events, quotes Brit Hume, columnist Jack Anderson's former legman:

> "Those guys on the plane," said Hume, "claim that they're trying to be objective. They shouldn't try to be objective, they should try to be honest. And they're *not* being honest. Their so-called objectivity is just a guise for superficiality. They report what one candidate said, then they go and report what the other candidate said with equal credibility. They never get around to finding out if the guy is telling the truth. They just pass the speeches along without trying to confirm the substance of what the candidates are saying. What they pass off as objectivity is just a mindless kind of neutrality."[15]

Gene Wyckoff, himself a sought-after producer of campaign films for television, after telling how it's done in *The Image Candidates,* remarks, "Television's slavish devotion to the stopwatch may also serve to reduce the substance of political statements to incidental dialogue between dramatic characters in conflict. Newscasts typically edit a candidate's SOF [sound-on-film] remarks to the most pithy and provocative sentences and, without elaboration or evaluation of the condensed statement, juxtapose it with a contrary statement by the opposition."[16] As for more extended, face-to-face confrontations of candidates on news-feature programs, Wyckoff continues,

> Even when the candidates are given more time to answer and rebut answers of questions about campaign issues, viewers may be forced to judge style rather than substance of the arguments because candidates are often in serious disagreement as to the basic facts and such disagreements are rarely (if ever) set straight by the professional television journalists conducting the program. The failure should not be dismissed with the comment that the professional television journalists might not be prepared to inform the viewer where the truth lies. Technically it is quite feasible (and hardly more expensive) to record candidate confrontations on videotape and delay broadcast twenty-four or forty-eight hours until the facts cited by the candidates can be authenticated and appraised by inserted remarks by the program moderators.
>
> But however feasible in a technical sense, any appraisal of political candidates or their remarks by television newsmen would constitute a cardinal sin against the medium's most holy commandment: *Thou shalt not offend.*[17]

Whether motivated by fear of offending listeners or of being cut by the copy desk, journalists who consider themselves merely a conduit are serving the politician and shortchanging the electorate. A journalist who broke away from the conduit role in the 1972 campaign was NBC correspondent Catherine Mackin. The incident was so unusual that it has been recounted by a number of media critics, including Edwin Diamond:

"Catherine Mackin has been campaigning with the President," John Chancellor noted on NBC the night of Sept. 28, "and she has some observations to make on the Nixon campaign style. . . ."

With that standard introduction, the *NBC Nightly News* switched to a film report by Cassie Mackin from Los Angeles. It looked like a typical item from the wind-in-the-hair school of TV journalism: Mackin doing a "standup" outside the hotel where President Nixon had spoken the night before, too late to make the network news programs. But the script that accompanied the routine clips of Richard (and Pat) Nixon shaking hands, climbing into helicopters, and appearing at the fund-raising dinner was sharp and unequivocal.

Mackin said that the Nixon campaign consists of "speeches before closed audiences—invited guests only. . . ." She reported that the press was getting only glimpses of Nixon as he campaigned. Then she added: "There is a serious question of whether President Nixon is setting up straw men by leaving the very strong impression that McGovern is making certain proposals which in fact he is not. . . ."

The film cut to Richard Nixon speaking of "some who believe" in defense budget cuts that "would make the United States the second-strongest nation . . . with the second-strongest Army . . . with the second-strongest Air Force. . . ." Then back to Mackin: "The President obviously meant McGovern's proposed defense budget, but his criticism never specified how the McGovern plan would weaken the country. On welfare, the President accuses McGovern of wanting to give those on welfare more than those who work— which is not true. On tax reform, the President says McGovern has called for 'confiscation of wealth'—which is not true."

It was a critical moment in NBC's coverage of the 1972 presidential campaign. Rather than merely re-amplifying a campaign attack, Cassie Mackin was offering a strong corrective—for NBC's audience of 10 million. Her gloss was too much for the men in the White House who monitor the media. NBC officials received three phone calls from Nixon Administration men protesting the Mackin item—the first call almost before the program's theme had faded.[18]

Aside from its forthrightness in interpretation, what made the Mackin newscast remarkable was its uniqueness. "Perhaps it was no coincidence that it was a woman who went for Nixon's jugular," Crouse commented in his account of the incident. "Mackin was an outsider. She had neither the opportunity nor the desire to travel with the all-male pack; therefore, she was not infected with the pack's chronic defensiveness and defeatism. Like Helen Thomas and Sarah McClendon, she could still call a spade a spade."[19]

The herd instinct in campaign coverage thus alluded to has been documented by more than one researcher. Political scientist Doris A. Graber, reporting on a content analysis of twenty newspapers she chose as a cross-section of the American press, declared, "The most striking finding of the analysis of press reporting of the 1968 presidential campaign is the great uniformity in coverage. Extant press information was essentially the same throughout the country."[20] Graber concluded,

Several reasons seem to account for the similarities in press coverage. In the first place, the origins of campaign news were surprisingly uniform. Forty-one percent of all campaign news was based on information supplied by presidential candidates and another 15 percent on information released by their running mates. Thus 56 percent of all campaign news was directly linked to the campaign efforts of the presidential and vice-presidential contenders.

Uniformity also resulted from the fact that news stories were encoded by a limited group of people. While some similarity undoubtedly springs from frequent use of wire service stories, this was not as heavy as we had anticipated. It ranged from a low of 7 percent for the New York *Times* to a high of 79 percent for the Bangor (Maine) *Daily News*. But the median was only 30 percent. Only seven of the 20 papers took as much as 40 percent of their campaign items from wire services.

Another reason for uniformity which was less influential than anticipated was use of syndicated columns. Fifteen percent of all items in the study came from columnists. But 75 percent of the columnists had columns in one paper only. Only 3 percent of the columnists had their work published in at least a third of the papers in this sample. . . .

In view of the limited unifying influence of columnists and wire service reports, one is left with the impression that common socialization, more than identity of encoders of news messages, accounted for the uniformity in campaign coverage. Newspaper personnel apparently shared a sense of what is newsworthy and how it should be presented.[21]

Part of the socialization to which Graber refers was specified by Crouse four years later as the reluctance of special correspondents, traveling with the candidates, to develop stories different from those filed by the wire services. They knew that back home in the newsroom, their copy would be compared with the wire service accounts and justification for deviations would be demanded.

That shared "sense of what is newsworthy"—though not pack journalism—is also apparent in reporting and interpreting the ultimate event in the political process, the election. In national elections, the broadcasting networks' elaborate systems for reporting and the computerized projection of vote totals have contributed to uniformity of presentation, if not always of results. For all their instantaneous delivery, however, they have not diminished the job of political journalists serving the newspaper audience. They must still have their own highly organized system for gathering results from precinct polling places and county auditors' offices in their areas, whether the election is local, state, or national. And the news for them, as for the broadcasters, is who won what office and by what margin.

Too often, they stop right there. The editors of *Columbia Journalism Review* have criticized the media generally for their "relatively casual treatment" in interpretation of election results, and they cite examples:

On election night [1972], John Chancellor asserted confidently on NBC that much of the Nixon majority represented a shift from the 1968 Wallace vote.

To say the least, this is a hypothesis worth study, but no reporter who has come to this publication's attention has actually gone to voting districts and tried to find proof.

Another example: *Time* asserted (Nov. 20) that Nixon's victory had "splintered" the New Deal coalition of minorities, and did cite a scattering of precinct returns to support its contention. But it reached back only to 1968, whereas a large organization should not find it beyond its grasp to determine whether in fact the Democratic coalition in 1968 was still Roosevelt's, and what stage 1972 represented in its evolution or dissolution over four decades. The possibilities are great. By halting the story of the election as soon as the counting stops, news media are discarding what is perhaps their best opportunity for reporting on the whole electorate.[22]

Not all the media, of course, do halt the story of the election when the counting stops. Even so, much of the postelection interpretation tends to be in the form of quotes from party chiefs as to how *they* interpreted the results or in the form of the journalist's impressionistic analysis that weighs such factors as economic trends, broadening of the suffrage, and type and cost of campaigns. Or a newspaper may report the enterprise of NBC News, which "interviewed· Republican voters as they left the polls, including both those who remained loyal to their candidates and those who voted Democratic. Among the loyalists, 26 percent said. . . ." And so forth. The readers' confidence is shaken when they discover later in the story that the NBC News sample was only 211 voters, and there is no indication of how many voters leaving the polls refused to answer the reporter's first question concerning party identification.[23]

The deep-delving analysis that ranges over decades to identify and hypothesize about voting behavior is left to the social scientists, and their findings, reported in scholarly journals, are rarely noted—let alone replicated—by the journalist.

Defining Issues

If the picture of political reality tends to be distorted by conventional reporting of events, that picture risks further distortion when the writer turns to the second function of political reporting: defining issues. In this effort, the writer may be hindered, rather than helped, by party platforms and the utterances of candidates.

Given the nonideological nature of the two major American political parties and their inclination to jostle each other for the middle of the road, it is not surprising that party platforms tend to be all things to all voters. They indulge in verbiage with little clear definition of positions on issues. As for the candidates, the strictures of the new campaigning often call for obscuring rather than defining issues. "The very pervasiveness of television may serve to inhibit meaningful debate on campaign issues," writes strategist Wyckoff. "When a candidate is making an in-person address to a banker's luncheon or a union convention, he can presume certain special knowledge or interests on the part of his audience and not risk boring them or talking over their heads—but not so via television, where a candidate has no way of knowing who is tuned in. His fundamental purpose—to win the election—may best be served by staying 'loose' and general on the issues."[24]

Whether or not party platforms are ambiguous and the candidates "stay loose" on the issues, the political journalist has a responsibility to put those issues in focus. Yet much of the criticism directed at campaign coverage springs from the fact that issues tend to be ignored in favor of who's ahead. Thomas E. Patterson, in an analysis of network news of the 1976 campaign, found that 60 percent of the coverage "focused on the horse race, compared to only 28 percent devoted to issues, candidate qualifications, and the like."[25] Nor are the networks alone in that emphasis. In its study of coverage of the 1979–80 primaries in three leading dailies, the *Washington Journalism Review* found that "The *Washington Post* ran more than five times as many stories on the horse race as on issues, 538 to 186. The *New York Times* and the *Chicago Tribune* both ran slightly less than twice as many stories on the horse race as on issues, 323 to 185 for the *Times* and 224 to 127 for the *Tribune*."[26]

Lyn Nofziger, Reagan's press secretary during the campaign, had a partial explanation for the imbalance. "What happens is reporters write a story once on an issue, and then they think that everybody has read it, so they decide they will not write about that again. They run away from the issues after they have written about them once, even though it might be the most important part of the campaign."[27]

The result is unfortunate. "The power of the press in America," Theodore H. White has written, "is a primordial one. It sets the agenda of public discussion; and this sweeping political power is unrestrained by any law."[28] In concurrence, political scientist Bernard Cohen has suggested that the mass media may not be very successful in telling their audiences what to think, but they are "stunningly successful in telling their audiences what to think *about*."[29] In study after study, communications researchers have demonstrated the importance of the press—and coverage of politics and elections—in setting the public's agenda, in helping to sort out and crystallize the issues of a campaign. Two leading authorities on agenda-setting research, Maxwell McCombs and Donald L. Shaw, say there is a strong relationship between the issues emphasized by the news media and those that eventually have salience for the individual reader or viewer.[30] What this means is that media coverage of campaigns has a more direct impact on the voter's perception of the important issues than was previously believed by social scientists.

One aspect of a campaign that should not be ignored by the political reporter in an effort to define issues is that of political advertising. Journalism professor Thomas Bowers believes the press should pay more attention to such advertising because of the part it plays in setting agendas. A thorough analysis of campaign advertising can tell the reporter where the candidate thinks he is weak, what issues he thinks the voters want to hear about, and what kind of image he is trying to project. In recent years, political advertising has often been based on the candidate's precampaign polls that indicate issues of concern to the voters. These data are analyzed by political operatives who decide how they will be used. Sometimes advertising is aimed at the general public, sometimes at specific audiences. For example, in the 1972 presidential campaign, the McGovern forces emphasized the Vietnam war in their advertising. They did this, not because the war was a "gut issue" with the voters, but because the candidate and his staff agreed that persons likely to contribute money to the campaign would be attracted by it.[31]

Whether the candidate is manipulating issues or straddling them by "staying loose," the responsibility of the political reporter is clear. The importance of the agenda-setting function of the media is such that the journalist must raise the questions and pursue the answers that define genuine issues before the electorate. If the answers from the candidates are not forthcoming, that, too, is news.

Portraying Personalities

Given the length of the ballot in most voting districts and the limitations of newspaper space, the political writer is faced with an almost insoluble problem in fulfilling the function of adequately portraying the candidates' personalities. And yet, under the terms of the new campaigning, the need for such portrayal is perhaps greater than ever. For the image presented on the television screen is, at best, superficial, one that needs the kind of fleshing out that only research, careful observation, and honest assessment in well-documented stories can provide. It is not realistic to expect this kind of portrayal of even the leading contenders in minor races, but too often the press falls short in profiling major candidates in major contests. In her analysis of the 1968 presidential campaign coverage, Graber concluded that "the press provided a very shallow portrait of the candidates based largely on general character traits. Readers learned little about the candidates' professional abilities."[32] More specifically, she reported,

Presidential qualities were discussed in similar manner by all papers. Papers varied in the actual number of references to personal and professional qualities described as important for the presidency, but the types and proportions of qualities mentioned were surprisingly uniform throughout the entire country. Only the special audience papers and the Sunday issues of general papers showed a somewhat different pattern.

With the single exception of the *National Observer*, personality attributes received the bulk of the stress. More than one third of all presidential qualities mentioned by newspapers dealt with character traits needed by the candidates. Presidential style ranked in second place, except for the *National*

Observer where it ranked first and the Chicago *Defender* [a black newspaper], *Wall Street Journal,* and three out of four Sunday papers where it ranked third. Professional image—the ability to project an image of capacity in crucial policy areas—ranked third for most papers. While the man and his image were widely discussed, his professional capacities were slighted. Ability in foreign affairs, race relations, or relations with the public received scant mention. Other vital abilities were ignored entirely. Remarks concerning the political philosophy of the candidates and their plans for organizational changes also were barely touched upon. Sunday papers, in particular, emphasized personal qualities to the exclusion of nearly all other criteria for judging presidential fitness.[33]

Investigating Support

The political writer's function in checking out support for candidates traditionally takes two directions: endorsement and financial backing. In neither is the investigation usually thorough enough. Suppose the reporter surveys all the county chairpersons in an effort to determine candidate preferences. Such questionnaires, if carefully devised, may serve as indicators of strength. But what if a high proportion of county chairpersons are leaders in name only? What if many have lost touch with their constituency and represent the opinion of only a small hard core of party loyalists? Then such a survey is no substitute for the kind of door-knocking in key areas that is counseled—and practiced—by the *Washington Post*'s David Broder and Haynes Johnson. As polling becomes more and more widely practiced, many news organizations are not content with either door-knocking or surveys of party leaders but instead conduct surveys of public opinion throughout all stages of campaigns.

Another kind of endorsement tactic that needs close scrutiny is the frequent claim, "endorsed by labor." What segments of labor? Which unions? Not even organized labor speaks in unison. Then there are the various "independent volunteers for . . ." and "independent citizens for . . ." and "independent voters for. . . ." A little independent checking by the reporter may disclose that volunteers–citizens–voters are one-to-a-handful of longtime partisans whose news releases are cleared, if not written, by the candidate's public-relations staff.

As for financial support, the high cost of campaigning plus the Watergate corruption have created a climate that has encouraged enactment of campaign disclosure laws in many states. These are of varying degrees of stringency, and the effectiveness of all of them depends on follow-through by the press. "Every candidate can follow a disclosure law to the letter, but the public will never know where the money came from or where it went unless newsmen relay the information," says political writer Timothy Harper. "In Iowa, where one of the toughest disclosure laws ever written went into effect last fall, too many journalists have chosen to ignore the new statute rather than assume knotty added responsibilities."[34]

Journalists who did not shirk the responsibilities of a new disclosure law in another state were a team of reporters for the *Roanoke* (Va.) *Times*, who employed a computer to study a gubernatorial race. They found that "the two candidates actually spent a third of a million dollars more than they reported," according to *Editor & Publisher*.

> The study . . . also uncovered several avenues, real and potential, for abusing the state's new election laws which require candidates to show near the end of the campaign where their money comes from and where it was spent. According to a story by [associate editor Forrest M.] Landon, "No less than 99 separate campaign committees, candidates' local headquarters, economic-interest groups and assorted organizations—some real, some imaginary or practically so—were raising money for [gubernatorial candidates] Howell and Godwin." This multiplicity of fund-raising operations, he said, prevented the voter from getting a full and accurate picture of where the money was coming from during the election's peak. Another method of concealing donations was splitting gifts to several different organizations, although the money originated from one benefactor, the study reported.[35]

The sophisticated analysis practiced by the *Roanoke Times* team is perhaps beyond the resources of most newspapers, but a careful examination of the required reports of income and expenditures by candidates and their committees is not. Such examination can be useful in indicating sources of support for candidates through contributions of a relatively new campaign adjunct, the Political Action Committee, but it will not disclose the contribution, financial or otherwise, of such organizations as the Moral Majority. They are not governed by campaign spending limits as long as they are not affiliated with or controlled by a candidate's campaign organization.

Identifying Trends

The job of political writers is not limited to reporting and interpreting events, defining issues, portraying candidates, and investigating support. Indeed, some of their most useful work in giving the reader a picture of political reality may lie in areas less readily perceived, and for that reason, all the more interesting. Politics is a dynamic process: Alignments shift, coalitions form and dissolve, new strivers for power enter the arena. The political writer is alert to signs of change and untiring in checking them out. Such enterprise resulted in a *Detroit News* story that reported that the country's schoolteachers were greatly increasing their contributions to "friendly" political candidates. John E. Peterson of the *News*'s Washington bureau began his story this way:

> Washington—When a suburban Detroit teacher returned from a vacation trip this summer, her mailbox contained a letter requesting a pledge to the National Education Association's (NEA) political action fund.

Eighty cents of each $1 she contributed, the letter said, would be used to support state and local candidates "friendly to education." The rest would go to the NEA's Washington headquarters for political use on the national scene.

Before the start of school this fall, the NEA had collected nearly $1.1 million in political donations from the 1.6 million classroom teachers and other educational professionals who make up its membership.[36]

The story went on to report that NEA officials expected to spend 125 times more than the organization had spent on campaigns two years earlier and that its objectives were vastly increased federal aid to education, or in the words of the reporter, "better working conditions."

Another "trend" story, much more elaborately based, concerning increased participation in politics by teachers, has already been cited in Chapter 5. That story grew out of an effort by the *Minneapolis Tribune* to analyze the action at party caucuses. The *Tribune* explained how it had covered them:

> From a carefully arranged list of the more than 3,900 precincts in Minnesota, a computer selected 100 by a random method. What happened in those precincts reflects accurately the state as a whole.
>
> For each precinct, one observer was recruited to attend the Republican caucus and another to attend the DFL [Democratic–Farmer–Labor]. Observers were thoroughly briefed about caucus procedures.
>
> Each observer was asked to note certain facts about the people attending, about the chairman, and about the business of the meeting. In addition, each observer also gave a questionnaire to each delegate elected.
>
> Observers phoned in some of their findings . . . and also were interviewed for their impressions about the meeting. Delegate questionnaires and information about the resolutions were mailed. The findings were coded and assembled for processing on a computer for analysis by the *Tribune*.[37]

One of the results of that analysis was the reader's awareness of an otherwise imperceptible trend: a new strength of teachers among DFL convention delegates disproportionate to their numbers among eligible voters.

Checking and Analyzing Public Opinion

The wide acceptance of public opinion polling in the political realm, for all its attendant controversy, speaks clearly to the political writer about the importance of gauging voter attitudes if readers are to gain a clear picture of political reality. The fact is that the picture is incomplete if the political journalist concentrates on events, issues, personalities, and support, to the exclusion of voters' reaction to any and all of these. The question for reporters remains: How can they best fulfill this function without distorting the picture?

The answer will probably depend, at least in part, on the resources made available to them by their publisher. But whether they can command an in-house survey team or subscribe to one of the polling organizations or neither of these, their concern will be with accuracy in polling and sophistication in reporting the results. These considerations apply in double measure to their assessment of a candidate's own polls.

In any case, the political writer should be familiar with at least the rudiments of survey research methodology described in Chapter 5. In cautioning the reporter to treat leaked survey results with skepticism, Philip Meyer has compiled a checklist, based on an advisory of the National Council on Public Polls (NCPP), that should serve as the minimum information needed to judge such results:

1. The identity of the sponsor of the survey.
2. The exact wording of the questions asked.
3. A definition of the population sampled.
4. The sample size and, where the survey design makes it relevant, the response rate.
5. Some indication of the allowance that should be made for sampling error.
6. Which results are based on part of the sample, e.g., probable voters, those who have heard of the candidate, or other subdivisions.
7. How the interviews were collected: in person in homes, by phone, by mail, on street corners, or wherever.
8. When the interviews were collected.[38]

Such information is important for the reader, as well as for the reporter, in assessing the significance of survey results. Some newspapers, as a matter of regular policy, precede every news report of a political poll with editorial comment pointing out what NCPP standards the poll does and does not meet.

It is this kind of consideration for the needs of the reader that can help to make coverage of politics a significant service by the media. The political process is too complex, and the voter's choice too important, for reporters to be willing to settle for less than the closest approximation of reality that they are capable of making.

NOTES

[1]John P. Robinson, "Perceived Media Bias and the 1968 Vote: Can the Media Affect Behavior After All?" *Journalism Quarterly* 49 (Summer 1972), 239–46. See also Robinson, "The Press as King-Maker: What Surveys from Last Five Campaigns Show," *Journalism Quarterly* 51 (Winter 1974), 587–94.

[2]John Sears, "The Press Elects the President," *Washington Journalism Review,* September 1980, p. 32.

[3]James D. Barber, *The Pulse of Politics: Electing Presidents in the Media Age* (New York: W. W. Norton & Co., 1980), p. 8.

[4]Frank J. Sorauf, *Party Politics in America,* 2nd ed. (Boston: Little, Brown, 1972), p. 84.

[5]Hugh A. Bone and Austin Ranney, *Politics and Voters,* 3rd ed. (New York: McGraw-Hill, 1971), p. 35.

[6]David S. Broder, "Politicians and Biased Political Information," in Richard W. Lee, ed., *Politics and the Press,* (Washington, D.C.: Acropolis Books, 1970), p. 63.

[7]Guido Stempel, "The Prestige Press Covers the 1960 Presidential Campaign," *Journalism Quarterly* 38 (Spring 1961), 157–63; "The Prestige Press in Two Presidential Elections," *Journalism Quarterly* 42 (Spring 1965), 15–21; Jae-won Lee, "Editorial Support and Campaign News: Content Analysis by Q-Method," *Journalism Quarterly* 49 (Winter 1972), 710–16; Ben H. Bagdikian, "The Fruits of Agnewism," *Columbia Journalism Review* 11 (January–February 1973), 9–21.

[8]Edward M. Glick, et al., *The Federal Government-Daily Press Relationship* (Washington, D.C.: American Institute for Political Communication, 1967).

[9]Sorauf, *Party Politics in America,* p. 1.

[10]Bone and Ranney, *Politics and Voters,* p. 1.

[11]Sears, "The Press Elects the President," p. 36.

[12]Herbert Asher, *Presidential Elections and American Politics* (Homewood, Ill.: The Dorsey Press, 1980), p. 261.

[13]Douglas Lowenstein, "Covering the Primaries," *Washington Journalism Review,* September 1980, p. 36.

[14]Ibid.

[15]Timothy Crouse, *The Boys on the Bus* (New York: Random House, 1972), p. 305.

[16]Gene Wyckoff, *The Image Candidates* (New York: Macmillan, 1968), p. 210.

[17]Ibid., p. 211.

[18]Edwin Diamond, "Fairness and Balance in the Evening News," *Columbia Journalism Review* 11 (January–February 1973), 22.

[19]Crouse, *Boys on the Bus,* p. 267.

[20]Doris A. Graber, "Press Coverage Patterns of Campaign News: The 1968 Presidential Race," *Journalism Quarterly* 48 (Autumn 1971), 502–12.

[21]Ibid., 511–12.

[22]Editors, "The Neglected Results," *Columbia Journalism Review* 11 (January–February 1973), 3.

[23]*Milwaukee Journal,* November 6, 1974, p. 26. The NBC sample totaled 8,000 voters.

[24]Wyckoff, *Image Candidates,* p. 7.

[25]Thomas E. Patterson, "The 1976 Horse Race," *The Wilson Quarterly,* Spring 1977, 73–77.

[26]Lowenstein, "Covering the Primaries," p. 39.

[27]Lyn Nofziger, quoted in *Candidates and Their Gurus Criticize Coverage,"* *Washington Journalism Review,* September 1980, p. 30.

[28]Theodore H. White, *The Making of the President 1972* (New York: Bantam, 1973), p. 327.

[29]Bernard C. Cohen, *The Press and Foreign Policy* (Princeton, N.J.: Princeton University Press, 1963).

[30]See Donald L. Shaw and Maxwell E. McCombs, *The Emergence of American Political Issues: The Agenda-Setting Function of the Press* (St. Paul, Minn.: West Publishing Co., 1976).

[31]Thomas Bowers, "Political Advertising: Setting the Candidate's Agenda," paper delivered at the Media and Agenda-Setting Function Conference, Syracuse, N.Y., October 25–28, 1974.

[32]Graber, "Press Coverage Patterns," 512.

[33]Ibid., 506–7.

[34]Timothy Harper, "Disclosures on the Campaign Trail," *Quill* 62 (March 1974), 24.

[35]*Editor & Publisher,* March 2, 1974, p. 10.

[36]*Detroit News,* October 28, 1974, p. 1.

[37]*Minneapolis Tribune,* March 3, 1974, p. 9A.

[38]Philip Meyer, *Precision Journalism* (Bloomington: Indiana University Press, 1973), pp. 185–86.

SUGGESTED READINGS

ASHER, HERBERT. *Presidential Elections and American Politics.* Homewood, Ill.: The Dorsey Press, 1980. The revised edition of this study of changes in campaigns, electorate, and political discourse between 1952 and 1976 has a new chapter on the media and presidential politics, signifying the increased importance the author attaches to media influence on presidential selection.

BARBER, JAMES DAVID. *The Lawmakers.* New Haven, Conn.: Yale University Press, 1965. Presents state legislators as representing four types of behavior on the basis of personality characteristics.

————. *The Pulse of Politics.* New York: W. W. Norton & Co., 1980. Media influence is stressed in this case for a cyclical theory of presidential elections dominated successively by themes of conflict, conscience, and conciliation between 1900 and 1980.

BOGART, LEO. *Silent Politics.* New York: Wiley, 1972. Explains and evaluates public opinion polling in the context of politics and journalism.

CROUSE, TIMOTHY. *The Boys on the Bus.* New York: Random House, 1973. A sharply critical report of the methods and mores of political writers based on direct observation in the 1972 presidential campaign.

GRABER, DORIS. *Mass Media and American Politics.* Washington, D.C.: Congressional Quarterly Press, 1980. A thorough survey of issues, heavily emphasizing the effects of the press.

GREEN, MARK J., JAMES M. FALLOWS, AND DAVID R. ZWICK. *Who Runs Congress?* New York: Bantam/Grossman, 1972. Describes congressional organization and operation in a useful perspective for the journalist. Another view of the congressman is offered by REP. DONALD RIEGLE, in *O Congress* (New York: Popular Library 1972). In *Congress: The Electoral Connection* (New Haven, Conn.: Yale University Press, 1974), political scientist DAVID MAYHEW examines the behavior of members of Congress from the standpoint of news and publicity.

HIEBERT, RAY E., et al., eds. *The Political Image Merchants: Strategies for the Seventies.* Washington, D.C.: Acropolis Books Ltd., 1975. The "new" politics discussed in a collection of conference papers, of which the most useful are those of participating campaign managers.

KELLEY, STANLEY. *Professional Public Relations and Political Power.* Baltimore, Md.: The Johns Hopkins Press, 1956. This early examination of the role of public relations in politics is still one of the best.

MEYER, PHILIP. *Precision Journalism: A Reporter's Introduction to Social Science Methods.* Bloomington: Indiana University Press, 1973. This "bible" of social science methodology has particular relevance for the political writer.

PETERS, CHARLES. *How Washington Really Works.* Reading, Mass.: Addison-Wesley, 1980. The editor-in-chief of *Washington Monthly* provides an entertaining eye-opener on the potential for political reporting.

ROBINSON, JOHN P.   "The Press as King-Maker: What Surveys From the Last Five Campaigns Show." *Journalism Quarterly* 51 (Winter 1974), 587–94. A summary of studies supporting the author's thesis that newspaper endorsement influences voters' choices.

ROLL, CHARLES W., JR., AND ALBERT H. CANTRIL.   *Polls, Their Use and Misuse in Politics.* New York: Basic Books, 1972. A pair of professionals find ignorance about polling among media and media users. This is a readable effort to dispel it.

10

Covering
the Legislative Process

You can find out more about what's going on at the state capitol by
spending one night drinking with the capitol press corps than you can
in months of reading the papers those reporters write for.

Molly Ivins, Houston Journalism Review

At every level of government, from the municipal council to the state
legislature to the Congress, legislative bodies meet to consider laws. An idea
for a law may originate with the lawmakers themselves, departmental administrators, citizens, or lobbyists, but whatever the source, there is a typical process by which an idea becomes a law. The idea is first expressed in a
bill, drafted to conform to other laws and court rulings. The bill is introduced in the law-making body, which usually refers it to one of its committees for study. The committee may amend, revise, ignore, kill, or pass the
bill; if it is of sufficient interest, the committee may hold a public hearing at
which citizens and representatives of affected groups may add their views.
If released from committee, the bill is considered by the entire legislative
body, which may amend, defeat, refer to another committee, or approve
the measure, with or without debate. If the legislative body consists of two
houses, this procedure is followed in each of them, with differences resolved by a joint conference committee. Finally, if passed, the bill is considered by the appropriate executive—mayor, governor, or president—who
vetoes or approves it. The law-making body may vote to sustain or override
a veto.

Covering the legislative process, whether it is at the local, state, or
federal level, requires intensive effort by public affairs reporters. Under-

standing the process by which a bill becomes a law is only the beginning. Reporters must weigh the myriad proposals in terms of their significance for readers and viewers. They must consider the important ones in relationship to other laws and court decisions. They must examine the pressures that determine defeat or passage. How can the reporters assigned to cover a legislative body—be it city council, state legislature, or national Congress—provide the public with information that is both important and interesting? How can they cover "events" (for example, "The city council today passed an ordinance prohibiting all-night massage parlors") and at the same time, set those events in context? In short, how can they best cover the legislative process?

FUNCTIONS OF COVERAGE

Understanding the functions of legislative coverage provides a foundation:

Providing information   In representative government, an informed citizenry is considered essential. From colonial times, American governmental institutions have, in theory at least, depended on the people for their authority. Clearly, the media, as principal conveyers of information about society's needs, can help the citizen to seek laws that benefit the society. Political scientist Delmar Dunn notes that the press can "lift a matter from the mire of obscurity to the light of intense attention," and in doing so, "alerts additional groups and decision makers to their stakes in the outcome" of a decision.[1]

Serving as watchdog   From colonial times to the present, an antagonism, sometimes latent and sometimes open, has pervaded the relationship between citizen and government. Traditionally, the press has been one of the social institutions that monitor the performance of government and government officials. "A policy-maker very often judges the success of an endeavor by the extent to which it generates press comment," according to Dunn. "If the press praises or criticizes them [officials' proposals or activities], they are affected by what they read. In fact, the press's critique of policy-makers' performances encourages them to act in ways that the press perceives as favorable."[2]

Promoting Change   The press can promote change that benefits society by exposing evil. If mental hospitals are dungeons, intensive press coverage can force corrective action by the legislature. If poverty and hunger are real, but invisible, problems, the press can instigate action by revealing the conditions. "The policy-maker," Dunn writes, "often seems desperate in his attempt to learn about his environment," and the press can help provide essential facts. Because officials "use the press to gauge public thinking," the press can influence the policy-making process.[3]

Dunn's observations have been confirmed in study after study of the legislative process. In a fascinating analysis of how an aggressive, cause-oriented member of Congress can team up with a newspaper, researcher Susan Miller examined how California Congressman Peter Stark worked closely with the *Los Angeles Times* in 1974 to expose the plight of American citizens languishing in Mexican jails. Stark's aide struck a bargain with the *Times* to "share the story with them if they agreed to go big." Stark opened confidential files to the paper with a pledge of confidentiality on sources. In turn, the office agreed not to release the information to any other reporter.[4] A series of articles in the *Los Angeles Times* followed, and these in turn prompted further efforts by Stark's office to give the issue wide exposure through a Congressional hearing. The snowball effect took over, and a spate of hearings, coverage, and hearings developed. "The symbiosis between Congress and the media can be enhanced by collaboration," Miller concluded. "But it also exists quite apart from any conscious effort. Reporters feed off Congress. Congress feeds off reporters."[5]

But that is not to say that public officials always welcome the press' attention. "I've gotten burned," Stark told Miller. "Some reporters I try to avoid because we always seem to have misunderstandings about what it was I said. . . . And some things happen you wish they wouldn't write about. The *Los Angeles Times* did a less than complimentary piece about my automobiles just after I came here. . . . But that's the way it goes. . . . Generally, if you're open, honest, don't bullshit, play it straight, you're okay."[6]

Tension in press–government relations lies just beneath the surface of most issues, and public affairs reporters are likely to confront government officials more than once early in their careers. The relationship may be placid as the new reporter takes over a beat, but as any experienced reporter will attest, it will turn contentious with the first hard-hitting story. The watchdog role of the press has a long history. "If the press were to fulfill its role in truthfully reporting to the people, it was inevitable that the press would occasionally pose a threat to government and those in similar positions of power," asserts Robert W. Greene, who headed the probe of Investigative Reporters & Editors, Inc., into the 1976 death of Arizona reporter Don Bolles.[7] The role of the media is no less critical in the small community than in Phoenix nor the functions less clearly drawn.

EVALUATIONS OF COVERAGE

For several months every two years—and in an increasing number of states, every year—state legislatures meet and pass thousands of laws. Many are routine, such as a law to change the state animal from the groundhog to the deer or to grant bonding authority to a school district to raise school-construction funds. But some are very complex, such as laws on taxation, property, public education, and the conduct of criminal trials. State laws, generally, have immediate and direct impact on the lives of citizens, perhaps more so than the ordinances of a city or village council, whose impact is within a municipality, or the laws of Congress, whose effect is often filtered through several layers of bureaucracy.

Yet, despite the importance of state legislatures, press coverage, in the eyes of many observers, has been, with exceptions, inadequate. "The legislator's most commonly heard concerns," writes former state capitol reporter Thomas B. Littlewood, "are that reporters do not dig deeply enough or interpret wisely enough; do not have the time or inclination to comprehend the subtle shadings and political nuances of the legislative arena; and—by far the most serious allegation—may not really understand the legislative process."[8]

Other observers criticize a cynicism toward genuine reform on the part of reporters covering the legislative process. One acerbic account concludes that the cynicism tends to "move from a healthy to a pronounced state, inclining the media toward agreement with the status quo. . . .The political process makes reporters so close to it that the way it operates is the way they believe it must operate."[9]

The process by which an idea becomes law, at the local, state, or federal level, is complex, and there are many actors and influencing ingredients in the making of any legislative decision. Too often, the reporter is caught up in the decision itself and ignores the behind-the-scenes pressures that resulted in the legislation, as well as the more apparent effect of the legislation on the lives of the readers. "The legislative process in the states is messy—really, it defies all of the American instincts for order—and extremely subtle," says Alan Rosenthal of the Eagleton Institute of Politics at Rutgers University. "At times it may be impossible to report it clearly and consistently, since it is not always clear and consistent itself."[10] Furthermore, the path by which a bill becomes a law can lead the reporter into fragmentary reporting, in that each time a bill is debated or voted on, there is an "event" to report, and the importance of a bill may be "watered down" in a series of fragmentary news stories. "Newspaper philosophy still keys on a breaking news story," observes Joe Weisman, a political columnist for the Chicago *Sun-Times* and a veteran of statehouse coverage in Springfield, Illinois. "And the legislature least lends itself to this theory."[11]

If coverage of the legislative process is censured by such critics, reporters and legislators involved in the process also are critical of the reporting. Carol Hilton, a student of the media, found in a 1967 study that many lawmakers "criticize the media broadly for having an appetite for sensationalism, for jazzing up coverage and rushing into print (or on the air) with half-researched stories." She also found that some reporters felt they were on a "useless errand" and that "a wide audience is achieved only by titillating copy."[12] A replication of her research ten years later concluded that legislators and reporters "had similar views" but that only the reporters recognized that fact.[13] Other recent studies have found that, on one hand, reporters "tend to hold a very favorable perspective toward the legislature as an institution of government. On the other hand, they tend to view legislators' qualities and roles in a negative fashion."[14]

COMPONENTS OF THE PROCESS

Like legislative bodies themselves, the press in its legislative coverage must engage in a dynamic process. The public may perceive this process as the visible, regular, and special sessions of city councils, state legislatures, and the Congress, but it is much more than that. It is a pattern of activity and leadership. It is also a manifestation of the complex interrelationships among other branches of government and various constituencies.

The Body Organizes

Through party caucuses and formal and informal meetings, legislative leadership emerges after each new election. Sometimes the jousting for leadership goes on for months, even years. The patterns can occur at the state, city, and village level. The reporter observing this process needs to watch for leadership patterns, appointments to key committees, and particularly sharp conflicts that flare up. These factors may not have great meaning when they occur, but they may determine the course of legislation for the next few months. The observant reporter who knows legislative voting records from previous sessions will have early clues about the way certain legislative proposals might fare.

Party Relationships Solidify

Relationships within and between the majority and minority parties in legislative bodies provide interesting copy. In a few instances, legislative bodies are nonpartisan, but even in these cases patterns of support or nonsupport for various bills chart a picture of political philosophy in action.

Molly Ivins, the former editor of the *Texas Observer,* now with the *New York Times,* has denounced newspapers in her home state for their lifeless coverage of the legislature. Ivins says the legislature is a vital, exciting place, yet too many legislative correspondents turn out stories that omit all the color and spontaneity. One way to avoid this lack is to cover the battles among party leaders and the procedural conflicts that sometimes stir spirited debate.

Agendas Are Set

Who determines what a legislature will do during a session? This is a question that reporters covering any type of law-making body must ask frequently, and it is a question that is answered differently depending on the locale and the political situation. In many legislatures, the chief executive (governor or mayor) has a major role in setting the agenda. He or she may set it through a "state of the state" message or through selected, topical messages (for example, health or energy). As the administrator of the state departments and agencies, the governor may marshal efforts to push the program through the legislature. In analyzing these messages, reporters need to distinguish between the maintenance functions of government and new programs. Relationships between the chief executive and commissioner or departmental director may have a strong influence on subsequent action. These relationships are best observed by following the activities of the executive's legislative liaison staff and legislators themselves who are close to the executive. This story from the *Chicago Tribune* shows how an astute legislative reporter kept pace with an emerging legislative package:

> Governor Walker's administration is studying a series of controversial criminal justice reforms, including the elimination of prison paroles in favor of flat-time sentences with more liberal early-release provisions than now exist. Before the consideration of the 15 proposals the Walker administration had not become greatly involved in trying to change the state's criminal justice system. . . . A spokesman for the administration cautioned that "all these proposals are only on the drawing board. Don't jump to the conclusion that all of them will be introduced as bills.[15]

Understanding what issues will come before a legislature and why is a difficult task and requires a close view of both executive–legislative interaction and the relationships among certain legislators, their constituents, and lobbyists. This interplay determines the agenda. The press itself, of course, often has a role by pointing out needs or by providing publicity for persuasive spokespersons for various causes and issues.

Lobbies Function

Special interest groups, which lobby for legislation, sometimes provide the spark for illuminating legislative stories. Reporters can often provide depth for a story about a bill by finding out what motivated its introduction and what groups are supporting it. They can do so not only through interviews and observation of lobbyists at work but also through a careful assessment of their newsletters and legislative materials. Often groups with interests ranging from gun control to public welfare will publish special bulletins during a legislative session to monitor and assess progress on actions in which they are interested.

Trends Develop

At several junctures during a legislative session, a reporter may want to assess the context and perspective of the lawmakers' activities. Which ways are they headed? Is the executive's program making headway? What does all this legislative activity mean to the average citizen? Legislative coverage should try to synthesize the meaning of single-instance bills and find a pattern of activity.

COVERAGE OF SESSIONS

From the town or city hall to the state and national capitols, the complexity of the legislative process increases, as do the problems of coverage for the reporter. At the town, city, or county level, reporters in search of the behind-the-scenes story may find themselves drawn to public records in search of a pattern. Or they may find themselves relying on the official meeting of the council and its official actions, which they follow up with careful interviews.

City Councils

Most beginning reporters are likely to find themselves assigned early in their careers to the meetings and official actions of a municipal council. Depending on the aggressiveness of the reporter's publication, tradition, and access to records and key municipal personnel, that coverage may vary from little more than a bulletin board of official council minutes to enterprising, investigative probes of the quality of city government. Public affairs reporters, as a first step, should obviously become familiar with the structure of the body they are covering. Several types of structure characterize local government in the United States, including "strong mayor," "weak mayor," commission, and city manager systems. These types, and their modifications, are discussed in a variety of political science books, and the local municipal library can also provide the reporter with the basics of the municipal structure. In addition to their overall structure, municipal governments are organized into various departments and bureaus, such as finance, assessment, police, health, public works, licenses, and legal. These divisions have different functions and duties depending on the size and type of the municipal government, and the reporter should obviously understand their operations.

The reporter covering local legislative bodies must also understand the powers under which the local council functions. Most municipal governments operate under charters granted by the state legislature and amended from time to time by the voters. These charters grant municipal law-making bodies certain authority, such as the right to pass ordinances, but often that power is limited. The reporter needs to know the ways in which the local governmental body relates to the state legislature and to the federal government, particularly in such matters as mass transit and housing, in which federal funding and jurisdiction are often involved. Whatever the relationships, reporters will often find that the major portion of their responsibilities in covering the council requires surveillance of the body's committees in which most of the discussion and decision making take place.

But not all of it. Local councils, particularly in smaller communities, often are cozy gatherings of political leaders who may have close ties to the community's businesses, including its newspaper. More than one reporter covering city hall has encountered singular foot dragging when he has set out to do an aggressive investigative story.

The reporter who does look behind the scenes and ask such questions as "Who runs this city?" is likely to turn up some fascinating news stories that examine the entire decision-making process, from formal governmental structure to the personalities of officials—and nonofficials. In a series entitled "St. Paul [Minn.] Decision Makers," reporter David Nimmer found that on a decision to build a civic center, "St. Paul suffered from a 'sugar daddy' complex—Let one of our millionaires do it for us. And there was a limit to what the wealthy men were willing to do." He found, further, that

> members of the city council, with perhaps one exception, never took any key leadership roles:
> Council members were generally in the position of reacting to what the businessmen and the MIC [Metropolitan Improvement Committee] had proposed.
> Mayor Thomas Byrne was the only Council member who played a critical part in Civic Center decision-making, and he did that this spring when he informed businessmen that he wasn't about to see the project go down the drain because of doubts over the design of a particular building.
> Even when the councilmen weren't eager to support a proposal, such as the voter referendum on auditorium expansion, MIC leaders were able to persuade them with apparent ease.[16]

The examination of a community's power structure often leads to fascinating stories about the ways government and business work together in American municipalities. In Rochester, New York, for example, reporter Richard Whitmire found a leadership vacuum at the top of the city's ranks which was sapping the community's progress. But he also found the city's major law firm wielded considerable influence despite its low profile.[17]

Even day-to-day coverage of municipal government should probe beneath the surface of events. *Boston Globe* reporter Gerry O'Neill advises the city hall reporter "always to have the germ of a news analysis or an investigative piece in the back of your mind."

> For example, the press office releases two pages of appointments by the mayor. In this list is a job for city auctioneer. So you write the formula story saying the mayor appointed 47 people today. But you come back the next day to this guy who's city auctioneer.
>   What's he do? Well, he conducts two auctions a year. What's he get paid to do? More than a high school teacher with a master's degree and two years' experience. How long does the job last? A lifetime. Who the hell is this guy? Well, he's a lawyer who worked on the mayor's campaign. Has he ever done an auction before? He's not sure. He thought he might have done one in college. Could he give you an example of his technique? I'll spare you the rendition of the Lucky Strike commercial he did over the phone. . . .

The goal, says O'Neill, "should be to write about things that city hall officials do not want in the paper."[18] The list of subjects is nearly endless. Here are just a few, suggested by experienced reporters of local governments:

> City charters. An *Oregon Journal* reporter checked an old city charter and discovered a $7,000 fund the charter allocated to the mayor and council.
>
> Garbage disposal. *Newsday* reporters counted garbage pickups and found how a contract firm had cheated taxpayers out of $5 million.
>
> Zoning variances. The parking space for 150 cars at a proposed shopping center suddenly drops to 40.
>
> Airline ticket requisitions. Is it first class?
>
> Bank deposits. Many are in noninterest-bearing accounts.
>
> Building codes. Are the materials adequate?
>
> Bond issues. Who's the bond counsel and the underwriter and what are they paid?
>
> Campaign contributions. Who's giving money?
>
> Contracts. What are the specifications and who can bid?
>
> Credit cards. What do the travel records show? Which travel agency has the account?
>
> Payrolls, work records. Who shows up for work?
>
> Roads. Where do they go and who profits from their existence?
>
> School districts. Who handles the bonds, the supplies, the hiring?
>
> Taxes. Who has reduced assessments? Who has access to the lien rolls on buying auctioned property?[19]

State Legislatures

Coverage of the state legislature, like coverage of the local law-making body, can lead the reporter to interpretive stories on how the legislative process works. State legislatures vary in size from several dozen members to well over 100, and increasingly, legislatures have supporting bureaucracies in the form of research staffs. Because the state legislature often

considers hundreds or thousands of bills during a typical session, the reporter may have difficulty making decisions on what to cover and in how
much detail. "Many newspapers try to simplify by publishing a legislative
checklist. . . ," write former reporters Ralph Whitehead, Jr., and Howard
Ziff, "showing the status of different bills at different times during the
session. While often helpful, this device can be seriously misleading. Merely
noting the progress of bills, such checklists are not always sensitive to crucial details."[20]

A major problem in covering state legislatures is lack of accurate
information. "For one thing," Whitehead and Ziff explain, "few legislators
stay around long enough to develop an expertise of their own. . . . Then
too, except for members of the leadership, most legislators, and most of
their committees, lack staff. For the use of its 180 members, the Vermont
legislature employs one research assistant, one fiscal analyst, one secretary
and two draftsmen. 'It's not like Washington, where you can stroll into the
offices of the Atomic Energy Commission and talk to somebody on the staff
who's one of the country's top half dozen experts on nuclear power.' "[21]

If lack of knowledge about issues is one problem, another is complexity. "If you make the thing so complex that nobody can figure it out,
including the people who operate it, then there is no way that anybody is
going to have access to it—media, expert or anybody else," asserts legislative observer Larry Margolis.[22] Public affairs reporting, he continues, requires the reporter to present material in a way readers and viewers can
grasp:

> If they have a chance to form an identification with someone, a mental image
> of who that person is, who is saying that, where is he in relation to me, what
> do I mean to him or what is all this having to do with me, then they begin to
> lock onto that image, to that picture, to that identification in their mind. Then
> they begin to get interested and to follow; and it is high drama as far as they
> are concerned. . . .
>
>   The reason we read the sports pages and the comic strips is that we are able
> to identify and to form an identification with the main characters and partici-
> pants. We see these people all the time and we know how we feel about them
> and how to relate to them. We get a lot of copy that feeds all of that interest. I
> do not understand why the same considerations would not apply to govern-
> ment and public affairs reporting.[23]

This problem becomes acute as the legislative session draws to a close,
and legislators and reporters alike find themselves in marathon sessions in
which many bills are passed without debate or discussion. Reporter Paul
Hoffman describes this scene of the closing hours of the New York legislature, but his comments might well apply to other states:

> The legislature closed shop with a twenty-one hour marathon. Hundreds of
> bills were passed—nearly one-fourth of the session's total—including a major
> revision of the law governing strikes by public employees and a controversial

proposal for a state lottery. Both bills were mimeographed only minutes before the vote. Neither the lawmakers who approved them, nor the reporters who had to explain them had time to digest their contents, much less penetrate the maze of deals and compromises that lay behind them. Hundreds of other bills were killed, either on the floor of the legislature or in committee.

All this meant a stream of activity on the floor of the assembly and the senate, in the leaders' offices and capitol corridors, and in the executive chamber—a stream involving more than two hundred legislators and scores of aides, lobbyists, and state officials. No newspaper had enough manpower to cover everything that happened. Few newsmen had the stamina to stay with even one development for twenty-one hours—and then write about it.[24]

The reporter faced with trying to say what a new law means has a difficult time under ideal conditions, much less under conditions like those described by Hoffman. The reporter's readers may be well-served if he or she follows these suggestions: don't tackle too much, get to those who know, and look for the personal relationships.

Obviously, no reporter can write definitive stories on each of the hundreds or thousands of bills that go through the typical legislature each session or look behind the scenes at the various pressures that brought defeat or passage. Although there probably is a need to provide day-to-day "overviews," reporters should guard against overextending themselves. Unlike city councils, which tend to have a more leisurely pace, legislatures can be rat races, particularly near the end of a session, and reporters should make a conscious effort to avoid being caught up to the extent that perspective is lost.

As for those who know: lobbyists have earned reputations, sometimes deserved, as wheeler-dealers who pressure legislators behind the scenes to pass their pet bills. Although that characterization may be true in some cases, lobbyists are often valuable sources for the reporter as well as for the legislator. Professional lobbyists may have a thorough understanding of certain kinds of legislation, and though their view is likely to be biased, balancing one such source against another can help the reporter put individual pieces of legislation in context. The same is true of research staff personnel, which many legislators now recognize as essential, if expensive. Executive departments and agencies have to administer the laws that are passed, and the reporter should see departmental staffs as potential sources of information.

There are other aspects of covering the legislature that the public affairs reporter must be mindful of, too. For example, because legislators represent different constituencies, they may see the need to trade off votes on some issues to gain support for their favorite projects.

"At the desk ahead of mine in the fir-paneled legislative chamber sits a piano salesman," writes Richard L. Neuberger in a 1941 article which is still a classic on the legislative process. "Next to him is a haberdasher. To my right is a prominent lawyer, to my left a longshoreman. I can turn around and talk to a Ford dealer who was born in the Scottish highlands. We are a cross-section of our state. . . ."[25] The legislature today is staffed mostly by people whose interests are parochial and narrow. How can effective government be maintained by such part-timers in an age of increasing complexity? And how can the reporter participate in that process? In a perceptive article about the Maine legislature, *Maine Times* reporter Phyllis Austin examined the relationships behind the scenes:

> A legislator introduces a bill to raise the salary of a state post. A son of the legislator holds that post. But the amount of money is small.
> A legislator works to switch tax money to an agency he heads. But it is a legitimate agency and the position he holds with it is unpaid. He makes no financial gain.
> Are either or both of these conflicts of interest? When a specific case is cited, it becomes clear just how difficult it is to define conflict of interest. But the specific cases also shed light on what makes Maine's legislature tick. . . .[26]

How do public affairs reporters proceed when they want to write this kind of story? What resources can they use? The committee hearing, the debate on the floor, the vote for and against—these are easier to take hold of. But where does the reporter turn first to get a systematic story off the ground? Let's take an example. You're covering the legislature in a Western state where environmental issues are widely discussed and debated. A group of mining companies proposes to strip-mine for coal, but the group needs enabling legislation. One of its chief spokespersons in the legislature is a senator who is rumored to have some private interests in coal mining. You want to investigate what interests those might be and examine the real pros and cons behind the strip-mining issue.

You might begin here on two tracks, one, a careful review of the legislator's voting record on mining issues, and two, thorough research on coal mining. Sources would include legislative voting files and the debates and minutes of committee meetings. You might also turn to trade publications on coal mining and position papers by such environmental groups as the Sierra Club. The state department of taxation might provide projections on revenues generated by the coal-mining industry, and lobbyists in other industries, such as electric power, could provide data on the need for coal. You might well find yourself deep into newspaper stories in other states where coal mining or other types of mining are an issue. A statistical base on employment factors might be available from the state department of employment or the U.S. Department of Labor. You would then move on to middle-level interviews with mining experts, asking questions about the environmental impact, the employment projections, the effect on the state's tax base. Along the way, you would develop the ability to make valuable and realistic comparisons with what is happening in other states and regions. This evaluation would free you from the necessity of depending on the opposing groups' press releases, with their assumed biases.

In the examination of the senator, you might study land and deed records in areas where mining is proposed to see whether the senator has land interests there. You might also examine corporation papers to see whether the senator has an interest in a company that might benefit from mining, such as one that supplies and distributes tires for huge earth-moving equipment. You might examine the wills of the senator's parents and of other relatives to learn if the senator owns mining company stock. A check of various business professional directories might show whether the senator is an officer or on the board of directors of a company that would benefit from mining. Last, you should not overlook the senator's own statements, comparing them with his private votes or comments in committee hearings, which generally get less attention than the full-scale public meeting.

In the examination of both mining as an issue and the senator's interests, you would be constantly asking comparative questions in which statements with built-in prejudices are weighed against standards and performance. You might ask, Do the senator's public statements coincide with his votes recorded in committee? Do his private interests seem to be reflected in his votes? Has mining by the same mining group in other states met permit standards set by those states' pollution monitoring agencies? Have the mining companies helped or hindered efforts by other states to protect the environment while allowing mining to continue? How have the legislatures in other states responded to pressure by mining interests? With all these questions, and perhaps dozens more, you would soon begin to have a knowledge of the mining issue that would go well beyond that needed to cover individual bills as they came up in the Senate and House. Combining these investigative techniques with direct observation of, say, mining operations in other states, you would be able to get behind the public event to real issues.

Again, experienced legislative reporters suggest a long list of stories on state government that lend themselves to probing and analysis. Here are a few:

Budget bamboozles. Watch school bond issues and financial program scams. Where are the university's stadium revenues going?
Professors' payola. Where does the grant money come from and who gets it? Check professors who consult for corporations or sit on corporate boards. Does the university buy from those companies? Who signs the purchase orders?
Athletics. Recruiting and equitable funding abuses abound.
Agriculture. Who's selling short on fertilizer, meat, eggs? Who does the meat inspections? If the gasoline pump says a gallon, did you get that amount?
Ethics. Check the state ethics commission for economic statements of self-

interest by state officials. Watch lobbyist disclosure reports. [In one story, *Twin Falls* (Ida.) *Times-News* reporter David Morrissey found lobbyists spent more than $50,000 on food and drinks for legislators in 1977 alone.]

Gambling. The Nevada Gambling Commission records in Carson City are public records, and anyone running junkets from other states to Nevada has to be licensed.

Liquor. Records in this area touch companies, restaurants, motels, and outlet stores as well as the criminal records of the applicants for the permit.

Regulatory agencies. There are dozens, mostly with low profiles. What do they do with the barber licensing fees at the cosmetologists and hairdressers board?

Secretaries of state. Keep state corporation records and audits of branches of state and local government.

State bars. Some disciplinary hearing records on lawyers and other professionals are public.

Highway departments. Who has the road contracts? How is the trust-fund money allocated?[27]

But even under the best of circumstances, top-flight legislative reporting is not easy, even when the smell of corruption is high. In Pennsylvania, for example, *Philadelphia Inquirer* reporters dug into the governmental structure in Harrisburg to find a government in sad disrepair. They also established a factual basis for reform and repair by exposing a long list of corrupt practices, ranging from ghost employees to kickbacks to political patronage in college scholarships to double billing and lack of competitive bidding.[28] On a much smaller scale, the *Anniston* (Ala.) *Star* examined the progress of the Alabama legislature in the decade since it was rated one of the worst in the nation by the now-defunct Citizens Conference on State Legislatures and found the body has improved—some.[29] Perhaps the best development is the growing recognition that writing about state government need not be limited to politics and tales of back-room deals but can discuss substantive issues. The public affairs reporter in this area has many limitations, but many opportunities as well.

Congress

Much has been written that is critical of Washington correspondents and the coverage of Congress, yet more recent critics still find Capitol Hill coverage inadequate. Ben H. Bagdikian writes that "the American body politic is hemorrhaging from Executive people unwatched. But the remedy, a responsive and daily accountable Congress, has also gone largely unwatched in any way significant for local voters."[30] About 400 of these 1,400 correspondents cover Congress specifically," he explains, "but they also follow the herd, most of them working for national news organizations that concentrate on big issues and a few leaders. This is a natural and necessary concern, but it means that most members of Congress are left uncovered. This gap pretty much leaves the field to the printed press release and an even more effective instrument of political promotion: television footage represented as news when in fact, it is government-subsidized propaganda."[31]

Obviously, reporters assigned to Congress will have to develop their own ways of covering the news "events" from Capitol Hill and of researching and writing the systemic stories. But perhaps the biggest pitfall is the press release, which is all too available and easy for reporters to pick up. An American University team of student journalists found that

> Eighty percent of these papers' [suburban newspapers] coverage is based on the congressmen's press releases. It apparently is common practice for releases to go straight from the Hill and into a local newspaper word for word. Unbeknownst to the reader, a congressman's legislative boasts or self-serving quotes may be lifted whole from the releases and shoveled into print with no further checking. In one two-month period, we found 84 stories (in 29 papers) that were based on press releases, and nearly half (41) of them were verbatim reprints of the release.[32]

COVERAGE OF PUBLIC MEETINGS AND HEARINGS

On any given weekday or evening, the reporter is likely to find a number of public meetings going on in his or her community. There may be a specially called session of the county board of supervisors to hear citizen comments about a proposed widening of a highway. An environmental protection agency may be taking testimony from people in business about the need for a rubber-processing plant. The next night, it might hear from opponents of the plant. The district school board might be inviting comments from parents and taxpayers about the need—or lack of it—for an addition to the high-school gymnasium. An advisory committee on the problems of aging may be taking testimony from nursing-home operators as it considers recommended changes in a state's nursing-home regulations. In all these cases, the reporter is faced with several problems.

Scale   The public meeting often draws only the most outspoken of opponents and proponents on public issues. The vast majority of citizens, although they may be concerned about an issue, don't bother to come. Thus, because there may be important views unrepresented at a public hearing, reporters should ask themselves what other sources could make the story complete and balanced.

Size   The beginning reporter, particularly, tends to measure the support for or opposition to an issue by the number of people who turn out for a meeting, and the emotional level of their participation. Thus, a crowd of

2,000 that jams into a high-school auditorium to scream about a proposed desegregation plan may be taken to represent the community as a whole. Conversely, the reporter who is the only spectator as the county zoning board rules on variances may think people don't care about the proposals. The size of the audience may subtly lead reporters to "weight" their accounts: the larger the crowd, the longer the story; the smaller the crowd, the briefer the account.

Interest　Reporters may assume that if they are not interested in the contents of the meeting, then surely, the public is not either. "On one occasion," writes a state representative, "a reporter asked me if a certain bill I was introducing was 'sexy' or 'exciting.' I stated I wasn't sure, but I thought it was important. The reporter agreed that it was important but since it wasn't 'sexy' or 'exciting' or controversial, no story was written."[33]

Grandstanding　Some political officials see the public hearing as a forum to impress the audience with the "rightness" of their positions. That audience often includes the press. The reporter needs to measure what an official says in a public setting against that official's record on the issue or against what he or she says in private. "The only way for a reporter to look at an official is skeptically," writes journalism Professor William L. Rivers.[34] The investigative committee, Douglass Cater writes, "is geared to the production of headlines on a daily basis and even twice daily basis. It is able to create the news story which lingers week after week on the front pages to form an indelible impression on the public mind."[35]

Access　It is not unusual for public officials to meet, behind closed doors, in an "executive session" and make decisions that are then rubber-stamped at a later public meeting. Most states have laws prohibiting such closed sessions, and these apply sometimes to the meetings of municipal as well as state officials. But these laws are sometimes ignored, and the reporter should attempt to find out what decisions, if any, are being made outside the public meeting.

Impact　What happened in a public setting, such as a meeting, may not reveal the important forces that influence a legislative decision. The reporter needs to ask how important the meeting is to the outcome of an issue. Have decisions already been made? Will the public debate influence the officials? The reporter must follow up the meeting with questions about its importance. Often, decisions made in such settings are only part of the picture. Always, reporters must keep in mind their chief job: providing the reader with the *meaning* of an issue and how the public meeting fits into that meaning. Reporters must evaluate the substance of the meeting in relationship to the needs of their audience. In doing so, they will often be led to the systemic story. The reporter in such situations should maintain a high level of skepticism, if not disbelief. In an article about investigative reporting, former *New York Times* reporter Robert M. Smith writes about the frustration of being lied to. "There is an old bromide imparted to young Washington reporters. Always ask yourself, they are told, 'Why is this bastard lying to me?' Being lied to becomes so much a part of the investigative reporter's life that once or twice a year he asks himself, 'Why is this guy telling me the truth?' "[36] Reporters who cover the legislative process need to be aware that lying does occur, or at a minimum, that often what they see in the public forum is only part—often a small part—of the story.

How can the public affairs reporter cover a public meeting and avoid the problems inherent in the discussion? Let's take a theoretical example from the first part of this section—a meeting of the school board to consider the need for an addition to the high-school gymnasium—and look at how you as a reporter might cover it.

The meeting is to be held at the school district's board room, and when you arrive half an hour before the meeting is to start, you find the room already filled with parents, coaches, teachers, students, and other interested citizens. In a corner, you spot the chairman of the high-school English department, an outspoken teacher popular with her students and generally critical of spending for sports facilities at the expense of more academic programs. You also notice a couple of "meeting regulars," people who come to school board meetings frequently and who are generally critical of spending funds that require additional property taxes. And you also note the presence of the high-school football coach, a popular figure in the community since last fall's team finished with a 10–0 record. You scan the room more carefully and realize that you do not see someone you expected: a statistics and economics professor at the local college who has served as chairman of the community's planning commission and who is generally regarded locally as an unbiased expert on public financing and cost-benefit analysis. You make a mental note of the professor's absence and jot the professor's name on a page of your notebook under the heading "should contact."

The meeting is lively but orderly. The English teacher makes a case for needed textbooks and says the present gymnasium is adequate. The football coach says he could get more students involved in high-school sports if there were more practice facilities. One of the "regulars" argues that property taxes are already too high and that the proposed addition to the gymnasium would cost too much. Board members listen intently, and one, with a reputation for "playing to the audience," assures the group that the board will do its best to make the right decision. A vote is taken, and the addition is approved unanimously. Several persons in the audience seem disgruntled, and the English teacher shrugs and leaves.

As you leave, you begin to think about what happened and what pieces are missing. To be sure, the meeting attracted a large crowd, but several important sources, including the professor, were absent. Back at the office, you get on the telephone and begin to fill in the holes in the story. The professor tells you that the addition will cost too much in light of population trends that project a leveling off of the tax base in the community and provides you with cost-benefit statistics. You call the English teacher, and she further describes the inadequate high-school library and the need for books in the English program. You plan your report of the meeting. One story, a relatively short one, describes the meeting; another, much longer, presents the professor's views and those of the English teacher. You supplement the package with an out-of-date reading list for an English course, provided by the English teacher, and a table of cost statistics. The group of articles runs in the next day's paper, and the reader, instead of getting only a report on the board's action and the meeting, gets reports that put that action in context.

CONTINUITY OF COVERAGE

The process by which a bill moves through the legislative process is complex, from introduction to various hearings in committee to the debate and vote on the floor. Whether the proposal is a local ordinance, a bill in a state legislature, or a piece of congressional legislation, the reporter needs to develop ways of keeping track of the proposal's progress. The job is complicated by the practice of "gutting" proposed legislation. For example, a state legislator may introduce a measure that establishes an environmental protection agency to regulate state power companies. In committee, another legislator may come along with an amendment to the proposal that strikes everything after the enacting clause and inserts entirely new language that gives the proposed agency "advisory" power only. So the first pitfall to avoid is "labeling" a piece of legislation in a way that would mislead the reader or tell the reader little about what the proposal would accomplish. As one legislator points out, "No-fault insurance, no-fault divorce, environmental rights act, equal rights amendments, fair pupil dismissal act, are just a few of these that have passed in the last two years. In every case, the bill as passed is far different from the bill as originally prepared by the author."[37] Shrewd legislators know that a certain kind of bill, sent to a hostile committee, will be permanently "postponed." A state legislative agriculture committee, for example, may have a disproportionate number of farmers and may not be very favorable to a bill allowing synthetic milk products to be sold widely. So one part of keeping track of legislation is to watch the kind of "setting" in which a bill winds up. That will often give the reporter a clue to the bill's chances of getting out to the floor.

Legislatures themselves have begun to develop rather sophisticated methods of keeping track of legislation. Ordinarily, clerks of each body of the legislature function as repositories for legislation and steer bills to the right committees. This practice is normally under the guidance of a rules committee of the legislature. Reporters should become familiar with these and other legislative components because, obviously, it is difficult for them to trace a bill unless they understand the procedure by which bills move. Legislatures also keep journals of their proceedings, and these are helpful to reporters too.

THE ACTORS: LAWMAKERS, AIDES, AND LOBBYISTS

The Congress, as Bagdikian suggests, is particularly subject to press coverage of a few "stars" at the expense of most of its members. But every legislative body has leaders. These may be either formal leaders, such as the majority and minority whips, or the chairpersons of major committees or the speaker of the house or president of the city council. Often, these individuals are party caucus leaders as well as legislative leaders, and their influence and power may vary with the size and makeup of the legislative body. Political scientist Dunn suggests that the press is used for a number of political purposes, including building program support, achieving personal publicity, providing neutral information, and testing public reaction with a "trial balloon,"[38] and legislative leaders are probably more likely than others to employ the press for these purposes. The perceptive reporter recognizes these uses and is cautious about self-serving statements from legislative leaders. Dunn explains that "the legislative leader, for his part, knows that his colleagues learn much of what they know about a bill from the papers, and that they measure public reaction to a proposition by reading the papers. He therefore believes that his success with a bill is often commensurate with his success in publicizing it."[39]

From the reporter's point of view, an undue emphasis on legislative leaders may result in a myopia that ignores, or at least diminishes, the importance of the views of so-called ordinary legislators. Legislators, particularly those with several years' experience, recognize the effect of favorable press coverage, perhaps more so than new legislators. In a study of Texas legislative coverage, for example, journalism researcher John Merwin found that "Subjects serving in the Texas Legislature more than two years rated newspapers significantly more potent than their colleagues serving two years or less. Perhaps after one session in the Legislature the new legislator becomes more acutely aware of the potency of newspapers because of personal experience with adverse editorial comment and news stories."[40] The result may be coverage that focuses on leaders at the expense of other legislators, that leaves the neophytes with relatively low profiles, even to their own constituents.

The real pros in the legislative process are the managerial people. Certainly, the legislative aide or research staff person is a valuable source for the reporter. Such persons can often steer the reporter to the relevant background material on important legislative issues and can just as often supply the names of other "experts" both in and out of government. A well-staffed city manager's office, with experts on population trends, housing, transportation needs, and other crucial issues, can be invaluable to the reporter looking for hard information that is likely to be less biased than the public statements of interested officials. The same is true of the legislative research staff.

Lobbyists are among the most durable of legislative figures and often exert immense influence on the legislative process. They are usually experts in their fields, and although they are almost certainly biased toward a particular position, their range of knowledge may include opposing viewpoints. There are many kinds of lobbyists, ranging from a corporation attorney for a major industry, such as mining or railroads, to "citizen" lobbyists for the League of Women Voters. In many states and in the Congress, lobbyists greatly outnumber lawmakers. The relationship between them is frequently clouded, and every capital city, during a legislative session, is awash with rumors of sumptuous dinners paid for by "big lobbies" for legislators and, sometimes, the press. More sober examination, however, suggests that the lobby provides an important service to lawmakers by presenting the opposing positions of special interest groups. Yet the key question is still how much influence the lobbies exert; and recently, states have begun to enact strict lobbyist-disclosure laws and rules.

In an article examining a professional lobbyist, John N. Cole, editor of the *Maine Times,* wrote that Loyall Sewall, a lobbyist, "will write, or have a hand in writing, nearly half the bills in any given legislature." Sewall "has no real power base, no vote, and usually represents a minority view. But he often prevails, because he maintains his credibility, performs a unique and otherwise unobtainable legal service, and is on duty on the third floor every day of every session."[41] There is one group of statehouse regulars," according to Whitehead and Ziff, "that serves as a stable source of information: the lobbyists. A 1969 study of lobbying in four states—Utah, Oregon, North Carolina, Massachusetts—reports that the typical lobbyist has been on the job for an average of ten years."[42]

OTHER SOURCES
FOR COVERAGE

The resources available to the reporter covering an aspect of the legislative process are growing. Organizations, associations, libraries, and research staffs all can help provide the background materials necessary to report the daily events of legislation with context.

Law libraries in many state capitols contain compilations of state laws, and often, the laws of nearby states. Many also have records of state legislation, including committee minutes and background documents on important issues. Many state historical societies collect important state documents and historical sources.

Increasingly, legislatures are providing themselves with research staffs to develop "fact statements" on various issues. Also, many large cities have research personnel, sometimes under the wing of the city manager or city coordinator, who help plan the city's direction in such fields as transit and housing. These research groups draw on the resources within various state and municipal departments. The New York Department of Transportation, for example, maintains a planning and research division that supplies data on traffic flow, movement patterns, and forecasts for urban travel.

A number of organizations can help the reporter learn what is being done in the same field in other parts of the country. Such organizations include the National League of Cities, the Council of State Governments, the Eagleton Institute of Politics at Rutgers University, the National Conference of State Legislative Leaders, the Ford Foundation, and Common Cause. Other such groups may be valuable at the local level, such as citizens' leagues and the League of Women Voters.

CONCLUSIONS AND SUMMARY

Legislative coverage is among the most demanding assignments for public affairs reporters, and the obstacles to sound, informative coverage are many. Reporters need to watch, particularly, the *process* by which proposals become law or are defeated, for in doing so, they will gain an understanding of the pressures and influences that affect specific proposals.

Understanding the process, however, will serve little purpose unless reporters succeed in interesting their readers in that process by showing them how its results have an effect on their daily lives. After all, that's the assumption with which legislative coverage began.

NOTES

[1]Delmar D. Dunn, *Public Officials and the Press* (Reading, Mass.: Addison-Wesley, 1969). See particularly chap. 9, "The Impact of the Press on the Policy-Making Process," pp. 165–71.
[2]Ibid., pp. 169–70.
[3]Ibid., pp. 167–68.

[4]Susan H. Miller, "Reporters and Congressmen: Living in Symbiosis," *Journalism Monographs* 53 (January 1978). 10.

[5]Ibid., 22.

[6]Ibid., 22.

[7]Robert W. Greene, "Not in Vengeance, But to Inform," speech upon receipt in 1977 of the John Peter Zenger Award for Freedom of the Press and the Public's Right to Know, conferred annually by the University of Arizona.

[8]Thomas B. Littlewood, "What's Wrong with Statehouse Coverage," *Columbia Journalism Review* 10 (March–April 1972), 42. See also Paul Simon, "Improving Statehouse Coverage," *Columbia Journalism Review* 12 (September–October 1973), 51–53.

[9]John Mello, "Probers Blast Reporters on State House Coverage," *Editor & Publisher*, February 28, 1981, p. 22. Mello cites a Massachusetts report of a final report by the Special Commission Concerning State and County Buildings on corruption in state and county building contracts.

[10]Quoted by Ralph Whitehead, Jr., and Howard M. Ziff in "Statehouse Coverage: Lobbyists Outlast Journalists," *Columbia Journalism Review* 12 (January–February 1974), 12.

[11]Ibid.

[12]Carol S. Hilton, "Reporting the Legislature: A Study of Newsmen and Their Sources," unpublished M.A. thesis, University of Washington, 1966.

[13]Carolyn Steward Dyer and Oguz B. Nayman, "Under the Capitol Dome: A Survey of Relationships Between Legislative Reporters and Legislators," *Journalism Quarterly*, Autumn 1977.

[14]Charles W. Wiggins and J. Paul Yarbrough, "Reporters and the Legislative System: A Study of Perceptions and Performance," paper delivered at the Midwest Political Science Association, Chicago, Ill., May 3–5, 1973. See also Walter Gieber and Walter Johnson, "The City Hall Beat: A Study of the Roles of Sources and Reporters," *Journalism Quarterly* 38 (Summer 1961), 289–97; Arthur García, "A Study of the Opinions and Attitudes of California's Capital Correspondents," *Journalism Quarterly* 44 (Summer 1967), 330–33; and John Merwin, "How Texas Legislators View News Coverage of Their Work," *Journalism Quarterly* 48 (Summer 1971), 269–74.

[15]"Walker Weighing 15 Justice Reforms," *Chicago Tribune*, February 12, 1975, p. 1.

[16]David Nimmer, "St. Paul Decision Makers," *Minneapolis Star*, June 20, 1969, p. 1.

[17]Richard Whitmire, "Does Anyone Run Rochester?" *Rochester* (N.Y.) *Times-Union*, March 6, 1980, p. 1.

[18]Gerry O'Neill, "City Hall" panel discussion, Investigative Reporters and Editors National Conference, 1978; reprinted in *The Best from IRE Conference: Denver, 1978* (Columbia, Mo.: IRE, Inc., 1978).

[19]"Local Angles Worth Pursuing," *The IRE Journal*, October–November 1978, pp. 10–11.

[20]Whitehead and Ziff, "Statehouse Coverage," 10.

[21]Ibid., 11–12.

[22]Larry Margolis, speech at the National Conference on State Government Reporting, Orlando, Fla., February 1977. See also Thomas B. Littlewood, "The Trials of Statehouse Journalism," *Saturday Review* 49 (December 10, 1966).

[23]Ibid.

[24]Paul Hoffman, "The Neglected Statehouse," *Columbia Journalism Review* 6 (Summer 1967), 22–23.

[25]Richard L. Neuberger, "I Go to the Legislature," *Survey Graphic*, July 1941, p. 373; reprinted in Robert L. Morlan, *Capitol, Courthouse and City Hall*, (Boston: Houghton Mifflin, 1972), 4th ed., p. 105. See also Hans A. Linde and David B. Frohnmayer, "Prescription for the Citizen Legislature: Cutting the Gordian Knot," *Oregon Law Review* 56:1 (1977), 8–29.

[26]Phyllis Austin, "What Interest Does Your Legislator Represent?" *Maine Times*, December 7, 1973, p. 1.

[27]Sandra Zec, "Investigating State Government Abuses," *The IRE Journal*, January–February 1979, pp. 10–11.

[28]John DeMott, "Stalking the Wild and Elusive State Legislature," *The IRE Journal*, January–February 1979, pp. 6–7. See also William Ecenbarger, Thomas Ferrick, Jr., and Jane Shoemaker, "Pennsylvania's Assembly: Out of Control," *Philadelphia Inquirer*, September 10–18, 1978, and reprint booklet.

[29]Mike Sherman, "How Does Alabama's Legislature Rate?" *Aniston* (Ala.) *Star*, March 12, 1981, p. 1.

[30]Ben H. Bagdikian, "Congress and the Media: Partners in Propaganda," *Columbia Journalism Review* 12 (January–February 1974), 10. See also Bernard C. Cohen, *The Press and Foreign Policy* (Princeton, N.J.: Princeton University Press, 1963); Dan D. Nimmo, *Newsgathering in Washington* (New York: Atherton Press, 1964); James Reston, *The Artillery of the Press* (New York: Harper & Row, 1967); and Leo Rosten, *The Washington Correspondents* (New York: Harcourt, Brace, 1937).

[31]Bagdikian, "Congress and the Media," 5.

[32]Lewis W. Wolfson, "The Local Congressman's Lament: Doesn't Anybody Know My Name?" *Washingtonian* 9 (February 1974), 130.

[33]Tom Berg and Charles Weaver, "Capitol Coverage: How Does It Look from the Statehouse?" *Twin Cities Journalism Review* 2 (July–August 1974), 14.

[34]William L. Rivers, ed., *The Adversaries: Politics and the Press* (Boston: Beacon Press, 1970), p. 253.

[35]Douglass Cater, "The Congressional Hearing as a Publicity Vehicle," *The Fourth Branch of Government* (Boston: Houghton Mifflin, 1959), p. 56.

[36]Robert M. Smith, "Why So Little Investigative Reporting?" (MORE) 3 (November 1973), 7.

[37]Berg and Weaver, "Capitol Coverage," 15.

[38]Dunn, *Public Officials and the Press*, p. 116.

[39]Ibid., p. 119.

[40]John Merwin, "How Texas Legislators View News Coverage of Their Work," *Journalism Quarterly* 48 (Summer 1971), 274.

[41]John N. Cole, "The Lobbyist," *Maine Times*, February 23, 1973, p. 2.

[42]Whitehead and Ziff, "Statehouse Coverage," 12.

SUGGESTED READINGS

BLANCHARD, ROBERT O., ED.   *Congress and the News Media*. New York: Hastings House, 1974. Contains many provocative articles on Congressional coverage.

HESS, STEPHEN.   *The Washington Reporters*. Washington, D.C.: The Brookings Institution, 1981. Examines capitol news gathering through survey of almost 500 reporters and analysis of their stories.

KRISTOL, IRVING.   "The Underdeveloped Profession." *The Public Interest* 6 (Winter 1967), 36.

SIGAL, LEON V.   *Reporters and Officials: The Organization and Politics of Newsmaking*. Lexington, Mass.: D. C. Heath and Company, 1973. Studies news decisions at the *New York Times* and the *Washington Post*.

11

Urban Journalism

We will transmit this city not only not less, but greater, better and more beautiful than it was transmitted to us.

from the oath of the Athenian City-State

More and more, for the men charged with governance of our cities, politics has become the art of the impossible.

Daniel P. Moynihan, 1969

For most of recorded history, cities have been both the salvation of civilized life and its bane. The city made possible commerce, and therefore growth and the creation of wealth. It also imposed a structure on the life of its inhabitants that created problems of social and political relations. In modern times, those problems have been manageable. Only in the last thirty years have the problems of the cities escalated to the point of crisis. In the United States, urban crisis—conditions that threaten the continued functioning of cities—has been the dominant political constant. But it has meant different things at different times in the years following World War II.

In 1950, urban crisis meant the loss of population from the central cities to new suburbs, an explosive change that led to the Balkanization of government and services. It was accompanied by a massive migration of rural and Southern blacks to the cities of the North, accelerating the exodus of middle-class whites to the suburbs. It was a crisis of social problems—poverty, crime, slums. Society's principal response to the crisis was urban redevelopment: demolition of old housing and its replacement with publicly financed apartment projects.

By the 1960s, the urban crisis had become a two-headed monster. One phase was the series of ghetto revolts, starting in 1964, that swept like a firestorm through Watts, Newark, Detroit, Chicago, and dozens of other cities. The other phase was what Daniel Bell and Virginia Held called "the community revolution," the appearance of neighborhood groups to oppose urban redevelopment and gain a voice in political decision making.[1] The social upheaval of the 1950s had been joined by political chaos. Doubt arose concerning the cities' ability to cope with traffic congestion, air pollution, housing shortages, and other political demands.[2]

By the late 1970s, two new developments added heat to the urban cauldron. Frostbelt cities, chiefly in the Northeast and the Midwest, were rapidly losing population and industry, and with them the means to pay for municipal services. The Sunbelt cities of the South and Southwest were the beneficiaries of shifting population and industrial base. But the gains were accompanied by the result of rapid growth: the accelerated need for services, from schools to sewers, demanded by a growing population. By 1980, the urban crisis was further complicated by a national economy turned sour, aging cities more dependent than ever on federal funds (some for as much as half of their budgets) and a theme new and foreign to the American ear: Less is more. The need to conserve in an era of shrinking resources compounded the problems of a largely urban nation already beset by class and racial friction, a burgeoning grass-roots tax revolt, uncontrolled inflation, environmental pollution, and a political structure that in some cities was near paralysis.

This fusion of accelerated growth, social conflict, and environmental decay spawned "urban journalism."

THE RISE OF URBAN JOURNALISM

Although the press from its early days had attempted to monitor the pathology of urban life, recognition of the crisis in the cities came late. It wasn't until the ghetto riots of the 1960s that the press took formal notice of a problem in the cities. And the problem, as it was seen then, centered chiefly on racial conflict. After the riots, news executives began a searching, painful, and often public examination of their roles in both the riots and the conditions that led up to them. Studies were conducted; conferences were held; reports were written. Much of the focus was on the behavior of journalists during the disturbances, a self-searching that produced numerous sets of guidelines on how to cover riots. The *Chicago Sun-Times*, for example, adopted "Eight Rules for Handling News of Racial Tension," ranging from "We do not report trivial incidents" to "We try to tell the story without slant or bias."[3]

The impetus for this approach came from a suspicion—sometimes an accusation—that news media practices may have been responsible for the escalation of minor disturbances into full-scale riots. The National Advisory Commission on Civil Disorders (the Kerner Commission) was asked to investigate this question of press influence on ghetto riots. It reported these conclusions:

> First, that despite incidents of sensationalism, inaccuracies, and distortions, newspapers, radio and television, on the whole, made a real effort to give a balanced, factual account of the 1967 disorders. Second, despite this effort, the portrayal of the violence that occurred last summer failed to reflect accurately its scale and character. The overall effect was, we believe, an exaggeration of both mood and event.
>
> Third, and ultimately most important, we believe that the media have thus far failed to report adequately on the causes and consequences of civil disorders and the underlying problems of race relations.[4]

The report went on to criticize the media for reflecting "the biases, the paternalism, the indifference of white America" to black and other minority groups.[5] It also urged bringing more members of minority groups into journalism as practitioners, to remedy its conviction that "the press has too long basked in a white world, looking out of it, if at all, with white men's eyes and a white perspective."[6]

Many newspapers and broadcast operations attempted to correct this myopia in the late 1960s. Their stories described the horrors of ghetto life. They attempted to explore the multiple causes of minority unemployment and underemployment, of educational inequality, of social discrimination. Blacks began to appear regularly on television. News executives searched for minority journalists, and finding few with desired training or experience, launched training and scholarship programs. Aspects of minority life long ignored, such as social and organizational news, found a place in the paper. Language that expressed bias or perpetuated stereotypes began to recede from the mass media.

Some of the effects of that sudden minority consciousness are still evident in newsrooms today. Many of them vanished, however, as the memory of Watts and Newark waned, and the media reverted to traditional news values. Events make news, and riots are easier to report about than the subtleties of job discrimination or lack of transportation. As one critic observed,

> Today, although blacks can be seen on television, and although some "white" media seriously attempt to cover the urban ghetto experience, most metropolitan and suburban newspapers and broadcast stations think of blacks only in terms of crime stories and bussing stories. Mainstream American media write white. News is covered by whites for whites. Feature sections rarely recognize the existence of blacks. Columns on beauty hints are of value only

to white women. It is a small wonder that blacks often ignore white newspapers and feel the need for a black press.[7]

Although concentrated coverage of black issues and neighborhoods waned in the 1970s, urban journalism itself mushroomed. It became the pepperoni pizza of the news business—hot and popular, with a mélange of ingredients. As awareness of the urban crisis infiltrated the newsroom, editors broadened coverage of the dozen or more topical areas that mark its boundaries: municipal finance, land use, housing, education, transportation, unemployment, social services, intergovernmental relations, demography, medical resources. The promise of an evolving urban journalism was an approach to news-gathering and news-writing that would accommodate complex subject matter in a manner understandable and relevant to a public already reeling from information overload.

In a decade of development, the amorphous specialty of urban journalism has lived up to many of its promises. It has gained an identity: There is now a small but growing literature and an index classification in *Journalism Quarterly*. It has gained support: The Urban Journalism Center was established at Northwestern University, and urban course work has been introduced in the curriculum at a number of schools of journalism. It has gained adherents, including an Urban Writers Society. It has also achieved some success in helping to break down the artificial barriers to holistic journalism, the "beat" system.

What it hasn't yet achieved is a definition. Most reporting specialties are defined by subject matter. Writing styles are defined by method of presentation. Urban journalism, a hybrid of both content and method, evades easy identification. Its subject matter runs through many existing journalistic specialties; its style varies with content and purpose. It is as much a state of mind as a specific genre, testimony to a conceptual change in news definition and practice throughout journalism. It embodies at its core the "process-centered" approach to news described earlier in this book. It demands context and breadth to achieve its goals of monitoring trends and explaining developments.

Urban journalism is a specialty in fact rather than in name at most large newspapers. Some writers, like author and syndicated columnist Neal Peirce, identify themselves as urban specialists. The *Milwaukee Journal* has an "urban desk." Long Island's *Newsday* has a "projects department" that deals with urban problems. At most newspapers, however, reporters who adopt an urban focus carry titles that range from environmental reporter to social issues writer. Whatever the designation, the function is similar: to identify and analyze urban issues. The once-distinctive approach to news by the urban specialist—contextual, interpretive reporting—has in fact been adopted by most of the news profession in the past few years, making urban journalism a genre that is losing its distinctiveness.

URBAN JOURNALISM
IN PRACTICE

There is another way to look at urban reporting, however, that goes beyond the simple coverage of selected subjects. A common thread links all the urban problem topics. Each involves several—and often competing—interest groups. Each involves decision processes that cut across conventional beat lines. Each affects layers of civic and social strata other than the parties directly involved in a single news event. In this perspective, urban reporting serves to integrate the multidimensional reality of complex social systems. These are systems in which events rarely occur in isolation, in which the shock waves of decisions travel past the intended limits of their points of origin.

The urban reporter's function, then, is to sort out what communication researcher Jack Lyle describes as the "complex systems of interrelated parts" that constitute urban problems and solutions. For the reporter, urban problems do not start and stop on the steps of city hall or the county courthouse. Though necessarily local in nature, an urban subject may involve several levels of government and any number of formal and informal civic organizations. A decision to develop a mass transit system, for example, may include participation by federal and state agencies, local government, and citizens' organizations of several kinds. In addition, the effects of the transit decision may be felt by other groups and individuals not direct parties to the process—retail businessmen, employers, bankers, commuters, taxi drivers, residents along the transit route—including some not even aware of the implications it has for them. The decision also may have profound meaning for other communities and their constituent groups, both short term and long term. The reporter's horizon must include all these in order to present the dynamics of the situation.

The process of urban reporting, under this definition, begins with the systematic identification of (1) the interest groups that *should* be represented in stories as sources of information and (2) the various audiences for the specific subject, so that information serving their needs may be included. Making these procedures explicit helps the urban reporter avoid missing significant elements. For instance, when the police chief and the city council meet to discuss rising juvenile crime, the urban approach suggests that judges, probation officials, criminologists, community help organizations, and similar groups may be relevant to the story. So may, for that matter, seemingly unrelated agencies such as schools and building inspection departments.

As with other reporting specialties, urban journalism implies specialized knowledge. Because the field includes so many subjects, formal training may range from public administration, land-use planning, and economics, for some reporters, to architecture, sociology, and criminal justice studies for others. This training enables the urban specialist to see more clearly than the generalist the dimensions of public issues. Journalism Professor Gene Burd describes the result this way:

> Because of the complexity of cities, the urban specialist is better trained than the general assignment reporter to see the relation of cause and effect. He is better able to detect defective building code enforcement than report on slum fires; better able to analyze poor street planning than report on auto accident fatalities; and better able to detect high tension areas than report on mass murders.[8]

Urban problems don't often respect news beat boundaries. The action taken on a shopping center proposal in one suburb is likely to have profound implications for nearby suburbs and the central city itself. A housing program in the inner city may have some of its story roots in the state capital's political beat. The beat structure works against such cross-sectional reporting, however. Burd suggests an "urban renewal" program in newspaper city rooms to adapt to these conditions. Such a program could involve the organization of reporting teams around urban subjects and urban functions—land development, social problems, public services. Reporters on the teams could continue to operate on narrower beat levels, with an urban "generalist" overseeing each team to assure integration. Such teamwork might result in reports on water supply and control rather than an occasional flash flood; on highway planning and politics rather than the freeway jam; on slum conditions and causes rather than the tenement fire.[9] At least one major newspaper, the late *Minneapolis Star,* reorganized its reporting staff along those general lines, ten years after Burd first suggested the approach.

USING SOCIAL INDICATORS

In Chapter 5, we introduced social indicators, readily available statistics that provide insight into more general conditions about the population or community under study. Social indicators and the pool of census data described in Chapter 4 are important tools for the urban issues reporter. They provide validation and authentication for claims and conclusions made by human sources. It is the rare story about urban problems that isn't based at least in part on statistics.

The idea for a story may originate with a statistic. Early in 1981, for example, the Census Bureau announced that surveys showed a drop in the use of public transportation by workers from 1970 to 1977 in large metropolitan areas. The news was startling because the United States had been in the grip of a gasoline shortage since the Arab oil embargo of 1973. The government was encouraging workers to commute by bus or join van and car pools. Gasoline prices had risen dramatically during the period, giving workers additional incentive to leave their cars at home. The reported drop in the patronage of public transportation begged for examination.

The census data could have been a starting point for reporters to inquire about what is essentially an urban issue: the availability, quality, and use of public transit. Natural questions flowing from the announcement might include these:

> Does the pattern hold true in this region? Local ridership data are available from state and local transit authorities.
>
> Can the drop be explained by a reduction in service? A rise in fares? By changing residential or employment patterns? By expansion of ride-sharing programs?
>
> Do local authorities have plans to counter the trend?
>
> What do commuters say about their use or nonuse of public transportation? A survey would be necessary here.

In some cases, reporters will generate story ideas from other sources and turn to social indicators to illuminate the subject. A team of reporters for *Newsday* spent more than six months preparing a series of articles examining urban problems on Long Island, New York. The result of their efforts, an impressive series of more than twenty articles, examined local government, taxes, the economy, transportation, education, energy, culture, housing—all the elements of the urban community.[10] Statistics were at the heart of most of the stories, blended skillfully with readable prose. Consider this example, on the industrial economy of Long Island:

> When it came time to move his business from New Cassel to larger quarters, Milton Fieg carefully investigated several prospective sites in Suffolk. After a long search, he found the perfect place—in Pennsylvania. . . .
>
> "We needed more room but couldn't expand where we were," Fieg said. "We finally decided to move out for tax reasons." Other factors, he said, were low-cost financing offered by Pennsylvania and cheaper construction and land costs there. . . .
>
> The move cost 28 people their jobs. They are among the more than 12,000 workers who have been left unemployed since 1961 as a result of manufacturing firms moving off the Island. By itself, the out-migration of firms might be only another nagging problem tugging at the Nassau-Suffolk economy. But considered with other ailments, it becomes a symptom of deeper economic ills undermining the stability of the bicounty area.[11]

After that humanized introduction, the story goes on to detail the scope of the problem, in both statistical and individual terms. The *Newsday* series, directed by Suffolk editor Robert W. Greene, not only painted a picture of the area's condition but also sought solutions for each of the problems examined. It is representative of exemplary urban journalism.

As in other reporting areas, the urban beat sometimes demands original quantitative research. The continuing debate over redevelopment of downtown districts in older cities is one such circumstance. Proponents of downtown renewal argue that the health of a city's central core is vital to the well-being of the region. Opponents challenge that notion and question the propriety of using municipal bonding powers and taxes to aid developers of downtown business buildings. A test of the argument was devised by San Francisco journalists Bruce Brugmann and Greggar Sletteland. They analyzed city budgets and tax reports to see if downtown business property was a boon or a burden to taxpayers. After examining mountains of paper, they found that it cost the San Francisco treasury $5 million more a year to provide services to downtown business buildings than the properties paid in taxes.[12]

RACE RELATIONS REVISITED

As the memory of the urban riots of the late 1960s has faded from news media consciousness, so has the intensity of coverage of minority groups and neighborhoods. Squeaky wheels get the grease in the news business, too. But news organizations haven't reverted to the indifference toward minorities they displayed in an earlier era. There are still some reporters specializing in minority coverage, and an incident like the Miami riot of 1980 spurs a flurry of interpretive stories across the country, examining local conditions.

Day-to-day coverage of minority affairs is a demanding, delicate assignment. Reporters assigned to this topic must first overcome the inertia and disinterest in their own newsrooms, a common attitude toward "soft news" subjects. But if lack of media attention to the interests of racial minorities is, as the Kerner Commission suggested, a cause of unrest, then reporters covering minority relations have a rare journalistic opportunity to improve directly the quality of life in their communities. To realize that opportunity, obstacles that don't confront other urban affairs reporters must be overcome. Foremost among them is the need to develop trusting and trustworthy news sources. The white reporter working in the Hispanic, black, or American Indian communities may encounter language barriers, indifference, and cynicism along with more common news-gathering barriers. Reporters must get to know the welfare recipient as well as the welfare director, the postman as well as the NAACP president, the pool hall operator as well as the mortuary owner, the factory worker as well as the minister. Visible leaders of minority organizations sometimes don't represent the real opinion of the community.

Race relations presents a broad landscape to the reporter. It includes coverage of routine organizations, from fraternal groups to political associations. It includes coverage of the civil rights and equal opportunity programs of government and business. It includes searching out those individuals worthy of news attention because of achievement, activities, or personality. And it requires, most of all, awareness of the larger forces at work in the minority community and society at large. Sensitivities are great and source relationships fragile in urban minority communities. Not covering an event is likely to be interpreted as evidence of racism, not as a judgment on news value based on available space and manpower. Some community groups expect overt participation by reporters in their activities as a sign of support and sympathy. A story critical of a group or individual may destroy irreplaceable sources. Human relations reporters must develop suitable mechanisms to cope with these and other ethical dilemmas.

In one important area, media coverage of minority issues has improved markedly in the last ten years: the monitoring of social and economic indicators. Journalists are now quick to recognize and react to statistical data that have bearing on the status of minorities, particularly in regard to employment, education, and income. It was the absence of this early-warning approach to news that led to white America's shock and incomprehension at the riots of the 1960s.

In addition to being alert to developments and trends, many news organizations have undertaken comprehensive examinations of minority conditions. Two impressive recent efforts, by the *San Bernardino* (Calif.) *Sun* and the *Fort Meyers* (Fla.) *News-Press,* provide excellent examples of urban reporting techniques. Consider this sampling of stories from the *Sun*'s 144-page tabloid supplement, "Skin Deep, A Study of Minorities."[13] On minority employment:

> Jobs, occupations—in short, who gets a piece of the dollar—is the number one concern in minority communities. It's also the number one problem. . . .
> Nationally, the minority unemployment rate was 2.4 times the white rate in 1978—the widest gap between the two groups since the federal government began recording employment statistics.
> The local picture is identical.

On housing:

> The real estate agent shuffled through a pile of contracts and forms on her desk until she found a clean sheet of paper.
> "When I came to town," she said, peering over the top of her glasses, "I appreciated someone telling me where the blacks and Chicanos are, so I'm doing the same for you."
> With that, she began drawing a rough map. . . . She circled the West Side— a predominantly minority area—in red. "Stay away from here," she told the anglo visitor.
> The statement was illegal, a violation of both California and federal fair housing laws, but it was only one of many such comments made by San Bernardino Valley real estate agents during a *Sun* study of discrimination in local housing.

On political power:

> Blacks and hispanics in San Bernardino County are no longer in the back of
> the political bus, but they're not in front either.
> It's been 12 years since San Bernardino hispanic Robert Flores said, "We
> must elect those who look like us, think like us, act like us and feel like us
> because they have suffered like us and we can talk to them."
> It's been 10 years since Harry Davidson, a black San Bernardino resident,
> said, "We feel the city on the move has been moving away from the black
> community."
> It's now 1980, a new decade, and while things have taken a turn for the
> better, the same pleas are still being made—but perhaps not as loudly.
> Blacks and hispanics, the two largest minority groups in the county, de-
> scribe a sense of impotency when they talk about politics: "There's no power;
> there's no power when you're poor."

The thirty-five stories in the *Sun* supplement employed an arsenal of journalistic tools—records searches, government statistics, attitude surveys, experiments, interviews, and documentary research. Many of the same methods were used by the staff of the Fort Meyers newspaper in developing
"Dunbar: A Community Profile." The *News-Press* series, reprinted in a
fifty-six-page special edition, presents a stark picture of Dunbar, a pre-
dominantly black suburb of Fort Meyers. The series was introduced with
this explanation from the newspaper:

> Many blacks are capable of joking about the stereotyped thinking that too
> often permeates their very existence. They recognize that many whites simply
> do not have enough information about blacks to make valid judgments.
> That's precisely why the *News-Press*, starting today, is running an extensive
> series of articles about the Dunbar community. The series is aimed at giving
> all residents of Lee County a chance to shape a valid view of Dunbar and the
> nearly 12,000 persons who live there.
> Such a series is long overdue. . . . The *News-Press* is just as guilty as the rest
> of the media for ignoring the facts about Dunbar and we've spent many
> months working to correct that.[14]

The efforts by the *Sun* and the *News-Press* to address the needs of
minority residents and the larger need of the majority community to become aware of conditions are outstanding, but not unique. Other newspapers have conducted similar, if less ambitious, projects. The test of the
urban journalism model described in this chapter will be the continuation
of that kind of monitoring over time on a systematic basis.

REPORTING ON EDUCATION

Coverage of education as a special subject was a journalistic staple long
before the urban crisis became a household word. Why, then, consider

such reporting in a chapter on urban journalism? One reason is that public education has been at the very center of the urban maelstrom for the last three decades.

Ask people to name the biggest problem in the schools today and as likely as not they'll say "busing." The movement of pupils from one school neighborhood to another to satisfy court-ordered desegregation policies is the latest in a series of controversies that have engulfed public education for almost thirty years. Conflict over integration has dominated education news in much of the nation since the Supreme Court decision barring "separate but equal" schools.

Education as an urban issue, however, goes much beyond integration and race relations. The entire process of suburbanization has had profound impact on urban schools. Declining population in the central cities means smaller school enrollments and a smaller tax base to support the schools. New suburbs face the opposite problem: rising enrollments and the overnight need for new buildings and staff. The latter problem is particularly troublesome today in the rapidly growing Sunbelt cities. School finance is a principal focus for education writers.

Even without population shifts, urban school enrollments have declined because of private school growth, a development brought on, in part at least, by parental response to public school integration. The vexing economic squeeze on public schools has led to demands for increased state and federal aid to local school districts. It has also led to cutbacks in school programs for some districts. Here's how one New Jersey daily newspaper, in a series of articles on school problems, introduced the issue:

> Less than 15 miles separate Plainfield and the Bridgewater-Raritan Regional school district. But except for similarities in structure and enrollment, they're worlds apart.
>
> The great differences in wealth and educational resources that divide these two districts—and occur in varying degrees between urban and suburban schools throughout the state—undermine the foundations of public education in New Jersey.
>
> Suburban districts like Bridgewater-Raritan have strong fiscal advantages that allow higher school spending. They can draw a greater level of financing from commercial and industrial development, many of which moved from aging urban centers to pleasant surroundings and the property-tax haven of the suburbs. Compared to an urban district like Plainfield, it takes considerably less effort for suburban districts like Bridgewater-Raritan to appropriate tax revenue for school purposes.[15]

It should be evident that education reporters must be conversant with public finance and tax matters. Today approximately 40 percent of all local governmental expenditures are devoted to education. But budgets and taxes are just one dimension of news coverage. Court actions that affect the schools, state and federal legislation on education, and activities in the classrooms are other areas that must be monitored. Attending school board meetings and relying on publicity handouts from the superintendent's office won't do the job in an age when education is at the vortex of urban concerns. The education beat demands interpretive and investigative reporting beyond spot coverage of events.

Although education writers are responsible for coverage of legal, legislative, and fiscal matters affecting the schools, they also have a responsibility to report on developments in education itself. Education is a dynamic field, where innovation is common—and often controversial (the "new math" of the 1960s and sex education classes are examples). Since parents make up a large part of the audience for education news, the quality of classroom education is of primary interest. Many parents distrust fads in education and want objective, detailed reports of experimental programs. Innovations such as magnet schools, learning centers, and curriculum changes are among the array of topics that deserve early attention from the press.

When dealing with those subjects, reporters must guard against two dangers: One is relying solely on program officials for information about new courses or services. Although it may be difficult for reporters to obtain independent evaluation of experimental programs, the effort must be made. Two possible sources for evaluation are university faculty and professional journals, which may have articles on similar programs. Parental and student reactions to new programs also have a place in news stories.

The second danger in these stories is lapsing into educationese, an affliction common to teachers and administrators. Parents are interested in what is happening to their children, but jargon-filled stories about "enriched learning experiences" or "cognitive development approaches" are likely to turn them off. The burden is on the reporter to translate the language of the pedagogue to the idiom of the living room. Consider this example from the New Jersey newspaper series previously mentioned:

> Myrtle Pratt peered at her students over the granny-style glasses that sat on the bridge of her nose. She took attendance. It was the start of what she called another of her typical compensatory (remedial) education classes.
>
> Five of the 13 students enrolled in her ninth-grade reading class were absent. Many of those who were there were too restless to stay in their seats for the duration of the 45-minute period.
>
> And in the back of the room, attention was focused on the teddybear radio a young lady brought to class, rather than on the mimeographed assignment sheet that had just been passed out.[16]

Reporter Michael A. Fletcher went on from there to describe and appraise the compensatory education program in Plainfield, New Jersey, schools. It's evident from the start that he didn't rely on a handout or merely an interview with the program coordinator; he went to the classroom for first-hand observation.

Education writers cover events and processes intimately connected to other systems in the urban milieu. The schools can't be regarded in isolation from other forces in the social, political, and economic systems. At the same time, they report on subject matter that requires specialized knowledge and close relationships with professionals. The combination of tasks requires a reach and vision as demanding as that of any other specialist in the public affairs spectrum.

OTHER URBAN ISSUES

The range of urban issues is broad, and we have touched on only a few thus far. If there is a common theme among these varied topics, it is the need for skillful utilization of demographic data and other statistics to help interpret and evaluate conditions. Most urban topics require specialized knowledge, and all permit a variety of stylistic approaches. A few of these topics and approaches will be examined through examples of various stories.

Politics and Power

Whatever the issue, an element of any urban story is decision making—who says "go" or "stop." The power structure in cities is a subject worthy of examination by itself, a job undertaken by newspapers in many communities. It should also be considered as a component of any urban issues story. In the following excerpts from a series in the *Rochester* (N.Y.) *Times-Union,* reporter Richard Whitmire combined survey research and extensive interviewing to help answer the very basic question, "Who runs Rochester?"

> With its wealthy industries and sophisticated culture, Rochester should be the kind of city that attracts people talented at wielding power.
> In the past, Rochester has seen lots of power brokers. But now it's hard to find a power broker worthy of the title in Monroe County.
> In fact, this city and this county have probably never had a bigger leadership vacuum.
> It shows in the potholes in the streets. A power elite would never let the little things slide—the things so many people care about. . . .

In a companion story, Whitmire supported his conclusion of a power vacuum with survey findings:

> The names and faces you see on the chart accompanying this story are the cream of Rochester's political power structure.

Those names come from our survey, which asked 147 community observers: Who wields political influence? Answers came from neighborhood group leaders, political scientists, businessmen, politicians, community activists, lawyers. . . .
That's the list of the power structure, but—as our survey clearly showed—even the power structure thinks there's a power vacuum here.[17]

The story documents the conclusion through interviews with survey respondents.

State of the Cities

The urban crisis spawned a continuing examination in the press of the condition of the cities. This investigation often takes the form of "quality of life" studies—using social indicators to assess urban conditions and compare them to other cities. Sometimes surveys are employed to record public perception of urban conditions. More often, the appraisals come from urban affairs experts and from statistical indicators. As the 1970s came to a close, urban reporters were writing about widespread observations of a turnaround in the central cities—a revitalization of the urban cores through redevelopment and gentrification. The *Minneapolis Star* decided to look at the phenomenon and came up with a counterappraisal, as this story by reporter Robert Guenther indicates:

"Back to the city."
"The urban renaissance."
The catch-phrases roll off tongues these days in conversations about the large, industrial cities of North America.
The words conjure an image of a flood of young couples from [the affluent suburbs], their Volvos loaded with Perrier water, jogging attire and down-filled comforters, pulling trailers filled with ten-speed bicycles and wood-burning equipment up to their newly rehabilitated Victorian homes in an aging but fashionable section of the city.
The urban crisis, according to a recent article in Harper's magazine by T. D. Allman, is gone. It has left town and moved to the suburbs.
News magazines have echoed that assessment in articles titled, "St. Louis: A Dying City Bounces Back," "Baltimore's Comeback" and "America's Troubled Cities: Better Times Ahead?"
But the voguish view that the cities are turning around clashes with available data and assessments of several of the nation's leading experts on cities.[18]

Guenther buttresses his thesis with an array of statistics suggesting that there has been little change in the underlying problems of the cities.

Housing

Perhaps no urban subject has attracted as much attention as housing. It has been invoked as the cornerstone of the employment problem, the key to school integration, and the underlying cause of the urban malaise.

Much of the federal government's intervention in city problems has been in the form of housing aid and redevelopment funds. Whatever the larger view, housing translates into cost, quality, and availability, in the minds of newspaper audiences. Looking at one facet of the housing issue, the Monroe, Louisiana, newspapers investigated slum housing. Reporters Charles Haddad and Eleanor Rushing chose as the targets of their investigation the slum landlords, the tenants, and city officials responsible for enforcement of housing codes. This is how their series began:

> Monroe needs substandard housing. Many of the city's residents can find nowhere else to live.
> The city's poor—elderly, disabled and handicapped people on low fixed incomes, young mothers without husbands raising small children, unskilled workers with small salaries and the unemployed—cannot afford Monroe's homes.
> Instead, they live in small wooden shacks much like those of sharecroppers built nearly 100 years ago.
> Such a house is at 1022½ Breard St. The story of how it was built 80 years ago and why it stands today illustrates the substandard housing problem in Monroe.[19]

The series of articles appeared in a twelve-page supplement to the *World* and *News-Star* which included efforts to explore housing alternatives and solutions to the slum problem.

THE LANDSCAPE OF URBAN REPORTING

The preceding examples of urban reporting have several common elements. They deal with significant and widespread concerns. They represent journalistic enterprise in the sense that the stories didn't originate with a press conference or public meeting. They require investigation in that the information needed for the stories isn't readily available. Although only a few topics were illustrated, the list could easily be expanded. Health, environmental, and scientific subjects often have urban implications. The *San Jose* (Calif.) *Mercury News,* for example, in 1980 examined how electronics firms in "Silicon Valley" were endangering the health of workers in Santa Clara County because of the use of poisonous chemicals.[20] A weekly newspaper, the *Monticello* (Minn.) *Times,* explored the subject of drug and alcohol abuse in 1981 and discovered that a suburban community isn't exempt from those big-city problems.[21]

The landscape of urban issues is large, and like the universe, expanding. As the nation moves into the 1980s, new problems are surfacing, and new social and political responses are emerging. We seem to be at a point in the United States of reforming the reforms of the previous generation.

The notion that government should be the principal source of social action, dominant for a half century, has been shaken in the past decade. After years of increasing centralization, we appear to be moving toward decentralization.

Federal grants to state and local governments rose from about $20 billion in 1970 to $80 billion in 1980. Even taking inflation into account, those figures represent a major shift in policy about who will deliver public services. State and local expenditures are approaching 20 percent of the gross national product—more than twice the level of 1955—and the prospects are for an even greater role for state and local governments. The battles of the 1980s may be fought over the locale for federal expenditures: in the devastated older cities of the industrial North or in the emerging metropolises of the South and Southwest.

On another level, local government is undergoing structural change. As dollars shrink, consolidation of school districts is accelerating. There is a growth of regional governing bodies to provide services that cross traditional jurisdictions: transportation, land-use planning, health care, sanitation, waste disposal, air and water pollution. Some regions, such as Atlanta, Minneapolis–St. Paul, and Portland, Oregon, have opted for comprehensive metropolitan governing bodies with broad powers. They supplant in some cases the jurisdiction of the cities. Other regions have moved toward more limited and less formal cooperative units, such as the Southern California Association of Governments.

Still other changes making themselves felt in urban America have little to do with government. The shifting nature of the family unit, with late marriages for many people, is having its impact on the urban economy. Fewer children and more individual households are one result of this cultural upheaval. Energy shortages, inflation, an aging population, new technology, and changing moral and personal values are all having profound effects on urban life. The dynamism of postindustrial society poses both challenge and opportunity to the urban reporter of the 1980s.

NOTES

[1]Daniel Bell and Virginia Held, "The Community Revolution," *The Public Interest* 16 (Summer 1969), 142–77.

[2]John M. Mollenkopf, "The Post-War Politics of Urban Development," in John Walton and Donald E. Carns, *Cities in Change*, 2nd ed. (Boston: Allyn and Bacon, 1977), pp. 554–55.

[3]For examples of press reaction to urban riots in the 1960s, see Edmund M. Midura, ed., *Why Aren't We Getting Through?* (Washington, D.C.: Acropolis Books, 1971); Charles U. Daly, ed., *The Media and the Cities* (Chicago: University of Chicago Center for Policy Studies, University of Chicago Press, 1968); Richard Leonard, "Role of the Press in the Urban Crisis," *Quill*, May 1968, pp. 8–11; and "We Have

Learned Something About Reporting Riots," *Editor & Publisher*, September 2, 1967, p. 11.

⁴*Report of the National Advisory Commission on Civil Disorders* (New York: Bantam Books, 1968), p. 363.

⁵Ibid., p. 366.

⁶Ibid., p. 389.

⁷David B. Sachsman, "Mass Media and the Urban Environment," *Mass Comm Review* 1 (July 1974), 11.

⁸Gene Burd, "Urban Renewal in the City Room," *Quill* 56 (May 1968), 12.

⁹Ibid., 13.

¹⁰*Newsday*, March 19–31, 1978.

¹¹"Long Island at the Crossroads," special reprint of the *Newsday* series, p. 8.

¹²Bruce Brugmann and Greggar Sletteland, *The Ultimate Highrise* (San Francisco: San Francisco Bay Guardian, 1971).

¹³*San Bernardino Sun*, September 7, 1980.

¹⁴"Dunbar: A Community Profile," supplement to the *Fort Meyers News-Press*, December 3–11, 1978, p. 2A.

¹⁵*Bridgewater Courier-News*, July 23, 1980, p. 17.

¹⁶Ibid., p. 21.

¹⁷*Rochester Times-Union*, March 6, 1980, p. 2.

¹⁸*Minneapolis Star*, March 31, 1980, p. A1.

¹⁹*Monroe World* and *News-Star*, April 22, 1979.

²⁰*San Jose Mercury News*, April 6–8, 1980.

²¹*Monticello Times*, February 5, 1981, pp. 5–8.

SUGGESTED READINGS

CALLOW, ALEXANDER B., JR.   *American Urban History.* New York: Oxford, 1973. An interpretive reader tracing the development of cities in the United States.

GORHAM, WILLIAM, AND NATHAN GLAZER.   *The Urban Predicament.* Washington, D.C.: Urban Institute, 1976. Excellent overview of urban issues—finance, transportation, housing, crime—by authors who anticipated urban developments of the present decade.

HELMER, JOHN, AND NEIL A. EDDINGTON.   *Urbanman, The Psychology of Urban Survival.* New York: Free Press, 1973. Articles dealing with the social and psychological aspects of living in cities.

HUMMEL, RAYMOND C., AND JOHN M. NAGLE.   *Urban Education in America.* New York: Oxford, 1973. Overview of social, financial, political, and educational issues affecting city schools.

JANOWITZ, MORRIS.   *The Community Press in an Urban Setting*, 2nd ed. Chicago: University of Chicago Press, 1967. Now-classic study of role and function of community newspapers in metropolitan areas.

KALT, NEIL C., AND SHELDON S. ZALKIND.   *Urban Problems.* New York: Oxford, 1976. Readings and text presenting behavioral studies that bear on urban issues.

MERCER, CHARLES.   *Living in Cities.* Baltimore: Penguin, 1975. Examines the urban environment, principally from the standpoint of architecture and space, as it applies to psychological effects.

NATHAN, RICHARD P., AND MARY M. NATHAN.   *America's Governments.* New York: Wiley-Interscience, 1980. A factual book, drawn from census data, that covers the organization, finance, and employment of federal, state, and local governments.

NEWMARK, NORMA L., AND PATRICIA J. THOMPSON. *Self, Space and Shelter.* San Francisco: Canfield Press, 1977. Comprehensive treatment of housing fundamentals and issues.

ROSENTHAL, DONALD B., ed. *Urban Revitalization.* Beverly Hills, Calif.: Sage Publications, 1980. Collection covers many aspects of redevelopment, neighborhood planning, and government aid.

TICHENOR, PHILLIP J., GEORGE A. DONOHUE, AND CLARICE N. OLIEN. *Community Conflict & the Press.* Beverly Hills, Calif.: Sage Publications, 1980. Provocative and insightful report of studies analyzing the role of the press in relation to community structure.

VON ECKARDT, WOLF. *A Place to Live.* New York: Dell, 1967. An early and eloquent treatment of urban architecture and the deterioration of the cities.

WALTON, JOHN, AND DONALD E. CARNS. *Cities in Change,* 2nd ed. Boston: Allyn and Bacon, 1977. Collection of essays and articles covering the broad sweep of urban subjects, from culture to politics.

Periodical literature dealing with urban issues is as far-ranging as the disciplines that make up the urban environment. Each field offers professional journals for the reporter to monitor. Sage Publications of Beverly Hills is the publisher of several journals on urban subjects, as well as an annual review series.

12

Covering Business, Labor, and Consumer News

The business of America is business.

Calvin Coolidge

The thirtieth president of the United States may not have been everybody's favorite phrasemaker, but given the power wielded by business in this country, he must at times be credited with a certain insight. Some of the criticism leveled at the news media's coverage of business is grounded in the belief that they fail to share Coolidge's insight, and if they spent more time and space on business and less on government, the public would have a better understanding of where power in the country lies.

More effective than criticism, however, in advancing the claims of business for media attention has been the success of the *Wall Street Journal,* the top-circulation daily in the country in recent years; of *Business Week* and *Forbes'* magazines; and of beefed-up business sections of the *New York Times,* the *Los Angeles Times,* and other large dailies. All of these newspapers and periodicals have recently increased their commitments of personnel and space to business news, accounting in part for gains in circulation.

But these are the leaders. The rank and file continue to be vulnerable to attack on at least four grounds: insufficient space, or in the case of the broadcast media, time; superficiality of treatment; antibusiness bias; and inadequate training of personnel in economics, resulting in failure to understand how the system works. "If business got as much space as sports, your newspaper would be worth the price," runs a frequent complaint; and

"Releases on promotions and company earnings just aren't where it's at," runs another. Perhaps the most inclusive condemnation was uttered by Louis Banks of the Harvard Business School and a former editor of *Fortune:* "We are fed a daily diet of authoritative ignorance, most of which conveys a cheap-shot hostility to business and businessmen. Here is where the nation sees a persistently distorted image of its most productive and pervasive activity, business. . . . The reporters and the editors in the general media are woefully ignorant of the complexities and ambiguities of corporate operations, and being so, are easy targets for politicians or pressure group partisans with special axes to grind at the expense of business."[1]

Banks is not alone. A *Wall Street Journal*/Gallup Survey of chief executives of 282 large companies found that only 13 percent rated business journalists "very good" and 46 percent, "fairly good," whereas 29 percent rated them "poor" and 12 percent had no opinion. That evaluation is even less gratifying when compared to performance ratings of other business professionals by the same executives: accountants, 45 percent very good, 47 percent fairly good; lawyers, 39 percent very good, 43 percent fairly good; investment bankers, 28 percent very good, 48 percent fairly good.[2]

Although the survey rated business journalists, it should be noted that criticism is more often leveled at business stories by general assignment reporters in the general news pages than at those by business writers in the business pages.

Criticism of business coverage, however, is not entirely a one-way street. More than a few business writers counterattack with the charge that business is excessively secretive. Not all refusals to respond to inquiries are grounded in the legitimate fear of disclosing trade secrets to the competition. "We could do a better job of explaining business to the public if there were less of the fortress mentality among businessmen," is a not uncommon response by media people to their critics. Reporters also contend that business executives want to see only "good news" published, not negative or critical accounts.

Relationships between business and the media may vary in different parts of the country, depending on the individual media and the businesses they report. A study by University of Minnesota journalism students, directed by one of the authors and a colleague, found that Twin Cities businesspersons and the four dailies and four commercial television stations that report them are less antagonistic than each of the two groups perceives the other to be.[3]

Partly as a result of the spirited dialogue between business and news leaders, there are signs that the media are directing more space, staff, and concern toward their business pages.

What, then, are the new strategies for coverage of business news?

Some veteran business writers would argue that there is nothing new about investigation, interpretation, and research in the print treatment of business, that all these have been practiced for a long time. And indeed they have been on a few business pages. But much more familiar are the old staples: releases, rewritten and otherwise, of earnings and promotions and the tables of market quotations. Although these still have their place, they are no longer enough to satisfy the interest and curiosity of today's readers who want to know how the economic trend is likely to affect them, if another round of deregulation is going to mean another round of price hikes, and why the multinational conglomerate is divesting itself of its wine retailing outlets.

A look at some recent prize-winning economic reporting shows the extent to which some business writers are interpreting the economy as a whole, as well as specific situations, on the basis of extensive investigation and research. Richard C. Longworth and William Neikirk, economics writers for the *Chicago Tribune,* wrote a six-part, 20,000-word series on "The Changing American Worker" that won first place for newspapers of over 100,000 circulation from the University of Missouri School of Journalism Business Awards for 1980. For three months they interviewed experts, from economic theorists to union organizers—in one of the subsequent articles alone, they cited data of four different research organizations—and then talked to several hundred workers throughout the country. Their focus was on four factors: the impact on workers of computer technology, the huge increase of women in the work force, the declining strength of unions, and efforts to provide workers some measure of control over their work. The result of their carefully balanced gathering of facts and opinions, as well as analysis, provided readers with a new understanding of today's alienated worker in the face of business' needs for increased productivity.

A search of staggering proportions for documents, coupled with a cross-country trace of personal sources, constituted the six-month investigation of a bank's failure that won another first in the same competition. The reporter was Stephen Rassenfoss, twenty-seven years old, business writer for the *Clarion Ledger* of Jackson, Mississippi. The failed bank was the Fidelity Bank of Utica, Mississippi, and Rassenfoss's investigation proved the irony of that name. Federal and state banking regulators who closed the bank dropped a veil of silence to protect the solvency of a hastily chartered successor. An $8 million loss was explained merely as bad loans. Bank officers weren't talking; stockholders didn't know. The search for an explanation led Rassenfoss through more than 1,000 pages of U.S. Securities and Exchange Commission reports and thousands more of federal and state corporate records. The resulting four-part series, "Fidelity Bank: Anatomy of a Failure," was the first public disclosure of dealings that in time led to the convictions of three persons and guilty pleas by six others on charges of illegal use of loan money. "I had never thought of myself as an investigative reporter," Rassenfoss said in a telephone interview. "But I had pretty good training on the Chicago News Bureau. I had learned never to assume anything and always to ask every question you can think of, even the dumb ones."

Documentary research combined with interviews again constituted the investigation that led to another prize-winning business series in the University of Missouri competition. Philip Moeller, business editor of the *Louisville Courier-Journal,* burrowed through "mounds" of Interstate Commerce Commission regulations and rulings, as well as other government reports on railroads, in preparation for interviews with more than 100 different sources among railroad executives and government officials. The Louisville and Nashville Railroad, a vital factor in the economy of not only Louisville and Kentucky but also the central South, had lost its long-standing reputation for reliability through a mounting series of derailments in the late 1970s. The overt details—the who, what, where, and when—of that decline had been reported. Moeller determined to find out the why and the how. "The story ultimately boiled down to decisions made by present and former railroad executives and government officials," Moeller has written. But the explanation was so complex and wide-ranging that he needed an eight-part series to accomplish his objective in a fair and carefully balanced, thoroughly documented account.

Business writers' digging is not necessarily limited to corporate finance; their ability to write knowledgeably on economic matters may serve their newspaper well in fulfilling its function as a watchdog of government. Alan Guggenheim, a thirty-year-old business writer for the *Oregon Statesman Journal* of Salem, led a team of reporters in an investigation of a financial crisis in the government of Marion County. What they found was that a so-called "paper" loss of $8 million was a very real loss to taxpayers of more than twice that amount because of inept investment practices and gross overestimates of tax revenues. Their exposé resulted in the firing of several highly placed managers in the county government, as well as another award in the Missouri competition for business writers.

But how many business writers have the opportunity to invest time and effort in several weeks of digging into a complex economic problem or situation? Relatively few. The day-to-day or week-by-week coverage of the business news of a community is considerably less ambitious than the examples just cited. Relatively few developments in the economy justify that type of in-depth coverage. Nonetheless, investigation and research, as well as interpretation, are implicit in this definition of business reporting offered by Jim Fuller, veteran of twenty-odd years of business reporting, more than half of them for the *Minneapolis Tribune:*

> It is the coverage of the specifically economic side of our society: corporate sales and earnings, products and their costs and function, cost and availability of mortgages, trends in pay, the availability of jobs. Done properly, business

reporting is telling people about the things that immediately or ultimately affect their personal economics.[4]

In line with that definition, Fuller, writing in the *Twin Cities Journalism Review*, had suggestions about useful sources for aspiring business writers:

> People in the securities business—brokers, analysts, stock traders—know one hell of a lot about publicly-held companies. If you have questions about a publicly-held company, its recent financial performances, its management, call a brokerage firm and ask for the analyst who follows that company. If you can't get a name from the company telephone operator, call a broker and ask for the analyst's name. . . .
> Annual reports and, at least with bigger companies, 10K forms (expanded versions of annual reports that publicly-held companies must file with the Securities and Exchange Commission) usually are on file in the newspaper office. Or you can get one from a brokerage firm or the company itself. They're loaded with information about a company's finances, sales, earnings, plans for expansion, management.[5]

Also on the subject of sources, Isadore Barmash, assistant to the financial editor of the *New York Times* and a newsman of thirty years' experience, describes a practice he follows that could pay off in time. He keeps a file of all the business cards he has been given. "Many times I have sought to find someone with data or a lead to something I was working on and found him among my random cards."[6] Barmash is also a strong believer in maintaining contacts, once established, by occasional telephone calls to exchange information. "It amazes me how much people know about what's going on in fields other than their own."[7]

Fuller, like most of his colleagues in business reporting, finds competitors of firms he's writing about extremely useful sources. Oftentimes he can't use their names, but that's a worthwhile concession. And he thinks it's foolish not to use public relations people who "usually can give you the basic background quickly so that you can spend your time with top executives on important questions. The PR department also can tell you quickly what executive is most likely to have the answers you seek and sometimes can put you in touch with an executive you can't immediately reach on your own."[8]

Not all business writers would agree with Fuller. They would insist, instead, that too many "flacks" are overzealous in shielding top executives from the media, and because of their accent on the positive and muting of the negative, are lacking in candor. Generalizations about them are dangerous.

Fuller would probably get less disagreement concerning his advice on the care and feeding of business sources:

> In talking with businessmen, economists and such, the soft approach is almost always best. Unlike public officials, they usually don't have to talk to you. It is

sometimes necessary to play bully, but not very often. It's also easier, in most cases, to get a businessman to talk if he is in an atmosphere in which he feels comfortable—in his office or favorite lunch spot.[9]

Even more important than the soft approach is the knowledgeable, well-informed one. The standard precaution for interviewers—go prepared—is nowhere more applicable than in quizzing business sources. They tend to be wary of reporters. "But if the reporter does his or her homework, learns what motivates business people, is not afraid to ask the intelligent question but doesn't have to ask the dumb one, more than enough sources will break down," according to James L. Rowe, Jr., New York financial correspondent for the *Washington Post*.[10]

That "homework" cited by Rowe may consist of a variety of sources: the brokers, the analysts, the annual statements, the 10K forms (all previously referred to); any one of a number of standard reference works: *Commodity Year Book, Encyclopedia of Banking and Finance, Moody's Manual of Investments, Poor's Register of Corporations, Directors and Executives;* the relevant trade press, indexed in *Business Periodicals Index;* or in the event that the subject of the story has been involved in litigation, court records.

But what if after the reporter's most diligent application to homework the essential sources don't "break down"? References to "stonewalling" abound in the written experiences of business writers. Some industries—food, tobacco, pharmaceutical—have a reputation for being less open than others—airline, computer, and banking. "'There are still quite a few executive officers who are accustomed to giving orders and who resent the media for not taking them,'" the president of a business research group is quoted by A. Kent MacDougall, a writer on business for the *Los Angeles Times*. And MacDougall cites what is perhaps an extreme example of executive arrogance toward the media: "When a *Los Angeles Times* reporter phoned an oil company president to clarify a news release on a new gasoline pricing policy, he was told, 'Just run it the way I sent it in, sonny,'"[11] Such arrogance, although it has not been unusual, probably is declining and will continue to diminish as more and more businesspersons learn that when they refuse to deal with the media they do so at their own risk. "'No comment' can cause more harm to a company's image than good," MacDougall notes.

As James P. Gannon, executive editor of the *Des Moines Register*, observes, "It didn't help Ford Motor Co. to deny that it knew of any problem with its Pinto automobile, and it didn't help Firestone Tire to stonewall the press about the problems with its radial 500 tire. Those stories came out anyway, and the companies only worsened the situation."

Indeed, difficulty in getting information tends to confirm a reporter's suspicions that a company has something to hide, and may reinforce his determination to get the story by some other means. This can lead to a more critical story, and even an inaccurate one.[12]

Certainly the reporter, when rebuffed by a business source (as well as by any other) should insist that the story is going to be written in any case, and it would be to the source's advantage if the story were not incomplete or possibly inaccurate. Business sources may be particularly susceptible to such persuasion, especially if they reflect that any knowledgeable reporter is going to turn to their competitors to fill gaps in the data.

Of course such recalcitrance does not relieve reporters of one iota of responsibility for making their accounts as accurate as possible. All previous admonitions about accuracy can be doubled for the business writer. Irretrievable damage can be done to a business firm as well as to readers—to say nothing of the reputation of the reporter and his or her paper or station—by an inaccurate story. "No story should be written unless the reporter is just about 100 percent sure of his facts," Barmash writes.[13] And at another point, he cautions, "Never accept as final any facts or figures volunteered by someone who is not directly responsible for them."[14] Errors in reporting, he points out, are basically of two kinds:

> One is misunderstanding or misinterpreting what some one person or several have told you. The other is the basic one of erroneously reporting a fact or a figure. There are ways to prevent these. One is to go over with the prime source the comments he has made before they are published, but lots of reporters avoid this since it seems to indicate that they are unsure of themselves. Personally, I'd rather seem unsure than be inaccurate, but the only time I check back with a source is when I'm not entirely certain that I have accurately reflected his comment. And when it comes to figures, I have learned that it is well worthwhile, after I finish, to recheck all my figures. I find that the check back with the source and the checking of figures do catch potential errors.[15]

Reporters who are reluctant to double-check either comment or figures through fear of seeming unsure of themselves would do well to reflect that most sources would regard such care as an indication of thoroughness, not incompetence. Such indications—and the consequent reliability of the reporting—would do much to surmount the barriers of mistrust between business and the media.

As noted earlier in this chapter, the annual report of a business firm is a helpful source of information. It may vary from a glossy book, resplendent with graphics and artwork as lush as an issue of *Harper's Bazaar*, to a mimeographed sheet similar to the accountant's report for your high-school yearbook. And it will probably be accompanied by a news release that summarizes the high points of the report. Showcased or drab, it will disclose net income compared with previous years; volume of business compared to previous years; dividends paid to stockholders; taxes paid to government; and a variety of other information that may include plans for expansion, a review of new products introduced during the year, and an announcement of additions to plant and equipment.

All those figures may seem quite straightforward, but appearances can be misleading, and a knowledge of accounting is useful in the analysis that precedes interpretation. (The newspaper's accounting department can give you help here.) A frequent business gripe is that the media report profits "unsympathetically" instead of helping to educate the public to the need for even higher profits to spur capital investment. Despite such complaints, MacDougall writes,

> a close look at profit-reporting practices indicates that the news media's most serious shortcoming is not that it reports profits unsympathetically but that it does so simplistically. Too many journalists accept the illusory precision of corporate financial statements at face value. Too few question the accounting conventions that enable companies to report high profits to investors and the public, while at the same time reporting lower profits to the tax collector.
>
> As Harold M. Williams, chairman of the Securities and Exchange Commission, recently noted: 'Conflicting reports of record profits on the one hand and inadequate earnings to maintain and expand capacity on the other, serve only to confuse the public and political leaders. Further, they raise questions about the integrity of financial reporting. Unfortunately, daily press reports of record earnings fail to communicate the effects of changing prices in a meaningful way, and thus the confusion and conflicting claims are likely to continue. In such a conflict, business, serving up the weapons for its own destruction, is clearly and predictably the loser.[16]

Business is quite within its rights, MacDougall goes on to explain, in using accelerated depreciation in reporting profits to the Internal Revenue Service, for example, while using straight-line depreciation in reporting profits to investors and the public. And there's nothing to stop a corporation from reporting the value of its inventory at acquisition cost, rather than at replacement cost, to show a profit that is largely illusory. "Newspapers can be faulted," MacDougall writes,

> for failing to issue general alerts that corporate profit figures are unreliable, but they can hardly be blamed for failing to correct the figures that individual corporations report. There simply are too many corporations, their accounting practices are too complex, and they all tend to report their financial results at about the same time, flooding newspaper offices a few weeks after the close of each calendar quarter with news releases that typically are thick and difficult to digest—and sometimes are less than straightforward.[17]

Although the corporation's news release may be less than straightforward, the business writer's account should never be. Distortion or glossing over in a news release may be hard to detect, but as the business reporter's sophistication grows with experience, the angles that need probing and the statements that need extra verification will become more readily apparent.

With all data in hand, the business reporter turns to the writing task. If that differs from other journalistic writing, it is only because it imposes special demands for clarity. In writing the business story, Paul E. Steiger, financial editor of the *Los Angeles Times,* observes, "Our central problem is that of steering the narrow path between talking down to our specialized readers and talking over the heads of our general ones."[18] In steering that path, Steiger cautions against use of jargon (where unavoidable, explain it) and urges, "Don't be afraid to translate and popularize. Even more than general assignment reporters, business and economic writers must use analogy, anecdote and personification to convey the essential reality of the subject they are covering."[19]

Turn to any edition of the *Wall Street Journal,* and you'll find writing that exemplifies Steiger's strictures, and not only in the first-page features. You'll find other qualities, as well, such as a conversational tone, striking quotes from authority, and examples, as in this lead:

> New York—It really is possible to buy a place here for less than a million dollars, but you wouldn't know it from talking to some of the brokers.
> "New York is finished for the middle class," says A. Laurance Kaiser IV, vice president of Key Ventures, a New York real estate firm. Real estate ads say things like: "5 sty limestone residence . . . extraordinary value at $1,050,000." Or: "Elegant mansion . . . $3,200,000."[20]

Moreover, writing in the *Journal,* in addition to being clear, is often crisp and concise, whether describing broad economic trends in an industry or developments in an individual business, as in these article openings:

> According to Webster's Dictionary the "prime rate" is supposed to be "the most favorable rate of interest available on loans from banks."
> There's only one trouble with that definition: It's wrong.[21]
> New York—The American travel slump, which began last year, is apparently getting worse.[22]
> The market: millions of office desks in the paperless office of the future. The product: desk-top computer terminals with video tubes wired to computer files, or data bases.[23]
> San Francisco—Levi Strauss & Co., which built its reputation and empire mainly selling blue jeans to men, is moving aggressively into the women's wear field. Today that part of its business is as large as the entire company was just a decade ago.[24]

Nor are conciseness and color limited to the leads of *Journal* articles. The causes and effects of declining sales in a single firm and throughout an industry are explained clearly, concisely, and with a bit of sparkle throughout the following account of competition among the makers of running shoes.

JOGGING'S FADE FAILS TO PUSH NIKE OFF TRACK
By Victor F. Zonana
Staff Reporter of the *Wall Street Journal*

The running-shoe industry has run into trouble.

After riding the jogging boom of the late-1970s from practically nowhere to $750 million in sales last year, the industry is facing its first slow growth, or no growth, year. A shake-out looks imminent, as manufacturers retire capacity that has reached unsustainable levels, and as market shares of marginal brands plummet.

"Nothing lasts forever," says James Spring, president of Sports Marketing & Retail Technology Inc., a Wilton, Conn., market research firm. "Americans are fickle. The number of runners has leveled off " at about 20 million, he says, citing a recent Gallup Poll estimate. "The running shoe no longer has that fashion magic."

Makers Cut Back

As a result, Brooks Shoe Manufacturing Co., whose market share of about 15% puts it third in the field, in February laid off 10 clerical and administrative employees at its Hanover, Pa., headquarters, and 200 manufacturing workers in Puerto Rico. Etonic, a unit of Colgate Palmolive Co., with a 4% market slice, is deemphasizing its running-shoe line, and furloughing workers at its three Maine plants.

But industry leader Nike Inc., which went public last December, isn't feeling the pain. With 50% of the domestic running-shoe market, Nike foresaw the trend and started to diversify, even as the jogging craze boomed.

Today, running shoes make up only 43% of Nike's U.S. and international sales, which totaled $270 million in the fiscal year that ended May 31. Basketball shoes account for 24% of sales, with tennis and other racquet-sport shoes adding another 18%. Nike will offer hiking shoes and deck shoes this year.

Bucking the industry's bland performance, Nike reported a strong first half, with net income more than doubling to $13.1 million, or 80 cents a share, from $5.8 million, or 36 cents a share a year earlier. Sales jumped 93% to $213 million in the same period. Still, Nike's stock is trading below its $22 a share offering price, closing yesterday at $19.75 bid.

"We hope sales for fiscal year 1981 will top $430 million," says Philip H. Knight, Nike's president, who founded the company and is its major shareholder with a 46% stake. The 43-year-old Mr. Knight sketched out his blueprint for Nike in 1960, while studying at Stanford University's business school.

Competition for Tiger

Nike, named for the Greek goddess of victory, has grown phenomenally (1976 sales were $14.1 million) due to innovative shoe design and aggressive marketing. Its growth has been at the expense of West Germany's Adidas and Puma and Japan's Tiger, whose shoes dominated the running market in the early 1970s. Mr. Knight started in the athletic-shoe business in 1964 as Tiger's U.S. distributor but broke with the Japanese company in 1972. Most of Nike's shoes are made overseas, with South Korea supplying 58%, and Taiwan 21%.

Mr. Knight isn't sitting back. Nike, which until now has sold all its footwear under the Nike label, will this year introduce One, a line of shoes "to attract the price-sensitive segment of the market." Nike, with suggested retail shoe prices ranging from $23 to $63, and other major brands, such as Adidas, Brooks, and New Balance, have been facing tough competition from unbranded athletic shoes sold by department stores.

Nike and a handful of other U.S. manufacturers are also planning to invade Europe, where locally made Adidas and Puma dominate the market.

Nike, for example, has just opened an office in Amsterdam.
Flexibility Helps
"We're going after Adidas," says Mr. Knight, who is betting that Nike's softer, more flexible shoes can dislodge Adidas from the No. 1 spot in Europe. The strategy worked in the U.S., where Adidas' market share has dropped from 40% to about 20%. Adidas does business in the U.S. through four distributors, an unwieldy arrangement that industry sources say prevented the West German company from reacting quickly to American runners' preference for a softer, better-padded shoe.

Some observers think most of the smaller running-shoe makers that have sprung up in recent years will disappear, leaving the field to four or five manufacturers. "Nike, Adidas, Brooks and New Balance all seem secure," says Tim Graney, owner of Runners Feet, a California retail chain. "But for a retailer, it just doesn't pay to stock some of the smaller brands like Saucony, Pony, and even the once-mighty Puma," shoes that have 1% or less of the market.

"The running-shoe market has definitely flattened out," adds Bruce Tobin, franchise coordinator of Athlete's Foot Marketing Associates, which has 370 stores. "In a market like this, only the strong will survive."[25]

NEWS OF LABOR

An adjunct of business coverage that constitutes a specialization in a few newsrooms is reporting about labor. Time was—at mid-century, give or take a decade—when the labor reporter was an important specialist in many newsrooms. The 1930s had launched a new era in the history of the labor movement: The New Deal assured organized labor the right to bargain collectively, and John L. Lewis challenged the craft unions by organizing unskilled workers in industrial unions. Labor's gains in economic, political, and social power made news constantly, and it was the kind of news that needed knowledgeable reporters who had earned the trust of otherwise distrustful labor sources. Most often, those sources were union officials, and reporters tended to think of labor exclusively as organized, blue-collar, production-line labor.

But in the 1970s, the labor force changed in a number of significant ways: Women became a much larger component; the proportion of white-collar to blue-collar shifted as the number of service workers swelled to more than double the number of production workers; new technology diminished the ranks—and the clout—of such powerful unions as the longshoremen, the coal miners, and workers in the printing trades. The unions had never accounted for a majority of workers; in the 1970s, only one worker in five belonged to a union.

As a consequence, coverage of labor by the media changed. In some newsrooms, the beat was all but abandoned as other areas of concern, such as energy and the environment, asserted claims on space and staff. In others, the emphasis in labor coverage shifted from disputes between unions and management to consideration of such concerns as causes and effects of stress and tension in the workplace, the trend toward more flexible work scheduling, worker input into decision making, efforts to involve employees in improvement of production, personnel policies designed to forestall unionization of employees, union efforts to expand membership, and many more.

The reporter engaged in this kind of labor coverage needs, then, to be able to deal broadly in social and economic problems. But he or she also should be familiar with federal labor laws—the Wagner Labor Relations Act, the Fair Labor Standards Act, the Taft-Hartley Law, the Landrum-Griffin Labor Reform Act—as well as labor laws of the state(s) served by the newspaper or station. Do so-called right-to-work laws apply, for example?

The reporter also needs general knowledge of labor in the community: What proportion of workers are unionized? What is the history of labor-management relations in the community? To what extent are minorities included in union membership? How well enforced are safety regulations and laws governing working conditions? Who are the principal labor spokespersons in the community and what are their characteristics as news sources?

More specifically, the labor specialist will keep track of dates of expiration of union contracts in major industries and will try to keep informed about issues under negotiation. When contract negotiations are concluded without resort to strike (as most of them are), that's news, too, as union members have pointed out in criticizing the media for reporting only news of labor conflict. What will be the effect of the settlement on the local economy? Readers should be informed, as well, about labor's agenda for the state legislature and the progress of individual items on that agenda.

In the event of a strike, readers want to know the issues at stake, how many workers are out, efforts at settlement, offers and counteroffers, effects on the public. Interest in the strike varies, of course, depending on numbers affected, duration, conduct on picket lines, and other factors. The central facts—the progress of negotiation—are usually hard to get. "Outside the realm of diplomatic relations between the great powers, no field compares with collective bargaining in the reluctance of the parties to let the public know what is really going on," Abe H. Raskin, long-time premier labor reporter for the *New York Times,* has written. "The settled conviction of labor and management, in both public and private employment, is that the only time the rest of the world is entitled to any useful information is when an agreement has been reached and it is too late for anybody outside the charmed circle to do anything about it, no matter how damaging its economic consequences."[26]

Raskin recommends "developing responsible sources within labor and management and also among the third parties intimately involved in industrial relations. The Federal Mediation and Conciliation Service has scores of expert mediators on its staff who can be of inestimable help in supplying trustworthy information, provided their identity as sources is safeguarded."[27]

Strike coverage, then, may be the most frustrating assignment for the labor reporter, but it is not necessarily the most challenging, given the importance of labor in the economy and the complexity of issues arising from the workplace.

CONSUMER REPORTING

Another aspect of business coverage—though not necessarily an adjunct of the business pages—is consumer reporting. If business reporting sometimes ruffles feathers in the business community, consumer reporting invariably raises hackles in the same barnyard. It's not even safe from criticism by its proponents.

The term *consumer reporting* covers a fairly wide range of journalistic activity, from investigative reporting for the purpose of exposing, for example, price fixing in an industry through comparison shopping to the mix of entertainment and services that constitute the "action-line" phenomenon. It may also vary in stance from advocacy to the most rigorous effort to be impartial.

Recognition of the range is important in understanding changes that have taken place in this field. Ralph Nader gave the movement a boost that appeared to peak in 1974, at least in the number of designated consumer reporters. Francis Pollock, who was editor of Consumer Union's *Media & Consumer* monthly during its three-year life, puts the number at approximately 500 that year and probably less than half that number six years later. He ascribes the decline to several causes: a waning interest in consumer issues as the most egregious abuses were eliminated from the marketplace and reporter burnout from trying to stay on top of all the developments relevant to consumerism in credit, utilities, insurance, government regulations, and antitrust prosecution. But he also believes that consumer reporting has developed from a specialization to a diffusion throughout the newspaper, with more aggressive reporting of consumer interests, ranging from the food sections to the business pages.[28]

That impression would seem to agree with the observation of Irwin Landau, editorial director for Consumer Union and editor of *Consumer Reports* magazine. "All reporters should consider themselves watchdogs for the consumer," Landau says. "If I were the editor of a newspaper, I would first abolish the idea of a consumer reporter as a specialty. There's no such thing as a consumer reporter. Information of interest to consumers covers too wide a range."[29]

However broadly or narrowly defined, consumer reporting has had an impact. The late Sidney Margolis, dean of consumer writers, believed that without this type of investigative reporting, the consumer would not have made such important gains as "truth-in-lending and other credit reforms on federal and state levels; the new product safety laws; advances in regulations governing auto and tire safety; some reforms in food and cosmetic packaging; unit pricing and open dating of foods; the 1962 drug amendments requiring that drugs be proven efficacious as well as safe; the exposure and increasing regulations of multiple distributor investment schemes, and many other money-wasting deceptions whether actually illegal or barely inside the law."[30]

At least one observer of the field, however, thinks consumer reporting hasn't gone—and isn't going—far enough. Toby J. McIntosh, a reporter of antitrust and consumer news for the Bureau of National Affairs, after serving as a judge in a National Press Club competition in consumer journalism (120 entries) commented, "Consumer reporters appear reluctant to write the less-obviously sexy stories about anti-trust. Violations of anti-trust come in many forms, sometimes as blatant price-fixing, sometimes as more subtle 'structural' problems. Estimating their cost to consumers is an elusive algebra, but lack of competition throughout the economy undoubtedly costs each consumer hundreds of dollars annually. By comparison, other consumer problems are peanuts."[31]

Even so, publishers, particularly those of smaller papers whose advertising revenue may come from only a few major accounts, remain sensitive to consumer stories that may unsettle advertisers. The reporter must be rigorous in presenting documentation for every statement and insuring that the story is fair. Many consumer reports include sidebars in which the allegedly offending businesses are given a chance to respond to the charges.

How do consumer affairs reporters work? What methods do they use? What are the snares? David Nimmer, a reporter for WCCO-TV in Minneapolis, but formerly managing editor and before that consumer reporter for the *Minneapolis Star,* offers these guidelines:

> You can always do comparison shopping, as for liquor or food, or any product or service of which you might find comparable items at different outlets.
>
> If you work for a newspaper which is not able to hire a private laboratory, you may be able to get a state agency to do the testing, such as the department of weights and measures, to see if companies are giving a full gallon of milk or ice cream. Or you may be able to use the facilities at your state university, such as asking the business administration department to explain the ins and outs of a homeowners insurance policy.
>
> I'd say you should plan to spend two weeks at a minimum to find out just what it is you're looking for in a particular product or service. Talk to government experts; talk to the people in the business. For example, if you're look-

ing at television repair, you have to know what is reasonable for a television repairman to charge for a particular repair.

Most importantly, don't overwrite your facts. If you find, for instance, bacteria counts of 10 million in hamburger, you have to point out that 10 million is generally considered an acceptable level. And if you find one sample with 100 million bacteria count, you should point out that no one will die from eating the meat, because most of the bacteria will be destroyed in cooking. At the same time, point out that a lot of people have meat that is cleaner than that, and that the meat is not as clean as it ought to be."[32]

Whether you do comparison shopping as a consumer reporter or monitor union contracts as a labor reporter or investigate the collapse of a bank as a financial reporter, you will be working in an area of specialization that is assuming greater and greater importance in the minds of your readers and listeners. Coverage of business news will never be immune to criticism, but investigation, interpretation, and research by well-trained staffs can increase public understanding of the country's "most productive and pervasive activity."

NOTES

[1]Louis Banks, "Media Responsibility for Economic Literacy," speech given at the Annual John Hancock Awards for Excellence in Business and Financial Journalism, Boston, October 28, 1975, and quoted by S. Prakash Sethi, "The Schism Between Business and American News Media," *Journalism Quarterly,* Summer 1977, p. 241.

[2]The sample was drawn from *Fortune* magazine's listings of 1,300 large companies. The margin of sampling error was reported by the *Journal* to be plus or minus six percentage points. Interviews were by telephone. *Wall Street Journal,* December 2, 1980, p. 25.

[3]The study consisted of a content analysis of business news in the dailies, which found only 19 percent of the articles "reflecting negatively" on business, and surveys by questionnaire of 186 businesspersons, 81 journalists from the four dailies, and four commercial television stations as well as a separate sample of 14 full-time business writers. The study was directed by Professors Ismach and Daniel Wackman.

[4]Jim Fuller, "How-to's of Business News," *Twin Cities Journalism Review* 3 (August 1975), 29.

[5]Ibid., 30.

[6]Isadore Barmash, "The How and the Why of the Business Story," ed. William McPhatter, *The Business Beat: Its Impact and Its Problems* (Indianapolis, Ind.: Bobbs-Merrill Educational Publishing, 1980), p. 74.

[7]Ibid.

[8]Fuller, "How-to's of Business News," 30.

[9]Ibid., 29.

[10]James L. Rowe, Jr., "Why It Is Important to Build Good Business Sources," *The Bulletin of the American Society of Newspaper Editors,* October 1980, p. 14.

[11]A. Kent MacDougall, "Firms Often Learn Hard Way It Doesn't Pay to Clam Up," reprint from *Los Angeles Times,* undated.

[12]Ibid.

[13]Barmash, "The How and the Why," p. 75.

[14]Ibid., p. 77.

[15]Ibid., p. 82.

[16]A. Kent MacDougall, "In Reporting Profits, There Are Many Bottom Lines," reprint from *Los Angeles Times*, undated.

[17]Ibid.

[18]Paul E. Steiger, "How to Write Clearer Business/Economics Stories," *The Bulletin of the American Society of Newspaper Editors*, October 1980, p. 16.

[19]Ibid., p. 17.

[20]*Wall Street Journal*, March 2, 1981, p. 17.

[21]*Wall Street Journal*, February 27, 1981, p. 19.

[22]*Wall Street Journal*, March 6, 1981, p. 7.

[23]Ibid., p. 15.

[24]*Wall Street Journal*, March 4, 1981, p. 19.

[25]Victor F. Zonana, "Jogging's Fade Fails to Push Nike Off Track," *Wall Street Journal*, March 5, 1981, p. 27.

[26]Abe H. Raskin, "The Inside of Labor," ed. Louis M. Kohlmeier, Jr., Jon G. Udell, and Laird B. Anderson, *Reporting on Business and the Economy* (Englewood Cliffs, N.J.: Prentice-Hall, 1981), p. 200.

[27]Ibid., p. 202.

[28]Interview with Francis Pollock, March 13, 1981.

[29]Denis M. Hurley, "Beyond Nader," *Quill*, September 1980, p. 15.

[30]Sidney Margolis, "Enter the Specialist Consumer Reporter," *Media & Consumer* 1 (July 1973), 11.

[31]Toby J. McIntosh, "Chronic Insignificance," *Quill*, September 1980, p. 19.

[32]Interview with David Nimmer, April 14, 1974. See also David Nimmer, "How One Newspaper Tells the Consumer Story," *Editor & Publisher* 106 (March 17, 1973), 32, 34.

SUGGESTED READING

KOHLMEIER, LOUIS M., JR., JON G. UDELL, AND LAIRD B. ANDERSON, eds. *Reporting on Business and the Economy*. Englewood Cliffs, N.J.: Prentice-Hall, 1981. Ten business and economics writers, in addition to the three editors, contribute consistently useful chapters that range from general discussions of the American economy and economic journalism through focused attention to such issues as prices and inflation and wages and employment to consideration of covering economics for newspapers, magazines, and the broadcast media.

MCPHATTER, WILLIAM, ed. *The Business Beat, Its Impact & Its Problems*. Indianapolis, Ind.: Bobbs-Merrill Educational Publishing, 1980. The six essays are adapted from a lecture series by critics, defenders, and practitioners of business journalism, sponsored by the University of Missouri School of Journalism.

13

Covering Uncertainty: Science, Environment, and Medicine

> It is of great importance that the general public be given an opportunity to experience, consciously and intelligently, the efforts and results of scientific research. It is not sufficient that each result be taken up, elaborated, and applied to a few specialists in the field. Restricting the body of knowledge to a small group deadens the philosophical spirit of a people and leads to spiritual poverty.
>
> *Albert Einstein*

The coverage of science, technology, medicine, the environment, mental health, and a myriad of other scientific topics is one of the liveliest and most vital areas of public affairs journalism. From discoveries of health hazards to the cloning of animals and humans to nuclear power or the impact of automation on the work force, science writers and their journalistic cousins who go by other names are concerned with the impact of organized knowledge on the public. For the journalist navigating these complex waters, there is a need to understand the uncertainties of science and their effects on social problems. This has sometimes been called "the journalism of uncertainty."[1]

"Uncertainty," writes communication researcher Phillip Tichenor, "has long been recognized as inherent in the scientific process. Many of the unsettled questions might easily be ignored by journalists; but scientific disputes are not limited to the ivory tower, and show up in a wide range of public problems."[2]

What are these unsettled questions that the public worries about? Would supersonic transports destroy ozone in the upper atmosphere, or wouldn't they? Does radiation from a nuclear plant increase the risk of leukemia in nearby cities, or doesn't it? Is one's diet a potential cause of cancer, and if so, to what degree? Does it make sense to use results from the experimental feeding of megadoses of saccharin in human foods? Are fur hunters in fact threatening the harp seal with extinction or not? And what is the best way to prevent algae buildup and loss of dissolved oxygen in a particular river or lake?[3]

Some of the information necessary for evaluating these questions and developing coherent news stories is found with scientists and others in laboratories, but more often it is also debated in public places—at legislative hearings, at demonstrations and rallies, in journals and other periodicals, and in many other sources. Reporters dealing with these subjects, whether specialists or general assignment reporters pressed into service on a story involving a scientific issue or problem, are public affairs reporters. They try to gather the best possible information from a variety of sources in order to evaluate the arguments being advanced by various interests.

Most of the reporters concerned with the journalism of uncertainty have wide-ranging interests within their specialty. After all, what could be broader than the discussion of science, medicine, technology, and related fields? Science and environment journalists on metropolitan dailies usually have considerable flexibility in determining how they spend their time and just what they cover. A 1978 study of these specialists focused on what areas of science and science-related subjects occupied their energies. The reporters were asked to indicate what areas of science they covered and what percentage of their time was devoted to each of several subjects. The results, seen in the following table, show that the heaviest concentrations are in medical and environmental-energy reporting.

TABLE 1. Percentage of Time Devoted to Individual Subjects by Science Journalists on Metropolitan Daily Newspapers

Physical science	7%
Biological sciences	10%
Medicine	39%
Behavioral sciences	6%
Environment and energy	27%
Technology	11%

Source: *The Journal of Environmental Education*, Spring 1979, p. 10.

PUBLIC INTEREST IN SCIENCE NEWS

Perhaps because many journalists and journalism students shy away from science courses, there is a prevalent myth that the public isn't much interested in science. Although this myth was often challenged in national readership and reader preference studies, many reporters continued to believe it until the late 1970s and early 1980s. During that period readership studies conducted by the Newspaper Advertising Bureau and by individual newspapers demonstrated increasing public interest in science-related content.[4] Some studies even showed that readers sometimes preferred stories on public health, the environment, and energy to gossip columns and the comics! These findings were not lost on magazine publishers who launched several new science magazines aimed at the general reader.[5] Among them are *Omni, Science Digest, Science/80,* and *Discover,* which joined such well-established publications as *Science, Scientific American,* and *Science News.* In addition, space devoted to science and science-related stories in daily newspapers expanded to a greater percentage of the total newshole.

In spite of greater precision in readership studies, science journalists still differ over who should be their primary audience. In a study by one of the authors of this text and a colleague, science reporters on metropolitan daily newspapers (over 100,000 circulation) were asked, "Whom do you have in mind as you write your stories?"[6] The question yielded widely differing responses, although the overwhelming majority answered simply, "the layperson." Others mentioned education and specified the "average high school graduate" and "intelligent readers with some college education." The reporters also expressed special interest in readers "with concerns for new discoveries and techniques," people with some stake in the story, such as "the relative of a hospital patient." Others mentioned were "literate readers," "consumers," "the educated generalist with no scientific expertise," and a "lay audience easily capable of comprehending science material when translated into common language." A small number thought they were writing for professionals in science and scientific fields.

Again, as with the selection of actual subject matter, science reporters have a considerable amount of latitude for creativity in their conception of the audience they want to reach. Science readership is increasing, no doubt in part because of these imaginative ideas about the audience. The science news audience is not an amorphous mass; instead it is people who want news that will have meaning to them in their everyday lives. The successful science reporter knows and understands this requirement.

Of the various categories of science-related reporting we treat in this chapter—science and medicine, the environment, mental health and social welfare—all share some of the same barbs from critics.

CRITICISM OF SCIENCE-RELATED REPORTING

As we mentioned earlier, there are general assignment reporters who by luck of the draw cover an occasional science-related story, and there are science writers who are trained and experienced specialists. All too often the criticism of science news from the public and the scientific community does not distinguish between the copy produced by the general reporter and the specialist. Two of the most common criticisms of science reporting are polar opposites. Some critics complain that science news is too superficial, that it lacks context, understanding, and effective interpretation. Others complain that science news is too complex, aimed only at a small, elite audience with a "public be damned" arrogance. There are examples of both sins in science journalism, of course, but overall the impressive improvement in this kind of reporting over the years has often muted the critics' voices and won the admiration of the general public and the scientific community alike.

Another criticism is that science writers are likely to be coopted by their sources. At one time it was common practice for some science writers to see themselves simply as "interpreters" for the scientific community. This view often produced uncritical, conveyer-belt coverage. The trend is now clearly away from such simplistic treatment of science news, but as Phillip Tichenor warns, "since the prestige of a science writer rests to a considerable degree on acceptance in the scientific community, the possibilities for cooptation by sources are considerable."[7]

In the study of newspaper science writers previously mentioned, reporters were asked to characterize the relationship between source and science writer as it exists today. The overwhelming majority of reporters (thirty-eight or fifty-three percent) said the relationship was cooperative, twenty-three or thirty-two percent described it as neutral, and only two or 2.7 percent said it was adversarial. Another group in the same study (nine persons or thirteen percent) said the relationship varied so much from situation to situation that it was impossible to characterize it in any general sense. Clearly, science journalists cooperate with their sources to get information, but there is no evidence that they are slavishly parroting information as the individual scientist wants it to appear. More often reporters consult several sources in ascertaining the nature of an issue or problem.

Other criticisms of science journalism have less to do with reporters' performance than with the refusal of some key sources to cooperate. For a number of years scientific organizations kept the press at a distance. Information was released slowly and at the scientist's convenience. Medical journals still cause problems for reporters by insisting that information published in substantial part elsewhere has no place in their journals. This policy may sound innocuous, but it is not. Journals like the prestigious *New England Journal of Medicine* have sometimes refused to publish the results of a researcher's work if it has been discussed in the public press.[8] Naturally such a policy makes researchers quite reluctant to talk to the press even when the public interest would clearly be served. Sometimes the need to warn the public about a problem found in research is denied for months by the scientific community because of this rule. The rule is under assault today and it will no doubt be modified in time, but at present it clearly constitutes a barrier to the free flow of information.

These criticisms aside, it can be stated with some certainty that science-related news is probably the most sophisticated type of public affairs coverage, and those who find fault with it are simply identifying flaws in a generally sound field. Sometimes the criticism leads to a lively debate. A 1978 exchange between George Alexander of the *Los Angeles Times*, then president of the National Association of Science Writers, and officials of United Press International is indicative of this healthy criticism.[9] Alexander saw this UPI story:

> CHICAGO (UPI)—Mankind did not originate in earth's primordial slime, but may have come from a giant planet "Marduk" which orbits the sun far beyond the last known planet—so says Secharia Sitchin.
>
> Sitchin, author of a recent book called "The Twelfth Planet," doesn't believe conventional theories of evolution.
>
> Marduk is a hidden planet located beyond Pluto and is many times the size of earth, he said. It orbits the sun, passing near earth only once in 3,000 years.
>
> Sitchin has devoted the past 25 years trying to convince others—through research, decipherings of 3,000-year-old charts and world travel—that Marduk was known to ancient civilizations. He said the technologically advanced inhabitants of Marduk may have genetically created mankind.
>
> By his own admission, Sitchin said the theory "sounds crazy." But the 58-year-old New York businessman, in Chicago Wednesday for the Fifth World Conference of the Ancient Astronaut Society, said he is pleased to find United States Naval Observatory astronomers are beginning to share his view about the existence of another planet.
>
> "There is mounting astronomical evidence that there exists one more planet within our solar system," he said. "It is a planet many times the size of earth and the discovery of this planet will confirm ancient beliefs in its existence.
>
> "The big news of the week, however, is that astronomers of the Naval Observatory in Washington, D.C., confirmed the discovery by one of their colleagues, Dr. James W. Christy, that Pluto has a moon. They also calculated that Pluto is much smaller than hitherto believed.
>
> "The orbits of Haley's Comet were suspected a long time ago to have been caused by Planet X, but the irregularities in the orbit of Uranus and Neptune were attributed to Pluto. But now, because Pluto is not as big as originally thought, Pluto can no longer account for these irregularities. They say there must be one more planet farther out than Pluto to account for it, just as I have been saying all along."

Alexander was outraged and wrote the following to the UPI president:

> I feel compelled to call your attention to the attached story, written by Marcia Stepanek, moved out of your Chicago bureau. In its naivete and imbalance this story is precisely the sort of journalism which makes professional scientists grimace in disgust and science writers despair. Ms. Stepanek having obviously accepted Secharia Sitchin's bizarre—to say the least—theory as credible and consistent with reality, she can only encourage similar erroneous beliefs among the impressionable readers in our society.

Alexander complained that the writer had accepted the theory without contacting sources with other views—one or more informed adversaries since the claims were light years away from mainstream science. A UPI official in responding to the Alexander letter agreed that "it would have been prudent certainly to include at least a line in the Chicago story's claim about a twelfth planet, to the effect that recognized scientists discredit it. But, the official said, there were several references in the story which would give the reader fair warning that his theory should be taken with a grain of salt (for example, "Sitchin . . . doesn't believe conventional theories of evolution" . . . "Sitchin has devoted the past 25 years trying to convince others" . . . and "by his own admission . . . the theory sounds crazy."

COVERING THE ENVIRONMENT

In the hamlet of Topsham, Maine, two journalists launch a weekly newspaper, the *Maine Times,* and regularly publish hard-hitting articles about the impact of proposed oil refineries on the Maine coast. A few miles away in Portland, *Maine Sunday Telegram* reporter Bob Cummings examines just how much electric power will be produced by a hydroelectric project that would flood one of northern Maine's wild rivers. Halfway across the country, *Minneapolis Tribune* reporter Lewis Cope writes about environmental hazards caused by a high-voltage powerline. On the West Coast, *San Francisco Chronicle* reporter David Perlman examines the energy needs of California, a state with a growing supply of power. These articles, and many more like them in publications large and small, reflect the extensive coverage being devoted to environmental issues. Discussion of the environment has become "in," and the topic is not likely to diminish in importance when terms like *energy crisis, land-use planning, smog,* and *zero population growth* have become commonplace.

Yet covering the environment has not been, in some critics' view, as professional as it might be. Colorado environmentalist H. Peter Metzger argues that some journalists "simply refused to consider the possibility that the U.S. Army or the AEC [Atomic Energy Commission] could, for any reason, create a situation of hazard to the public." He also maintains that all too many writers on the environment have a "general incompetence" in technical matters.[10] Moreover, the "event" approach of traditional news reporting is not well suited to covering environmental issues. Says *Los Angeles Times* environmental reporter Larry Pryor,

> Environmental writing is ideally suited to interpretive reporting. Here the writer turns theorist as well as reporter. He investigates and draws together seemingly unrelated facts into an understandable pattern. This takes time— literally months for one story—as well as good sources and the ability to communicate with them on technical topics.[11]

Journalism researchers Leonard Sellars and David W. Jones, Jr., take a similar view:

> Environmental change is often incremental, an equilibrium which shifts slowly and cumulatively over a period of years, seldom becoming an "event" that would normally be considered reportable. Event reporting is a linear, compartmentalized procedure that obscures the fact that environmental change is a process. It perforce focuses our attention on man's projects rather than nature's processes.[12]

Some of the danger zones for the environmental reporter ought to be evident from these comments. Environmental stories are complex, and reporters should not rely on single sources; the translation of technical jargon is difficult; and environmental reporters may find themselves with a blind reliance on "experts" who present "doomsday" findings in "pseudo-events" such as news conferences.

Environmental coverage is, of course, complicated. Public policy decisions on the environment are based not only on scientific evidence but also on a sorting out of contrasting value systems. A major oil company may want one thing, the Sierra Club quite another. Both may marshal impressive scientific evidence to support their views. Both may also take moralistic positions: Free enterprise versus conservation of natural resources. Complex messages coming from diverse voices confront the reporter at every turn. At a public hearing, for example, spokespersons for ecology groups may claim that certain action will lead to a contaminated water supply. They may back their argument with a battery of high-powered scientific talent. Industrial spokespersons, on the other hand, may be equally persuasive. They may have even higher-powered scientific support because their witnesses are likely to be paid consultants, whereas the ecology groups quite often have relied on volunteer talent. For reporters this conflicting evidence means developing considerable sophistication in the particular field. They may want to seek out independent authorities with no ax to grind, read the leading journals, and consult with persons who can help them put the debate at the hearing in the proper context. The reporter must avoid becoming the moralist who always identifies with one side. At times, there are dozens of sides, all in disagreement. Writer Dennis J. Chase concludes,

> By and large, journalists have been content to report the crisis by attributing it—to a study, a report, or the judgment of a prominent scientist or government spokesman—with no serious attempt to verify the conclusions or locate flaws in the findings. Most of these findings are of the "doomsday" variety and have scared the daylights out of readers and viewers. . . . This is most demonstrable in the cases of air pollution, water pollution and the population "explosion"—the Three Horsemen of the Apocalypse—all crises at once, and all containing the same flaws of the self-contradictory, the non-evidentiary,

the non-verifiable, and the undefined. Eco-journalism (my term) is the journalistic practice of reporting ecological crises by ignoring, treating as unimportant, or mishandling the evidence on which the crises are based.[13]

These commentators suggest a changing role for the public affairs reporter who covers environmental topics. Rather than concentrating on the day-to-day events, reporters should turn their attention to broader issues and attempt to place events in context. What should be the objectives of the environmental reporter?

Expand understanding of the environment.   By writing about the environment, the reporter can help promote a broader understanding of ecological sciences and their importance. Although some might disagree that the reporter should advocate particular stands on environmental issues, it is hard to argue with the overall need of society to use natural resources in an intelligent fashion. The reporter, by providing careful analyses of proposals, can help decision-makers and the public make such choices.

Show the interrelationships of technical and social knowledge.   Environmental writer David Hendin says that to most persons, "environment is synonymous with pollution of the air and water. But not to the Negro in Harlem. . . . To this person environment is rats, leaks in the roof and peeling lead-base paints that kill his children when they eat it. To this person environment is bad plumbing, no job and no coat to wear when he goes out in the snow."[14]

Some environmental reporting is beginning to reflect these larger concerns. In his article on a proposed hydroelectric dam, Cummings writes,

> Last winter's energy scare made an almost magic word of Dickey-Lincoln [the name of the project].
> The project, which would flood the wild Saint John River to generate electricity, is being touted as the answer to Maine and New England's long quest for a cheap and plentiful source of power.
> The truth is somewhat less dramatic. Dickey-Lincoln would produce useful volumes of power. But construction of the dams won't solve either the energy crisis in general or New England's need in particular.[15]

Cummings carefully examines reports by the Army Corps of Engineers on the project's potential and concludes that the project would "increase the electricity available to New England homes, businesses and industries by the grand total of seven-tenths of one percent." Against this gain, he weighs the loss of the river as a recreation area for canoeists and anglers and the loss of forest products. In an interview, Cummings describes his approach to environmental reporting. The "beat" typically takes him out of the office several days a week, and his major sources include local environmentalists and state agencies, such as the Natural Resources Council and the Land Use Regulation Commission. "I try to avoid the day-to-day coverage. A good, thorough story is worth more, and is more valuable to the reader than covering each development as it happens. The reader doesn't care week to week, so I try to do stories that tell where the overall issue is going."[16]

This same approach—looking for "where the overall issue is going"—was used by *Chronicle* reporter Perlman in his article on uses of power in California:

> Deep in the heart of the Pacific Gas and Electric Co.—hushed and tightly guarded—stand the airconditioned, pastel-tinted consoles of the giant system's Energy Control Center.
> Skilled men tend the center, but in the automated symbolism of the world's most energy-intensive society, the men seem little more than acolytes.
> They serve the machines, and to a degree control them; but the system itself holds the ultimate power, for upon it depend the economic life and social tranquility of nearly 9 million people in Northern California. . . .
> How much of all this energy is really needed? How much will be needed in the decades to come? How can what's needed be provided without ecological disruption? These questions are crucial to the public, to utilities companies, to government agencies and to politicians.[17]

Although a number of magazines and newspapers have examined the impact of the Alaska pipeline on the natural tundra environment, freelance writer Patricia Monaghan took a different approach in a three-part series in the *Saint Paul* (Minn.) *Pioneer Press*. She examined the effect of the pipeline on Alaskan cities and social structure:

> But if Anchorage residents seem preoccupied with the massive construction project begun this spring, it is with good reason: Their city is the destination of tens of thousands of work-seekers who swarmed north this past summer in pursuit of what one welfare administrator bitterly calls "gold in the streets." . . .
> The number of migrants alone would cause problems, even if all were healthy, employed and law-abiding. Statistics suggest that as many as one-fifth of Anchorage's residents are newcomers who arrived after congressional approval of the pipeline project in April. Housing is scarce, schools bulging, and inflation soaring. Social services are strained to the limit.[18]

Such articles begin to put environmental issues in perspective, by recognizing that "impact" is not limited in effects to natural environments. So, clearly, the reporter assigned to cover environmental issues must bring broad understanding to the job. Hendin writes,

> The environment is a unique subject. And the environmental reporter is a unique person. He isn't a layman and he isn't a scientist or environmentalist. He has to lie somewhere in between.
> The problem here is that even the so-called environmentalists don't exactly know what an environmentalist is. He must be part biologist, part chemist,

part architect, part physicist, part sociologist, part lawyer, part engineer, and more.

And the environmental writer must be all of those things, to a lesser extent, of course, and he must be able to write and be hardnosed too.[19]

SCIENCE AND MEDICAL REPORTING

Science and medical reporting in the American press has a long and colorful history, and along with business news, it is probably the most firmly established area of specialty reporting.

Early science reporting tended toward sensationalism, exaggeration, and even hoaxes. The *New York Sun* in an 1835 series, for example, perpetrated the "moon hoax," reporting that a leading scientist had sighted "batlike men four feet tall bearing copper-colored fur, with yellow faces."[20] But by 1870, Horace Greeley was writing a regular science column (on scientific agriculture) for the *New York Tribune*. Other landmarks in science reporting were the introduction of Einstein's theory of relativity to newspaper readers by Carr Van Anda of the *New York Times* in 1919, the appointment of David Dietz as the first newspaper science editor by the Scripps-Howard newspapers in 1921, and the first Pulitzer Prize to a science writer (Alva Johnson of the *New York Times*) in 1923 for reporting scientists' acceptance of Darwin's theory of evolution.

Carolyn D. Hay, in a 1970 master's thesis entitled, "A History of Science Writing in the United States," distinguishes three phases of such writing:

> The "gee whiz" phase, exemplifying an old "yellow journalism" dictum that a good story should make the reader say "Gee Whiz."
> The present era of increasingly professional analytic reporting of science, which has been a full-time journalistic occupation since the 1920s.
> A new phase in which science writers study the possible effects on society of science and technology.[21]

Science writing's place in American journalism has been solidified by university training programs in science reporting; the acceptance of trained science writers by the media; an active professional organization (National Association of Science Writers); and a continuing body of research about science reporting, readership, and the diffusion of scientific ideas.

As Hay suggests, science and medical writers have gone through different stages of development. As the space program evolved in the 1950s and 1960s, and as government began to play an increasingly important role in all phases of science, science writers often acted as mere translators for science and technology. With the ecology movement and similar social movements in the late 1960s, however, science writers became more critical. Jeff Carruthers, a science writer for Canada's Free Press newspapers, says the result was conflict between an old school of science reporting that relied almost exclusively on scientists as sources of news and a new school that went to other sources, which were occasionally embarrassing to the scientist.

Although science and medical reporting (medical is often, though not always, subsumed under science) seem light years ahead of other specialties that are just getting started, they may not indeed be far ahead at all. Perlman, for one, says science "is not covered properly. The writing is subject to whims, fashions, and fads in the scientific field."[22] In 1971 when Perlman was president of the National Association of Science Writers, a survey conducted by that organization showed that "far fewer than 100 dailies have fulltime science writers. Most papers are just faking it."[23] To Boyce Rensberger, a television writer formerly with the *New York Times*, a major problem with science writing is that some "science writers are trying to write about things they don't understand. When you think about it, it's ludicrous. I have seen science writers struggling to write something they don't understand themselves even asking the source to read it to make sure they understood it and wrote it properly. They are assuming that if the source okays it, it is ready for the paper."[24]

In spite of its problems, science writing is an active and diverse field. And most writers migrate toward those subjects that especially interest them. Because science, technology, and other subjects the science reporter covers are so vast, there is considerable latitude in selection of topics. Writers like Mildred Spencer of the *Buffalo Evening News* like to cover biological science, medicine, and health, whereas Edward Edelson of the *New York Daily News* is more of a generalist who tries to cover all areas of science. Daniel Greenberg, formerly of *Science* magazine and now the director of his own science news service, specialized in the "politics of science."[25] Most science writers would agree that their assignments allow for considerable personal freedom as they advise the city desk about the science stories most appropriate for the day's coverage. Sometimes, of course, circumstances and events guide the science writer in selecting a story. But, in the main, the writers might cover the physical and biological sciences, space exploration, medicine and public health, environmental sciences, social and behavioral sciences, and technology.

The public needs rapidly transmitted, accurate information about science and technology for several reasons. It is up to the science writer, therefore, to provide

> Pragmatic advice about everyday life. Everything from weather information to items about personal health.
>
> Guidance on public issues. Before the critical, evaluative process ever begins, the knowledgeable citizen needs to know and understand a wide range of

subjects from nuclear power plants to the funding of the National Science Foundation.

Help in evaluating the relationship between science, technology, and society. When do advances in one area hamper developments in another? What is the nature of progress?

Similarly, in the subfields that make up science there are different categories of news. For example, medical news stories are usually of three kinds: (1) the condition of specific patients, (2) advancements in medicine and science, and (3) activities of hospitals and medically related organizations."[26] Because most scientific activity is in the public sector (even many private institutions rely on federal grants and contracts), it requires public understanding, and only through effective science writing can this occur. Here are three leads that demonstrate the functions just mentioned:

Pragmatic advice about everyday life.   Lou Joseph asked, "Is a thumb for sucking?" in an article in *Today's Health:*

> The parents of Linus probably aren't worried about his thumb sucking. At his age, it's cute. And Linus will never grow up.
> But as a real thumb-sucking child grows older, his parents begin to nibble on pencils and gnaw their fingernails when he doesn't quit.
> This vexing habit—thumb sucking, that is—not only worries parents but also generates considerable discussion and sometimes outright controversy among child health experts.[27]

Guidance on public issues.   In a story telling the public that knowledge about air pollution and its effects was insufficient to justify pollution scares, David Spurgeon of the *Toronto Globe and Mail* began with one scientist's view:

> Dr. H. N. MacFarland of York University gets annoyed whenever he hears some prophet of doom predict that air pollution will kill us all in 20 years.
> An expert in inhalation toxicology, he says there simply is not enough known to make such statements. He even gets mildly irritated about the use of an air-pollution index, because he says there is no way of telling what the effects on health will be when the index is over a certain level: the basic scientific knowledge is just not available.[28]

Evaluating the relationship between science, technology, and society.   In a television news story, George Dusheck of KQED-TV, San Francisco, began as follows:

> The Atomic Industrial Forum wound up its annual meeting at the St. Francis Hotel here today with a long and occasionally sharp debate on what the Forum calls "The Nuclear Controversy."

In one sense, the nuclear controversy is simply whether the United States shall depend more and more heavily on nuclear plants to supply its growing need for electrical power.

But in another sense, the nuclear controversy is about whether very large social decisions shall be made on technical or upon political grounds.[29]

The science writers' task is formidable. They must understand the scientific method and the particular nuances of scientists and their language. Often these demands mean dealing with mathematics and statistics, translating jargon, and coping with complex content. Similarly, sources for science news are quite varied, ranging from laboratories, scientific installations, and research institutions to journals and government reports. Scientific and professional meetings and conventions, such as the annual meetings of the American Association for the Advancement of Science, are also important sources of information. Not to be overlooked are personal interviews with local authorities on scientific subjects, whether or not they are scientists. As in other specialty reporting, science journalists must avoid simplistic translation and find varied bases for evaluation of the material they gather. Although science writers are moving closer to the methods of investigative reporting, they must take special care to avoid moral judgments and to evaluate scientific issues on a scientific basis.

Seasoned by coverage of demonstrations at scientific meetings, especially in the late 1960s and early 1970s, science reporters are moving toward a new style of tough-minded reporting. As John Lear of the *Saturday Review* has written, "If technology is to be brought under control, science reporters must move beyond mere description to evaluation that raises the hard questions."[30]

Although there has been increased investigative reporting in science journalism, it is still a modest part of science writers' output. Instead, there has been more emphasis on service journalism—stories that have a direct impact on the reader's needs or personal interests. As educator Warren Burkett has written, "Times change and research fancies change. In an uncertain age, it may be time editors and readers had help in living with uncertainty. Such advice may help relieve some of those itchy feelings that accompany many of the 'service' stories demanded by the newest new journalism."[31] Burkett is talking about stories like those on the pros and cons of vasectomies or how to cope with a nuclear accident.

COVERING MENTAL HEALTH AND SOCIAL WELFARE

Like the reporting of science and medicine, press coverage of mental health and social welfare has a colorful history. But unlike them, it has not been a highly successful field for specialty reporting. Only a few such reporters are working for newspapers and broadcast stations, though hundreds are writing for specialized publications. In spite of a long history of press involvement with mental health and social welfare issues, editors have shown some reluctance to invest their personnel resources in this type of coverage.

Yet the problems and issues of mental and social health have provided the press with considerable newsworthy material for many years. It may not have been the first time such a ploy was used, but Nellie Bly's "stunt" of the 1880s in which she feigned insanity in order to gain admission to a New York City asylum led to a classic exposé. Exposés of conditions in mental health and social welfare institutions became standard fare for the press. They were usually highly sensational, with little sensitivity for the people involved, and sought scapegoats for the conditions they disclosed. This situation began to change in the years after World War II. As Arthur J. Snider, distinguished science and medical reporter, suggests,

> Beginning in about 1945, there emerged a new type of story—an "exposé" with a constructive twist. Reporters entered mental hospitals and conducted investigations with the collaboration of superintendents and psychiatrists who were concerned over the lack of public interest in mental hospitals and the inability to obtain necessary funds from government agencies for operation, for rebuilding facilities that had deteriorated during the depression and for hiring staff. Today, most stories about state institutions are of this constructive type—calling attention to evils for the purpose of remedial action.[32]

In recent years the definition of mental health and social welfare has expanded greatly to encompass what are often referred to as "human services." In part this expansion is a consequence of the shift from isolated country asylums, homes for the elderly and juveniles, to community-based services. Furthermore, the term *mental health* has come to embrace, among other social maladjustments, alcoholism, drug abuse, and the problems of aging, adolescence, and minorities.

Coverage of mental health has often been rife with conflict between reporters and mental health professionals. As Paul I. Kliger, a Chicago community organizer, put it,

> The basic problem is communication. We have the uninformed journalist who knows nothing about mental health and the uninformed mental health professional who knows nothing about the media. The journalist comes to the mental health center looking for a good story. He brings with him all the usual popular beliefs and prejudices. He may come looking for an exposé or a more positive story to tell the public how well a center is doing.[33]

As early as 1956, the American Psychiatric Association, expressing concern over the lack of cooperation between mental health workers and the media, convened a conference to discuss mutual problems. Both sides agreed that it was in the public interest to cover mental health, and they attempted to work out an effective means of doing so. They agreed, as the conference report indicated, that "in supplying information and in presenting it to the public, members of both professions should avoid exaggeration, distortion, and sensationalism; seek to remove the stigmatization associated with mental illness; and bear in mind that some information about mental illness arouses anxiety."[34]

Snider lists three barriers that confront the writer trying to cover the mental health field: difficulty in conceptualizing the content of psychiatry, difficulty in communicating the language of psychiatry, and the negative attitude of psychiatrists toward the press. Although Snider concentrates on only *one* of the several professions (such as psychologists, social workers, and rehabilitation counselors) dealing with mental health and social welfare, his critique could apply to all.

Such organizations as the National Association for Mental Health, a citizens group; the American Psychological Association, a professional group; and the National Institute of Mental Health, a government agency, have expressed the view that adequate coverage of mental health—and the human condition—is crucial if the press is to tell the "people story" in human terms.

Mental health journalists face not only the barriers listed by Snider but also considerable confusion because of the many schools of thought and interpretations in this field. Often news sources will disagree about issues and it is necessary for the journalist to put these conflicts in context, indicating where they fit into the body of opinion about mental health. This confusion can be particularly disturbing in criminal trials where issues of tests for insanity are discussed. Witness, for example, the psychiatric testimony in the celebrated Jean Harris trial in 1981.

Functions for Mental Health and Social Welfare Reporters

Because these fields embrace both publicly and privately supported institutions, services, and programs, the reporter has an especially difficult task in helping the public to understand the nature, purpose, and availability of particular services. He or she must put the service into clear view in the news story, indicating how it is funded and to whom it is responsible. Functions for the mental health-social welfare reporter include the following:

Helping the public know and understand human services and how they can be utilized.

Examining the performance of officials who are responsible for those services through stories that monitor conditions, philosophies, and approaches.

Utilizing the content of the mental health field to cover larger social problems.

The first two functions are self-explanatory; the third may not be. Those who work in the mental health and social welfare field are specialists who possess considerable knowledge about the human condition. They ought to be used by the reporter as sources of news in stories about housing, urban crowding, abortion, and other significant social issues. A psychiatrist, sociologist, or other professional concerned with human problems, for example, may be a good source on certain types of crimes, for example, shoplifting.

Frank Angelo, a *Detroit Free Press* editor and former president of Sigma Delta Chi, has said that "the 'people story,' who they are and how they live, is the most important story of the decade—this one or any other." The reporter concerned with mental health issues can do much to capture the essence of this story. For example, this story from the now defunct *National Observer* demonstrates the kind of vital human information that can be delivered to the public:

> The door to a rickety, condemned shanty creaks open, exposing the distrusting gaze of an obese, 48-year-old Negro woman. Resigned to the regular intrusion of do-gooders, she admits the latest man-and-woman team with a shrug. An unconventional family waits inside: the woman's 72-year old, blind husband; her two illegitimate daughters, one 35 and pregnant and the other 12; and the pregnant daughter's three children. Leaking pipework has forced all seven of them into three murky rooms. The children run naked through the living room, where the stench from human excrement lying about is gagging. Cockroaches frolic openly.
>
> The woman interloper is a social worker, accustomed to such surroundings. But her partner, a psychiatrist, is radically far afield from the comfort of a tasteful office and cozy clientele. He is Dr. Fernando de Elejalde, director of an east Topeka community project, designed, as never before, to bring the services of a psychiatrist to the masses.[35]

Although many mental health and social welfare services are covered in the context of government agencies (see Chapter 8), reporters delving into this subject must make an effort to educate themselves about the nature of the field: the government organizations responsible for services, the professional groups who carry it out, and the citizen groups that monitor it and lobby for it. Further, there is a considerable body of knowledge in each of the fields concerned with human problems. Public information offices at the various professional organizations, such as the American Psychiatric Association, American Psychological Association, and National Association of Social Workers, publish glossaries, journals, and other helpful information. Similarly, important scholarly and professional publications and national meetings and conventions can serve as important sources.

Mental health and social welfare is a specialty that requires considerable knowledge on the part of the reporter. Unfortunately, there are few mental health and social welfare beats, and thus serious reporters must learn about this subject on their own so that they can apply the knowledge to general assignment work or a specialty like science writing or urban affairs.

CONCLUSION

The various kinds of science-related journalism discussed here have several similarities. All are concerned with systematic knowledge; all are concerned with the simplest possible explanation of complex facts; all require interpretation and analysis as well as straight reporting. Science journalism is a venerable and lively field that requires much from its practitioners. They must lead a spirited life of the mind, constantly probing not just for new information but also for new ways of thinking. And they must communicate this life effectively for their readers. For their trouble, though, science journalists are well recompensed: Although their work is regarded as highly specialized by some observers, it is really quite broad-based, allowing considerable creativity and freedom in deciding what to cover and how to cover it.

NOTES

[1] Phillip J. Tichenor, "Teaching and the Journalism of Uncertainty," *The Journal of Environmental Education*, Spring 1979, p. 5.

[2] Ibid., p. 7.

[3] Ibid., p. 5.

[4] Everette E. Dennis and James McCartney, "Science Journalists on Metropolitan Dailies, Methods, Values and Perceptions of their Work," *The Journal of Environmental Education*, Spring 1979, pp. 9–15.

[5] Newspaper Advertising Bureau, Inc., "Readership and Coverage of Science and Technology in Newspapers," (Reston, Va., 1978). Also see, William Bennett, "Science Hits the Newsstand," *Columbia Journalism Review*, January/February 1981, p. 53.; and Edwin Diamond, "Take a Great Editor, Add Great Writers, Throw Caution to the Wind," *Next*, February 1981, p. 57.

[6] Dennis and McCartney, "Science Journalists," p. 11.

[7] Phillip J. Tichenor, "Teaching and the Journalism of Uncertainty," pp. 5–8.

[8] See Dr. Arnold S. Relman, "Medical Meetings Should Be Backgrounders, Not News" and "Relman Stands Alone at Meeting With Reporters," in *National Association of Science Writers Newsletter*, November 1979, pp. 9–11. Also see Edward Edelson, "The Back of the Book," *NASW Newsletter*, December 1980, pp. 8–9.

[9] See *NASW Newsletter*, September 1978, pp. 7–9.

[10] H. Peter Metzger, "Wanted: Rocky Mountain Post," *The Unsatisfied Man: A Review of Colorado Journalism* 1 (November 1970), 3–4.

[11] Larry Pryor, "The Ecology Thicket," in ed. Clay Schoenfeld, *Interpreting Environmental Issues* (Madison, Wis.: Dembar Educational Research Services, 1972), p. 35.

[12]Leonard Sellers and David W. Jones, Jr., "Environment and the Mass Media," *Journal of Environmental Education* 5 (Fall 1973), 52.

[13]Dennis J. Chase, "Eco-journalism and the Failure of Crisis Reporting," *Quill* 60 (October 1972), 20–21.

[14]David Hendin, "Environmental Reporting," *Quill* 58 (August 1970), 16.

[15]Bob Cummings, "Dickey: Boon or Boondoggle?" *Maine Sunday Telegram,* April 7, 1974, p. 1.

[16]Interview by coauthor Stephen Hartgen with Cummings, June 27, 1974.

[17]David Perlman, "Electric Power Dilemma," *San Francisco Chronicle*, April 10, 1972, p. 1.

[18]Patricia Monaghan, "Boom Brings Social Problems to Anchorage," *St. Paul Pioneer Press,* December 3, 1974, p. 1.

[19]Hendin, "Environmental Reporting," 16.

[20]"Science Reporting Has Grown Out of Its 'Gee Whiz' Phase," *Editor & Publisher* 103 (September 12, 1970), p. 20. Also see Carolyn D. Hay, "A History of Science Writing in the United States," M.A. thesis, Northwestern University, 1970; and Hillier Krieghbaum, "Perspectives on Science Writing," *The Journal of Environmental Education,* Spring 1979, pp. 16–20.

[21]Hay, "History of Science Writing," *Editor & Publisher* 103 (September 12, 1970), 20.

[22]Everette E. Dennis, "A Report on the Science Writing Seminar," mimeographed (Eugene: University of Oregon, 1971), p. 3.

[23]Ibid.

[24]Ibid.

[25]See Daniel S. Greenberg, "The Politics of Science," *Bulletin of the American Society of Newspaper Editors,* December 1967, pp. 1–4.

[26]Howard Emerson, "Access to Medical News," *Freedom of Information Center Publication No. 163,* June 1966, p. 1.

[27]Lou Joseph, "Is a Thumb for Sucking," *Today's Health* 47 (December 1969), 32.

[28]David Spurgeon, "Knowledge Lacking for Pollution Scare, York Expert Insists," *Toronto Globe and Mail,* May 14, 1970, p. 1.

[29]George Dusheck, "TV Script—KQED-TV—San Francisco," reprinted in *National Association of Science Writers Clipsheet* 10 (April 1970).

[30]John Lear, "The Trouble with Science Writing," *Columbia Journalism Review* 9 (Summer 1970), 30–34.

[31]Warren Burkett, "Some Reflections on the Current Status of Science Writing," *NASW Newsletter,* September 1978, pp. 9–11.

[32]Arthur J. Snider, "Interpreting Mental Health: Concerns of the Science Writer," paper presented at Mental Health-Mass Media Conference, Kansas State University, Manhattan, Kansas, May 15, 1969, p. 1.

[33]Paul I. Kliger, "Understanding the Human Condition: Mental Health and the Mass Media," paper presented at the annual meeting of the American Orthopsychiatric Association, San Francisco, March 26, 1970, p. 3. See also Everette E. Dennis, "Improving Relations between Mental Health and the Mass Media," *Hospital & Community Psychiatry* 22 (June 1970), 39–41.

[34]American Psychiatric Association, *Psychiatry, the Press and the Public: Problems in Communication* (Washington, D.C.: American Psychiatric Association, 1956), pp. 47–48.

[35]Theodore W. Landphair, "Psychiatry Gets into the 'Action,'" *National Observer,* April 7, 1969, p. 20.

SUGGESTED READINGS

BURKETT, WARREN. *Writing Science News for the Mass Media,* 2d ed. Houston: Gulf Publishing Co., 1973. An excellent, though now somewhat dated, text on science writing.

KRIEGHBAUM, HILLIER. *Science and the Mass Media.* New York: New York University Press, 1967. A classic on the subject, which is also dated but still useful.

PERLMAN, DAVID. "Science and the Mass Media." *Daedulus,* Summer 1974, pp. 207–24. A thoughtful article by one of America's best-known science writers, who later became a city editor.

The best examples of science and environmental writing are found in works by such commentators as Jacob Bronoski, Loren Eisley, Rae Goodell, John McPhee, Marilyn Ferguson, and others.

A special edition of *The Journal of Environmental Education,* Spring 1979, was devoted to "Teaching Science and Environmental Writing" and contains articles sketching out problems in science journalism and science writing's history and current status. Useful for students as well as educators.

14

Strategies for Tomorrow

Technology, while adding daily to our physical ease, throws daily another loop of fine wire around our souls.

Adlai Stevenson

Nothing is more hazardous than prediction. Author Peter Drucker once warned, "the unsuspected and apparently insignificant [will] derail the massive and seemingly invincible trends of today."[1] The seemingly invincible trends in public affairs reporting today are the building blocks of this book. A focus on the audience's needs, interpretation of complex subjects, and the adoption of powerful new research methods were suggested as the guiding principles of contemporary reporting. The expectation, of course, is that they will also serve well in the future. But that is a matter for prediction, based on today's interpretations of yesterday's experiences and the one great unknown: tomorrow's changes.

The principal agents of change in journalism appear to be economics, the audience's desires, and technology. We already know a good deal about all three.

Rising production costs, intractable distribution problems, and increasing competition for advertising dollars will force profound changes on the daily newspaper industry in the closing years of the twentieth century. By the early 1970s, some editors were already predicting an accelerated rate of failures; a narrowing of news content to fit a smaller, more sophisticated audience; voluntary cutbacks in circulation to reduce costs;

and smaller page sizes (no larger than a paper towel, according to one prediction).[2] Some of the forecasts were realities before the end of the decade.

Audiences have already given a message to the newspaper industry: The average time spent with a daily newspaper is down to about fifteen minutes, according to some surveys. Newspaper sales have dropped from 1.3 per household in 1930 to .8 in 1979. Television is the preferred news medium for a majority of adults. In an age of communication overload, it isn't surprising that many people are no longer wedded to the word jam of newspapers. The printed word, however, hasn't been abandoned by the public. There is greater demand than ever before for specialized information, and readers are turning to magazines and newsletters that provide material of direct interest.

Technology has already planted the seeds of another communication revolution, hard on the heels of the broadcast revolution. Equipment to deliver news into the home electronically is tested and available. The "wired city," a visionary dream in the 1950s, is likely to become a reality in the 1990s. Industry sources expect more than 50 percent of the nation's homes to be connected to interactive cable systems by the end of this decade. Interactive cable permits home users to "talk back" to a computer, ordering information and services individualized to their needs.

The 1980s will be a transition period in this shift to computerized delivery of news, information, sales, and services. We appear to be on the threshold of the age of the electronic newspaper. Already, computerized information banks connected to remote terminals are being operated by industry and libraries. Computerized home-information systems—Ceefax, Telidon, Didon, Viewtron, Bildschirmtext, and others—have been tested in Europe, Canada, Japan, and the United States. Many have two-way communication capacity. Knight-Ridder, Dow-Jones, and other U.S. media giants are deeply involved in the new technology. Even small news organizations are buying into cable systems or leasing channel capacity. The question is not whether the electronic revolution will affect newspapers, but how and when.

Given these observations about the cutting points in mass communication today, where does that leave public affairs reporters? Will their methods of operation be changed substantially by economics, audience, and technology? Will there be more of them or less of them in the future? There is a truism in the trade that machines may replace printers, publishers, and editors, but there will always be a need for the live reporter. But truisms, as the Wright brothers proved, have a way of changing with conditions. The future role and scope of public affairs reporting must remain speculative. Consider, for example, this scenario:

The year is 1990, and a team of three reporters has just returned from covering a conference on prison reform. They confer for a few moments with an editor and then sit down at electronic keyboards. One writes a general story about the conference and its results, running 1,200 words, and follows this with a much briefer story, of 200 words, on the same material. The second reporter produces a lengthy story on the technical aspects of prison reform, geared to the information needs of penologists, lawyers, and other specialists. The third reporter pecks out an interpretive piece on the economic implications of the conference proposals for local, state, and federal treasuries. All their words, as their fingers touch the keys, are transmitted almost instantly to a computer that corrects for spelling, style, and certain factual errors. Computer A then passes the stories along to computer B, the central storage point for national news stories. Computer B makes an index summary of the stories available to regional news computer facilities around the nation. Within a matter of minutes after the stories are written, they are available to home users. All that is required is a glance at the "menu" of available stories listed on the home screen, punching out a series of digits on a telephone-like keyboard, and the story selected appears on the screen. If the news consumers want to retain the story for future reference, they can store it in their own minicomputer for later reference or have it produced on an inexpensive home printer wired to the television set.

Speculative? Yes, but it fits a vision that many managers and researchers share. The most popular guessing game in media circles at the dawn of the 1980s was whether the new electronic information delivery systems will eventually replace newspapers as we know them. Benjamin Bradlee, executive editor of the *Washington Post,* answered the question with finality in 1981: "No, television terminals won't replace newspapers."[3] His conviction is echoed by other editors from coast to coast. ("After all, you can't carry a terminal into the bathroom or onto a bus, can you?") But at the same time that editors are predicting survival of the traditional newspaper into the indefinite future, newspaper owners are investing heavily in electronic delivery systems. *Los Angeles Times* executive Angelo Musante, with as much conviction as Bradlee, told an industry conference in 1979, "Technology will change our audience, our product, and our organizations, whether we like it or not."[4]

Many industry observers are cautious in their predictions. Both Stanford University's James Rosse, a newspaper economist, and John Morton, a securities analyst who specializes in news media, expect little impact on newspaper circulation by interactive cable during the 1980s.[5] But after that? Neither would say.

Home terminals are no longer toys for a handful of computer buffs. A new generation of Americans is coming out of school as familiar with video terminals as previous generations were with blackboards. They should be receptive to home computers for news, advertising, sales, and other information—if it can be delivered conveniently and economically. The principal uncertainty revolves around the types of information the market will accept or demand. Some sources anticipate continued demand for the traditional newspaper because of its convenience and low cost. Others argue that interactive systems will erode enough of the newspaper's advertising base and news market to force major changes in newspaper format, size, content, and audiences. Whatever happens with delivery systems, though, it is likely that the public's appetite for information, including news, will not diminish. Existing news organizations, with their experience and personnel in place, are the most probable managers of the data bases in a digitalized tomorrow.

Perhaps no one knows what portent technology holds for public affairs reporting for the long-term future. Unless we become a nation of pacified robots like the characters in Ray Bradbury's ominous science fiction portrait *Fahrenheit* 451, however, the need for competent, professional reporting is likely to remain high. In these pages, a rationale and a set of unifying principles for the fruitful pursuit of public affairs reporting have been offered. Implicit in this presentation has been the belief that job skills alone are not enough for today's reporters. They must also thoroughly understand their readers and viewers and direct news efforts to serving their needs. Reporters must also have a thorough grasp of the workings of the society in which they live and a deep knowledge of the fields in which they write. Accomplished reporters must also learn to use nontraditional tools, such as social science research methods, both for gathering information and for evaluating that provided by others. And finally, reporters must develop professional standards (if not status) in order to function on a high ethical level. They must be able to resist the blandishments of the news source seeking special favor and of the publisher attempting to protect an advertiser.

This book is a beginning, not an end. It suggests strategies and approaches for the public affairs reporter. If adapted to the individual reporter's style and personality, they can help him or her attain the goals for effective coverage suggested in the foregoing paragraphs. But, of course, this is not enough. No book, no course of instruction can adequately prepare the public affairs reporter for the future. What individuals need to do is develop their own strategy, their own methods and procedures for keeping pace with the future. These are noble words transmitting noble ideas, but too often they ring hollow. Their emptiness stems from the fact that exhortation does not always lead to action. Well-trained journalists leave universities each year with ideals and good intentions, part of which tells them that they must stay current and at times leap ahead to be fully effective as public affairs reporters. But only a few succeed.

One of the greatest dangers is a primitive know-nothingism that pervades some newsrooms. This is an attitude that categorically and all too cheerfully rejects the work of communications researchers who are doing much to advance the art of human communication. (Admittedly, part of the problem can be traced to the researchers themselves, who often do a poor job of disseminating their findings where they can be used.) Similarly, the lessons of communication history are quickly forgotten. In this atmosphere, many reporters are not performing much differently than reporters did in 1920.

At the same time, there are thoughtful, attentive reporters who are doing much to advance the state of the art. Philip Meyer, whom we have mentioned repeatedly in this book, is one. He has become a middleman, translating the methods of research into language that makes sense to the practicing journalist. Other reporters such as Edwin Newman of NBC News have become knowledgeable students of the American language. Still others become skillful commentator-scholars, both within and outside their news organizations, such as Anthony Lewis of the *New York Times* or Fred Graham of CBS News. Reporters like these contribute to the intellectual life of the nation and to public understanding of the society and its problems.

Thus, there are good and bad examples. Reporters can avoid the know-nothing trap by developing an information retrieval system that keeps them in touch with current developments in journalism and mass communication as well as in selected subject areas they are covering. This is accomplished by systematic reading, by visits to libraries and universities. Some do it by offering to teach an occasional course at a nearby college or school. For every reporter a different style, geared to his or her own personality, is probably most appropriate. Such a strategy should include not only reading and synthesizing what is being written but also making active suggestions about what ought to be done. If, for example, communication research is to be truly relevant to the practitioner, the practitioner must have an input, must make suggestions about his or her own needs.

Earlier in this book we suggested that modern public affairs reporters need to acquire skills in writing and reporting as well as sustained substantive understanding of the things they will be covering. Writing skill should not imply a static formula that once acquired is never lost. The art of writing changes frequently. The journalistic form is changing and, with it, so are definitions of news. Similarly, skills for reporters, whether those from the social sciences or methods of interviewing, are also advancing. In the area of substantive knowledge, the information-retrieval methods mentioned earlier should address this problem.

The world of public affairs reporting is exciting and vital both to its practitioners and to the people who consume their work in newspapers and in newscasts. It has been our goal in this book to reflect on this vibrant field and to suggest ways for its improvement. The public affairs reporter is on the firing line, making sense out of society and translating this message back to citizens who can and must use it. In realizing this great purpose, the public affairs reporter helps to advance the social order.

NOTES

[1]Peter F. Drucker, *The Age of Discontinuity* (New York: Harper & Row, 1969), p. ix.

[2]See "Rising Newspaper Costs Reshaping Newspapers," *New York Times,* November 21, 1974, p. 79.

[3]Quoted in "The Media Decade," *Next,* January–February 1981, p. 40.

[4]Address before the winter meeting of the International Newspaper Advertising Executives Association, January 29, 1979.

[5]The assessments were made in lectures at the University of Minnesota, by Rosse on October 14, 1980, and by Morton on November 3, 1980.

SUGGESTED READINGS

SMITH, ANTHONY.   *Goodbye Gutenberg: The Newspaper Revolution of the 1980s.* New York: Oxford, 1980. Readable, nontechnical description of the dawn of the electronic information age.

GERBNER, GEORGE, LARRY P. GROSS, AND WILLIAM H. MELODY, EDS.   *Communication Technology and Social Policy.* New York: Wiley, 1973. Parts 2 and 4 offer still relevant examinations of policy questions posed by technology developments.

"The Media Decade." *Next,* January–February 1981, pp. 27–62. Popularized treatments of technological advances and their implications for newspapers, radio, television, magazines, and book publishing.

appendix a
The Guide to Legalese*

abstract of record: A complete history in short, abbreviated form of the case as found in the record.

abstract of title: A chronological history, in abbreviated form, of the ownership of a parcel of land.

accumulative sentence: A sentence, additional to others, imposed at the same time for several distinct offenses; one sentence to begin at the expiration of another.

action in personam (in per-sō-nam):   An action against the person, founded on a personal liability.

action in rem (in rem):   An action for the recovery of a specific object, usually an item of personal property such as an automobile.

adjudication: Giving or pronouncing a judgment or decree; also the judgment given.

adversary system: The system of trial practice in the United States and some other countries in which each of the opposing, or adversary, parties has full opportunity to present and establish opposing contentions before the court.

allegation: The assertion, declaration, or statement of a party to an action, made in a pleading, setting out what he expects to prove.

*Published by permission of the Pennsylvania Bar Association, 401 North Front Street, Harrisburg, Pennsylvania.

amicus curiae (a-mī'kus kū'ri-ē):   A friend of the court; one who interposes, with the permission of the court, and volunteers information upon some matter of law.

ancillary bill or suit: One growing out of and auxiliary to another action or suit, such as a proceeding for the enforcement of a judgment, or to set aside fraudulent transfers of property.

answer: A pleading by which defendant endeavors to resist the plaintiff's allegation of facts.

appearance: The formal proceeding by which defendant submits himself to the jurisdiction of the court.

appellant: The party appealing a decision or judgment—which he considers unfavorable—to a higher court.

appellate court: A court having jurisdiction of appeal and review; not a "trial court."

appellee: The party against whom an appeal is taken.

arraignment: In criminal practice, to bring a prisoner to the bar of the court to answer to a criminal charge.

arrest of judgment: The act of postponing the effect of a judgment already entered.

at issue: Whenever the parties to a suit come to a point in the pleadings which is affirmed on one side and denied on the other, they are said to be "at issue" and ready for trial.

attachment: A remedy by which plaintiff is enabled to acquire a lien upon property or effects of defendant for satisfaction of judgment which plaintiff may obtain in the future.

attorney of record: Attorney whose name appears in the permanent records or files of a case.

b

bail: To set at liberty a person arrested or imprisoned, on security being taken, for his appearance on a specified day and place.

bail bond: An obligation signed by the accused, with sureties, to secure his presence in court.

bailiff: A court attendant whose duties are to keep order in the courtroom and to have custody of the jury.

banc (bangk):   Bench; the place where a court permanently or regularly sits. A "sitting in banc" is a meeting of all of the judges of a court, as distinguished from the sitting of a single judge.

bench warrant: Process issued by the court itself, or "from the bench," for the attachment or arrest of a person.

best evidence: Primary evidence, as distinguished from secondary; the best and highest evidence of which the nature of the case is susceptible.

binding instruction: One in which the jury is told that if it finds certain conditions to be true it must find for plaintiff, or defendant, as the case might be.

bind over: To hold on bail for trial.

brief: A written or printed document prepared by counsel to file in court, usually setting forth both facts and law in support of his case.

burden of proof: In the law of evidence, the necessity or duty of affirmatively proving a fact or facts in dispute.

burglary: The breaking into and entering of a building with an intent to commit a serious crime.

c

calling the docket: The public calling of the docket or list of causes at commence-ment of term of court, for setting a time for trial or entering orders.

caption: The caption of a pleading, or other papers connected with a case in court, is the heading or introductory clause which shows the names of the parties, name of the court, number of the case, etc.

cause: A suit, litigation, or action, civil or criminal.

certiorari (s'er'shi-ō-rā'ri):   An original writ commanding judges or officers of inferior courts to certify or to return records of proceedings in a cause for judicial review.

challenge to the array: Questioning the qualifications of an entire jury panel, usually on the grounds of partiality or some fault in the process of summon-ing the panel.

chambers: Private office or room of a judge.

change of venue: The removal of a suit begun in one county or district to another, for trial, or from one court to another in the same county or district.

circumstantial evidence: All evidence of an indirect nature; the process of deci-sion by which court or jury may reason from circumstances known or proved to establish by inference the principal fact.

code: A collection, compendium, or revision of laws systematically arranged into chapters, table of contents, and index and promulgated by legislative authority.

codicil (kod'i-sil):   A supplement or an addition to a will.

commit: To send a person to prison, to an asylum, workhouse, or reformatory by lawful authority.

common law: Law which derives its authority solely from usages and customs of immemorial antiquity, or from the judgments and decrees of courts. Also called "case law."

commutation: The change of a punishment from a greater degree to a lesser degree, as from death to life imprisonment.

comparative negligence: The doctrine by which acts of opposing parties are com-pared in the degrees of "slight," "ordinary" and "gross" negligence, fre-quently on a percentage basis.

competency: In the law of evidence, the presence of those characteristics which render a witness legally fit and qualified to give testimony.

complainant: Synonymous with "plaintiff."

complaint: The first or initiatory pleading on the part of the complainant, or plaintiff, in a civil action.

concurrent sentence: Sentences for more than one crime in which the time of each is to be served concurrently, rather than successively.

condemnation: The legal process by which real estate of a private owner is taken for public use without his consent, but upon the award and payment of just compensation.

contempt of court: Any act calculated to embarrass, hinder, or obstruct a court in the administration of justice, or calculated to lessen its authority or dignity. Contempts are of two kinds: direct and indirect. Direct contempts are those committed in the immediate presence of the court; indirect is the term chiefly used with reference to the failure or refusal to obey a lawful order.

contract: An oral or written agreement between two or more parties which is enforceable by law.

corpus delicti: (kor'pus dē-lik'tī):   The body (material substance) upon which a crime has been committed, e.g., the corpse of a murdered man, the charred remains of a burned house.

corroborating evidence: Evidence supplementary to that already given and tending to strengthen or confirm it.

costs: An allowance for expenses in prosecuting or defending a suit. Ordinarily this does not include attorney's fees.

counterclaim: A claim presented by a defendant in opposition to the claim of a plaintiff.

court reporter: A person who transcribes by shorthand or stenographically takes down testimony during court proceedings.

courts of record: Those whose proceedings are permanently recorded, and which have the power to fine or imprison for contempt. Courts not of record are those of lesser authority whose proceedings are not permanently recorded.

criminal insanity: Lack of mental capacity to do or abstain from doing a particular act; inability to distinguish right from wrong.

cross-examination: The questioning of a witness in a trial, or in the taking of a deposition, by the party opposed to the one who produced the witness.

cumulative sentence: Separate sentences (each additional to the others) imposed against a person convicted upon an indictment containing several counts, each charging a different offense. (Same as accumulative sentence.)

d

damages: Pecuniary compensation which may be recovered in the courts by any person who has suffered loss, detriment, or injury to his person, property, or rights, through the unlawful act or negligence of another.

declaratory judgment: One which declares the rights of the parties or expresses the opinion of the court on a question of law, without ordering anything to be done.

decree: A decision or order of the court. A final decree is one which fully and finally disposes of the litigation; an interlocutory decree is a provisional or preliminary decree which is not final.

default: A "default" in an action at law occurs when a defendant omits to plead within the time allowed or fails to appear at the trial.

demur (dē-mer'):   To file a pleading (called "a demurrer"), admitting the truth of the facts in the complaint, or answer, but contending they are legally insufficient.

de novo (de nō'vō):   Anew, afresh. A "trial de novo" is the retrial of a case.

deposition: The testimony of a witness not taken in open court, but in pursuance of authority given by statute or rule of court to take testimony elsewhere.

directed verdict: An instruction by the judge to the jury to return a specific verdict.

direct evidence: Proof of facts by witnesses who saw acts done or heard words spoken as distinguished from circumstantial evidence, which is called indirect.

direct examination: The first interrogation of a witness by the party on whose behalf he is called.

discovery: A proceeding whereby one party to an action may be informed as to facts known by other parties or witnesses.

dismissal without prejudice: Permits the complainant to sue again on the same cause of action, while dismissal "with prejudice" bars the right to bring or maintain an action on the same claim or cause.

dissent: A term commonly used to denote the disagreement of one or more judges of a court with the decision of the majority.

domicile: That place where a person has his true and permanent home. A person may have several residences, but only one domicile.

double jeopardy: Common-law and constitutional prohibition against more than one prosecution for the same crime, transaction, or omission.

due process: Law in its regular course of administration through the courts of justice. The guarantee of due process requires that every man have the protection of a fair trial.

e

embezzlement: The fraudulent appropriation by a person to his own use or benefit of property or money entrusted to him by another.

eminent domain: The power to take private property for public use by condemnation.

enjoin: To require a person, by writ of injunction from a court of equity, to perform or to abstain or desist from some act.

entrapment: The act of officers or agents of a government in inducing a person to commit a crime not contemplated by him, for the purpose of instituting a criminal prosecution against him.

equitable action: An action which may be brought for the purpose of restraining the threatened infliction of wrongs or injuries, and the prevention of threatened illegal action. (Remedies not available at common law.)

equity, courts of: Courts which administer a legal remedy according to the system of equity, as distinguished from courts of common law.

escheat (es-chēt): In American law, the right of the state to an estate to which no one is able to make a valid claim.

escrow (es-krō): A writing, or deed, delivered by the grantor into the hands of a third person, to be held by the latter until the happening of a contingency or performance of a condition.

estoppel (es-top'el): A person's own act, or acceptance of facts, which preclude his later making claims to the contrary.

et al.: An abbreviation of et alii, meaning "and others."

et seq.: An abbreviation for et sequentes, or et sequentia, "and the following."

exception: A formal objection to an action of the court, during the trial of a cause, in refusing a request or overruling an objection; implying that the party excepting does not acquiesce in the decision of the court, but will seek to procure its reversal.

ex contractu (ex kon-trak'tu): In both civil and common law, rights and causes of action are divided into two classes: those arising ex contractu (from a contract) and ex delicto (from a wrong or tort).

ex delicto (ex de-lik'tō): Rights and causes of action arising from a wrong or "tort."

executor: A person named by the decedent in his will to carry out the provisions of that will.

exhibit: A paper, document, or other article produced and exhibited to a court during a trial or hearing.

ex parte (ex par'te): By or for one party; done for, in behalf of, or on the application of one party only.

expert evidence: Testimony given in relation to some scientific, technical, or professional matter by experts, i.e., persons qualified to speak authoritatively by reason of their special training, skill, or familiarity with the subject.

ex post facto (eks pōst fak'to):   After the fact; an act or fact occurring after some
  previous act or fact, and relating thereto.
extenuating circumstances: Circumstances which render a crime less aggravated,
  heinous, or reprehensible than it would otherwise be.
extradition: The surrender by one state to another of an individual accused or
  convicted of an offense outside its own territory, and within the territorial
  jurisdiction of the other.

f

fair comment: A term used in the law of libel, applying to statements made by a
  writer in an honest belief of their truth, relating to an official act, even though
  the statements are not true in fact.
fair preponderance: Evidence sufficient to create in the minds of the triers of fact
  the conviction that the party upon whom the burden is placed has established
  its case.
false arrest: Any unlawful physical restraint of another's liberty, whether in prison or elsewhere.
false pretenses: Designed misrepresentation of existing fact or condition whereby
  a person obtains another's money or goods.
felony: A crime of a graver nature than a misdemeanor. Generally, an offense
  punishable by death or imprisonment in a penitentiary.
fiduciary (fĭ-dū'shē-ā-rē):   A term derived from the Roman law, meaning a person
  holding the character of a trustee, in respect to the trust and confidence
  involved in it and the scrupulous good faith and candor which it requires.
forcible entry and detainer: [The taking of land and possessions and] summary
  proceeding for restoring possession of land to one who has been wrongfully
  deprived of possession.
forgery: The false making or material altering, with intent to defraud, of any
  writing which, if genuine, might be the foundation of a legal liability.
fraud: An intentional perversion of truth; deceitful practice or device resorted to
  with intent to deprive another of property or other right, or in some manner
  to do him injury.

g

garnishee (noun):   The person upon whom a garnishment is served; usually a
  debtor of the defendant in the action; (verb): to institute garnishment
  proceedings.
garnishment: A proceeding whereby property, money, or credits of a debtor in
  possession of another (the garnishee) are applied to the debts of the debtor.
general assignment: The voluntary transfer, by a debtor, of all his property to a
  trustee for the benefit of all of his creditors.
general demurrer: A demurrer which raises the question whether the pleading
  against which it is directed lacks the definite allegations essential to a cause of
  action or defense.
gratuitous guest: In automobile law, a person riding at the invitation of the owner
  of a vehicle, or his authorized agent, without payment of a consideration or a
  fare.
guardian ad litem (ad lī'tem):   A person appointed by a court to look after the
  interests of an infant whose property is involved in litigation.

h

habeas corpus (hā'be-as kor'pus):   "You have the body." The name given a variety of writs whose object is to bring a person before a court or judge. In most common usage, it is directed to the official or person detaining another, commanding him to produce the body of the prisoner or person detained so the court may determine if such person has been denied his liberty without due process of law.

harmless error: In appellate practice, an error committed by a lower court during a trial, but not prejudicial to the rights of the party and for which the court will not reverse the judgment.

hearsay: Evidence not proceeding from the personal knowledge of the witness.

holographic will: A testamentary instrument entirely written, dated, and signed by the testator in his own handwriting.

hostile witness: A witness who is subject to cross-examination by the party who called him to testify, because of his evident antagonism toward that party as exhibited in his direct examination.

hypothetical question: A combination of facts and circumstances, assumed or proved, stated in such a form as to constitute a coherent state of facts upon which the opinion of an expert can be asked by way of evidence in a trial.

i

impeachment of witness: An attack on the credibility of a witness by the testimony of other witnesses.

implied contract: A contract in which the promise made by the obligor is not expressed, but inferred by his conduct or implied in law.

imputed negligence: Negligence which is not directly attributable to the person himself, but which is the negligence of a person who is in privity with him, and with whose fault he is chargeable.

inadmissible: That which, under the established rules of evidence, cannot be admitted or received.

in banc: On the bench; all judges of the court sitting together to hear a cause.

in camera (in kam'e-ra):   In chambers; in private.

incompetent evidence: Evidence which is not admissible under the established rules of evidence.

indeterminate sentence: An indefinite sentence of "not less than" and "not more than" so many years, the exact term to be served being afterwards determined by parole authorities within the minimum and maximum limits set by the court or by statute.

indictment: An accusation in writing found and presented by a grand jury, charging that a person therein named has done some act, or been guilty of some omission, which, by law, is a crime.

inferior court: Any court subordinate to the chief appellate tribunal in a particular judicial system.

injunction: A mandatory or prohibitive writ issued by a court.

instruction: A direction given by the judge to the jury concerning the law of the case.

inter alia (in ter a'li-ä):   Among other things or matters.

inter alios (in'ter'a-li-ōs):   Among other persons, between others.

interlocutory: Provisional; temporary; not final. Refers to orders and decrees of a court.

interrogatories: Written questions propounded by one party and served on adversary, who must provide written answers thereto under oath.

intervention: A proceeding in a suit or action by which a third person is permitted by the court to make himself a party.

j

jurisprudence: The philosophy of law, or the science which treats of the principles of positive law and legal relations.

jury: A certain number of people, selected according to law, and sworn to inquire of certain matters of fact, and declare the truth upon evidence laid before them.

   grand jury: A jury whose duty is to receive complaints and accusations in criminal cases, hear the evidence and find bills of indictment in cases where they are satisfied a trial ought to be had.

   petit jury: The ordinary jury of twelve (or fewer) persons for the trial of a civil or criminal case. So called to distinguish it from the grand jury.

jury commissioner: An officer charged with the duty of selecting the names to be put into a jury wheel, or of drawing the panel of jurors for a particular term of court.

l

leading question: One which instructs a witness how to answer or puts into his mouth words to be echoed back; one which suggests to the witness the answer desired. Prohibited on direct examination.

letters rogatory (rog'a-tō-ri):   A request by one court of another court in an independent jurisdiction that a witness be examined upon interrogatories sent with the request.

levy: A seizure; the obtaining of money by legal process through seizure and sale of property. The raising of the money for which an execution has been issued.

libel: A method of defamation expressed by print, writing, pictures, or signs. In its most general sense any publication that is injurious to the reputation of another.

limitation: A certain time allowed by statute in which litigation must be brought.

lis pendens (līs pen'denz):   A pending suit.

locus delicti (lo kus de-lik'ti):   The place of the offense.

m

malfeasance: Evil doing; ill conduct; the commission of some act which is positively prohibited by law.

malicious prosecution: An action instituted with intention of injuring defendant and without probable cause, and which terminates in favor of the person prosecuted.

mandamus (man-dā'mus):   The name of a writ which issues from a court of superior jurisdiction, directed to an inferior court, commanding the performance of a particular act.

mandate: A judicial command or precept proceeding from a court or judicial officer, directing the proper officer to enforce a judgment, sentence, or decree.

manslaughter: The unlawful killing of another without malice; may be either voluntary, upon a sudden impulse, or involuntary, in the commission of some unlawful act.

master: An officer of the court, usually an attorney, appointed for the purpose of taking testimony and making a report to the court. Used most frequently in divorce cases.

material evidence: Such as is relevant and goes to the substantial issues in dispute.

mesne (mēn):   Intermediate; intervening.

misdemeanor: Offenses less than felonies; generally those punishable by fine or imprisonment other than in penitentiaries.

misfeasance: A misdeed or trespass. The improper performance of some act which a person may lawfully do.

mistrial: An erroneous or invalid trial; a trial which cannot stand in law because of lack of jurisdiction, wrong drawing of jurors, or disregard of some other fundamental requisite.

mitigating circumstance: One which does not constitute a justification or excuse of an offense, but which may be considered as reducing the degree of moral culpability.

moot: Unsettled; undecided. A moot point is one not settled by judicial decisions.

moral turpitude: Conduct contrary to honesty, modesty, or good morals.

multiplicity of actions: Numerous and unnecessary attempts to litigate the same right.

municipal courts: In the judicial organization of some states, courts whose territorial authority is confined to the city or community.

murder: The unlawful killing of a human being by another with malice aforethought, either expressed or implied.

n

ne exeat (nē ek'sē-at):   A writ which forbids the person to whom it is addressed to leave the country, the state, or the jurisdiction of the court.

negligence: The omission to do something which a reasonable man, guided by ordinary considerations, would do; or the doing of something which a reasonable and prudent man would not do.

next friend: One acting for the benefit of an infant or other person without being regularly appointed as guardian.

nisi prius (nī'sī prī'us):   Courts for the initial trials of issues of fact, as distinguished from appellate courts.

no bill: This phrase, endorsed by a grand jury on an indictment, is equivalent to "not found" or "not a true bill." It means that, in the opinion of the jury, evidence was insufficient to warrant the return of a formal charge.

nolle prosequi (nol'e pros' e-kwī):   A formal entry upon the record by the plaintiff in a civil suit, or the prosecuting officer in a criminal case, by which he declares that he "will not further prosecute" the case.

nolo contendere (nō'lō kon-ten'de-rē):   A pleading, usually used by defendants in criminal cases, which literally means I will not contest it.

nominal party: One who is joined as a party or defendant merely because the technical rules of pleading require his presence in the record.

non compos mentis (non kom'pos men'tis):   Not sound of mind; insane.

non obstante veredicto (non ob-stan'te ve-re-dik'to):   Notwithstanding the verdict. A judgment entered by order of court for one party, although there has been a jury verdict against him.

notice to produce: In practice, a notice in writing requiring the opposite party to produce a certain described paper or document at the trial.

o

objection: The act of taking exception to some statement or procedure in trial. Used to call the court's attention to improper evidence or procedure.

of counsel: A phrase commonly applied to counsel employed to assist in the preparation or management of the case, or its presentation on appeal, but who is not the principal attorney of record.

opinion evidence: Evidence of what the witness thinks, believes, or infers in regard to a fact in dispute, as distinguished from his personal knowledge of the facts; not admissible except (under certain limitations) in the case of experts.

ordinary: A judicial officer, in several of the states, clothed by statute with powers in regard to wills, probate, administration, and guardianship.

out of court: One who has no legal status in court is said to be "out of court," i.e., he is not before the court. For example, when a plaintiff, by some act of omission or commission, shows that he is unable to maintain his action he is frequently said to have put himself "out of court."

p

panel: A list of jurors to serve in a particular court, or for the trial of a particular action; denotes either the whole body of persons summoned as jurors for a particular term of court or those selected by the clerk by lot.

parties: The persons who are actively concerned in the prosecution or defense of a legal proceeding.

peremptory challenge: The challenge which the prosecution or defense may use to reject a certain number of prospective jurors without assigning any cause.

plaintiff: A person who brings an action; the party who complains or sues in a personal action and is so named, on the record.

plaintiff in error: The party who obtains a writ of error to have a judgment or other proceeding at law reviewed by an appellate court.

pleading: The process by which the parties in a suit or action alternately present written statements of their contentions, each responsive to that which precedes and each serving to narrow the field of controversy, until there evolves a single point, affirmed on one side and denied on the other, called the "issue" upon which they then go to trial.

polling the jury: A practice whereby the jurors are asked individually whether they assented, and still assent, to the verdict.

power of attorney: An instrument authorizing another to act as one's agent or attorney.

praecipe (prē'si-pe):   An original writ commanding the defendant to do the thing required; also, an order addressed to the clerk of a court, requesting him to issue a particular writ.

prejudicial error: Synonymous with "reversible error"; an error which warrants the appellate court in reversing the judgment before it.

preliminary hearing: Synonymous with "preliminary examination"; the hearing given a person charged with crime by a magistrate or judge to determine whether he should be held for trial.

preponderance of evidence: Greater weight of evidence, or evidence which is more credible and convincing to the mind, not necessarily the greater number of witnesses.

presentment: An informal statement in writing by a grand jury to the court that a public offense has been committed, from their own knowledge or observation, without any bill of indictment laid before them.

presumption of fact: An inference as to the truth or falsity of any proposition or fact, drawn by a process of reasoning in the absence of actual certainty of its truth or falsity, or until such certainty can be ascertained.

presumption of law: A rule of law that courts and judges shall draw a particular inference from a particular evidence.

probate: The act or process of proving a will.

probation: In modern criminal administration, allowing a person convicted of some minor offense (particularly juvenile offenders) to go at large, under a suspension of sentence, during good behavior, and generally under the supervision or guardianship of a probation officer.

prosecutor: One who instigates the prosecution upon which an accused is arrested or who prefers an accusation against the party whom he suspects to be guilty; also one who takes charge of a case and performs the function of trial lawyer for the people.

prosecutrix: A female prosecutor.

q

quaere (kēw're):   A query; question; doubt.

quash: To overthrow; vacate; to annul or void a summons or indictment.

quasi judicial (kwā'sī):   Authority or discretion vested in an officer wherein his acts partake of a judicial character.

quid pro quo: "What for what," a fair return or consideration.

quo warranto (kwō wo-ran'tō):   A writ issuable by the state, through which it demands an individual to show by what right he exercises an authority which can only be exercised through grant or franchise emanating from the state.

r

reasonable doubt: An accused person is entitled to acquittal if, in the minds of the jury, his guilt has not been proved beyond a "reasonable doubt"; that state of the minds of jurors in which they cannot say they feel an abiding conviction as to the truth of the charge.

rebuttal: The introduction of rebutting evidence; the showing that statements of witnesses as to what occurred is not true; the stage of a trial at which such evidence may be introduced.

redirect examination: Follows cross-examination, and is had by the party who first examined the witness.

referee: A person to whom a cause pending in a court is referred by the court to take testimony, hear the parties and report thereon to the court. He is an officer exercising judicial powers and is an arm of the court for a specific purpose.

removal, order of: An order by a court directing the transfer of a case to another court.

reply: When a case is tried or argued in court, the argument of the plaintiff in answer to that of the defendant. A pleading in response to an answer.

rest: A party is said to "rest" or "rest his case" when he has presented all the evidence he intends to offer.

retainer: Act of the client in employing his attorney or counsel, and also denotes the fee which the client pays when he retains the attorney to act for him.

robbery: The taking or stealing of property from another with force or the threat of force.

rule nisi, or rule to show cause (nī'sī):   A court order obtained on motion by either party to show cause why the particular relief sought should not be granted.

rule of court: An order made by a court having competent jurisdiction. Rules of court are either general or special; the former are the regulations by which the practice of the court is governed; the latter are special orders made in particular cases.

s

search and seizure, unreasonable: In general, an examination without authority of law of one's premises or person with a view to discovering stolen contraband or illicit property or some evidence of guilt to be used in prosecuting a crime.

search warrant: An order in writing, issued by a justice or magistrate in the name of the state, directing an officer to search a specified house or other premises for stolen property. Usually required as a condition precedent to a legal search and seizure.

self-defense: The protection of one's person or property against some injury attempted by another. The law of "self defense" justifies an act done in the reasonable belief of immediate danger. When acting in justifiable self-defense, a person may not be punished criminally nor held responsible for civil damages.

separate maintenance: Allowance granted to a wife for support of herself and children while she is living apart from her husband but not divorced from him.

separation of witnesses: An order of the court requiring all witnesses to remain outside the courtroom until each is called to testify, except the plaintiff or defendant.

sheriff: An officer of a county, chosen by popular election, whose principal duties are aid of criminal and civil courts; chief preserver of the peace. He serves processes, summons juries, executes judgments and holds judicial sales.

sine qua non (sī'ne kwā non):   An indispensable requisite.

slander: Base and defamatory spoken words tending to prejudice another in his reputation, business, or means of livelihood. "Libel" and "slander" both are methods of defamation, the former being expressed by print, writings, pictures, or signs; the latter orally.

specific performance: A mandatory order in equity. Where damages would be inadequate compensation for the breach of a contract, the contractor will be compelled to perform specifically what he has agreed to do.

stare decisis: (sta're de-si'sis):   The doctrine that, when a court has once laid down a principle of law as applicable to a certain set of facts, it will adhere to that principle and apply it to future cases where the facts are substantially the same.

state's evidence: Testimony, given by an accomplice or participant in a crime, tending to convict others.

statute: The written law in contradistinction to the unwritten law.

stay: A stopping or arresting of a judicial proceeding by order of the court.

stipulation: An agreement by attorneys on opposite sides of a case as to any matter pertaining to the proceedings or trial. It is not binding unless assented to by the parties, and most stipulations must be in writing.

subpoena (su-pē'na):   A process to cause a witness to appear and give testimony before a court or magistrate.

subpoena duces tecum (su-pē na dū sēz tē kum):   A process by which the court commands a witness to produce certain documents or records in a trial.

substantive law: The law dealing with rights, duties, and liabilities, as distinguished from adjective law, which is the law regulating procedure.

summons: A writ directing the sheriff or other officer to notify the named person that an action has been commenced against him in court and that he is required to appear, on the day named, and answer the complaint in such action.

supersedeas (sū-per-sē-dē-as):   A writ containing a command to stay proceedings at law, such as the enforcement of a judgment pending an appeal.

t

talesman (tālz'man):   A person summoned to act as a juror from among the bystanders in a court.

testimony: Evidence given by a competent witness, under oath; as distinguished from evidence derived from writings and other sources.

tort: An injury or wrong committed, either with or without force, to the person or property of another.

transcript: The official record of proceedings in a trial or hearing.

transitory: Actions are "transitory" when they might have taken place anywhere, and are "local" when they could occur only in some particular place.

traverse: In pleading, traverse signifies a denial. When a defendant denies any material allegation of fact in the plaintiff's declaration, he is said to traverse it.

trial de novo (dē nō'vō):   A new trial or retrial had in an appellate court in which the whole case is gone into as if no trial had been had in a lower court.

true bill: In criminal practice, the endorsement made in a grand jury upon a bill of indictment when they find it sufficient evidence to warrant a criminal charge.

u

undue influence: Whatever destroys free will and causes a person to do something he would not do if left to himself.

unlawful detainer: A detention of real estate without the consent of the owner or other person entitled to its possession.

usury: The taking of more for the use of money than the law allows.

v

venire (vē-ni rē):   Technically, a writ summoning persons to court to act as jurors; popularly used as meaning the body of names thus summoned.

venire facias de novo (fā'she-as dē nō'vō):   A fresh or new venire, which the court grants when there has been some impropriety or irregularity in returning the jury, or where the verdict is so imperfect or ambiguous that no judgment can be given upon it.

veniremen (vē'nī'rē-men):   Members of a panel of jurors.

venue (ven'ū):   The particular county, city, or geographical area in which a court with jurisdiction may hear and determine a case.

verdict: In practice, the formal and unanimous decision or finding made by a jury, reported to the court, and accepted by it.

voir dire (vwor dēr):   To speak the truth. The phrase denotes the preliminary examination which the court may make of one presented as a witness or juror as to his qualifications.

W

waiver of immunity: A means authorized by statutes by which a witness, in advance of giving testimony or producing evidence, may renounce the fundamental right guaranteed by the constitution that no person shall be compelled to be a witness against himself.

warrant of arrest: A writ issued by a magistrate, justice or other competent authority, to a sheriff or other officer, requiring him to arrest the person therein named and bring him before the magistrate or court to answer to a specified charge.

weight of evidence: The balance or preponderance of evidence; the inclination of the greater amount of credible evidence, offered in a trial, to support one side of the issue rather than the other.

willful: A "willful" act is one done intentionally, without justifiable cause, as distinguished from an act done carelessly or inadvertently.

with prejudice: The term, as applied to a judgment of dismissal, is as conclusive of rights of parties as if action had been prosecuted to final adjudication adverse to the plaintiff.

witness: One who testifies to what he has seen, heard, or otherwise observed.

writ: An order issuing from a court requiring the performance of a specified act, or giving authority and commission to have it done.

writ of error coram nobis (ko'ram no'bis):   A common law writ, the purpose of which is to correct a judgment in the same court in which it was rendered, on the ground of error of fact.

appendix b
Federal and State
Court Structure

Though this book is not designed to provide a comprehensive overview of court structure and jurisdiction, a brief sketch of the court structure in the United States may be helpful. Courts vary widely from state to state, and reporters covering the legal process should be familiar with the nuances of the structure in their area.

FEDERAL COURT STRUCTURE

The Constitution of the United States (Article III, Section 1) vests the judicial power of the nation "in one supreme Court, and in such inferior Courts as the Congress may from time to time ordain and establish." The Supreme Court, with nine justices, has included within its powers that of judicial review in cases involving constitutionality, that is, whether federal or state laws and lower court rulings conform with the Constitution.

There are two other courts in the federal court system that the reporter may cover. These are the federal district court and the circuit court of appeals. The circuit court is an intermediate court between the district court and the Supreme Court. There are eleven circuits in the United States, each with its own judges. Each circuit includes at least three states, except the District of Columbia circuit. In addition to reviewing, on appeal, cases from the district courts, circuit courts review the administrative actions of some federal administrative agencies for errors of law. Many cases that are appealed to the circuit courts receive their final review there. Under certain circumstances, a case may bypass the circuit court and go directly for review from the district court to the Supreme Court. For example, in the case of the Watergate tapes, the Supreme Court was asked to rule on questions of executive privilege directly from the district court level.

The federal district court is the federal court most likely to be covered by the public affairs reporter. There are ninety-four district courts in the fifty states and territories. Each state has at least one federal district court, and some states have two or three. New York State has four. These courts have original jurisdiction in cases involving federal statutes, federal constitutionality, and some reviews of state court rulings, such as the deprivation of constitutional rights.

Federal courts also have jurisdiction in cases where the United States is a party to the action and in cases involving disputes between states, between a state and citizens of another state, and between citizens of different states. Federal courts also have jurisdiction in cases involving ambassadors and foreign states.

Federal districts normally have a prosecutor, called a U.S. attorney, who represents the federal government in criminal cases and in cases

United States Court System

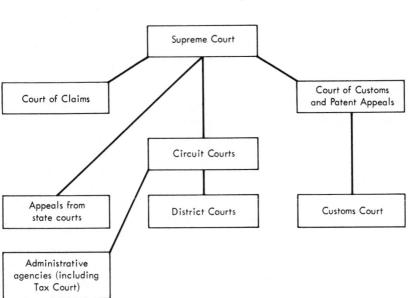

where the United States is a party to the action. These attorneys and their assistants may be helped by staff from the U.S. Department of Justice.

There are other courts in the federal system with which the reporter may have contact on an infrequent basis. One is the U.S. Court of Claims, which handles cases in which a monetary claim is made against the United States. Another is the U.S. Court of Customs and Patent Appeals, which hears appeals from the Customs Court, the Patent Office, and the Tariff Commission. There are also U.S. Tax Courts, which hear cases, often on appeal, involving IRS rulings. Although these specialized courts do not often make the news, the public affairs and investigative reporter should know of their existence. A company that has had a recent case in a tax court, for example, at either the state or federal level, may have filed documents revealing its holdings and corporate structure, information which is difficult to obtain unless it is filed as part of a "public record."

Federal courts have their own rules of procedure, and reporters assigned to cover them should begin with acquainting themselves with the courts' operations and functions.[1]

STATE COURT STRUCTURE

As with the U.S. Constitution, state constitutions vest their judicial power in a supreme court and in other inferior courts that are created by state legislatures. There is considerable variety in the structure of courts at the state level, and there is considerable variety in what these courts are called.

Typically, a state will have a supreme court or an intermediate supreme court of appeals, whose major function is to hear cases on appeal from lower courts in the state system. At the state level, judges usually are appointed to the bench by the governor and then stand for election to regular terms. Judges on federal courts, by the way, are appointed by the president and confirmed by the Senate. They do not stand for election.

Beneath the supreme court at the state level, the court system varies considerably with the size of the state and its major metropolitan areas. State district courts, sometimes called circuit courts, superior courts, or county courts, are usually organized by county in large metropolitan areas and by districts that may include several counties in rural areas. Normally, such courts have original jurisdiction to hear felony cases, civil suits where the damages are over a certain amount, divorces, juvenile cases, equity cases, and matters dealing with real estate and probate. Sometimes, the court will have specific judges assigned to specific divisions, such as juvenile and divorce (sometimes called family court). The district or county courts are probably the main source of important trial news for the reporter. It is here that major crimes are tried and where major civil suits are argued.

Beneath the district or county courts in the state court structure there

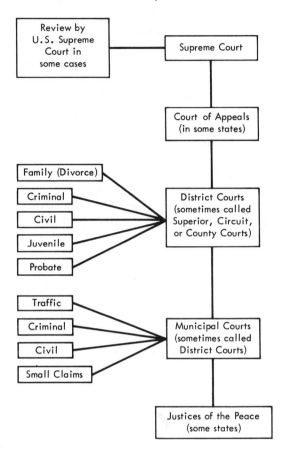

State Court System

is also considerable variety. The reporter may find municipal courts, which handle misdemeanors and act as courts of first appearance for felony cases, which are then referred to district courts for arraignment and trial. Traffic offenses normally are handled at the municipal court level. So are small claims, which are sometimes handled by a separate division called small claims or conciliation courts. Minor civil suits are often handled at this level as well.

Beneath the municipal courts, some states have a justice of the peace system, which usually consists of individuals (not necessarily learned in the law) who can hear certain minor offenses, such as certain traffic violations.

Prosecution of cases at the state level is normally divided among three types of prosecutors. Typically, most felonies will be prosecuted by a county attorney, sometimes called a state's attorney or district attorney. These officials are generally elected. The district attorney sometimes handles investigations through grand juries and has considerable discretion about if and when a person should be charged with a crime.

The district attorney may have assistants, who are generally hired by the attorney. They may have civil service status, and thus, may be less "political" than the district attorney, who must keep his or her eye on the upcoming election.

States generally also have an attorney general, who is also an elected official. The attorney general's office represents the state in civil suits and may handle some criminal cases. Some attorney general's offices have consumer protection divisions, organized crime investigation units, and other quasi-legal, quasi-law enforcement functions.

Misdemeanors and municipal ordinance violations are sometimes prosecuted by the district attorney's office, particularly in sparsely populated areas. In urban areas, there may be a city attorney who handles such prosecutions. A city attorney is normally an appointee of the village or city council.

NOTE

[1]House Committee on the Judiciary, *The United States Courts* (Washington, D.C.: U.S. Government Printing Office, 1973).

appendix c

Criminal Justice
and Criminal Trial Process

Criminal cases are handled in different ways in different states, but most criminal court matters follow a typical pattern.

THE CRIMINAL PROCESS
FROM ARREST TO SENTENCING

A criminal case in court begins with either an arrest or a "tag" charge, such as for a traffic violation. Most states have different categories of crimes, and they are handled in different ways and in different courts. These crimes are characterized as felonies, gross misdemeanors, misdemeanors, and ordinance violations.

Felonies are serious crimes for which a term in a penitentiary may be imposed. Such crimes include treason, murder, rape, and robbery.[1]

Gross misdemeanors are less serious crimes, which usually carry a jail term (not in a penitentiary) of between ninety days and one year. Gross misdemeanors often include certain thefts, depending on the dollar value of the loss, and inciting a riot.

Misdemeanors are statutory offenses for which a fine (often up to $300) or jail term (usually less than ninety days in other than a penitentiary) may be imposed. Traffic violations are usually misdemeanors, as are such offenses as simple assault, when a life is not threatened. Aggravated assaults, in which the victim is in "great bodily harm," are usually considered felonies.

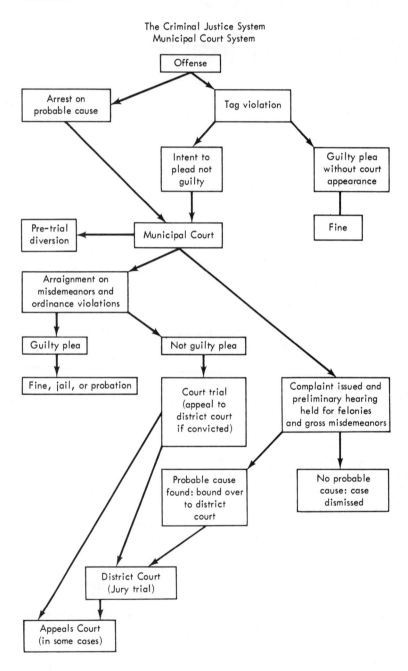

The Criminal Justice System
Municipal Court System

Ordinance violations are infringements of a municipal law rather than of a state law. These violations normally carry a penalty of up to ninety days in jail or a fine or both.

Normally, felonies and gross misdemeanors must be tried in the court of original jurisdiction, usually the district (or county or superior) court. Misdemeanors and ordinance violations may be handled in the court of limited jurisdiction—the municipal court or by a justice of the peace; a conviction there may be appealed to the district court.

The municipal court also handles the initial court appearance of defendants arrested for committing a felony or gross misdemeanor. A preliminary hearing is held, and if probable cause is established, the case is then referred to—bound over to—the district court for arraignment and trial.

In felony cases where police believe they have enough evidence, they will draw up a legal document, called a complaint, which is presented to a judge. A warrant for arrest on probable cause is then issued, based on the complaint.

The reporter who finds defendants appearing in court on such complaints needs to exercise considerable caution. A complaint is not a verdict, not even an indictment. It does not establish guilt. It merely asserts that there is probable cause to believe that a crime has been committed and probable cause to believe that the defendant committed it. A complaint does not convict the defendant of anything.

Because the charge is a felony, the defendant would appear first in municipal court for a preliminary hearing, at which the state would attempt to show through witnesses that there is, indeed, probable cause to believe that (1) a crime or crimes were committed and (2) that the defendant named in the complaint committed it. In the preliminary hearing, the defense may attempt to rebut the state's case by attacking the credibility of the witnesses. If probable cause is established, the judge will bind the defendant over to the district (higher) court for arraignment and trial. At the district court, the complaint will be superseded by a court document called an information. An information, issued by the court, is similar to a complaint in that it informs the defendant of the charges against him or her.

In cases involving homicides, most prosecutors use the indictment process. The indictment, issued by a grand jury, constitutes the finding of probable cause and brings the defendant directly to the trial court of original jurisdiction without going through the preliminary hearing. Indictments may also be sought by prosecutors for lesser felonies.

Once in district court, the typical felony case becomes more complex. There is normally an arraignment before the judge, at which a formal plea of guilty or not guilty is entered, and this may be followed by motions, the setting of a trial date, and pretrial evidentiary hearings. Most criminal cases never go to trial. The typical defendant pleads guilty to the charge for an agreed-on limited sentence or to a reduced charge. This process, called

The Criminal Justice System:
District Court Process

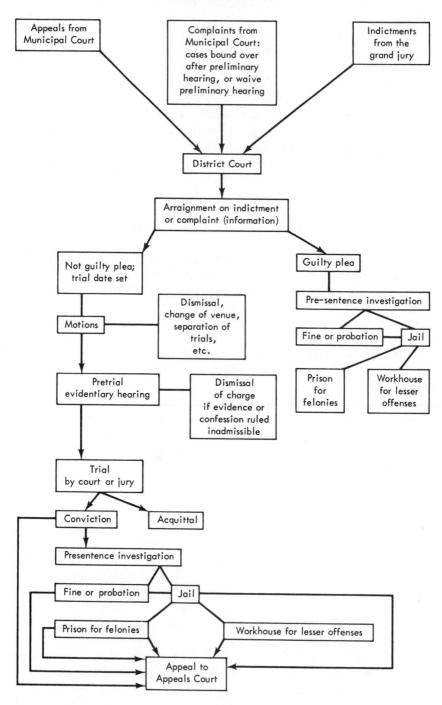

plea bargaining, involves negotiations between the defense attorney and the prosecutor with the approval of the judge.

Often, the case will be disposed of following an evidentiary hearing prior to trial. In these hearings, the judge hears testimony on evidence to be introduced at trial and rules whether the evidence is admissible or not. He or she may also rule on the admissibility of a "confession" by the defendant and whether the confession was given in a constitutional manner.

Covering a pretrial evidentiary hearing presents special problems for the court reporter. If certain evidence is ruled admissible, the reporter might well report that fact, as well as the nature of the evidence. But if the evidence is ruled inadmissible, the reporter who specifically identified the evidence might be prejudicing potential jurors.

There are numerous kinds of motions that may be filed in a criminal trial—either before arraignment, before the trial, or during the trial. A change of venue motion, for example, asks that the trial be moved to another county or district because circumstances, often pretrial publicity, are believed to make it impossible to impanel a fair and impartial jury. If there are codefendants in a case, they may all move that their trials be conducted separately. A motion to dismiss the charge or the indictment may be based on grounds that it was improperly drafted. Such motions normally precede arraignment. Some may be filed after, but heard before, the trial. Defense attorneys are particularly prone to present the court with a variety of motions.

Cases that go to trial are handled according to rules of procedure that are described generally in the next section of this appendix. Following a trial with a guilty verdict, a judge may sentence a defendant directly from the bench or may withhold sentencing until a presentence investigation is completed, normally by a division of the court or welfare department. A presentence investigation is normally confidential, and it often includes the defendant's previous criminal record, if any, and background information on employment, family, home, and personality. Investigators often recommend a particular kind of sentence, and judges frequently take such recommendations into account, though they are not bound by them.[2]

THE CRIMINAL JURY TRIAL: STRUCTURE AND PROCESS

A criminal trial begins with the selection of a jury from a panel of potential jurors, called veniremen. Potential jurors are chosen from the district in which the trial court has jurisdiction, and potential jurors normally undergo careful questioning by the judge and defense and prosecution. This process is called *voir dire,* and it may take considerable time. A potential

Criminal Trial Process

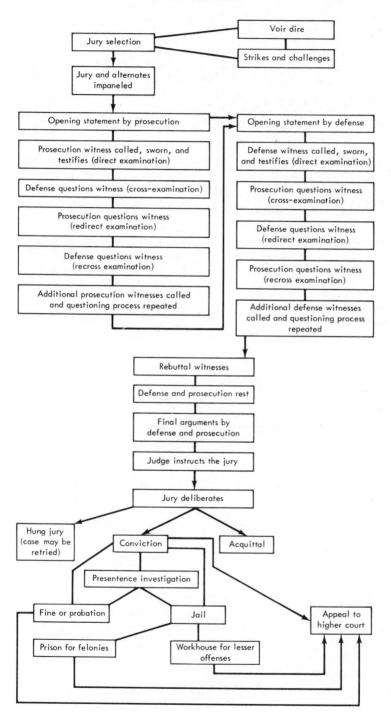

juror may be challenged or *struck* for *cause*, meaning there is some reason that he or she is unacceptable. A juror may also be struck by either the prosecution or defense in a *peremptory challenge,* in which no reason need be given.

Some attorneys consider jury selection the most important part of any criminal trial. They argue that potential jurors come to a trial with lifetimes of experiences which incline them in one way or another and that no amount of testimony, however persuasive, is likely to change basic beliefs. It is therefore crucial, they argue, that the right jury be impaneled. Others disagree with this approach, arguing that juries are fully capable of laying aside prejudices to consider cases on their merits.

Once a jury is impaneled, it is normally instructed not to read news accounts of the trial or to watch broadcast accounts. The jury may be sequestered if the judge believes it may become tainted by outside influences.

Following the selection of a jury, the prosecution in the typical criminal trial will make an opening statement, explaining to the jury what it intends to prove. The prosecution's statement, like that of the defense, is not testimony. The opening statements are usually very important because they give the court reporter a capsule of both sides of the case.

Depending on the rules of criminal procedure, and perhaps on the tactics of the attorneys, the defense may withhold its opening statement until after completion of the prosecution's case.

The next step in a trial is the calling of witnesses. Witnesses for the prosecution, called *state's witnesses,* are called first, and each is questioned first by the prosecuting attorney under what is called *direct examination.* After questioning is completed, the defense may question the witness in a process called *cross-examination.* The prosecutor may then question the witness again on items brought up in the cross-examination; this questioning is termed *redirect examination.* It may be followed with a recross-examination.

The same process is followed with each witness and is conducted in the same way when the defense begins to call witnesses. A defense witness will be questioned first—direct examination—by the defense counsel; he or she may then be questioned—cross-examination—by the prosecutor.

One witness may contradict another, and the purpose of calling a particular witness may not be clearly stated but only inferred. Reporters must take special care to balance their reports: a too-heavy emphasis on either the prosecution or defense performance is likely to bring protests. At the same time, they must watch out for the grandstand play by an attorney, the remark intended as much for the press as for the jury.

Unlike television "trials," very few criminal cases have dramatic moments when "the truth" is suddenly revealed. Witnesses provide pieces of a puzzle, and the experienced attorney presents witnesses to the jury in a careful, methodical fashion, building the case brick by brick.

After the prosecution and defense have called their witnesses, each may call "rebuttal" witnesses to attack specific points made by the other side. Both sides then rest their cases and prepare for final arguments. Final arguments may provide the reporter with an outline of what each side believes it has shown, but the reporter should realize that final arguments, like opening statements, are not testimony.

The judge will then instruct, or *charge*, the jury, telling them what aspects of the law they are to consider and the meaning of certain legal terms, such as "proof beyond a reasonable doubt." The judge's instructions to the jury are often crucial in the outcome of the case, and both defense and prosecution normally submit various rules of law that they would like the judge to give the jury. The option to include them in the charge or not, of course, is the judge's.

After the jury has been instructed, it will deliberate until it reaches a verdict or an impasse. A unanimous vote is usually required for conviction, although several states allow less-than-unanimous votes in some cases. If a jury cannot agree on a verdict, it may be declared a *hung* jury by the judge, and a new trial is ordered. If the defendant is convicted, sentencing may be immediate or follow a presentence investigation by probation officers.

NOTES

[1]Legal terms often have very precise definitions. See Henry C. Black, *Black's Law Dictionary* (St. Paul, Minn.: West Publishing, 1968).

[2]There are several summaries of the criminal trial process. One of the best is by Jerold H. Israel and Wayne R. LaFave, *Criminal Procedure in a Nutshell* (St. Paul, Minn.: West Publishing, 1971). See also the other titles in the "nutshell" series, including Ernest Gelhorn, *Administrative Law;* Paul F. Rothstein, *Evidence;* and Delmar Karlen, *Procedure Before Trial.*

appendix d
Sources of Information

Reporters, according to a newsroom adage, are as good as their sources. The quality of information obtained determines to a large extent the quality of the story produced. Throughout this text, we have emphasized the importance of thorough research in the planning and development of news stories, from personal interviews through the spectrum of other sources: library materials, statistics, public records and documents, and original field research.

Public records and documents offer a vast storehouse of information to reporters, as do nongovernmental agencies and organizations. This appendix lists directories, guidebooks, and the names and addresses of organizations and agencies that may be useful as sources.* The directories and guides describe the types of information available, but imagination and resourcefulness are required to plumb the extent it is available to the press.

---

*Listings in this section have been drawn from directories and from the following publications: *Raising Hell: A Citizens Guide to the Fine Art of Investigation* (San Francisco: Mother Jones Magazine, 1978); *How to Use the Federal FOI Act* (Washington, D.C.: FOI Service Center, 1980); *Healthy People* (Washington, D.C.: U.S. Department of Health, Education and Welfare, 1979); and Louis M. Kohlmeier, Jr., Jon G. Udell, and Laird B. Anderson, *Reporting on Business and the Economy* (Englewood Cliffs, N.J.: Prentice-Hall, 1981).

The Federal FOI Act

Although most state and local records are considered public, laws regarding their availability vary from state to state. Reporters must familiarize themselves with the laws in their own states. However, all federal materials are controlled uniformly by two laws, one relating to privacy, the other to information. The principal statute governing the release of federal information is the Freedom of Information Act, enacted in 1966 and revised in 1974 to strengthen its provisions. It guarantees access to federal documents and records unless the material comes under one of nine categories of exempt information. These range from internal operating memoranda to bank reports, business trade secrets, certain national security matters, and personnel files.

The act requires all federal entities to provide information in their files upon request of any person, within specified time limits (usually ten days). A "reasonable" charge for clerical and copying charges is permitted, but even these fees may be waived for journalists and academic researchers. Often, a simple phone call to the agency will produce the desired information. Most large agencies have a special person designated to process FOI requests. Sometimes, a formal letter of request is required. If an agency doesn't comply, the person making the request can file a lawsuit in federal court.

Reporters should become familiar with procedures required to obtain information under the act, and two publications can be helpful. One is *A Citizen's Guide on How to Use the Freedom of Information Act and the Privacy Act in Requesting Government Documents.* Published by the House Committee on Government Operations in 1977, it is available through the Superintendent of Documents, U.S. Government Printing Office, Washington, D.C. 20402, at a cost of two dollars. The other guide, *How to Use the Federal FOI Act,* is published by the FOI Service Center, a joint project of the Society of Professional Journalists, Sigma Delta Chi, and the Reporters Committee for Freedom of the Press. It is a complete do-it-yourself handbook for requesting federal documents and is available from the FOI Service Center, c/o Reporters Committee, 1125 15th St., N.W., Washington, D.C. 20005, at a cost of fifty cents.

DIRECTORIES AND GUIDES

A Directory of Information Resources in the United States. Washington, D.C.: U.S. Government Printing Office, 1974 and later revisions. Describes publications available from federal agencies and in the physical, biological, and social sciences.

County and City Data Book. Washington, D.C.: U.S. Government Printing Office, revised periodically. This is a Census Bureau publication, a supplement to the *Statistical Abstract of the United States,* providing data on political subdivisions.

DANIELLS, LORNA. *Business Information Sources.* Berkeley: University of California Press, 1976.

STANLEY R. GREENFIELD, ed.   *National Directory of Addresses and Telephone Numbers.* New York: Nicholas Publishing and Bantam Books, 1977. Lists business and government organizations by category and alphabetically.

MURPHY, HARRY J. *Where's What: Sources of Information for Federal Investigators,* New York: Warner Books, 1976. A CIA study now available to the public.

Open the Books: How to Research a Corporation. Chicago: Midwest Academy. Basic guide to research methods.

RIVERS, WILLIAM. *Finding Facts.* Englewood Cliffs, N.J.: Prentice-Hall, 1975; and Todd, Alden. *Finding Facts Fast.* New York: Morrow, 1972. Handbooks on research techniques and information sources.

U.S. Government Manual. Washington, D.C.: U.S. Government Printing Office, revised yearly. Lists purposes, programs, and top personnel of most federal agencies.

Washington Information Directory. Washington, D.C.: Congressional *Quarterly,* revised yearly. Lists federal departments and agencies by subject.

FEDERAL GOVERNMENT ADDRESSES AND TELEPHONE NUMBERS (WASHINGTON, D.C. AREA CODE 202)

Executive Departments

Agriculture Department
14th St. and Independence Ave., S.W.
Zip 20250   447-4026

Commerce Department
14th St. and Constitution Ave., N.W.
Zip 20230   377-4901

Commerce/Census
568-1220

Defense Department
The Pentagon
Zip 20301   697-5131

Education Department
400 Maryland Ave., S.W.
Zip 20202   426-6573

Energy Department
1000 Independence Ave., S.W.
Zip 20585   252-5806

Health and Human Services (HHS)
200 Independence Ave., S.W.
Zip 20201   245-6345

HHS/Food and Drug Administration
5600 Fishers Lane
Rockville, MD 20857
(301) 443-3285

HHS/National Institutes of Health
9000 Rockville Pike
Bethesda, MD 20205
(301) 496-2535

HHS/Public Health Service
5600 Fishers Lane
Rockville, MD 20857
(301) 245-6867

HHS/Social Security Administration
200 Independence Ave., S.W.
Zip 20201   245-1272

Housing and Urban Development
451 7th St., S.W.
Zip 20410   755-5284

Interior Department
18th and C Sts., N.W.
Zip 20240   343-3171

Justice Department
10th St. and Constitution Ave., N.W.
Zip 20530   633-2014

Justice/FBI
9th St. and Pennsylvania Ave., N.W.
Zip 20535   324-3691

Labor Department
200 Constitution Ave., N.W.
Zip 20210   523-7316

Office of Management and Budget
Old Executive Office Bldg.
Zip 20503   395-4790

State Department
2201 C St., N.W.
Zip 20520   632-2492

Transportation Department
400 7th St., S.W.
Zip 20590   426-4321

Treasury Department
15th St. and Pennsylvania Ave., N.W.
Zip 20220   566-2041

Treasury/Internal Revenue Service
1111 Constitution Ave., N.W.
Zip 20224   566-4024

Treasury/Secret Service
1800 G St., N.W.
Zip 20223   535-5708

Agencies

Central Intelligence Agency
Zip 20505   (703) 351-1100

Civil Aeronautics Board
1825 Connecticut Ave., N.W.
Zip 20428   673-5990

Consumer Product Safety
  Commission
1111 18th St., N.W.
Zip 20207   634-7780

Council on Environmental Quality
722 Jackson Place, N.W.
Zip 20006   383-1415

Environmental Protection Agency
401 M St., N.W.
Zip 20506   634-7040

Federal Communications
  Commission
1919 M St., N.W.
Zip 20554   632-7260

Federal Election Commission
1325 K St., N.W.
Zip 20463   523-4068

Federal Trade Commission
6th St. and Pennsylvania Ave., N.W.
Zip 20580   523-3830

General Services Administration
18th and F Sts., N.W.
Zip 20405   566-1231

Interstate Commerce Commission
12th St. and Constitution Ave., N.W.
Zip 20423   275-7252

National Labor Relations Board
1717 Pennsylvania Ave., N.W.
Zip 20570   632-4950

National Transportation Safety
  Board
800 Independence Ave., S.W.
Zip 20594   472-6100

Nuclear Regulatory Commission
1717 H St., N.W.
Zip 20555   492-7715

Occupational Safety and Health
  Review Commission
1825 K St., N.W.
Zip 20006   634-7943

Office of Personnel Management
1900 E St., N.W.
Zip 20415   632-5491

Securities & Exchange Commission
500 N. Capitol St., N.W.
Zip 20549   272-2650

Selective Service System
600 E St., N.W.
Zip 20435   724-0419

Small Business Administration
1441 L St., N.W.
Zip 20416   653-6822

U.S. Postal Service
475 L'Enfant Plaza West, S.W.
Zip 20260   245-4144

Veterans Administration
810 Vermont Ave.
Zip 20420   389-2741

Water Resources Council
2120 L St., N.W.
Zip 20037   254-6303

PRIVATE SECTOR ORGANIZATIONS

Trade organizations, professional associations, lobbying and public interest groups, trade organizations, and other private sector organizations are compilers and disseminators of statistics, information, and documents. This section presents a selected list of organizations and their addresses, classified according to popular categories: business, economics, and finance; consumer interests; health and medicine; environment and land use; labor; mass media; transportation; and miscellaneous.

Business, Economics, and Finance

American Enterprise Institute
1150 17th St., N.W.
Washington, DC 20036

Brookings Institution
1775 Massachusetts Ave., N.W.
Washington, DC 20005

The Business Roundtable
405 Lexington Ave.
New York, NY 10017

Center for the Study of American
   Business
Washington University
St. Louis, MO 63130

Chamber of Commerce of the
   United States
1615 H St., N.W.
Washington, DC 20062

The Conference Board
845 Third Ave.
New York, NY 10022

Export-Import Bank
811 Vermont Ave., N.W.
Washington, DC 20571

National Association of
   Manufacturers
1776 F St., N.W.
Washington, DC 20006

World Bank
1818 H St., N.W.
Washington, DC 20006

Consumer Interests

Agribusiness Accountability Project
1000 Wisconsin Ave., N.W.
Washington, DC 20007

Consumer Federation of America
1012 14th St., N.W.
Washington, DC 20005

Consumer Information Institute
1225 19th St., N.W.
Washington, DC 20036

Consumers Union
256 Washington St.
Mount Vernon, NY 10550

Corporate Accountability Research
  Group
1346 Connecticut Ave., N.W.
Washington, DC 20036

Council of Better Business Bureaus
1150 17th St., N.W.
Washington, DC 20036

National Association of Food Chains
1725 I St., N.W.
Washington, DC 20006

National Consumer Congress
1346 Connecticut Ave., N.W.
Washington, DC 20036

National Consumers League
1785 Massachusetts Ave., N.W.
Washington, DC 20036

Super Market Institute
303 E. Ohio St.
Chicago, IL 60611

Health and Medicine

American Cancer Society
777 Third Ave.
New York, NY 10017

American College of Sports Medicine
1440 Monroe St.
Madison, WI 53706

American Dental Association
211 E. Chicago Ave.
Chicago, IL 60611

American Heart Association
7320 Greenville Ave.
Dallas, TX 75231

American Lung Association
1740 Broadway
New York, NY 10019

American Medical Association
535 N. Dearborn St.
Chicago, IL 60610

American Red Cross
18th and E Sts., N.W.
Washington, DC 20006

American Social Health Association
260 Sheridan Ave.
Palo Alto, CA 94306

Blue Cross and Blue Shield
840 N. Lake Shore Dr.
Chicago, IL 60611

Center for Disease Control
Atlanta, GA 30333

Mental Health Association
1800 N. Kent St.
Arlington, VA 22209

National Center for Health
  Education
211 Sutter St.
San Francisco, CA 94108

National Clearinghouse for Family
  Planning Information
6110 Executive Blvd.
Rockville, MD 29852

National Council on Alcoholism
733 Third Ave.
New York, NY 10017

National Institutes of Health
Bethesda, MD 20205

National Safety Council
444 N. Michigan Ave.
Chicago, IL 60611

Nutrition Foundation
888 17th St., N.W.
Washington, DC 20006

Planned Parenthood Federation of
  America
810 Seventh Ave.
New York, NY 10019

President's Council on Physical
  Fitness and Sports
400 6th St., S.W.
Washington, DC 20201

Surgeon General of the U.S.
200 Independence Ave., S.W.
Washington, DC 20201

Environment and Land Use

American Industrial Development
  Council
215 W. Pershing Rd.
Kansas City, MO 64108

American Institute of Architects
1735 New York Ave., N.W.
Washington, DC 20006

American Institute of Planners
1776 Massachusetts Ave., N.W.
Washington, DC 20036

American Petroleum Institute
1801 K St., N.W.
Washington, DC 20006

American Public Works Association
1313 E. 60th St.
Chicago, IL 60637

American Society of Planning
  Officials
1313 E. 60th St.
Chicago, IL 60637

Council of State Governments
Iron Works Pike
Lexington, KY 40505

Council on Municipal Performance
84 Fifth Ave.
New York, NY 10011

Council on Population and the
  Environment
100 E. Ohio St.
Chicago, IL 60611

Environmental Defense Fund
162 Old Town Rd.
East Setauket, NY 11733

Friends of the Earth
529 Commercial St.
San Francisco, CA 94111

National Association of Conservation
  Districts
1025 Vermont Ave., N.W.
Washington, DC 20005

National Association of Counties
1735 New York Ave., N.W.
Washington, DC 20006

National Association of Regional
  Councils
1700 K St., N.W.
Washington, DC 20006

National Association of State
  Development Agencies
1015 20th St., N.W.
Washington, DC 20006

National Coal Association
1130 17th St., N.W.
Washington, DC 20036

National Industrial Zoning
  Committee
2459 Dorset Rd.
Columbus, OH 43221

National Recreation and Park
  Association
1601 Kent St.
Arlington, VA 22209

National Water Resources
  Association
897 National Press Building
Washington, DC 20045

National Wildlife Federation
1412 16th St., N.W.
Washington, DC 20036

National Resources Defense Council
15 W. 44th St.
New York, NY 10036

The Urban Institute
2100 M St., N.W.
Washington, DC 20036

Water Resources Congress
1130 17th St., N.W.
Washington, DC 20036

Water Resources Council (a federal
  agency)
2120 L St., N.W.
Washington, DC 20037

Sierra Club
1050 Mills Tower
220 Bush St.
San Francisco, CA 94104

Labor Relations

AFL–CIO
815 16th St., N.W.
Washington, DC 20006

George Meany Center for Labor
  Studies
10000 New Hampshire Ave.
Silver Springs, MD 20904

International Brotherhood of
  Teamsters
25 Louisiana Ave., N.W.
Washington, DC 20001

Labor Management Relations Service
  (government)
1620 I St., N.W.
Washington, DC 20036

Labor Policy Association
1717 Pennsylvania Ave., N.W.
Washington, DC 20006

National Commission on Productivity
  and Work Quality
2000 M St., N.W.
Washington, DC 20036

National Labor Management
  Foundation
2000 L St., N.W.
Washington, DC 20036

National Right to Work Committee
1990 M St., N.W.
Washington, DC 20036

United Auto Workers
Solidarity House
8000 E. Jefferson Ave.
Detroit, MI 48214

United Mine Workers of America
900 15th St., N.W.
Washington, DC 20005

Mass Media

More extensive listings of trade and professional organizations in the field of mass communication can be found in the *Editor & Publisher International Yearbook,* revised annually, and in the January issues of *Journalism Educator,* published by the Association for Education in Journalism.

The Advertising Council, Inc.
825 Third Ave.,
New York, NY 10022

American Association of Advertising
  Agencies
200 Park Ave.
New York, NY 10017

American Federation of Television
  and   Radio Artists—AFL-CIO
1350 Ave. of the Americas
New York, NY 10015

American Newspaper Publishers
  Association
Box 17407
Dulles International Airport
Washington, DC 20041

American Society of Newspaper
  Editors
Box 551
1350 Sullivan Trail
Easton, PA 18042

Associated Press Managing Editors
50 Rockefeller Plaza
New York, NY 10020

Freedom of Information Center
P.O. Box 858
Columbia, MO 65205

Magazine Publishers Association
575 Lexington Ave.
New York, NY 10022

National Association of Broadcasters
1771 N St., N.W.
Washington, DC 20036

National News Council
One Lincoln Plaza
New York, NY 10023

National Newspaper Association
1627 K St., N.W.
Washington, DC 20006

Newspaper Advertising Bureau
485 Lexington Ave.
New York, NY 10017

The Newspaper Guild
1125 15th St., N.W.
Washington, DC 20005

Public Relations Society of America
845 Third Ave.
New York, NY 10022

Radio Television News Directors
    Association
1735 DeSales St., N.W.
Washington, DC 20036

Reporters Committee for Freedom of
    the Press
1125 15th St., N.W.
Washington, DC 20005

Society of Professional Journalists,
    Sigma Delta Chi
840 N. Lake Shore Dr.
Chicago, IL 60611

Women in Communications, Inc.
P.O. Box 9561
Austin, TX 78766

Transportation

American Association of State
    Highway   and Transportation
    Officials
341 National Press Bldg.
Washington, DC 20004

American Public Transit Association
1100 17th St., N.W.
Washington, DC 20036

Highway Action Coalition
1346 Connecticut Ave., N.W.
Washington, DC 20036

Institute for Public Transportation
211 E. 43rd St.
New York, NY 10017

Institute of Traffic Engineers
1815 Fort Meyer Dr.
Arlington, VA 22209

National Association of Railroad
    Passengers
417 New Jersey Ave., S.E.
Washington, DC 20003

Urban Mass Transit Administration
    (federal)
400 7th St., S.W.
Washington, DC 20590

U.S. Railway Association (federal)
2100 Second St., S.W.
Washington, DC 20595

Miscellaneous

Agency for International
    Development
Washington, DC 20523

American Bar Association
1155 E. 60th St.
Chicago, IL 60637

American Farm Bureau Federation
425 13th St., N.W.
Washington, DC 20004

Bureau of Labor Statistics
U.S. Department of Labor
Washington, DC 20212

Congressional Budget Office
U.S. Congress
Washington, DC 20515

Congressional Joint Economic
  Committee
Dirksen Senate Office Building
Washington, DC 20510

Council of Economic Advisers
Office of the President
Washington, DC 20506

Equal Employment Opportunity
  Commission
Washington, DC 20506

Federal Mediation and Conciliation
  Service
Washington, DC 20427

Federal Reserve Board
Washington, DC 20551

Occupational Safety and Health
  Administration
U.S. Department of Labor
Washington, DC 20210

The Population Institute
100 Maryland Ave., N.E.
Washington, DC 20002

U.S. International Trade
  Commission
Washington, DC 20436

Index